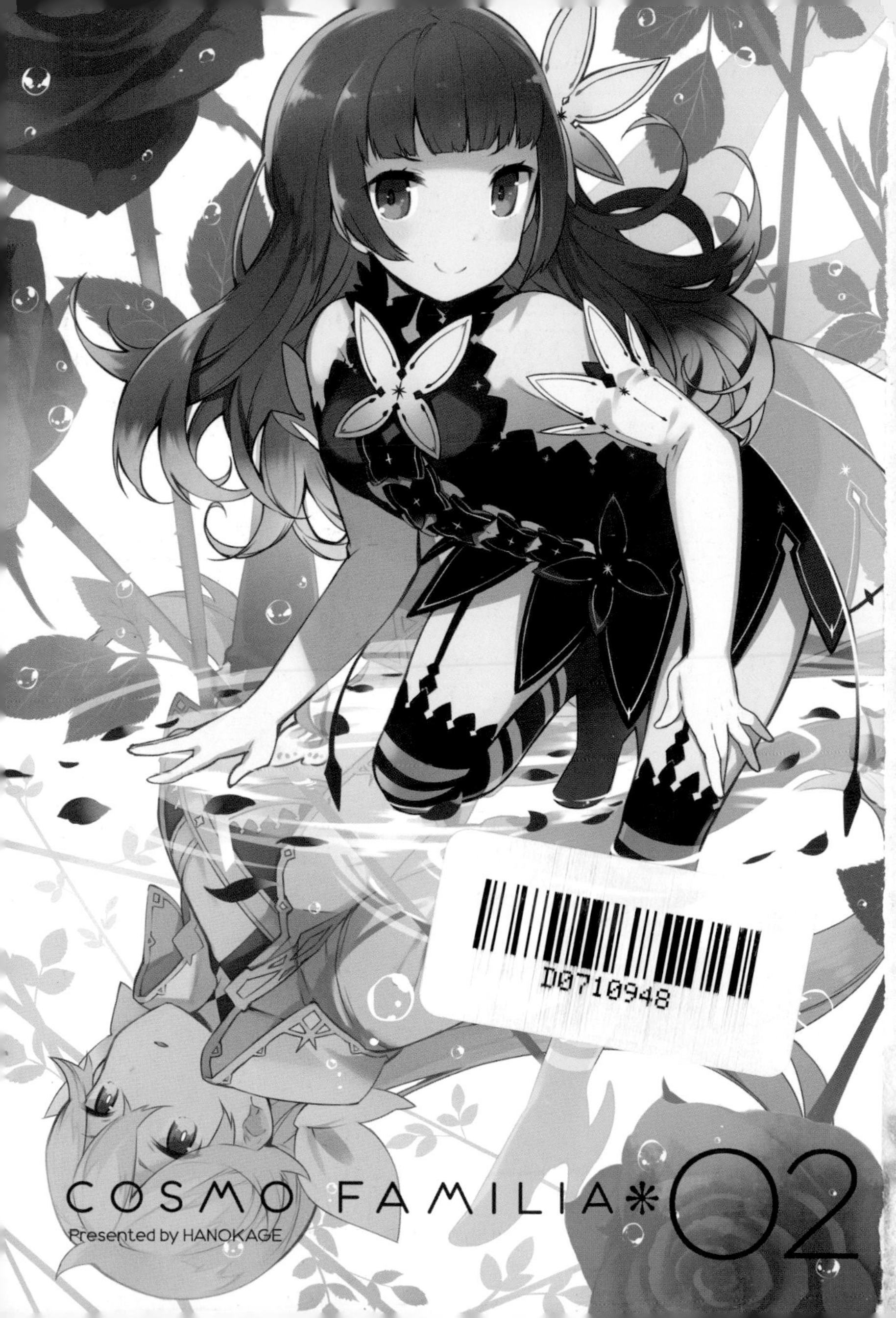
COSMO FAMILIA*02
Presented by HANOKAGE

# CONTENTS

Cosmo Familia Vol. 02
Presented by HANOKAGE

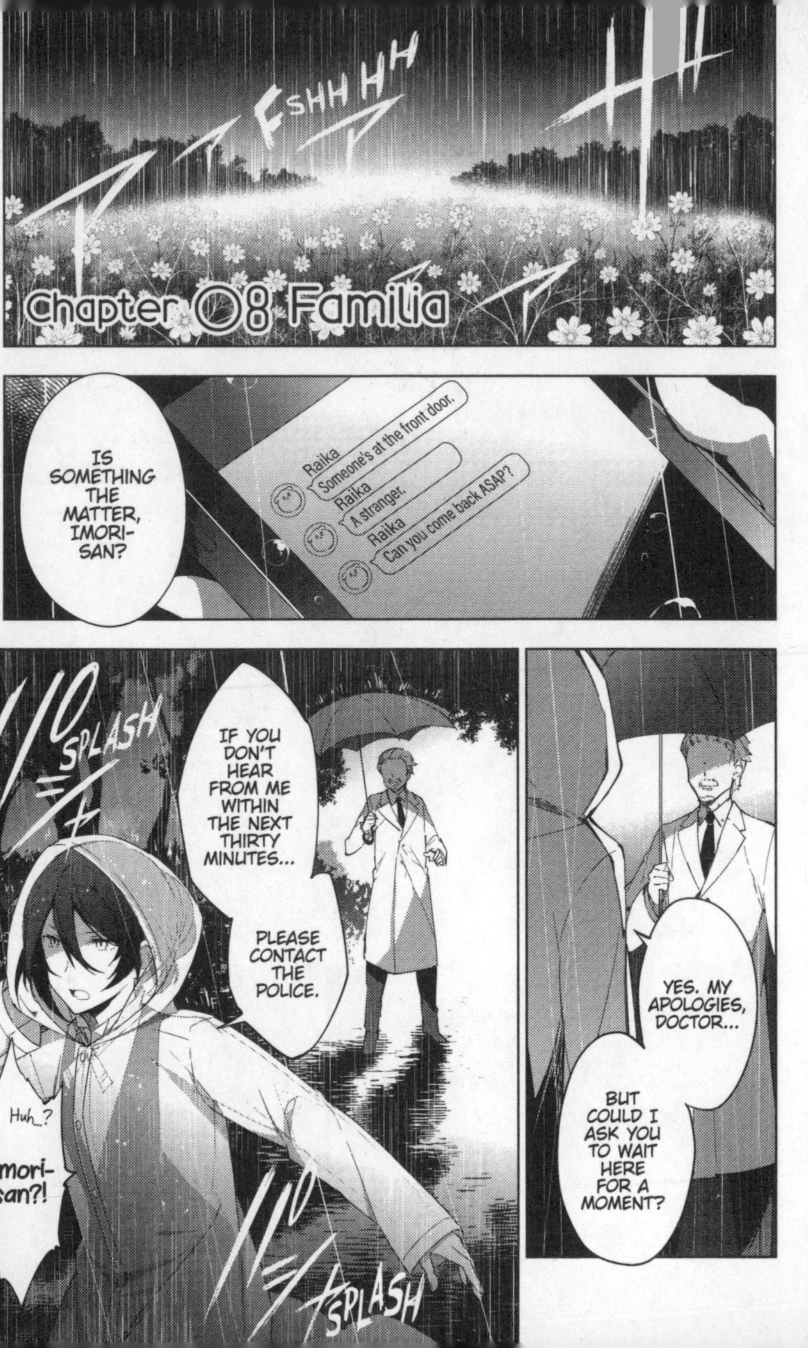
FSHHHH
Chapter 08 Familia
Raika
Someone's at the front door.
Raika
A stranger.
Raika
Can you come back ASAP?
IS SOMETHING THE MATTER, IMORI-SAN?
YES. MY APOLOGIES, DOCTOR...
BUT COULD I ASK YOU TO WAIT HERE FOR A MOMENT?
SPLASH
IF YOU DON'T HEAR FROM ME WITHIN THE NEXT THIRTY MINUTES...
PLEASE CONTACT THE POLICE.
Huh...?
Imori-san?!
SPLASH

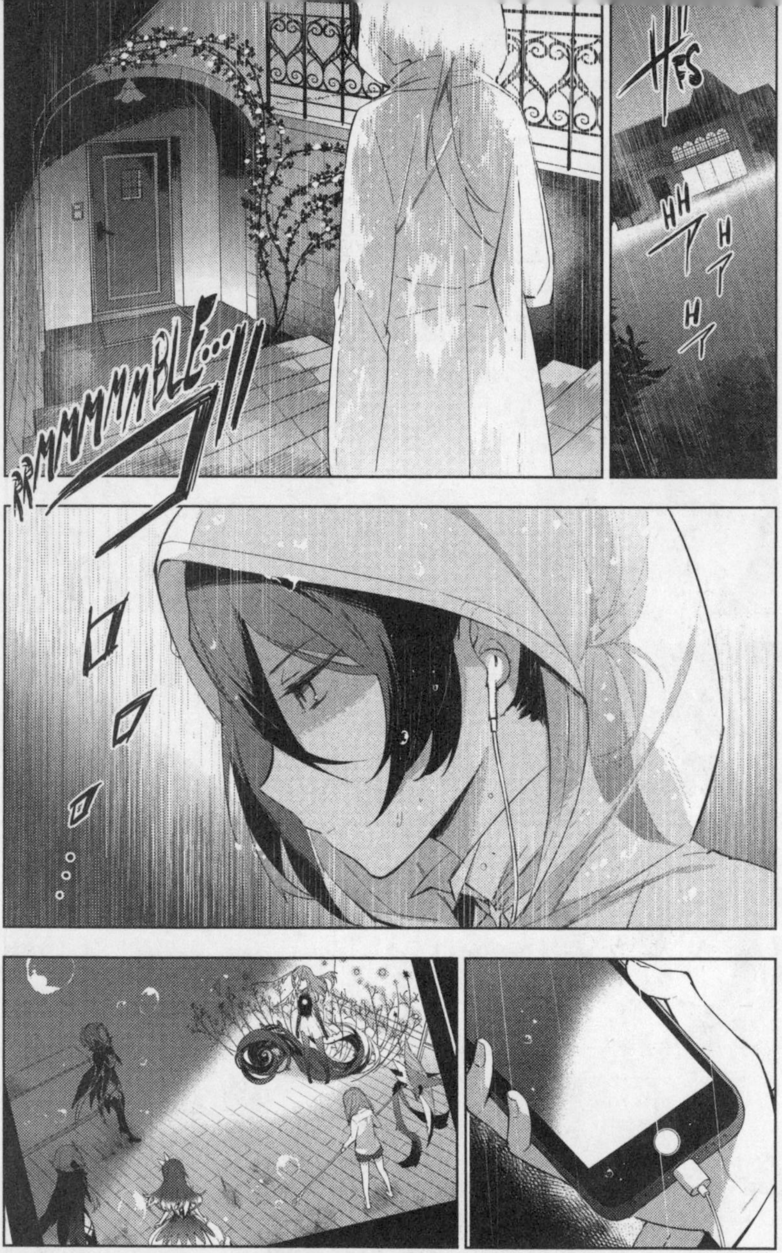
HFS
HH
H
H
RRMMMMMMBLE...!!

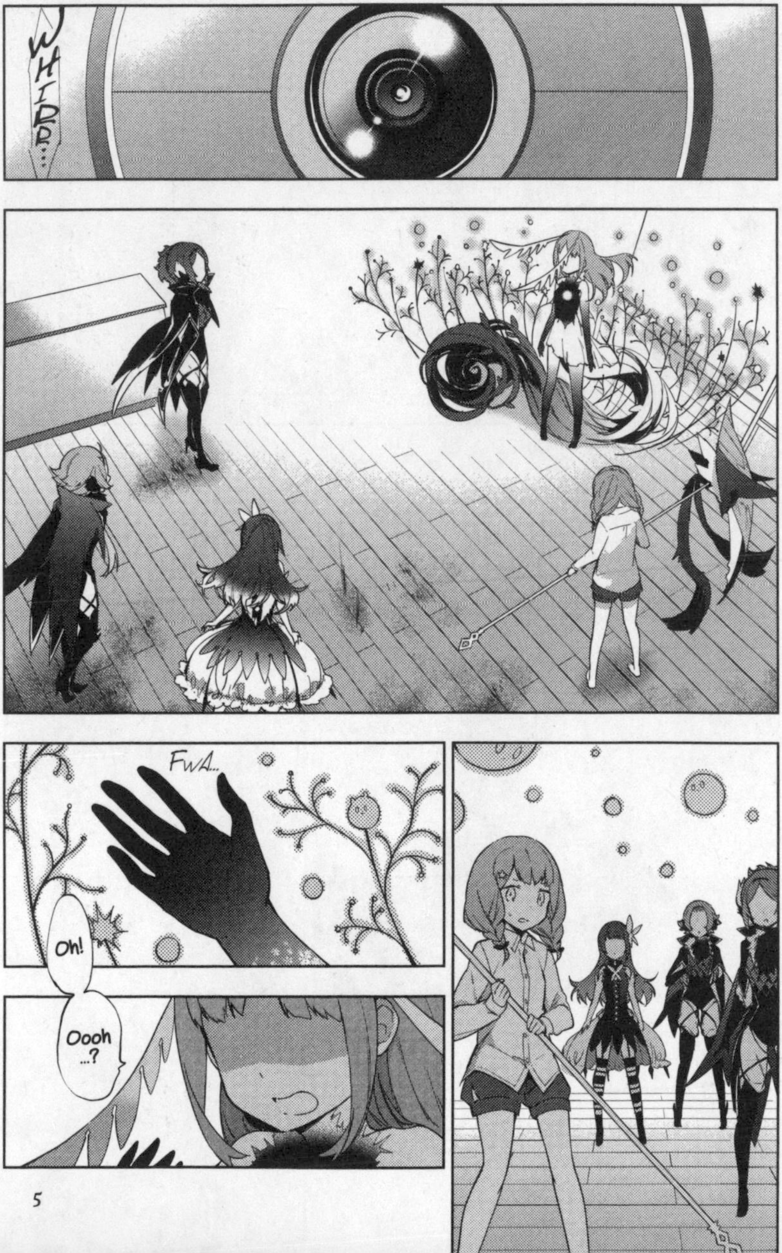
WHIRR...
FWA...
Oh!
Oooh
...?

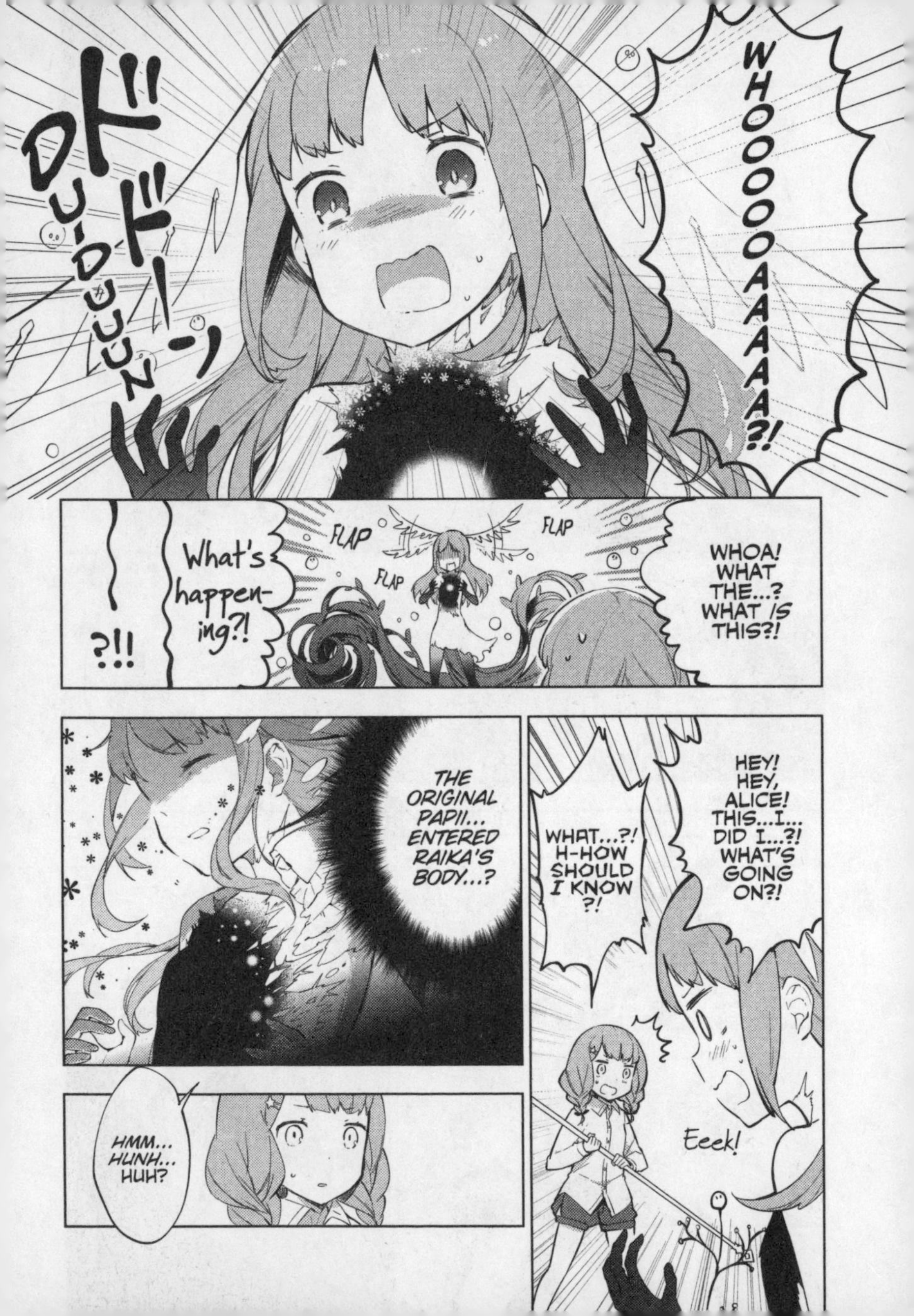
WHOOOOOAAAAAA?!
ドドーン
DU-DUUUN
WHOA! WHAT THE...? WHAT IS THIS?!
FLAP
FLAP
FLAP
What's happen-ing?!
—?!!
HEY! HEY, ALICE! THIS...I... DID I...?! WHAT'S GOING ON?!
WHAT...?! H-HOW SHOULD I KNOW?!
Eeek!
THE ORIGINAL PAPII... ENTERED RAIKA'S BODY...?
HMM... HUNH... HUH?

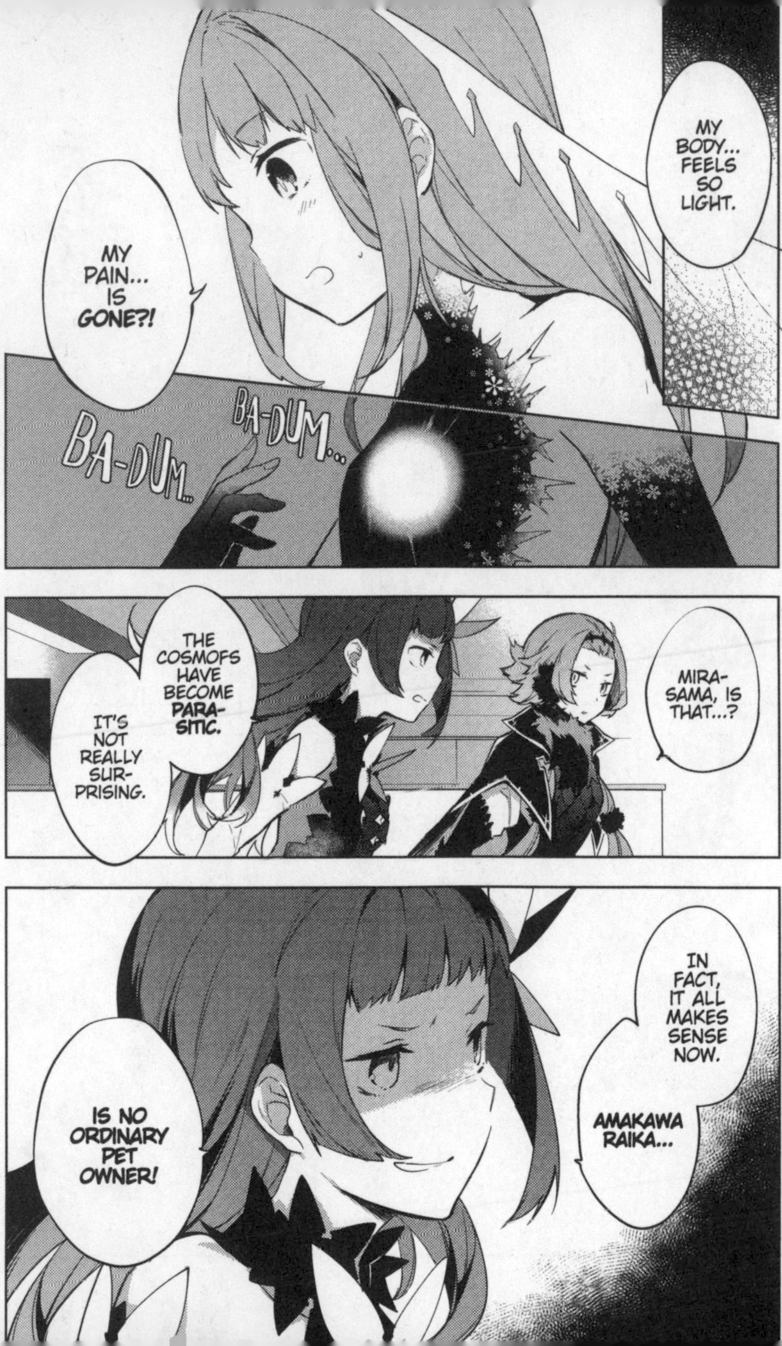
MY BODY... FEELS SO LIGHT.
MY PAIN... IS GONE?!
BA-DUM...
BA-DUM...
MIRA-SAMA, IS THAT...?
THE COSMOFS HAVE BECOME PARA-SITIC.
IT'S NOT REALLY SUR-PRISING.
IN FACT, IT ALL MAKES SENSE NOW.
AMAKAWA RAIKA...
IS NO ORDINARY PET OWNER!

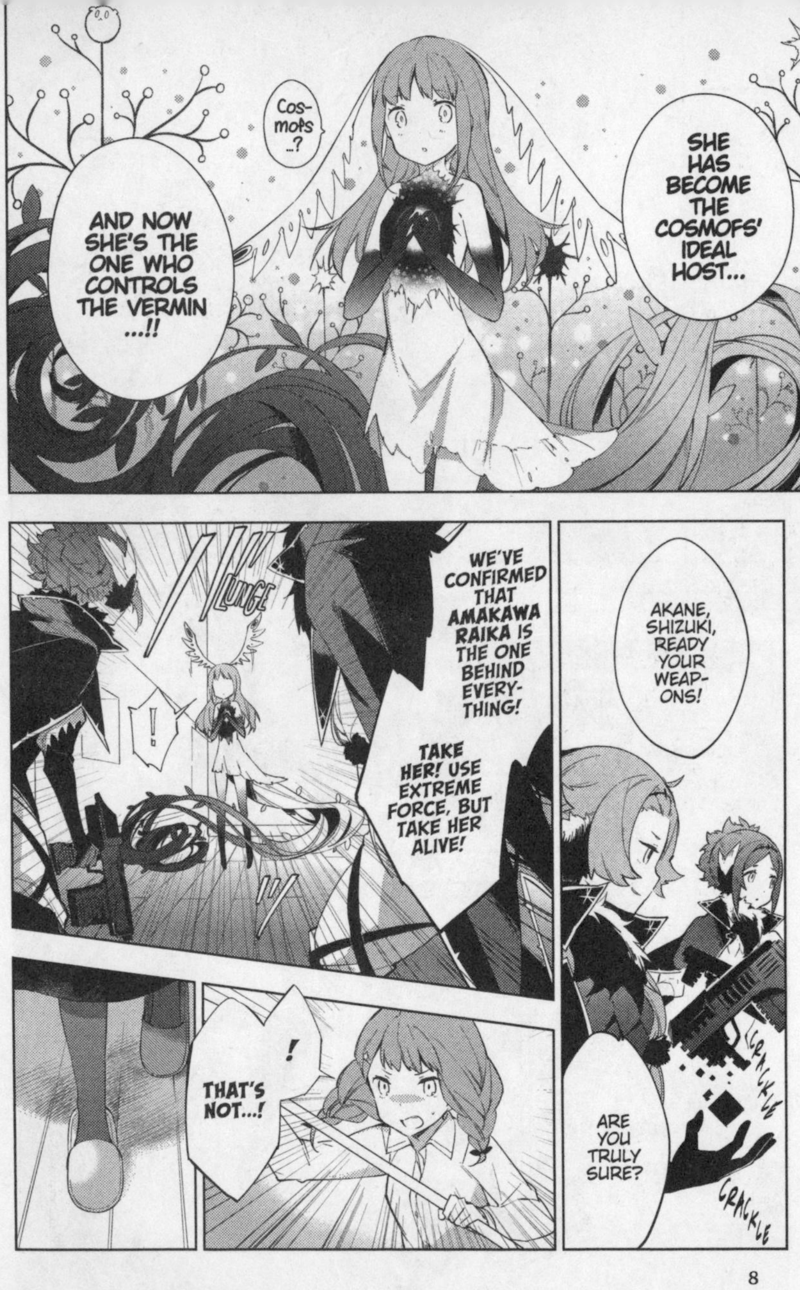
SHE HAS BECOME THE COSMOFS' IDEAL HOST...
Cos-mofs ...?
AND NOW SHE'S THE ONE WHO CONTROLS THE VERMIN ...!!
AKANE, SHIZUKI, READY YOUR WEAP-ONS!
CRACKLE
ARE YOU TRULY SURE?
CRACKLE
WE'VE CONFIRMED THAT AMAKAWA RAIKA IS THE ONE BEHIND EVERY-THING!
LUNGE
!!
TAKE HER! USE EXTREME FORCE, BUT TAKE HER ALIVE!
!
THAT'S NOT...!

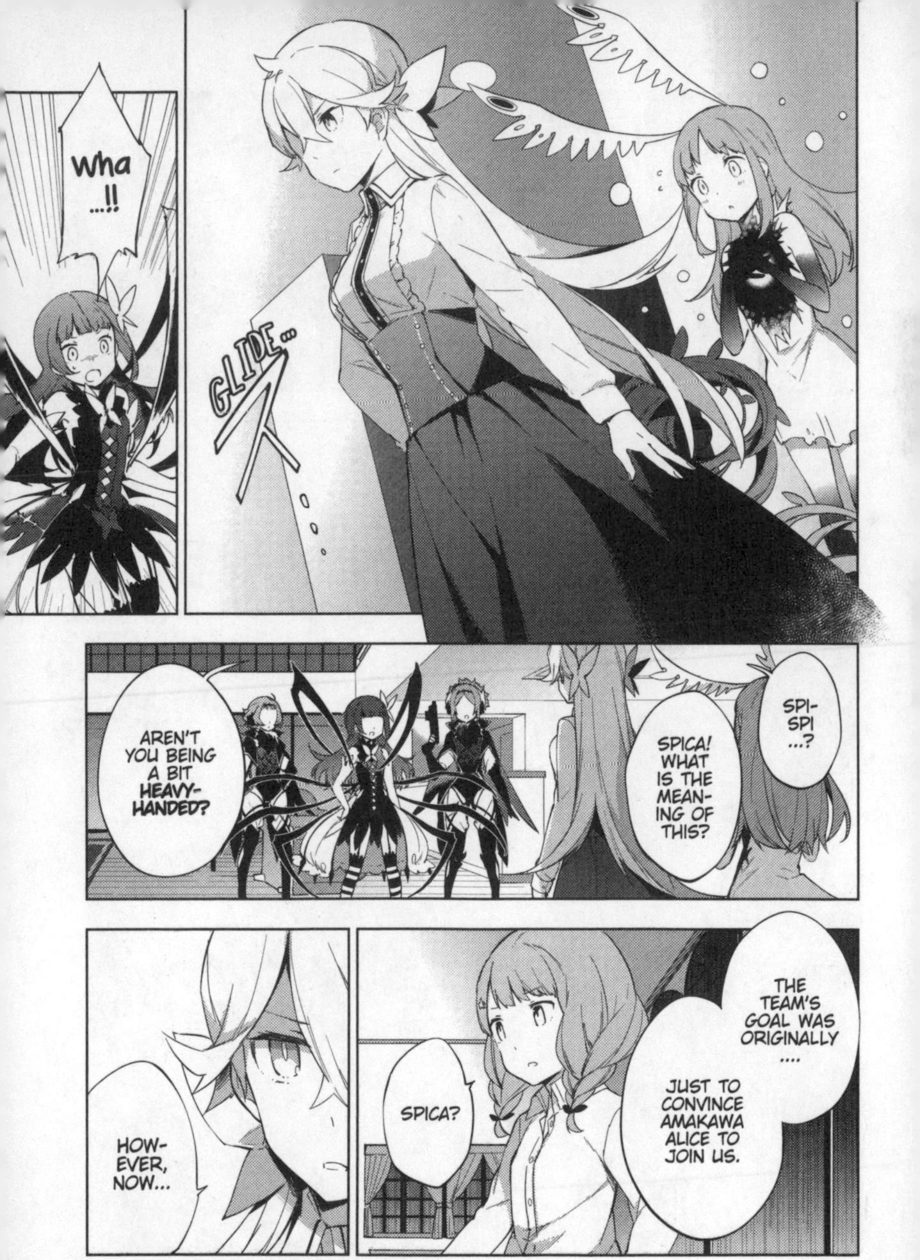
GLIDE...
Wha ...!!
SPI-SPI ...?
SPICA! WHAT IS THE MEAN-ING OF THIS?
AREN'T YOU BEING A BIT HEAVY-HANDED?
THE TEAM'S GOAL WAS ORIGINALLY ....
JUST TO CONVINCE AMAKAWA ALICE TO JOIN US.
SPICA?
HOW-EVER, NOW...

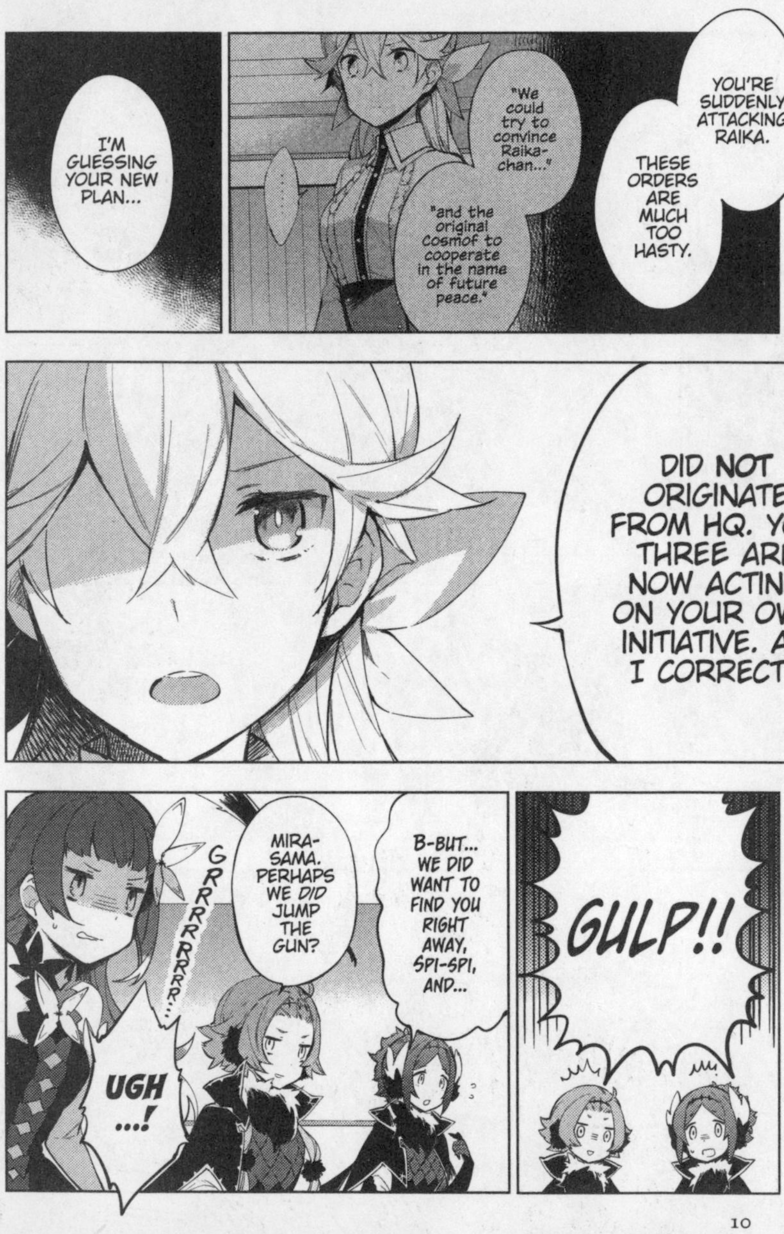
YOU'RE SUDDENLY ATTACKING RAIKA.
THESE ORDERS ARE MUCH TOO HASTY.
"We could try to convince Raika-chan..."
"and the original Cosmof to cooperate in the name of future peace."
...
I'M GUESSING YOUR NEW PLAN...
DID NOT ORIGINATE FROM HQ. YOU THREE ARE NOW ACTING ON YOUR OWN INITIATIVE. AM I CORRECT?
GULP!!
B-BUT... WE DID WANT TO FIND YOU RIGHT AWAY, SPI-SPI, AND...
MIRA-SAMA. PERHAPS WE *DID* JUMP THE GUN?
GRRRRRRRR...
UGH ...!

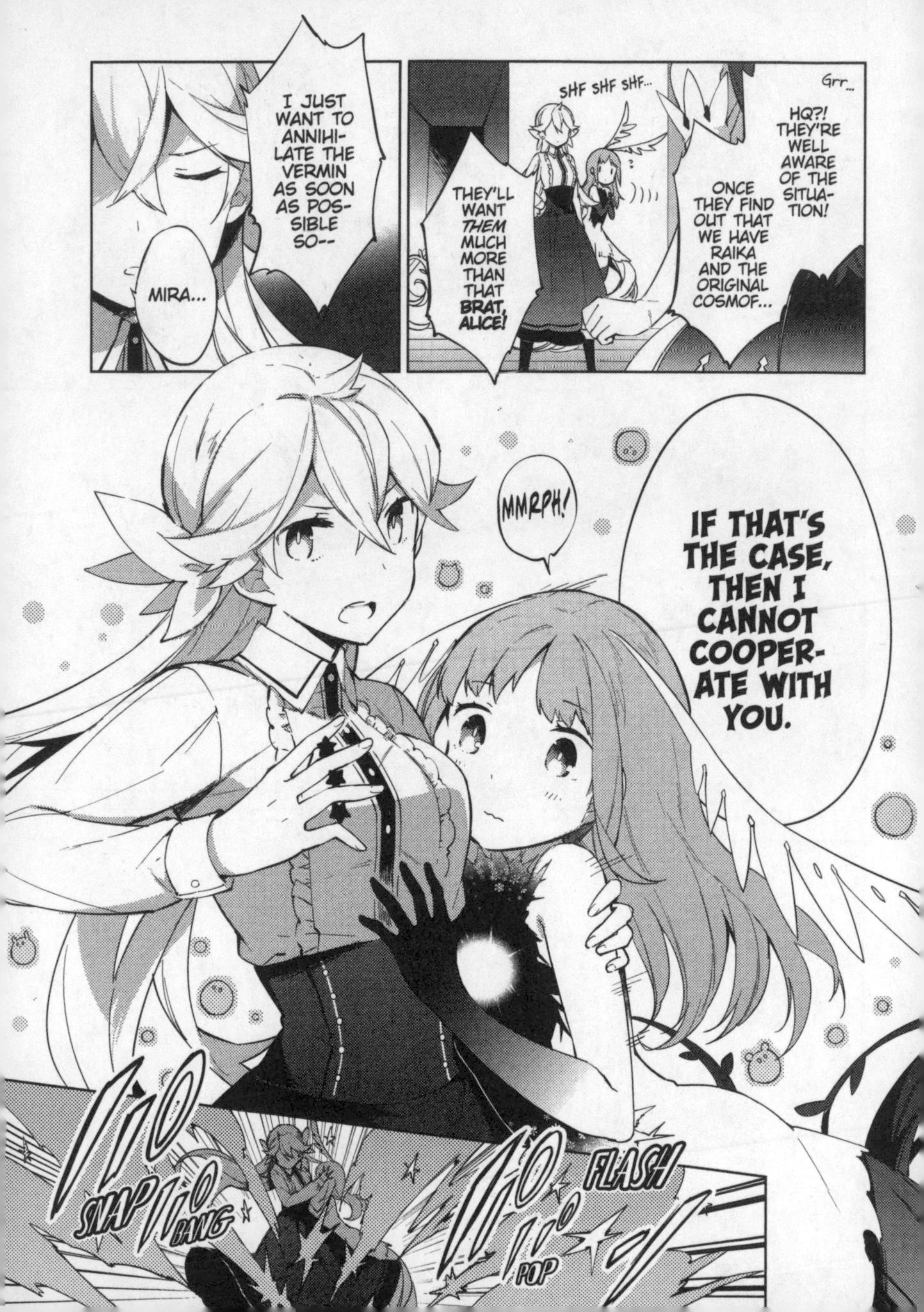
Grr...
HQ?! THEY'RE WELL AWARE OF THE SITUATION!
ONCE THEY FIND OUT THAT WE HAVE RAIKA AND THE ORIGINAL COSMOF...
SHF SHF SHF...
THEY'LL WANT *THEM* MUCH MORE THAN THAT BRAT, ALICE!
I JUST WANT TO ANNIHILATE THE VERMIN AS SOON AS POSSIBLE SO--
MIRA...
IF THAT'S THE CASE, THEN I CANNOT COOPERATE WITH YOU.
MMRPH!
FLASH
POP
BANG
SNAP

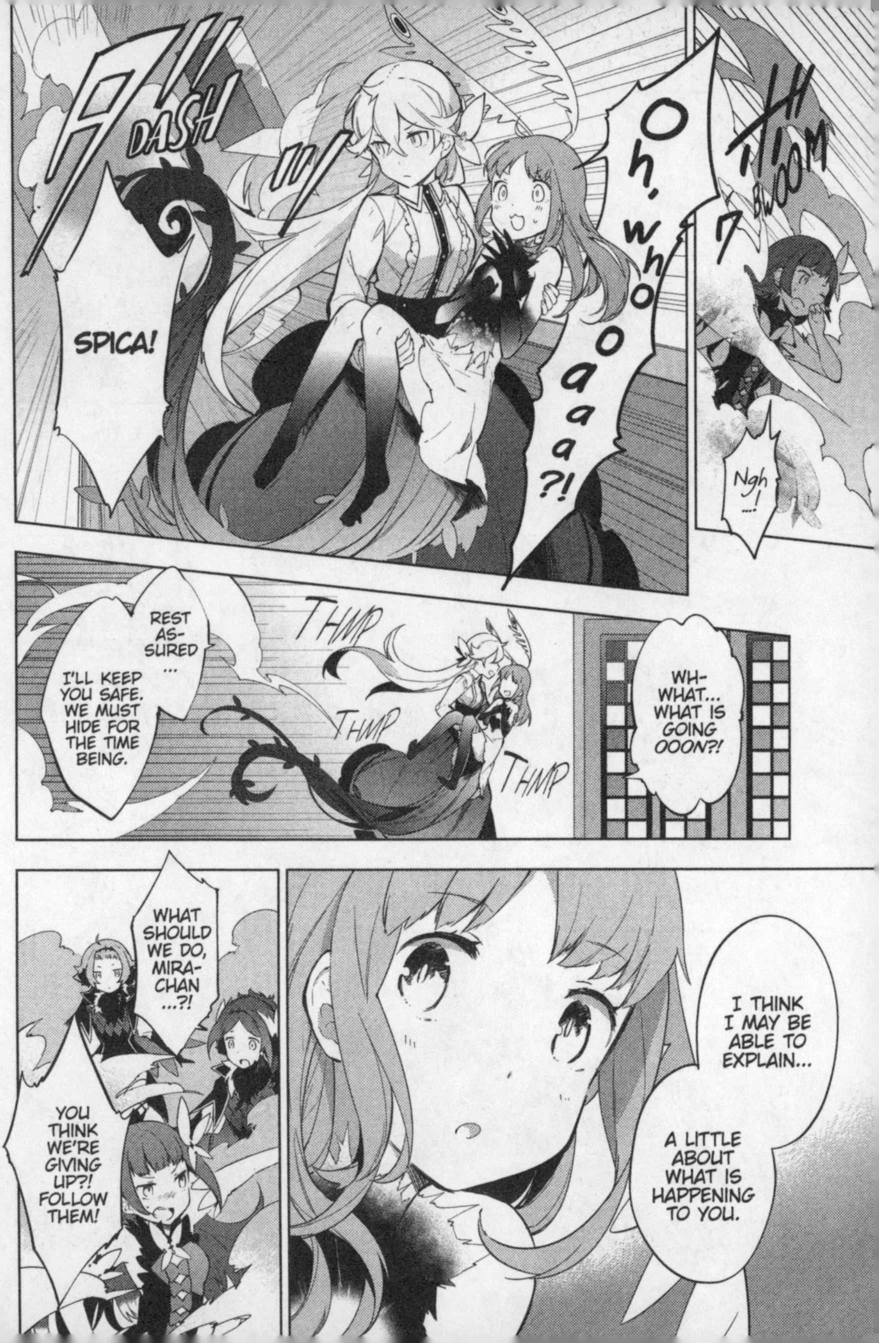
BWOOM
Ngh...!
Oh, whoooaaaa?!
DASH
SPICA!
WH-WHAT... WHAT IS GOING OOON?!
REST AS-SURED...
I'LL KEEP YOU SAFE. WE MUST HIDE FOR THE TIME BEING.
THMP
THMP
THMP
I THINK I MAY BE ABLE TO EXPLAIN...
A LITTLE ABOUT WHAT IS HAPPENING TO YOU.
WHAT SHOULD WE DO, MIRA-CHAN...?!
YOU THINK WE'RE GIVING UP?! FOLLOW THEM!

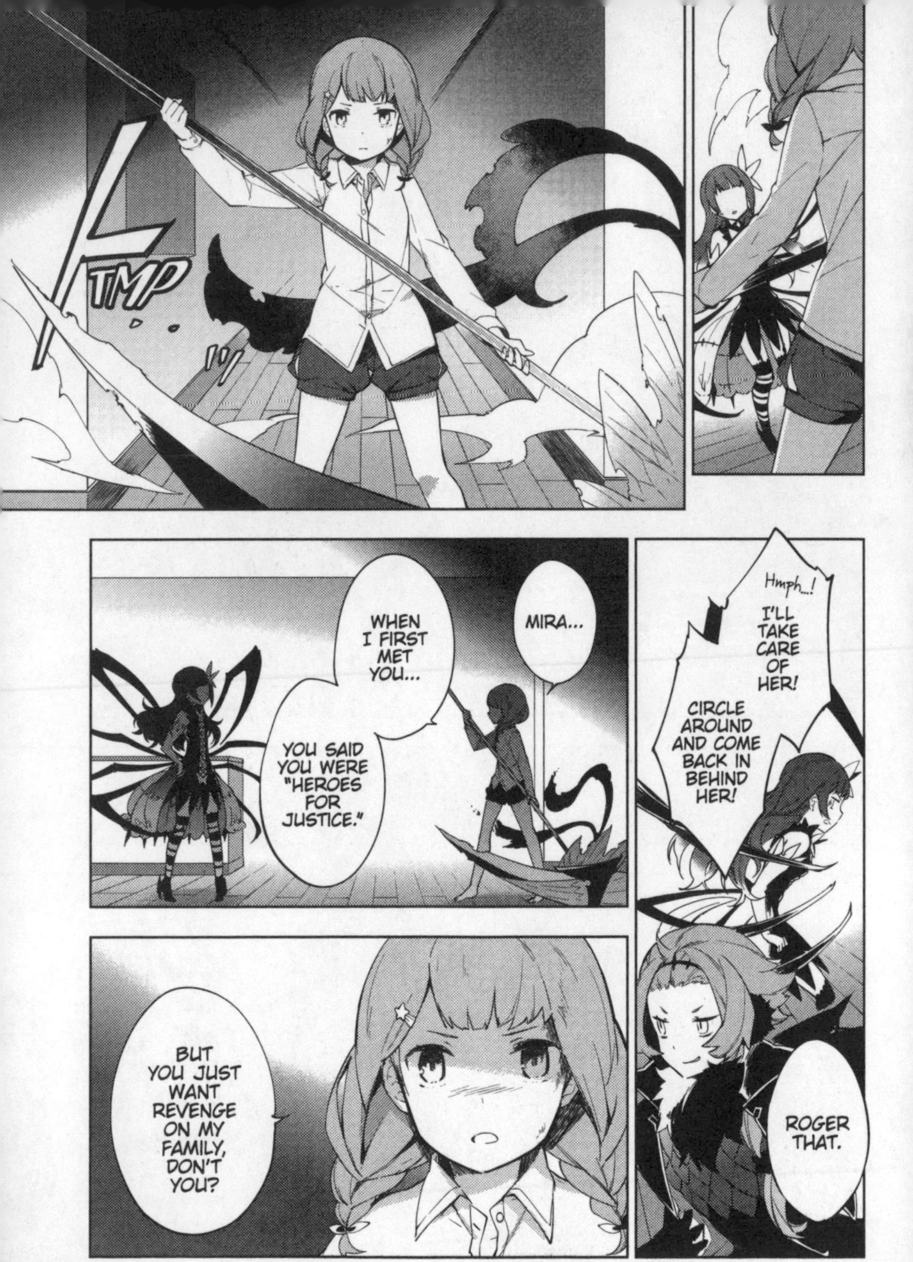
FTMP
Hmph...!
I'LL TAKE CARE OF HER!
CIRCLE AROUND AND COME BACK IN BEHIND HER!
ROGER THAT.
MIRA...
WHEN I FIRST MET YOU...
YOU SAID YOU WERE "HEROES FOR JUSTICE."
BUT YOU JUST WANT REVENGE ON MY FAMILY, DON'T YOU?

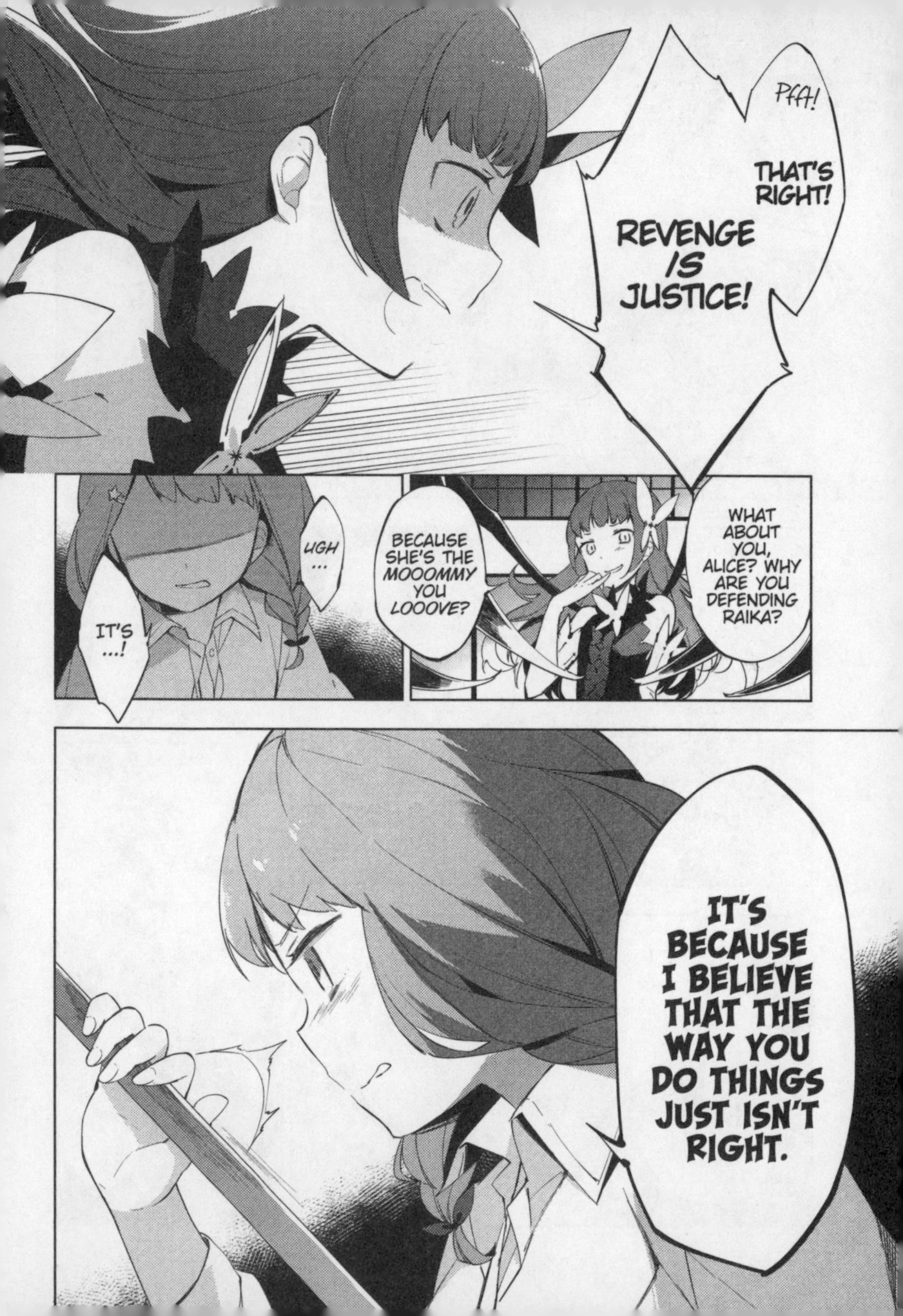
Pfft!
THAT'S RIGHT! REVENGE *IS* JUSTICE!
WHAT ABOUT YOU, ALICE? WHY ARE YOU DEFENDING RAIKA?
BECAUSE SHE'S THE *MOOOMMY* YOU LOOOVE?
UGH ...
IT'S ...!
IT'S BECAUSE I BELIEVE THAT THE WAY YOU DO THINGS JUST ISN'T RIGHT.

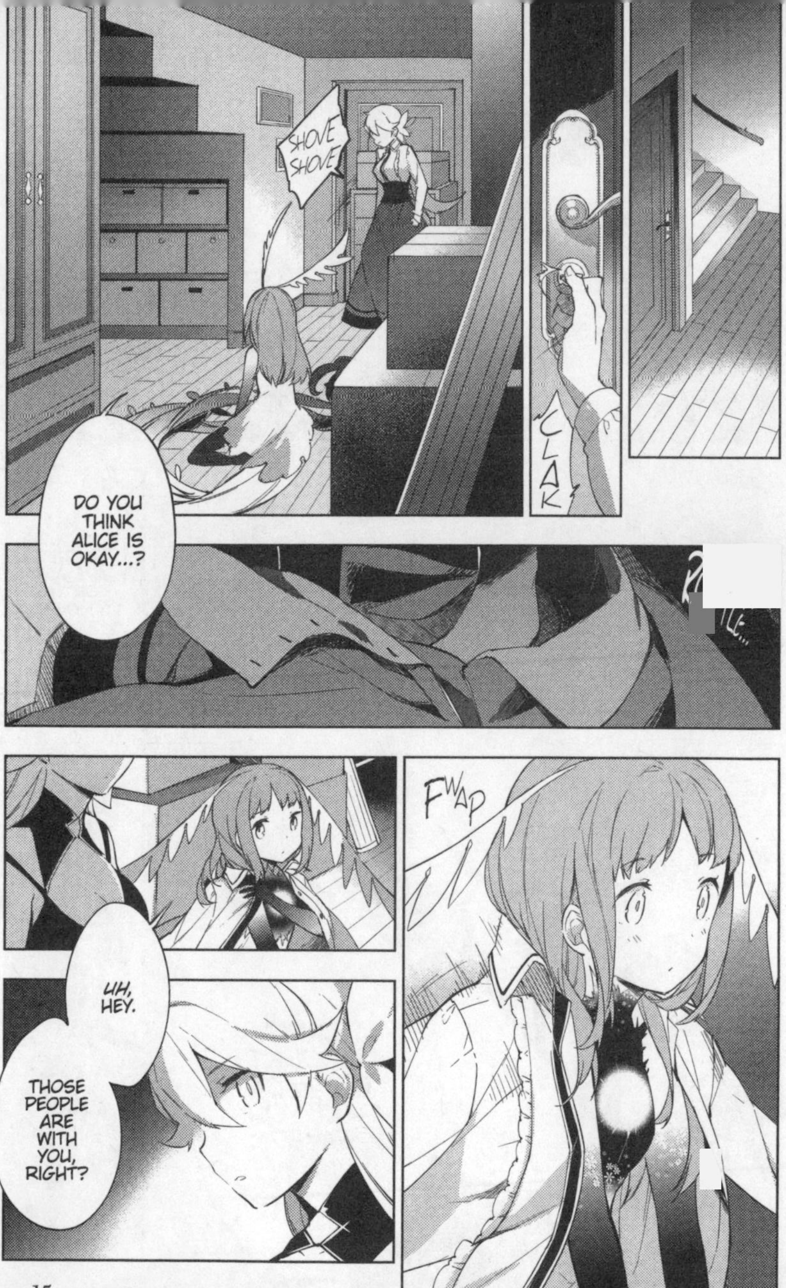
CLAK
SHOVE SHOVE
DO YOU THINK ALICE IS OKAY...?
FWAP
UH, HEY.
THOSE PEOPLE ARE WITH YOU, RIGHT?

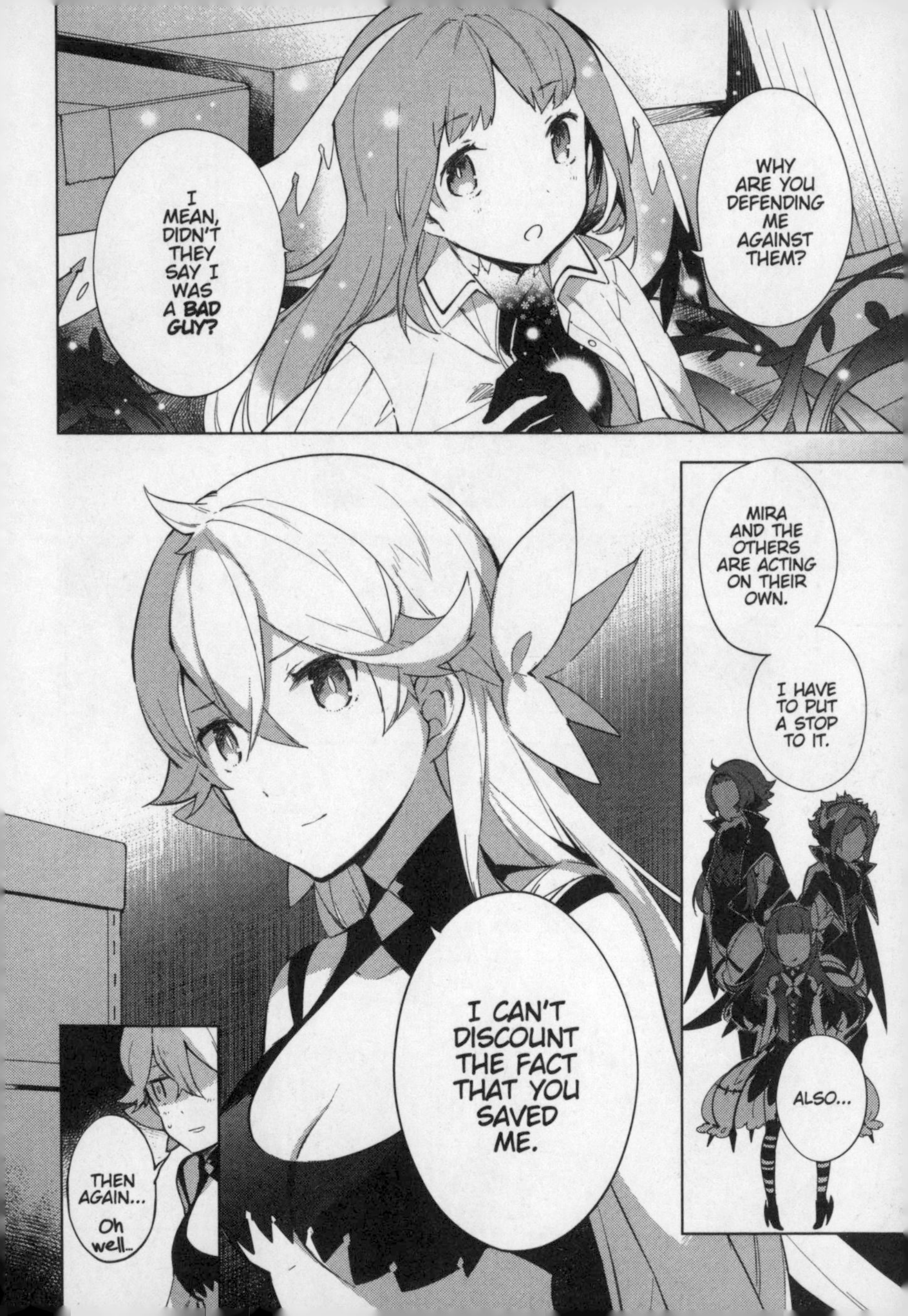
WHY ARE YOU DEFENDING ME AGAINST THEM?
I MEAN, DIDN'T THEY SAY I WAS A BAD GUY?
MIRA AND THE OTHERS ARE ACTING ON THEIR OWN.
I HAVE TO PUT A STOP TO IT.
ALSO...
I CAN'T DISCOUNT THE FACT THAT YOU SAVED ME.
THEN AGAIN...
Oh well...

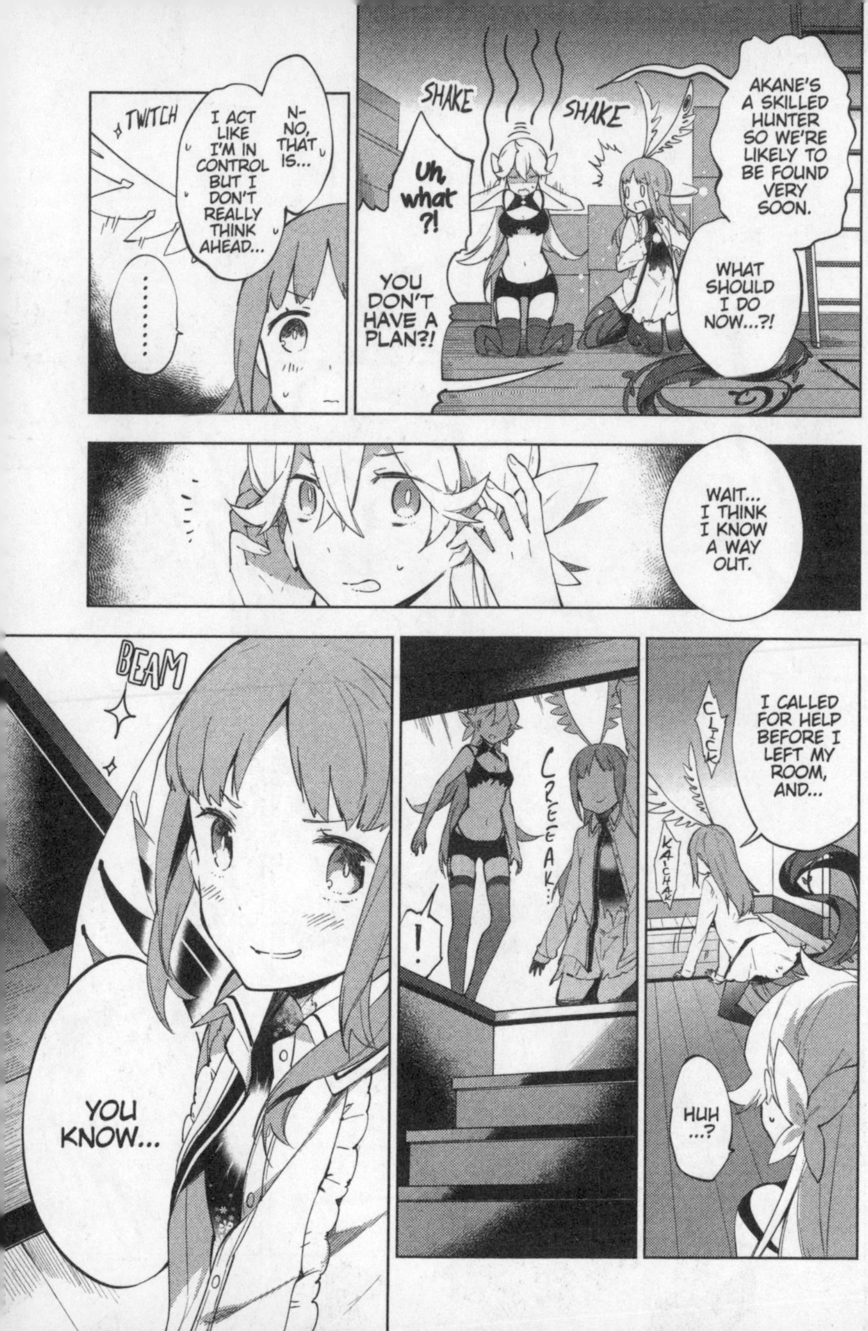
AKANE'S A SKILLED HUNTER SO WE'RE LIKELY TO BE FOUND VERY SOON.
SHAKE
SHAKE
Uh what ?!
WHAT SHOULD I DO NOW...?!
YOU DON'T HAVE A PLAN?!
N-NO, THAT IS...
I ACT LIKE I'M IN CONTROL BUT I DON'T REALLY THINK AHEAD...
TWITCH
......
WAIT... I THINK I KNOW A WAY OUT.
I CALLED FOR HELP BEFORE I LEFT MY ROOM, AND...
CLICK
KA-CHAK
HUH ...?
CREEEAK...
!
BEAM
YOU KNOW...

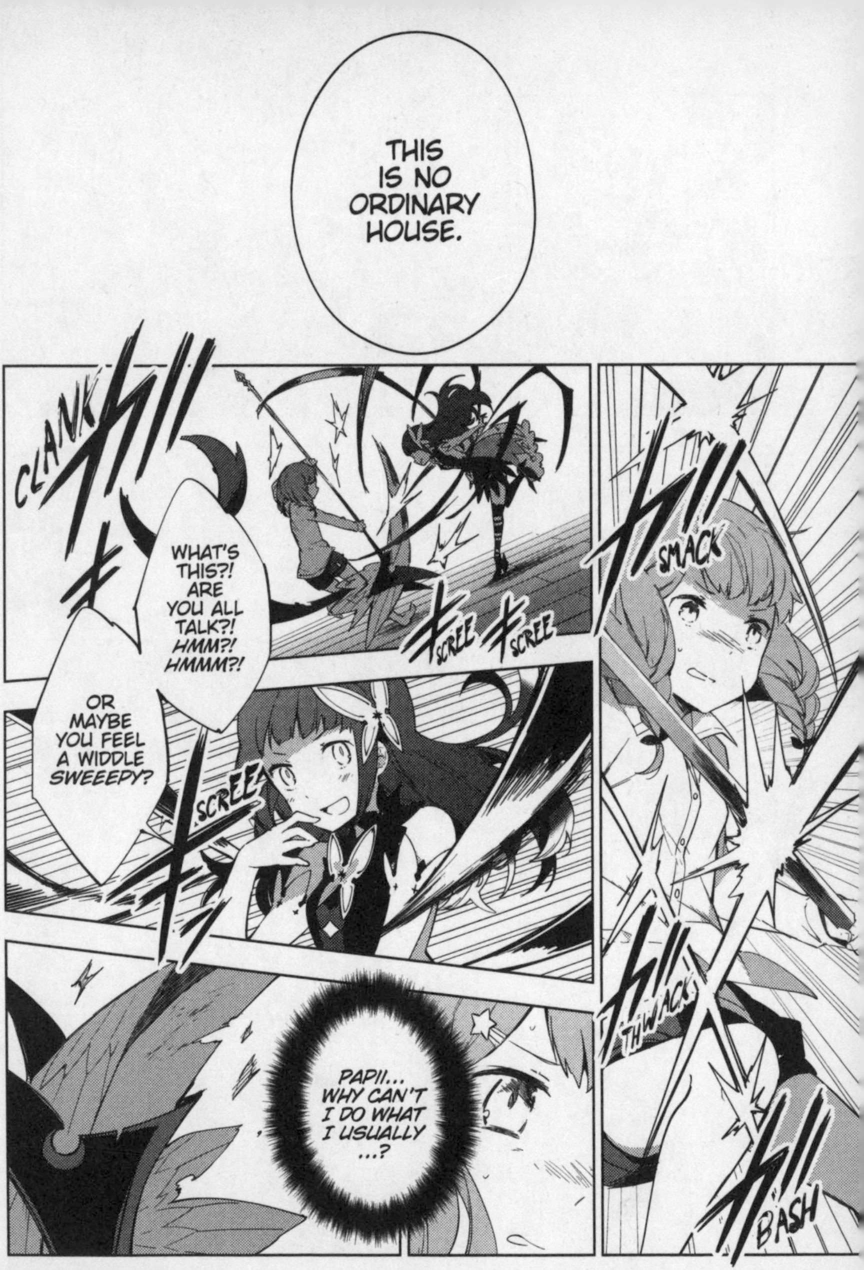
THIS IS NO ORDINARY HOUSE.
SMACK
THWACK
BASH
CLANK
WHAT'S THIS?! ARE YOU ALL TALK?! HMM?! HMMM?!
SCREE
SCREE
OR MAYBE YOU FEEL A WIDDLE SWEEEPY?
SCREE
PAPII... WHY CAN'T I DO WHAT I USUALLY ...?

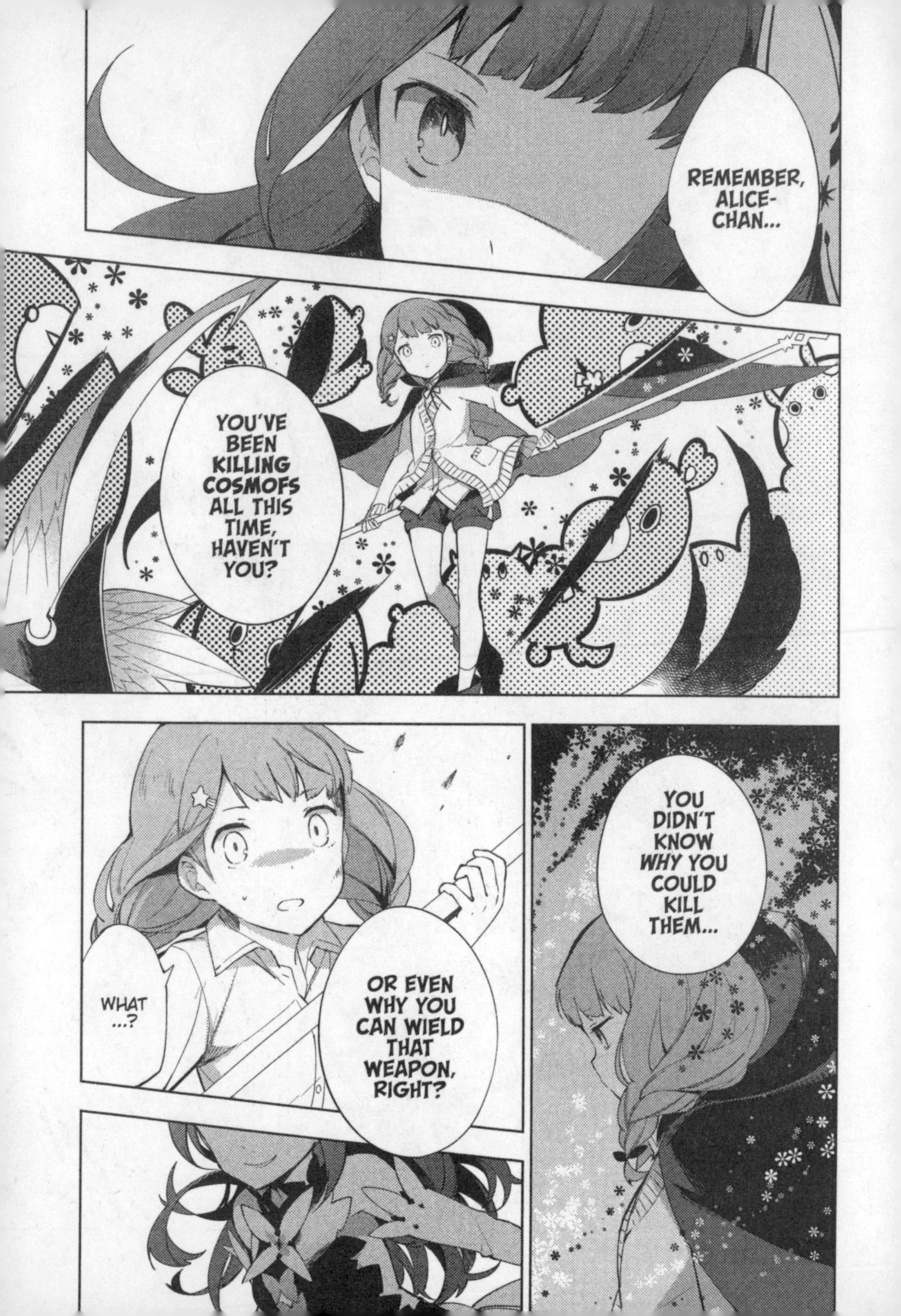
REMEMBER, ALICE-CHAN...
YOU'VE BEEN KILLING COSMOFS ALL THIS TIME, HAVEN'T YOU?
YOU DIDN'T KNOW *WHY* YOU COULD KILL THEM...
OR EVEN WHY YOU CAN WIELD THAT WEAPON, RIGHT?
WHAT ...?

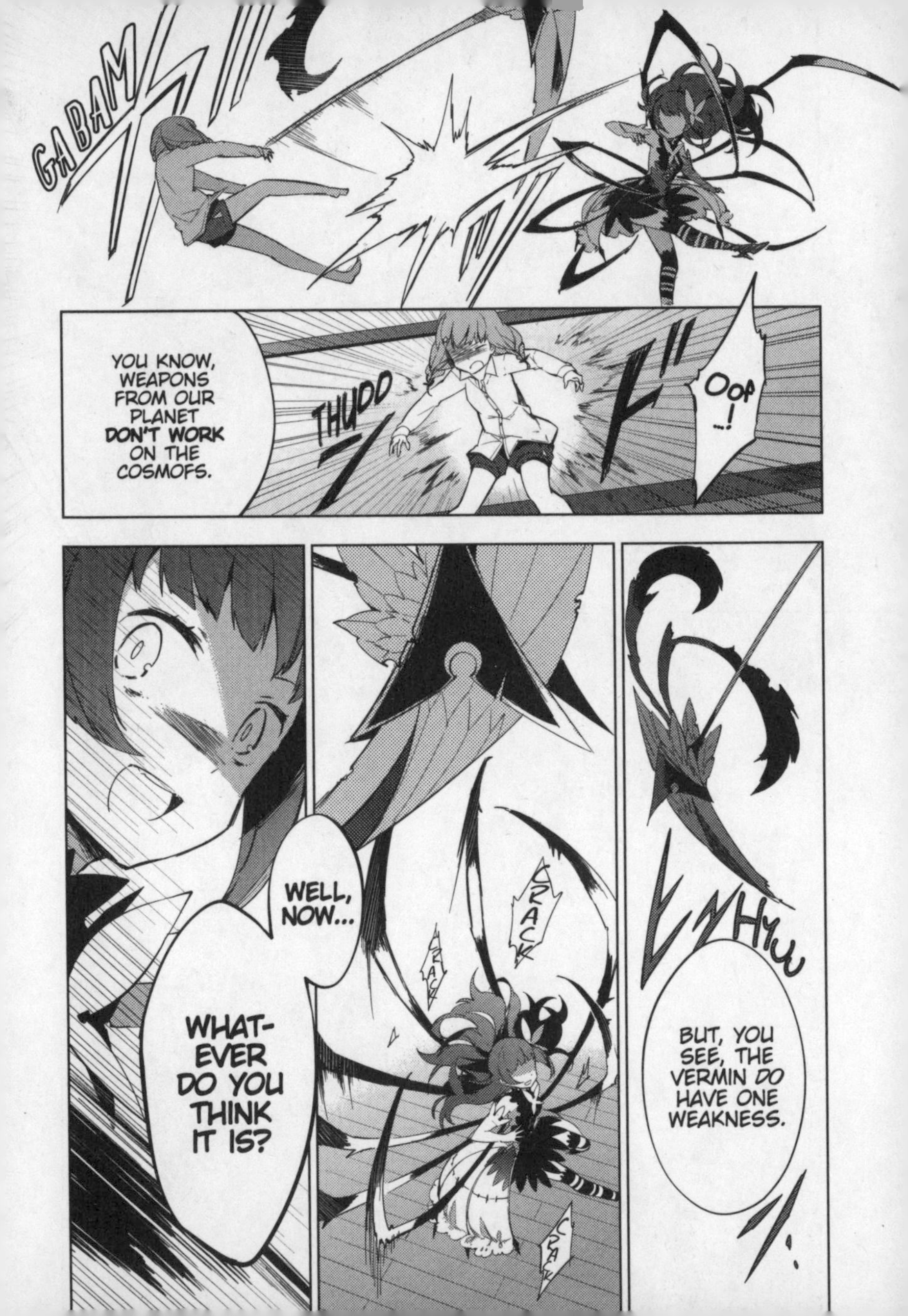
GABAM
Oof ..!
THUDD
YOU KNOW, WEAPONS FROM OUR PLANET **DON'T WORK** ON THE COSMOFS.
WHYUU
BUT, YOU SEE, THE VERMIN *DO* HAVE ONE WEAKNESS.
CRACK
CRACK
CRACK
WELL, NOW...
WHAT-EVER DO YOU THINK IT IS?

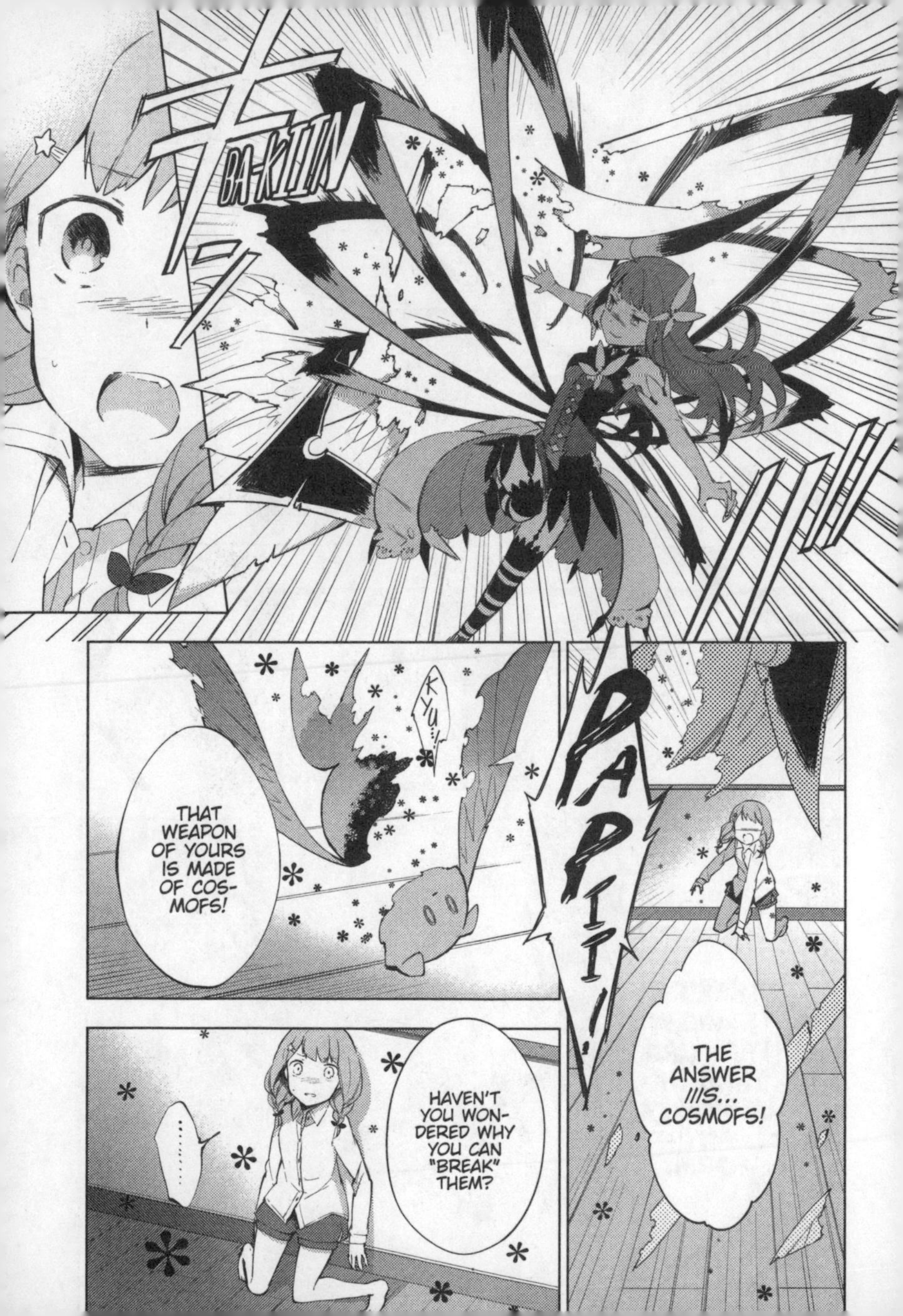
BA-KIIN
PAPIII!
THE ANSWER IIIS... COSMOFS!
KYU...!
THAT WEAPON OF YOURS IS MADE OF COS-MOFS!
HAVEN'T YOU WONDERED WHY YOU CAN "BREAK" THEM?
......

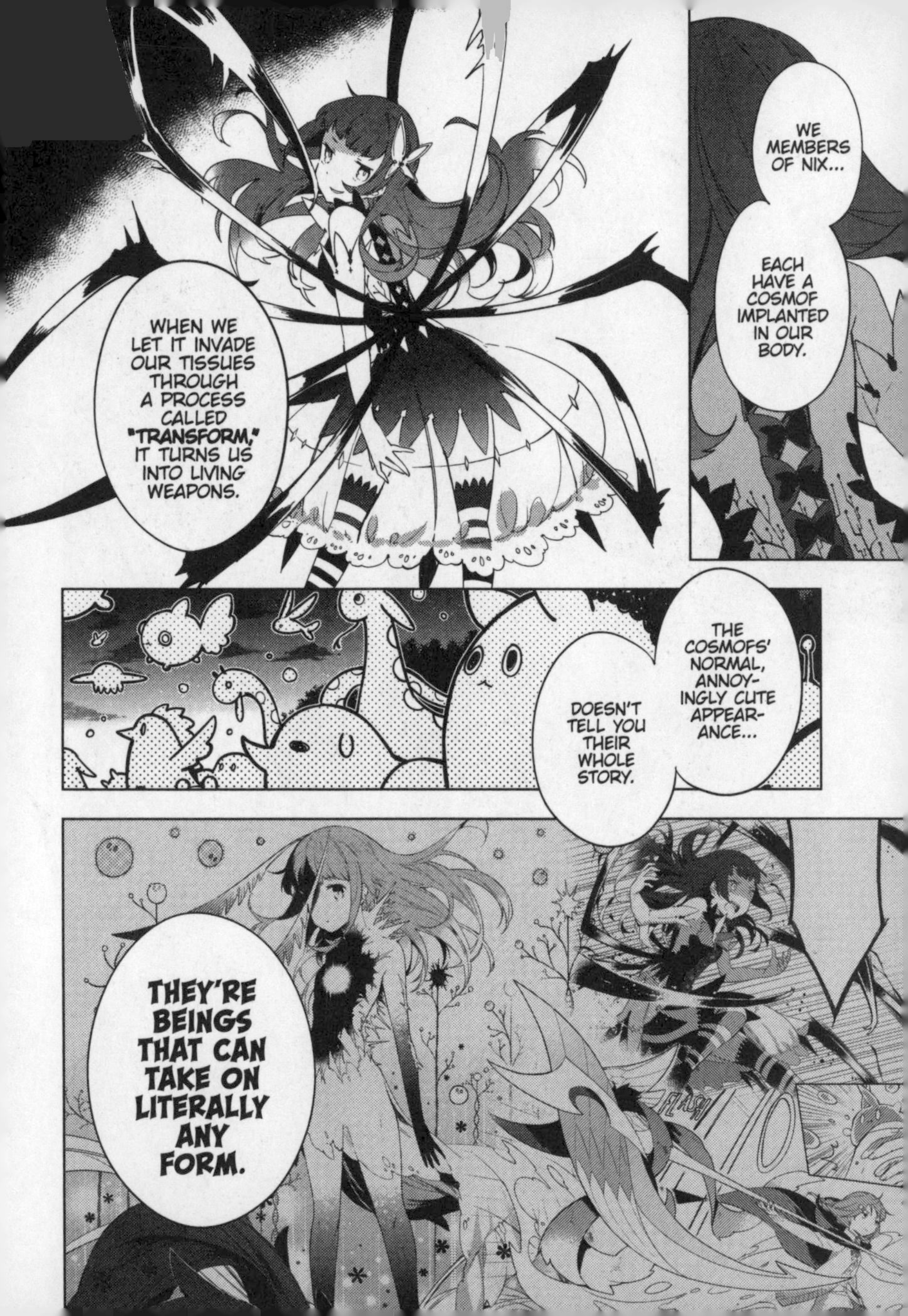
WE MEMBERS OF NIX...
EACH HAVE A COSMOF IMPLANTED IN OUR BODY.
WHEN WE LET IT INVADE OUR TISSUES THROUGH A PROCESS CALLED "TRANSFORM," IT TURNS US INTO LIVING WEAPONS.
THE COSMOFS' NORMAL, ANNOY-INGLY CUTE APPEAR-ANCE...
DOESN'T TELL YOU THEIR WHOLE STORY.
THEY'RE BEINGS THAT CAN TAKE ON LITERALLY ANY FORM.

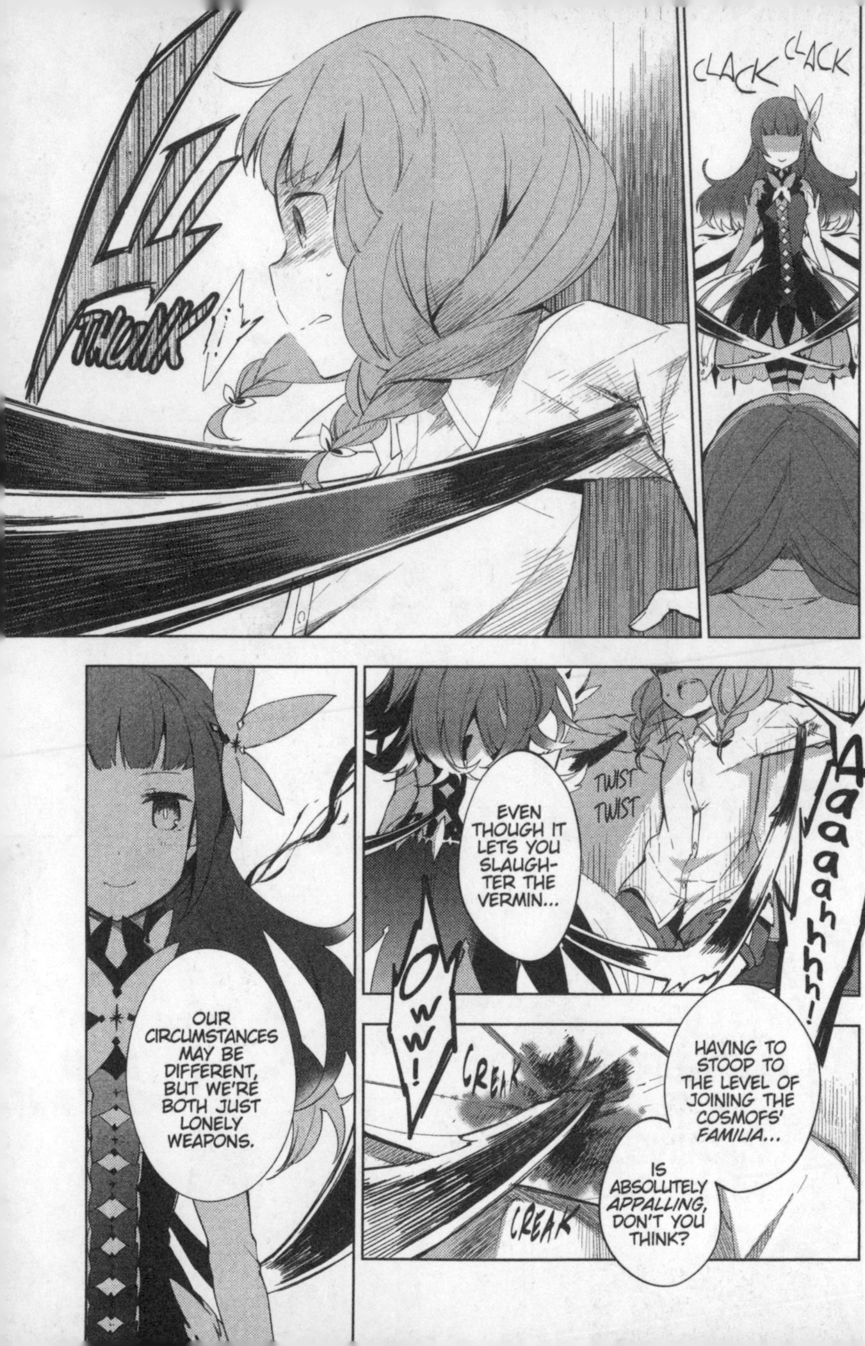
CLACK CLACK
THUNK
EVEN THOUGH IT LETS YOU SLAUGHTER THE VERMIN...
TWIST TWIST
Aaaaahhh!
OWW!
CREAK
HAVING TO STOOP TO THE LEVEL OF JOINING THE COSMOFS' *FAMILIA*...
IS ABSOLUTELY *APPALLING*, DON'T YOU THINK?
CREAK
OUR CIRCUMSTANCES MAY BE DIFFERENT, BUT WE'RE BOTH JUST LONELY WEAPONS.

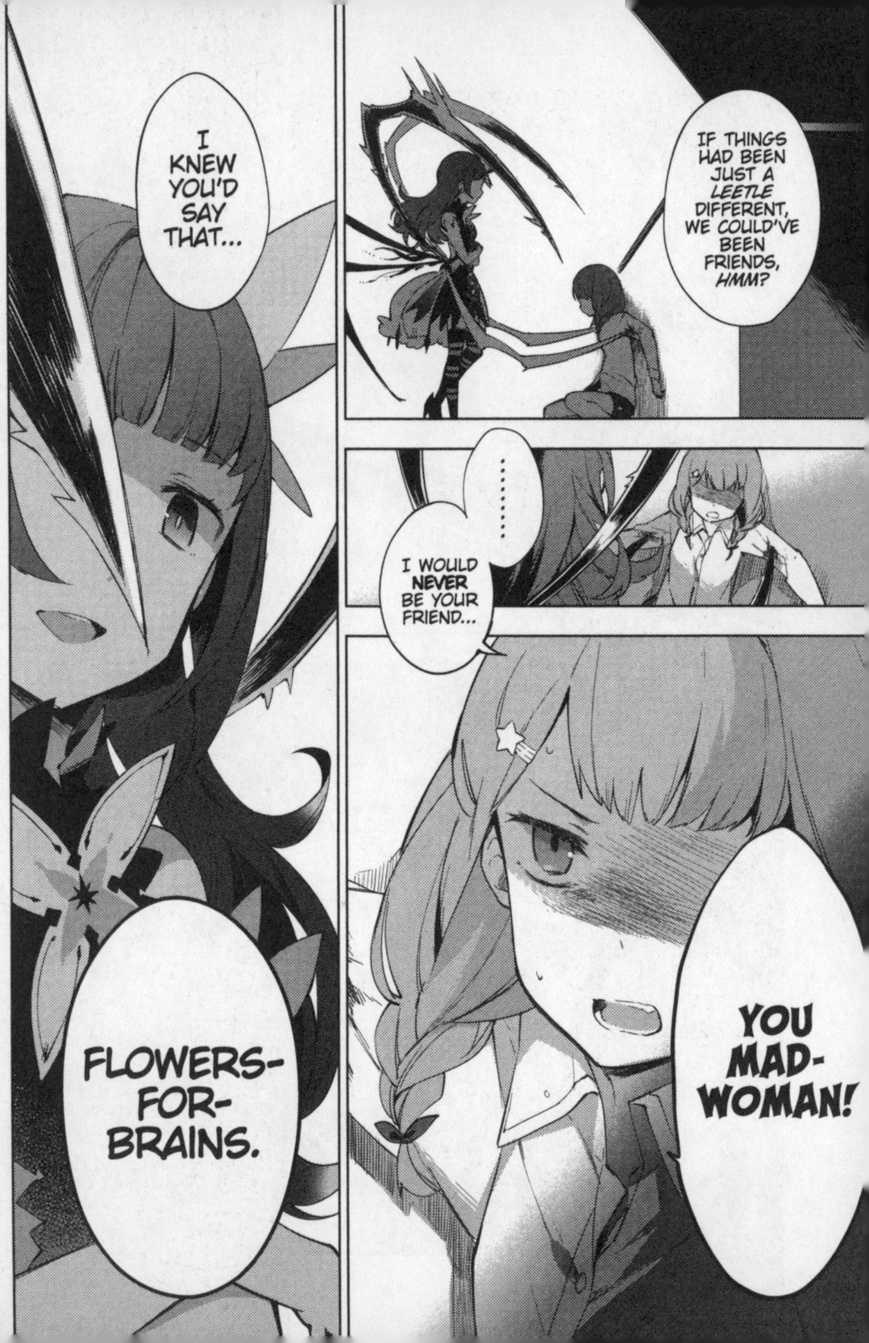
IF THINGS HAD BEEN JUST A *LEETLE* DIFFERENT, WE COULD'VE BEEN FRIENDS, *HMM?*
......
I WOULD **NEVER** BE YOUR FRIEND...
YOU MAD-WOMAN!
I KNEW YOU'D SAY THAT...
FLOWERS-FOR-BRAINS.

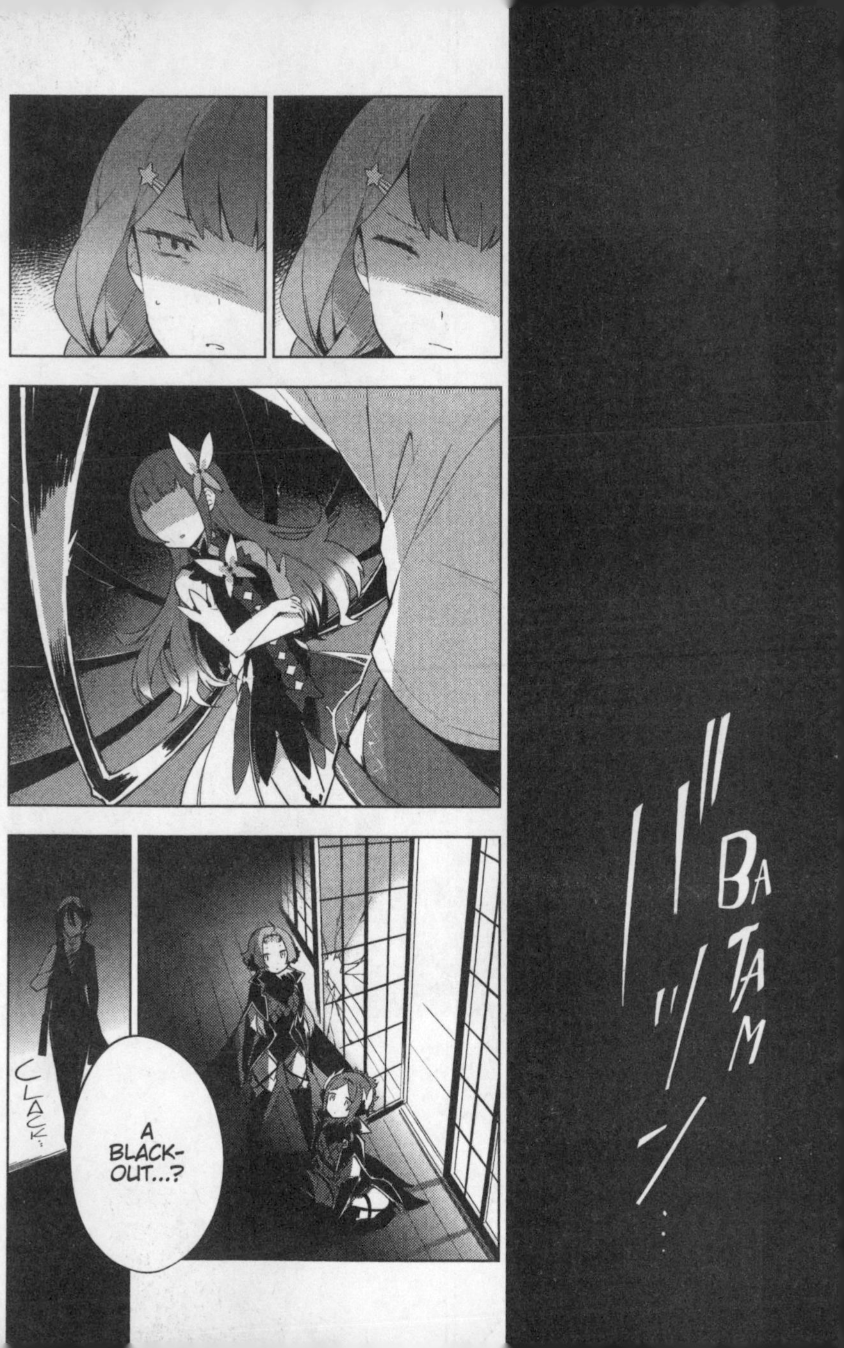
BATAM
CLACK..
A BLACK-OUT...?

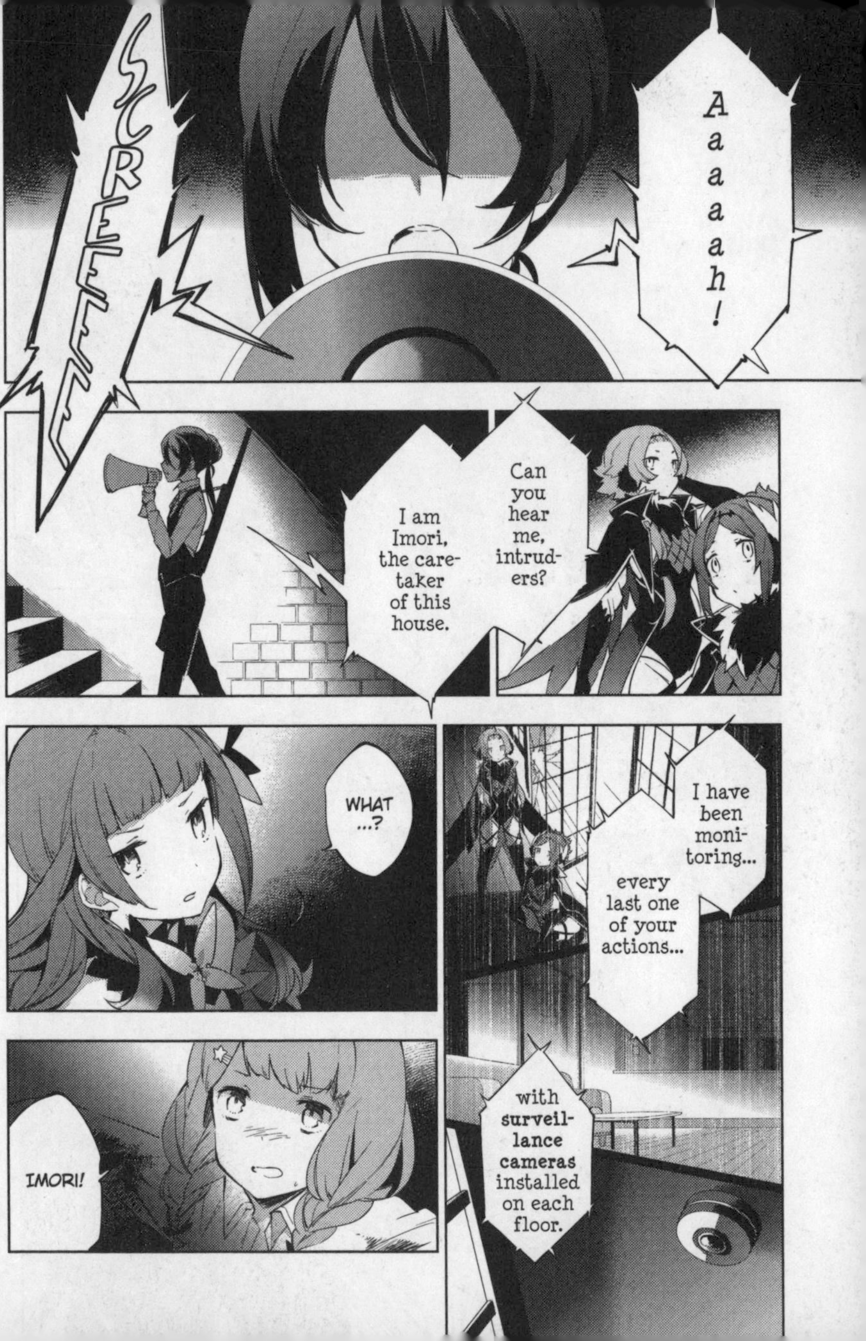
Aaaaah!
SCREEEEE
Can you hear me, intruders?
I am Imori, the caretaker of this house.
I have been monitoring...
every last one of your actions...
with **surveillance cameras** installed on each floor.
WHAT ...?
IMORI!

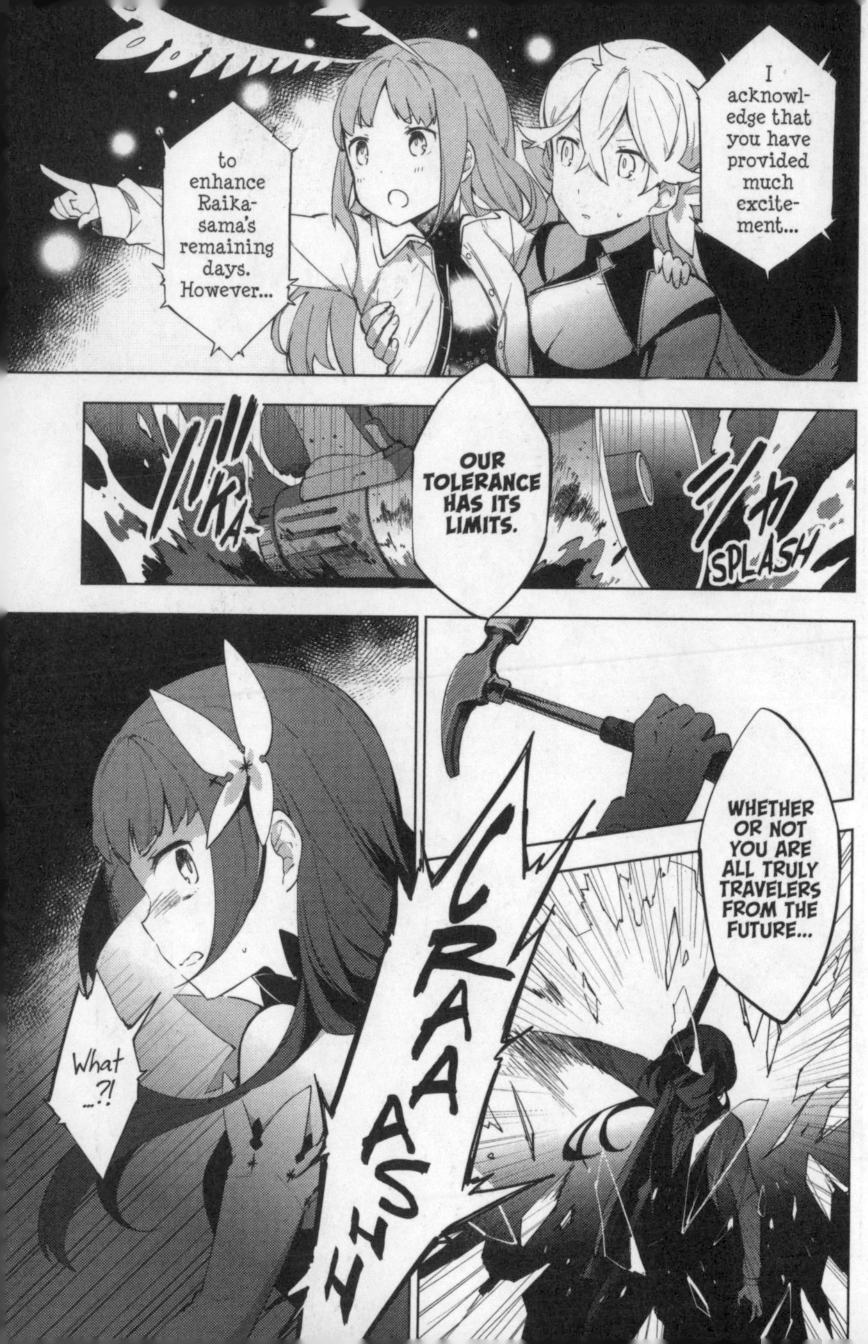
I acknowledge that you have provided much excitement...
to enhance Raika-sama's remaining days. However...
SPLASH
OUR TOLERANCE HAS ITS LIMITS.
WHETHER OR NOT YOU ARE ALL TRULY TRAVELERS FROM THE FUTURE...
CRAAASHH
What ...?!

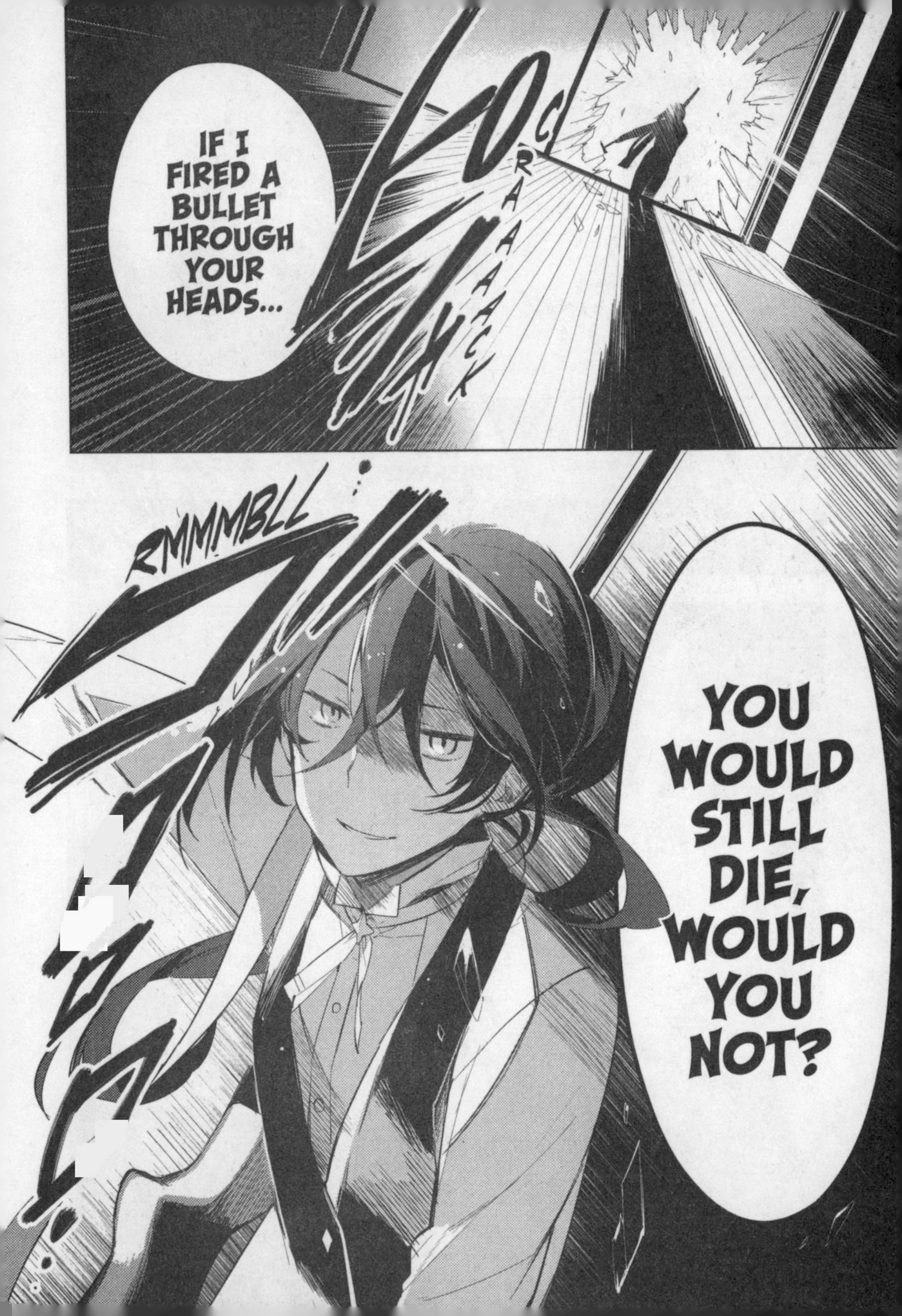
CRAAAAACK
IF I FIRED A BULLET THROUGH YOUR HEADS...
YOU WOULD STILL DIE, WOULD YOU NOT?
RMMMBLL

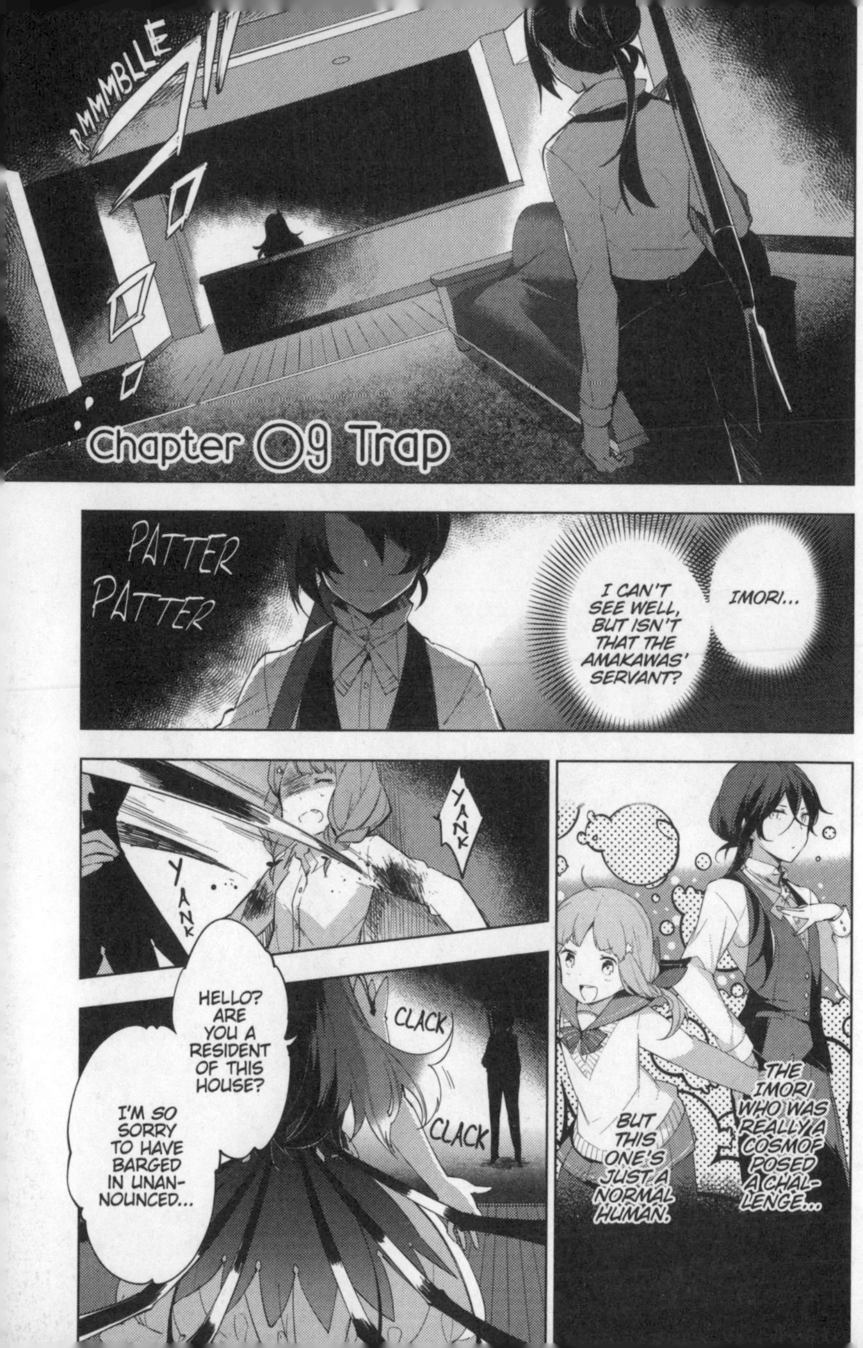
RMMMBLLE
Chapter 09 Trap
IMORI...
I CAN'T SEE WELL, BUT ISN'T THAT THE AMAKAWAS' SERVANT?
PATTER PATTER
THE IMORI WHO WAS REALLY A COSMOF POSED A CHALLENGE...
BUT THIS ONE'S JUST A NORMAL HUMAN.
YANK
YANK
CLACK
CLACK
HELLO? ARE YOU A RESIDENT OF THIS HOUSE?
I'M SO SORRY TO HAVE BARGED IN UNANNOUNCED...

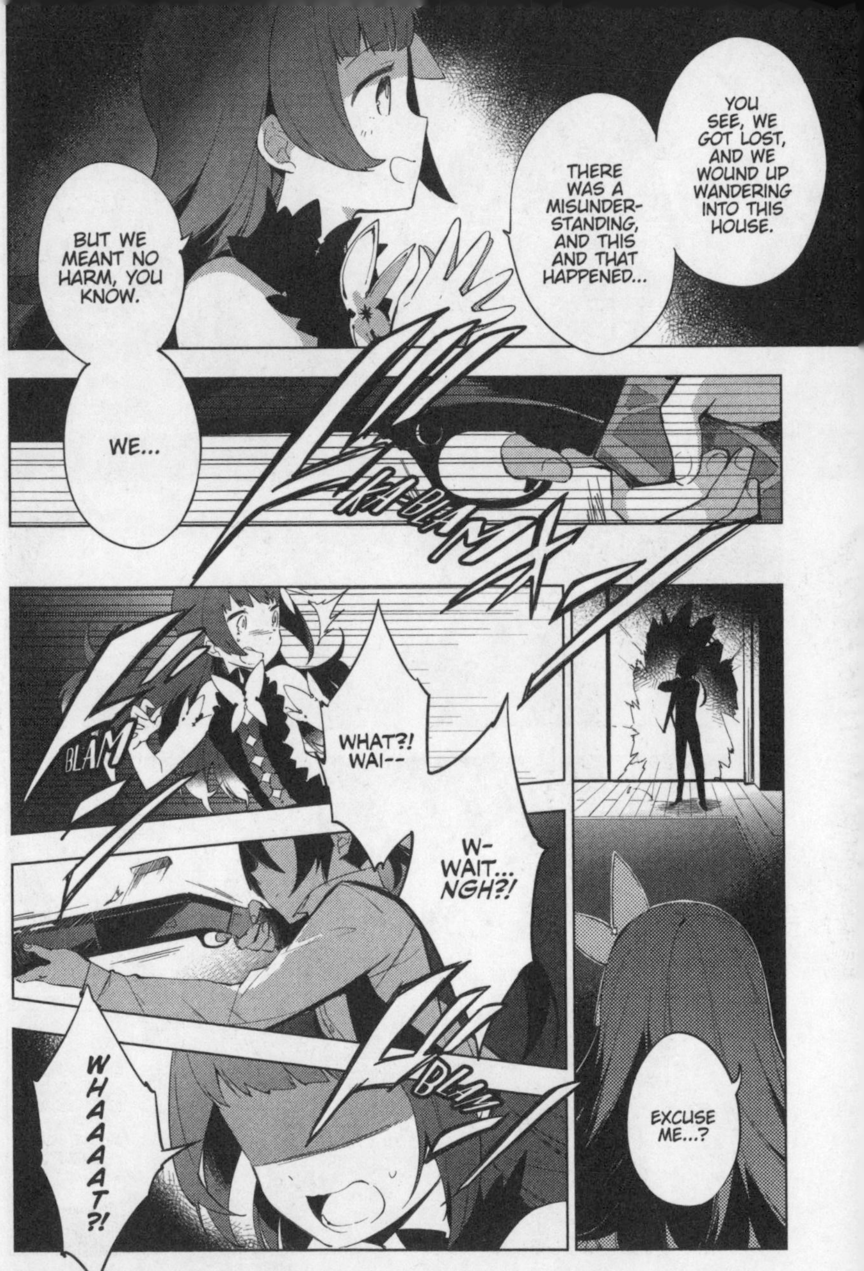
YOU SEE, WE GOT LOST, AND WE WOUND UP WANDERING INTO THIS HOUSE.
THERE WAS A MISUNDERSTANDING, AND THIS AND THAT HAPPENED...
BUT WE MEANT NO HARM, YOU KNOW.
WE...
KA-BLAM
WHAT?! WAI--
BLAM
W-WAIT... NGH?!
EXCUSE ME...?
BLAM
WHAAAAAT?!

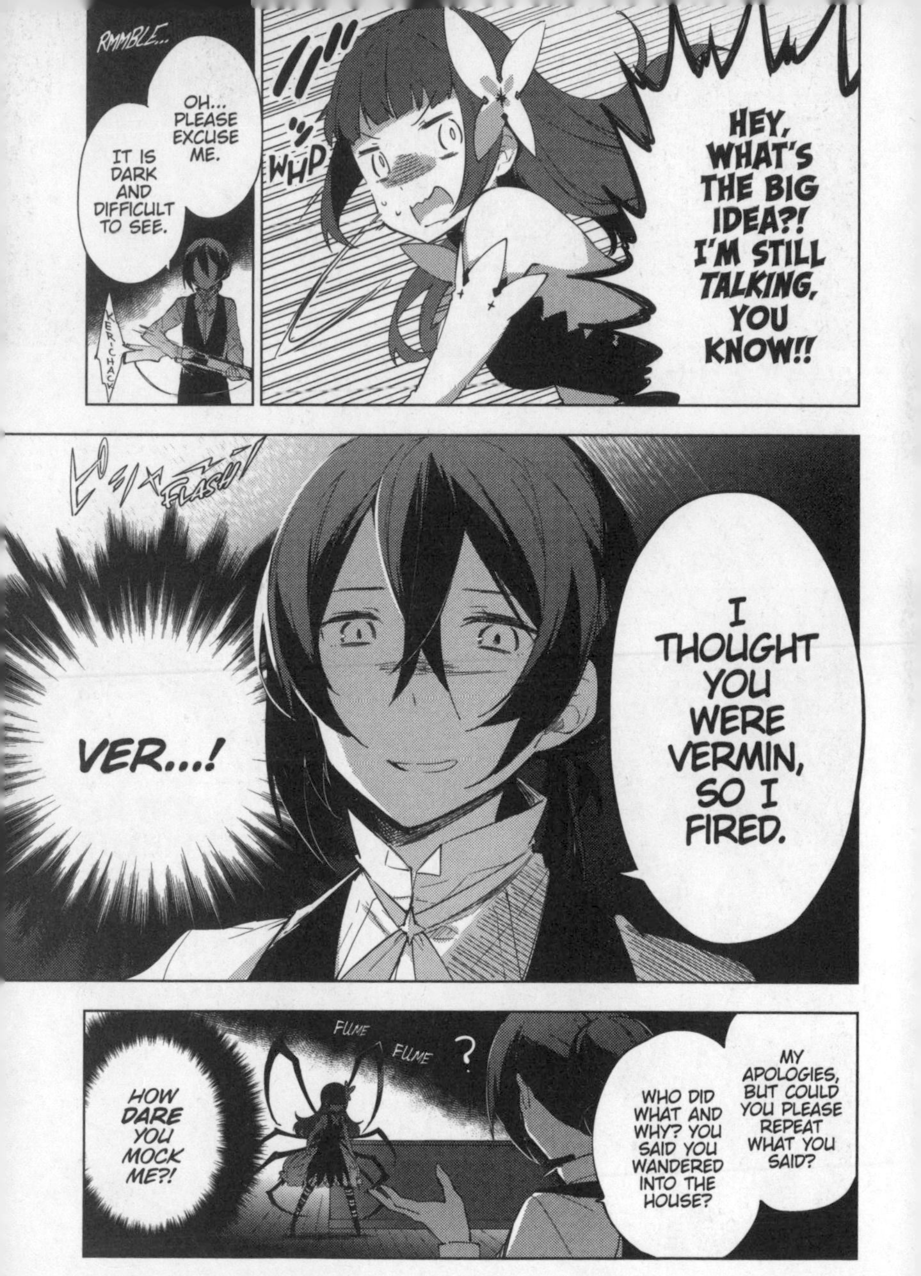
WHP
HEY, WHAT'S THE BIG IDEA?! I'M STILL TALKING, YOU KNOW!!
RMMBLE...
OH... PLEASE EXCUSE ME.
IT IS DARK AND DIFFICULT TO SEE.
KERICHACK
FLASH
I THOUGHT YOU WERE VERMIN, SO I FIRED.
VER...!
MY APOLOGIES, BUT COULD YOU PLEASE REPEAT WHAT YOU SAID?
WHO DID WHAT AND WHY? YOU SAID YOU WANDERED INTO THE HOUSE?
?
FUME
FUME
HOW DARE YOU MOCK ME?!

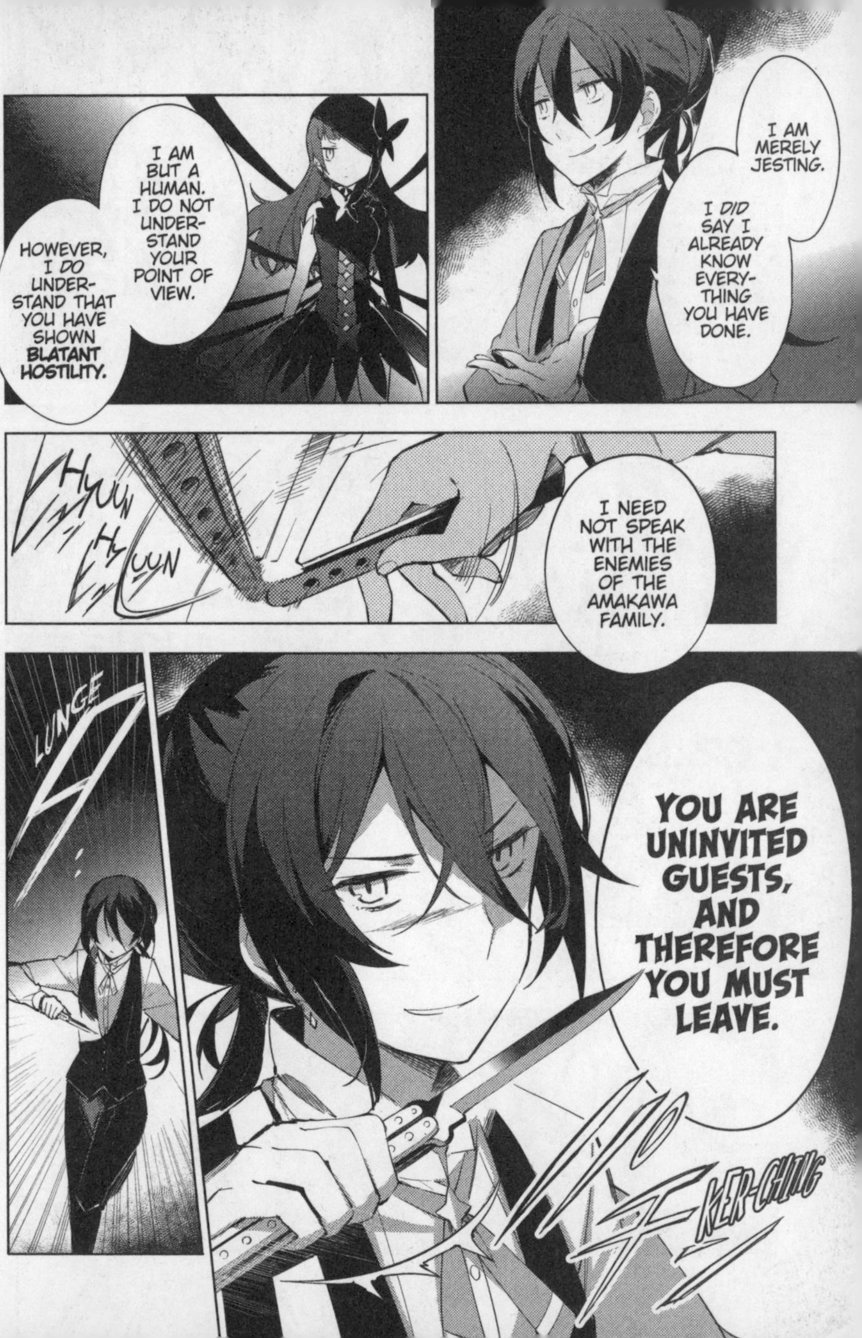

I AM MERELY JESTING.
I DID SAY I ALREADY KNOW EVERYTHING YOU HAVE DONE.
I AM BUT A HUMAN. I DO NOT UNDER-STAND YOUR POINT OF VIEW.
HOWEVER, I DO UNDER-STAND THAT YOU HAVE SHOWN BLATANT HOSTILITY.
I NEED NOT SPEAK WITH THE ENEMIES OF THE AMAKAWA FAMILY.
HYUUN
HYUUN
YOU ARE UNINVITED GUESTS, AND THEREFORE YOU MUST LEAVE.
KER-CHING
LUNGE

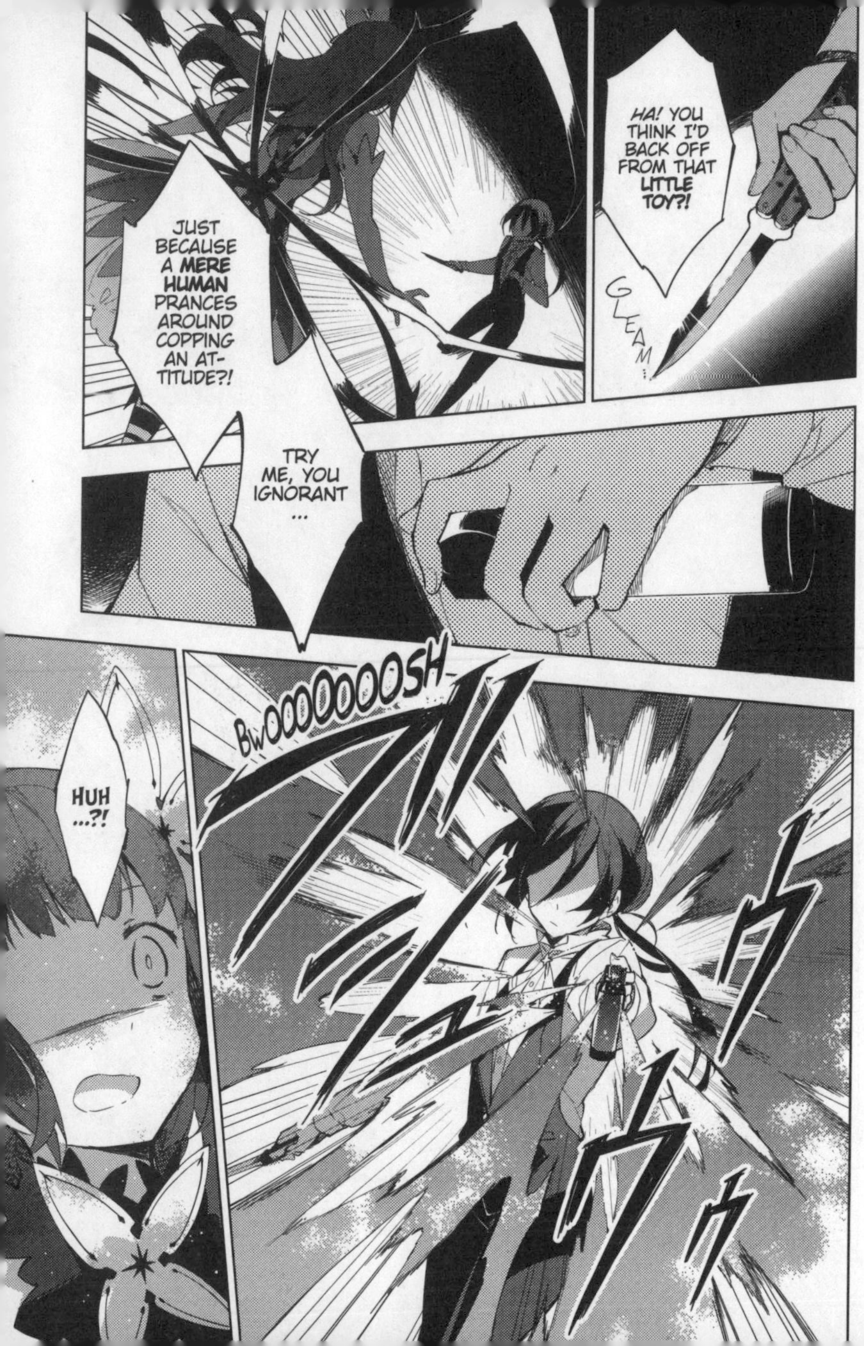
HA! YOU THINK I'D BACK OFF FROM THAT LITTLE TOY?!
GLEAM...
JUST BECAUSE A MERE HUMAN PRANCES AROUND COPPING AN AT-TITUDE?!
TRY ME, YOU IGNORANT ...
BWOOOOOOOSH
HUH ...?!

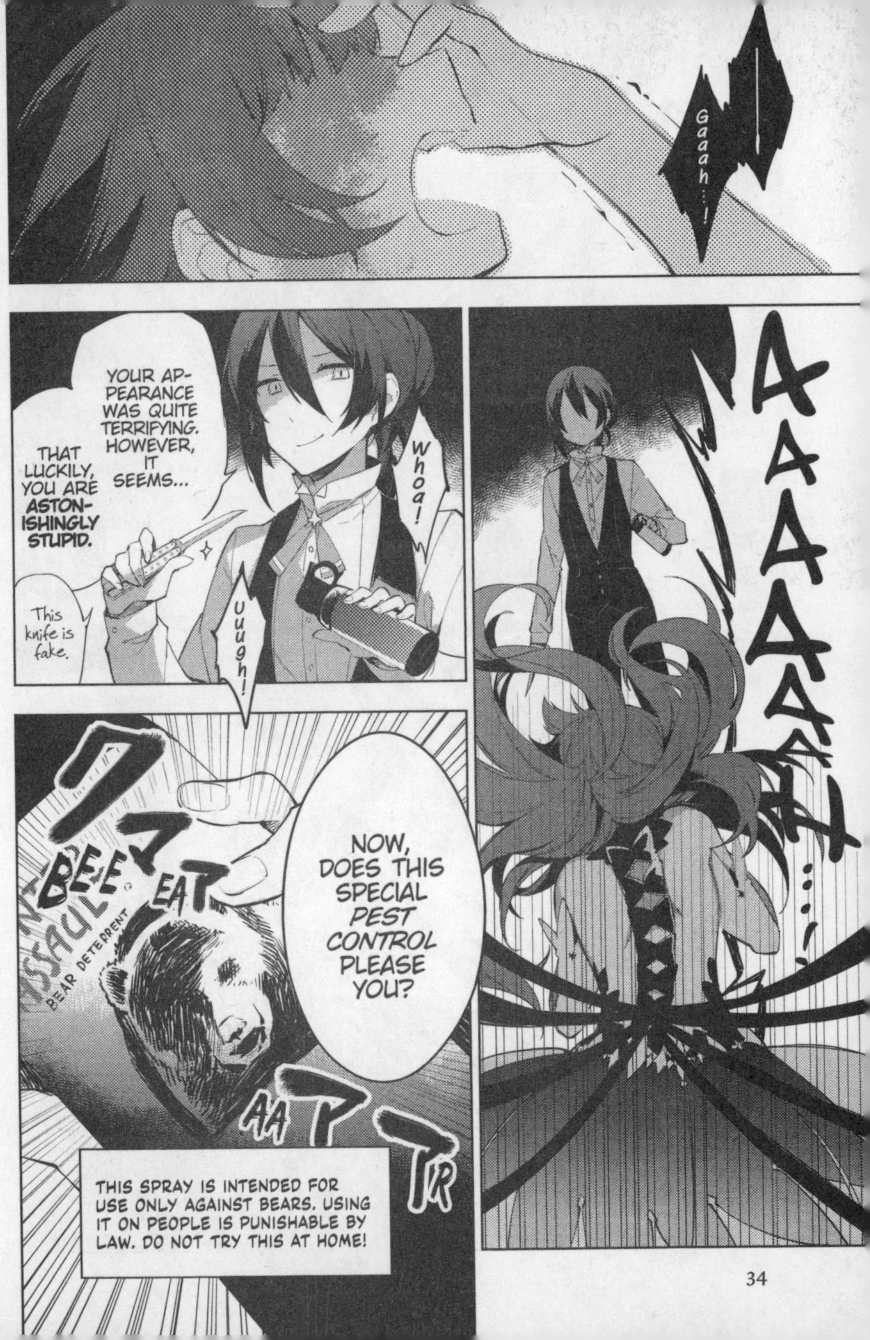

Gaaah...!
AAAAAAH...!
Whoa!
YOUR APPEARANCE WAS QUITE TERRIFYING. HOWEVER, IT SEEMS...
THAT LUCKILY, YOU ARE **ASTONISHINGLY STUPID.**
Uuugh!
This knife is fake.
NOW, DOES THIS SPECIAL *PEST CONTROL* PLEASE YOU?
BEAR DETERRENT
THIS SPRAY IS INTENDED FOR USE ONLY AGAINST BEARS. USING IT ON PEOPLE IS PUNISHABLE BY LAW. DO NOT TRY THIS AT HOME!

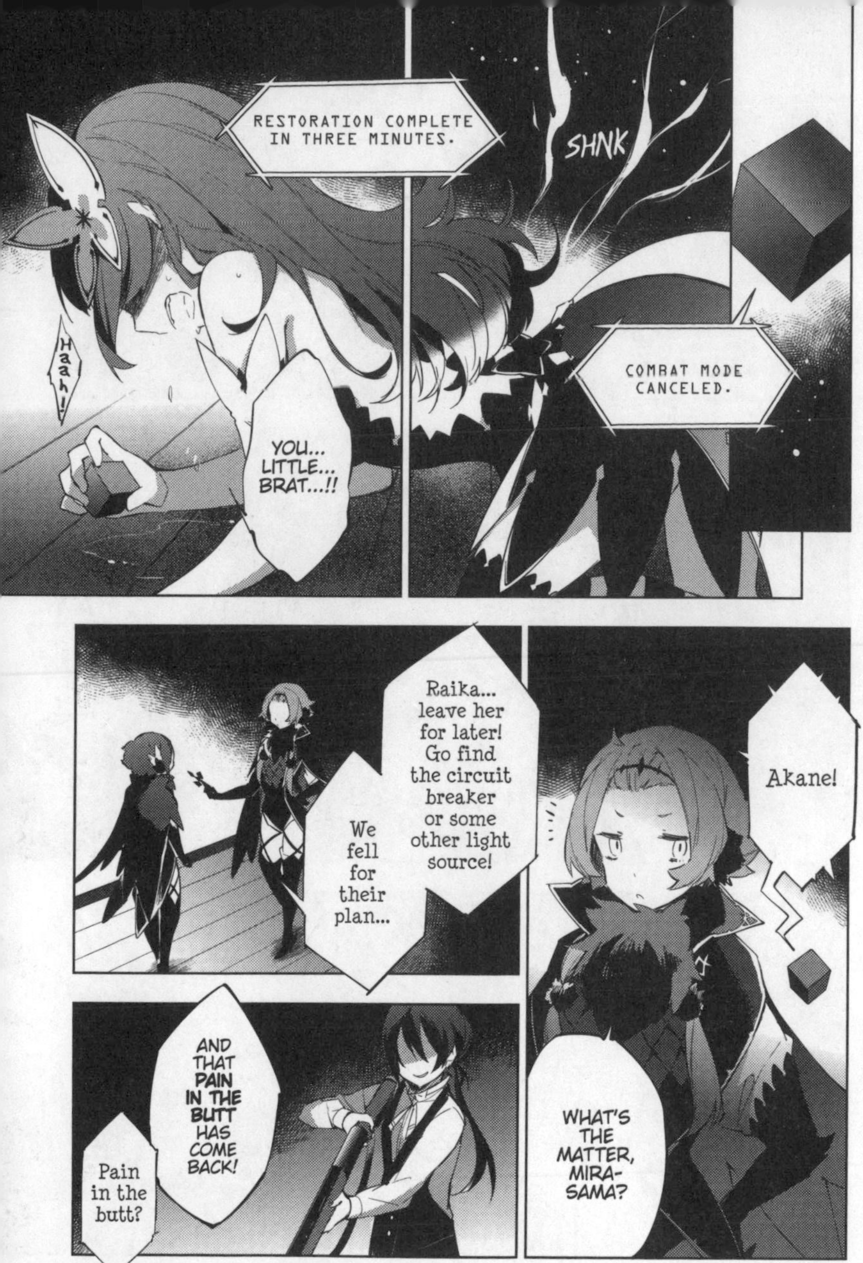
SHNK
COMBAT MODE CANCELED.
RESTORATION COMPLETE IN THREE MINUTES.
Haah!
YOU... LITTLE... BRAT...!!
Akane!
WHAT'S THE MATTER, MIRA-SAMA?
Raika... leave her for later! Go find the circuit breaker or some other light source!
We fell for their plan...
AND THAT PAIN IN THE BUTT HAS COME BACK!
Pain in the butt?

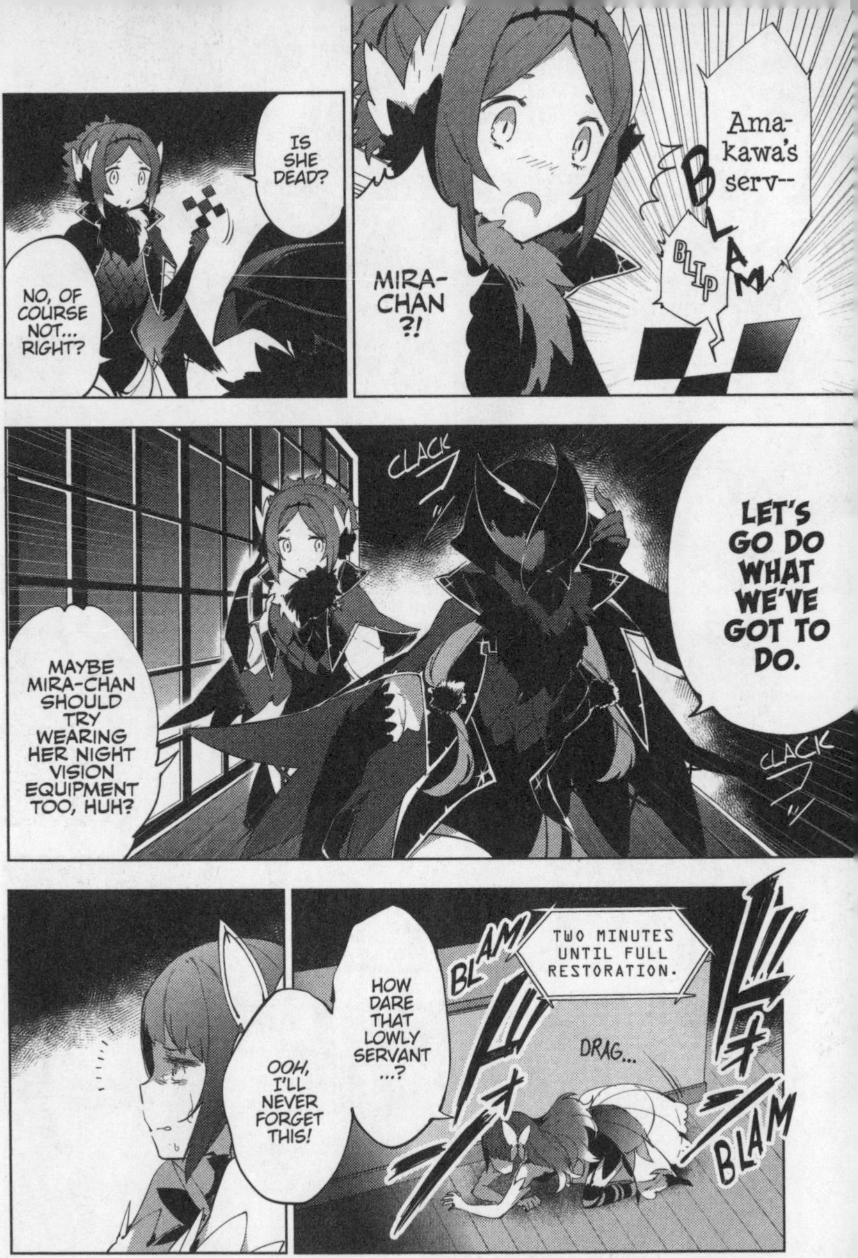
Ama-kawa's serv--
BLAM
BLIP
MIRA-CHAN?!
IS SHE DEAD?
NO, OF COURSE NOT... RIGHT?
CLACK
LET'S GO DO WHAT WE'VE GOT TO DO.
CLACK
MAYBE MIRA-CHAN SHOULD TRY WEARING HER NIGHT VISION EQUIPMENT TOO, HUH?
TWO MINUTES UNTIL FULL RESTORATION.
BLAM
DRAG...
BLAM
HOW DARE THAT LOWLY SERVANT ...?
OOH, I'LL NEVER FORGET THIS!

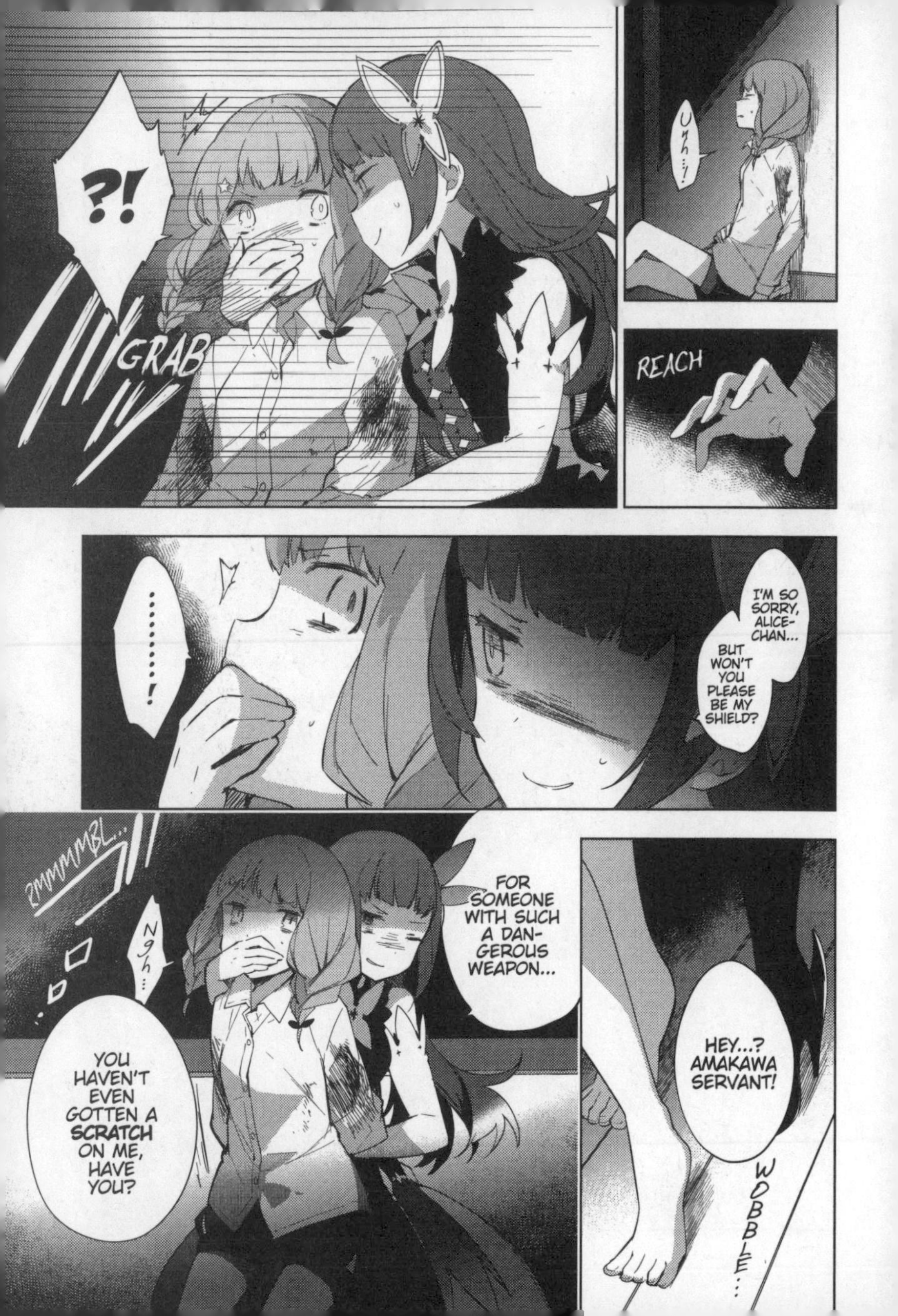

Urgh...!
REACH
?!
GRAB
I'M SO SORRY, ALICE-CHAN... BUT WON'T YOU PLEASE BE MY SHIELD?
.......!
HEY...? AMAKAWA SERVANT!
WOBBLE...
RMMMMBL...
FOR SOMEONE WITH SUCH A DAN-GEROUS WEAPON...
Ngh...
YOU HAVEN'T EVEN GOTTEN A SCRATCH ON ME, HAVE YOU?

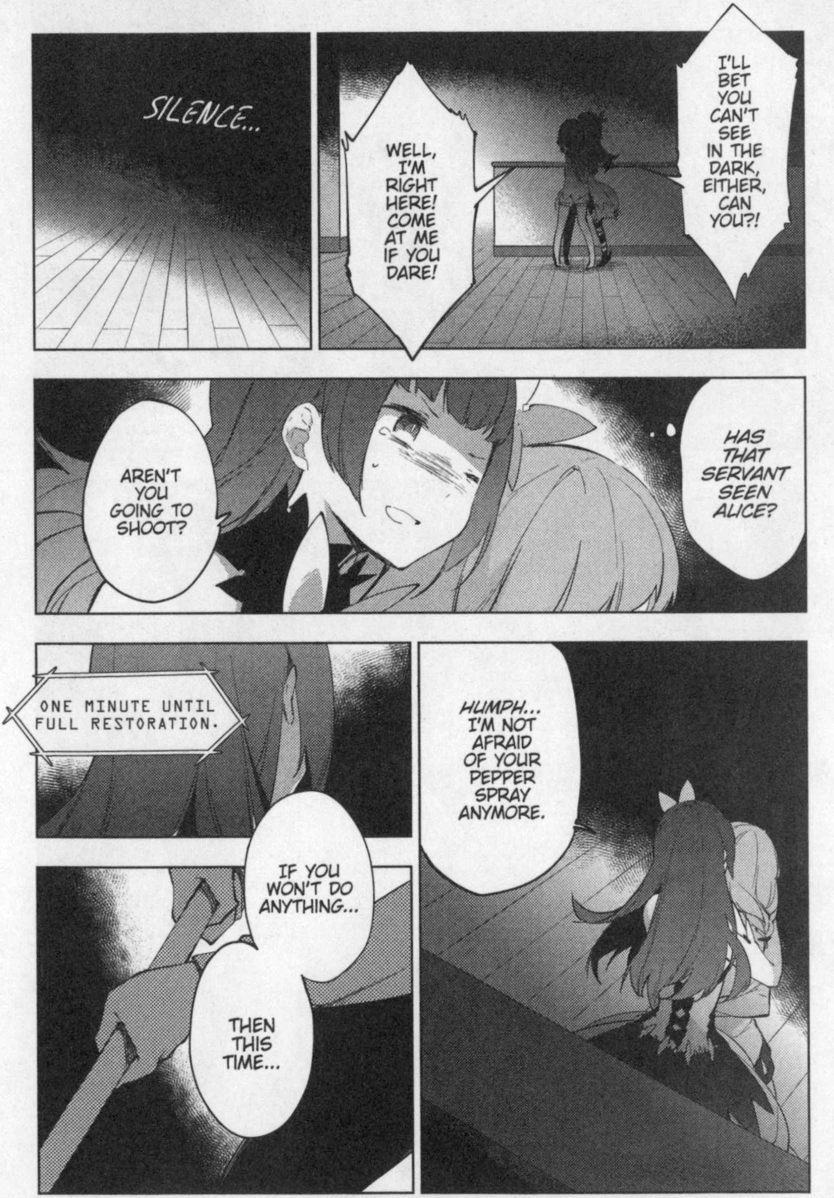
I'LL BET YOU CAN'T SEE IN THE DARK, EITHER, CAN YOU?!
WELL, I'M RIGHT HERE! COME AT ME IF YOU DARE!
SILENCE...
HAS THAT SERVANT SEEN ALICE?
AREN'T YOU GOING TO SHOOT?
HUMPH... I'M NOT AFRAID OF YOUR PEPPER SPRAY ANYMORE.
ONE MINUTE UNTIL FULL RESTORATION.
IF YOU WON'T DO ANYTHING...
THEN THIS TIME...

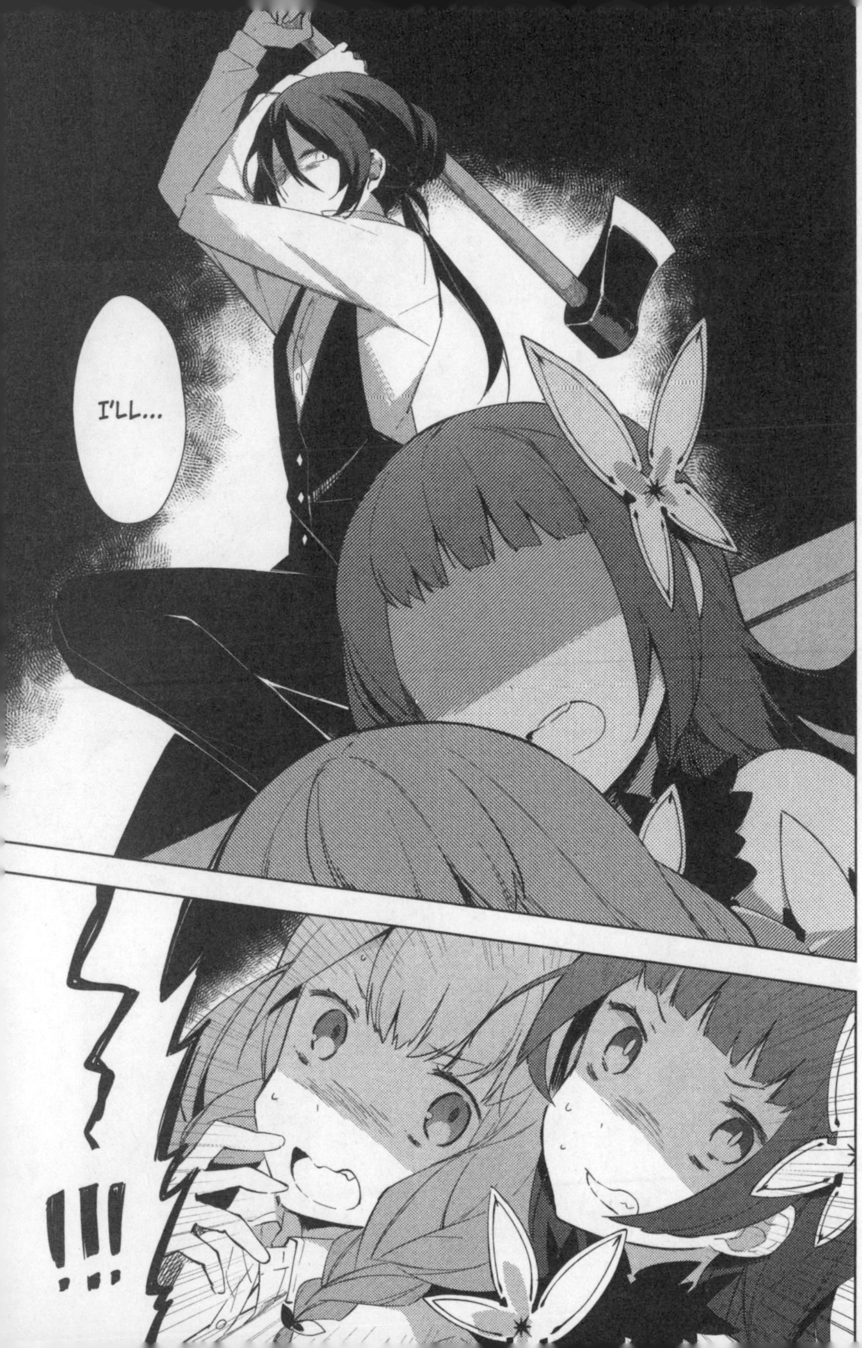
I'LL...
!!!

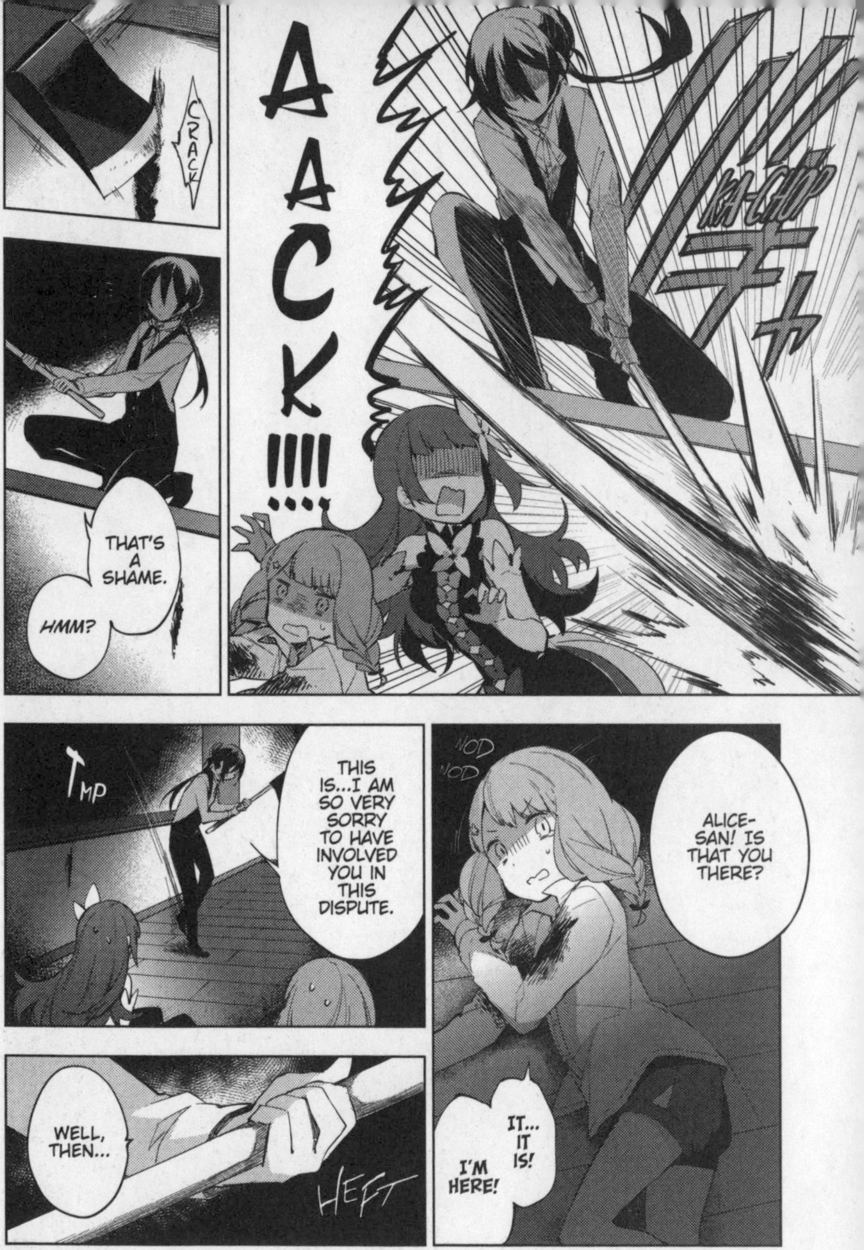
KA-CHIP
チャ
AACK!!!!....
CRACK
THAT'S A SHAME.
HMM?
NOD NOD
ALICE-SAN! IS THAT YOU THERE?
IT... IT IS!
I'M HERE!
TMP
THIS IS...I AM SO VERY SORRY TO HAVE INVOLVED YOU IN THIS DISPUTE.
WELL, THEN...
HEFT

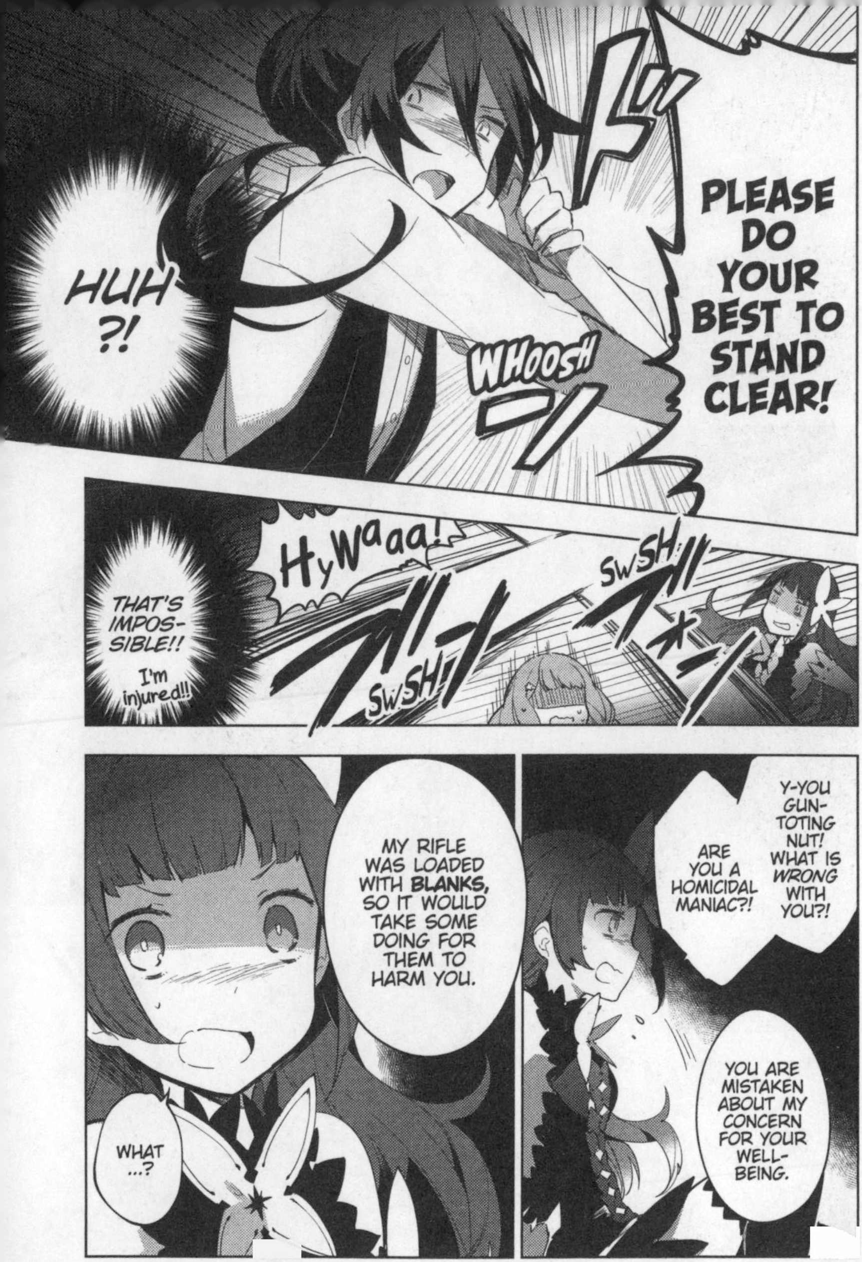
PLEASE DO YOUR BEST TO STAND CLEAR!
WHOOSH
HUH ?!
SWSH!
HyWaaa!
SWSH!
THAT'S IMPOSSIBLE!!
I'm injured!!
Y-YOU GUN-TOTING NUT! WHAT IS *WRONG* WITH YOU?!
ARE YOU A HOMICIDAL MANIAC?!
YOU ARE MISTAKEN ABOUT MY CONCERN FOR YOUR WELL-BEING.
MY RIFLE WAS LOADED WITH **BLANKS**, SO IT WOULD TAKE SOME DOING FOR THEM TO HARM YOU.
WHAT ...?

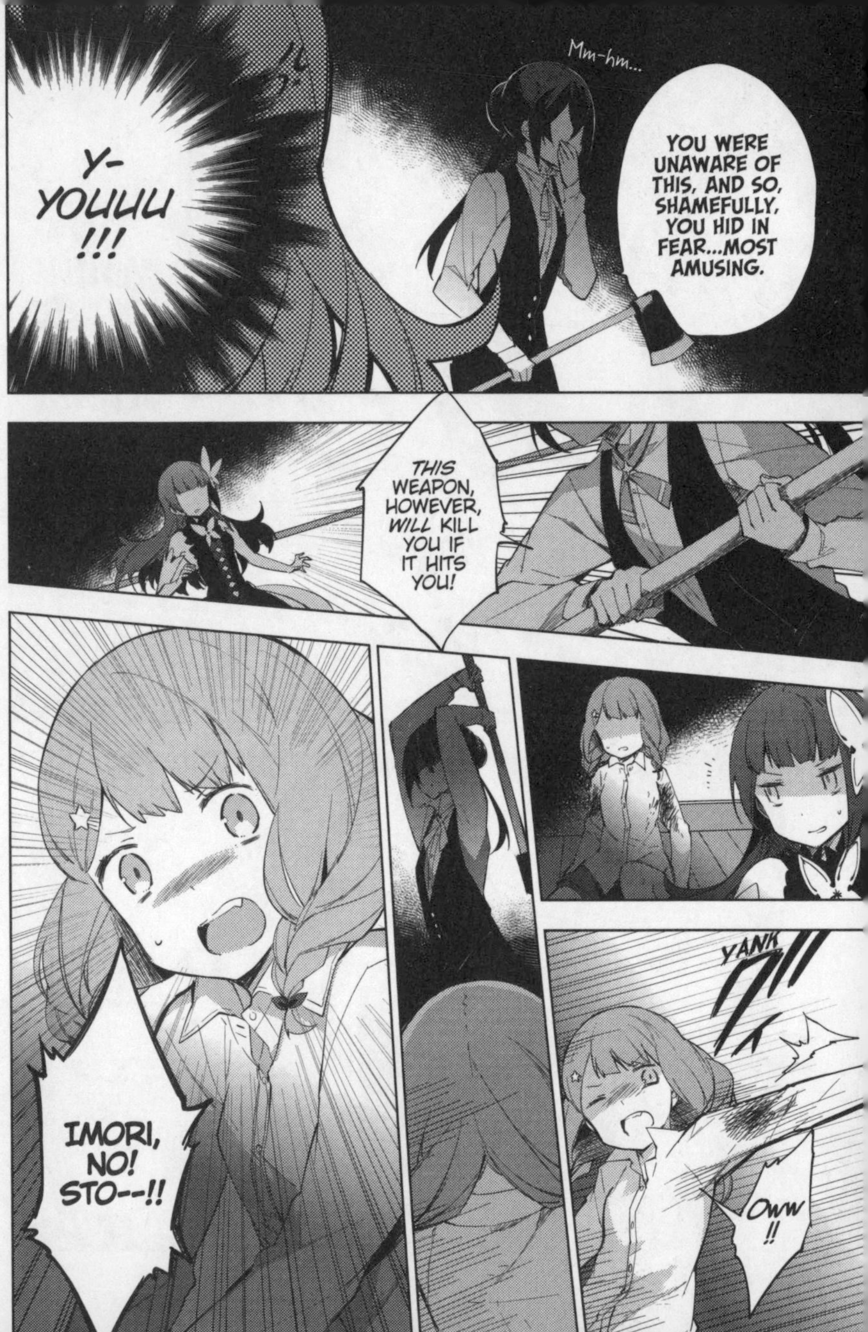
Mm-hm...
YOU WERE UNAWARE OF THIS, AND SO, SHAMEFULLY, YOU HID IN FEAR...MOST AMUSING.
Y-YOUUU!!!
THIS WEAPON, HOWEVER, WILL KILL YOU IF IT HITS YOU!
YANK
OWW!!
IMORI, NO! STO--!!

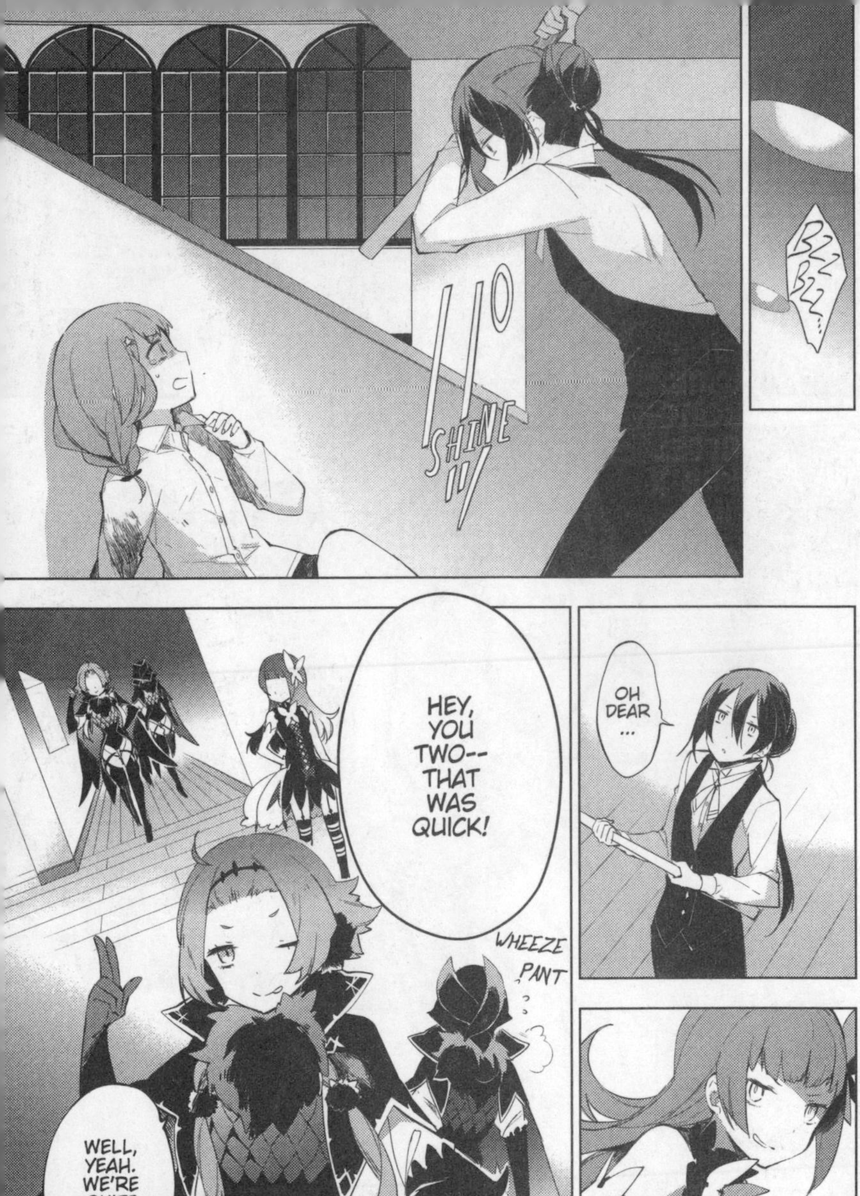
BZZ BZZ...
SHINE
OH DEAR ...
HEY, YOU TWO-- THAT WAS QUICK!
WHEEZE PANT
WELL, YEAH. WE'RE QUITE CAPABLE.

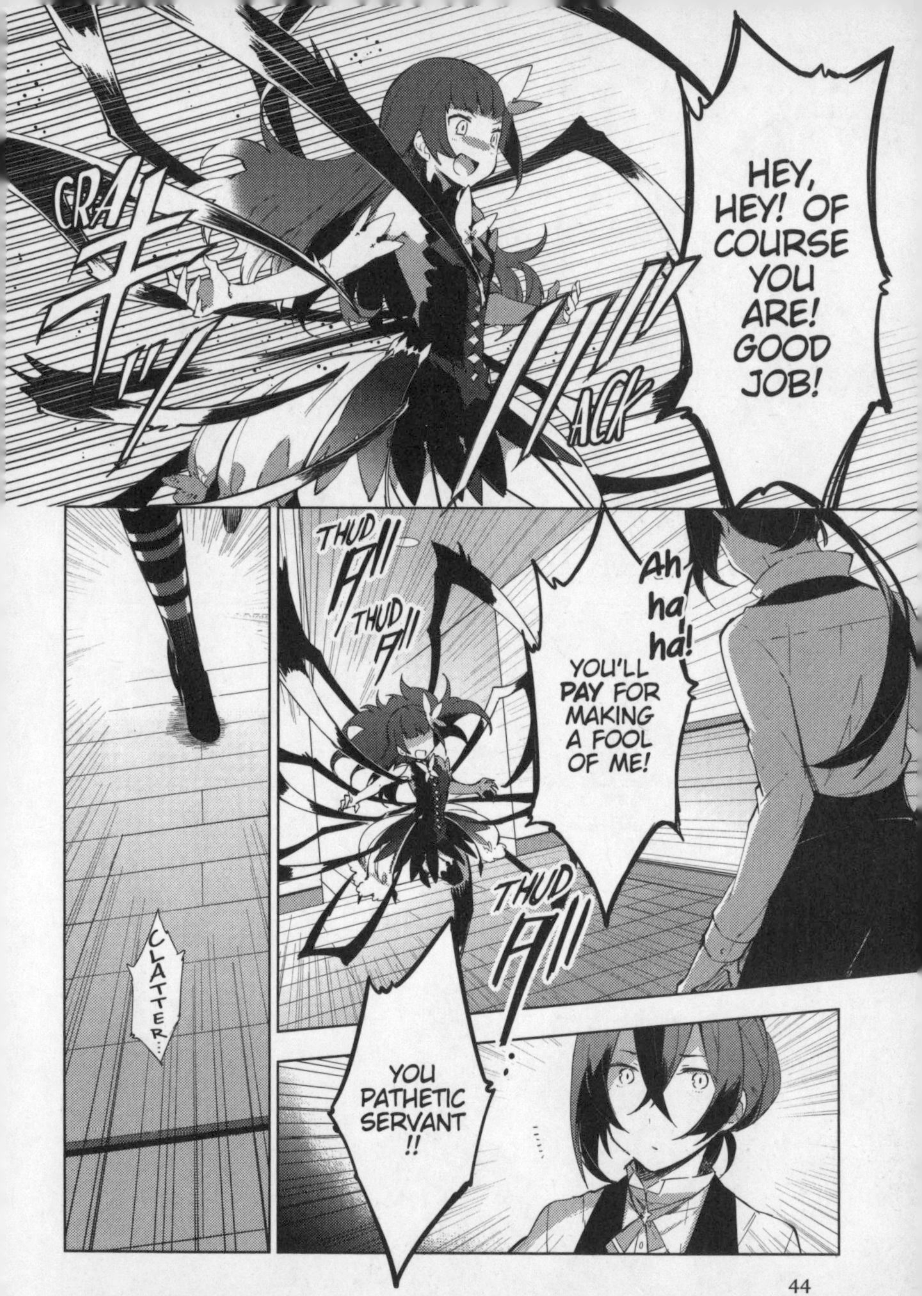
HEY, HEY! OF COURSE YOU ARE! GOOD JOB!
CRA
ACK
Ah ha ha!
YOU'LL PAY FOR MAKING A FOOL OF ME!
THUD
THUD
THUD
YOU PATHETIC SERVANT !!
......
CLATTER...

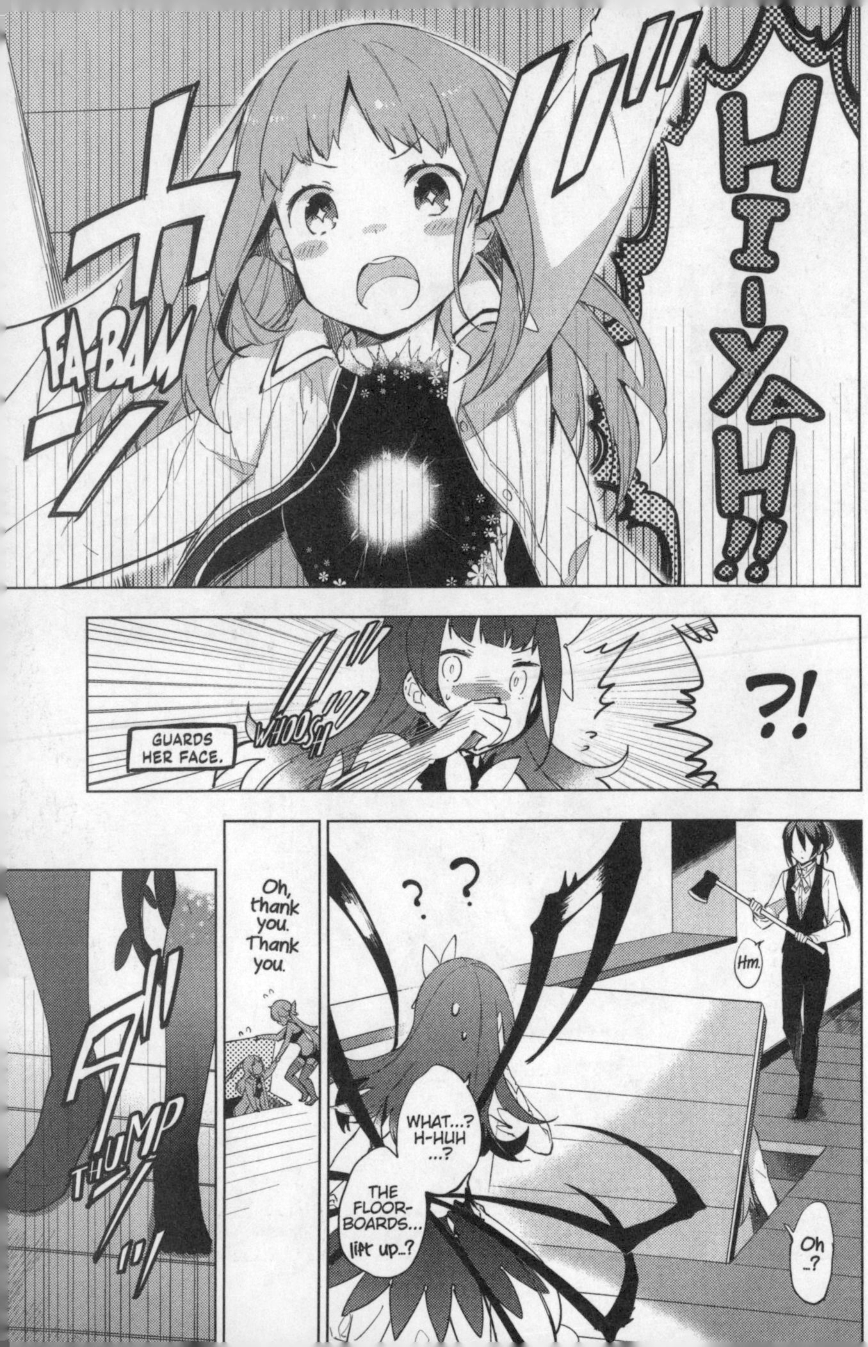
HI-YAH!!
FA-BAM
?!
WHOOSH
GUARDS HER FACE.
Hm.
Oh ...?
WHAT...? H-HUH ...?
THE FLOOR-BOARDS... lift up...?
Oh, thank you. Thank you.
THUMP

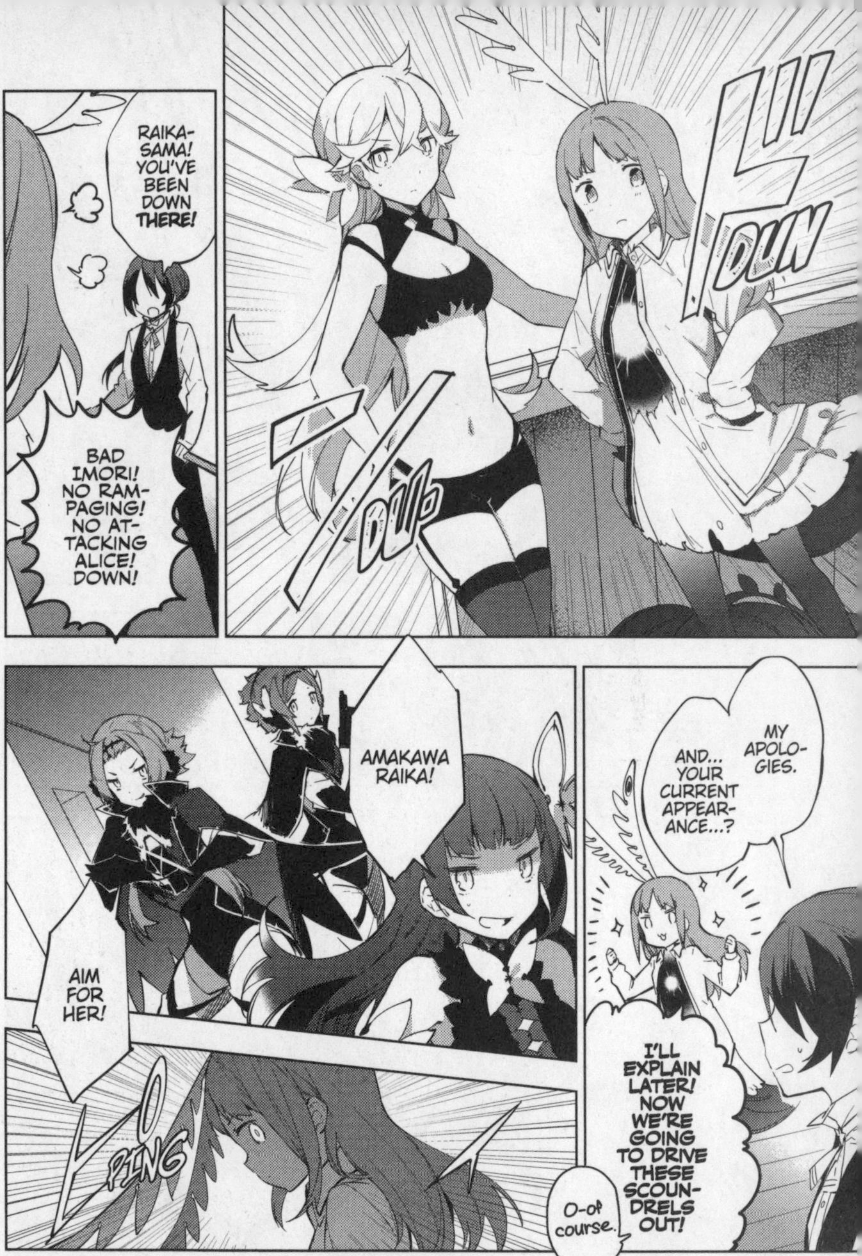
DUN
DUN
RAIKA-SAMA! YOU'VE BEEN DOWN THERE!
BAD IMORI! NO RAMPAGING! NO ATTACKING ALICE! DOWN!
MY APOLOGIES.
AND... YOUR CURRENT APPEARANCE...?
I'LL EXPLAIN LATER! NOW WE'RE GOING TO DRIVE THESE SCOUNDRELS OUT!
O-of course.
AMAKAWA RAIKA!
AIM FOR HER!
PING

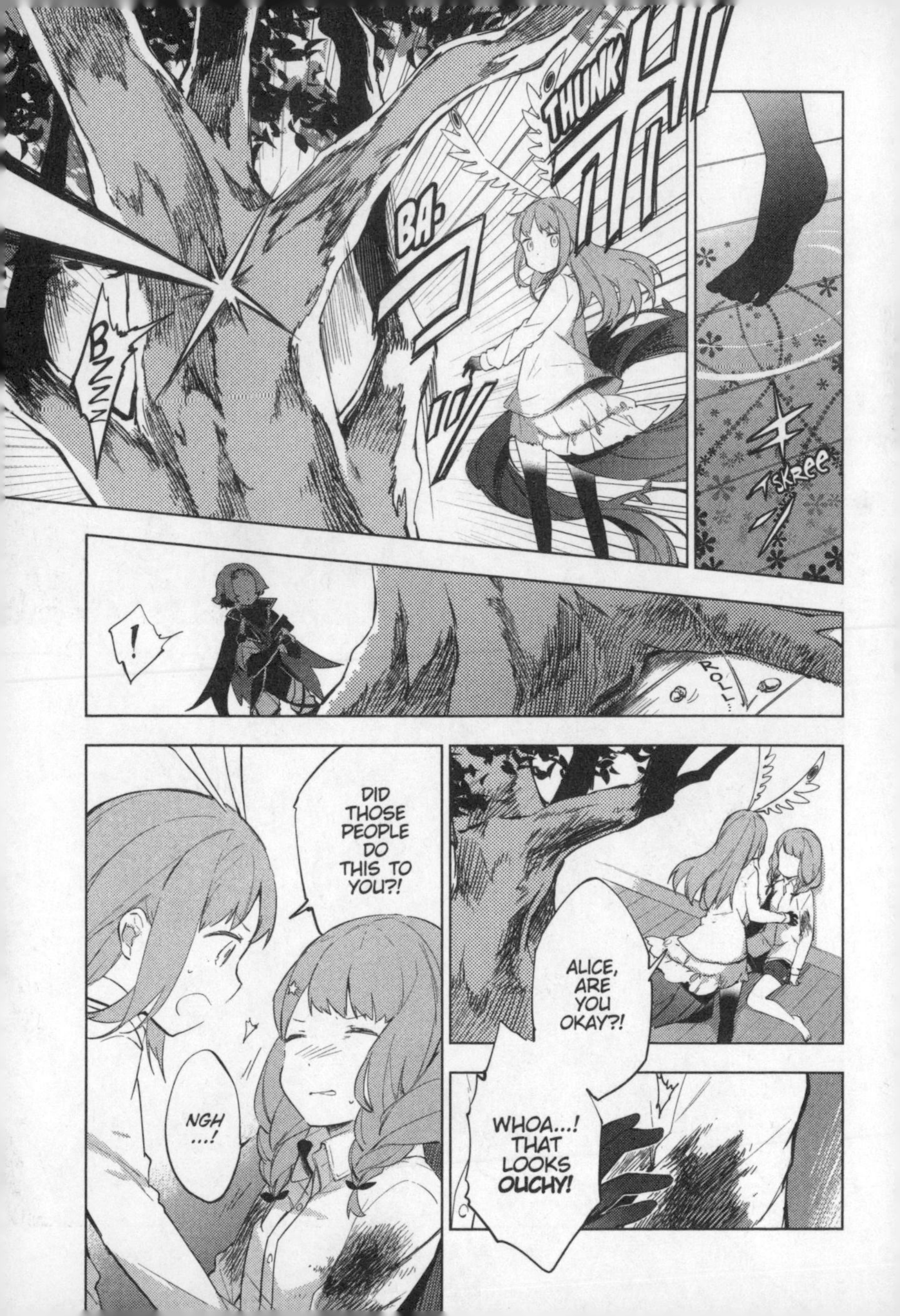
SKREE
THUNK
BA-
BZZZ
!
ROLL...
ALICE, ARE YOU OKAY?!
WHOA...! THAT LOOKS OUCHY!
DID THOSE PEOPLE DO THIS TO YOU?!
NGH ...!

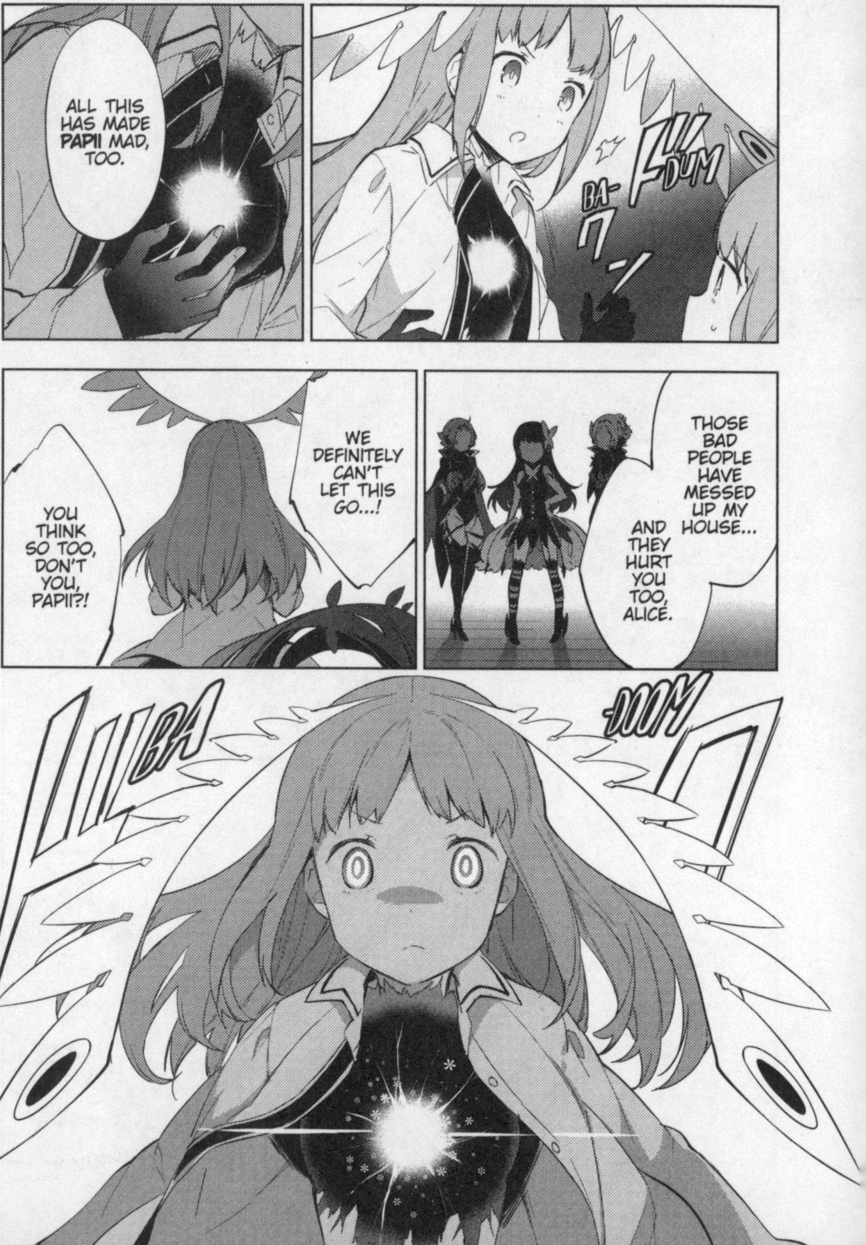
FLI
BA-DUM
ALL THIS HAS MADE PAPII MAD, TOO.
THOSE BAD PEOPLE HAVE MESSED UP MY HOUSE...
AND THEY HURT YOU TOO, ALICE.
WE DEFINITELY CAN'T LET THIS GO...!
YOU THINK SO TOO, DON'T YOU, PAPII?!
BA-DOOM

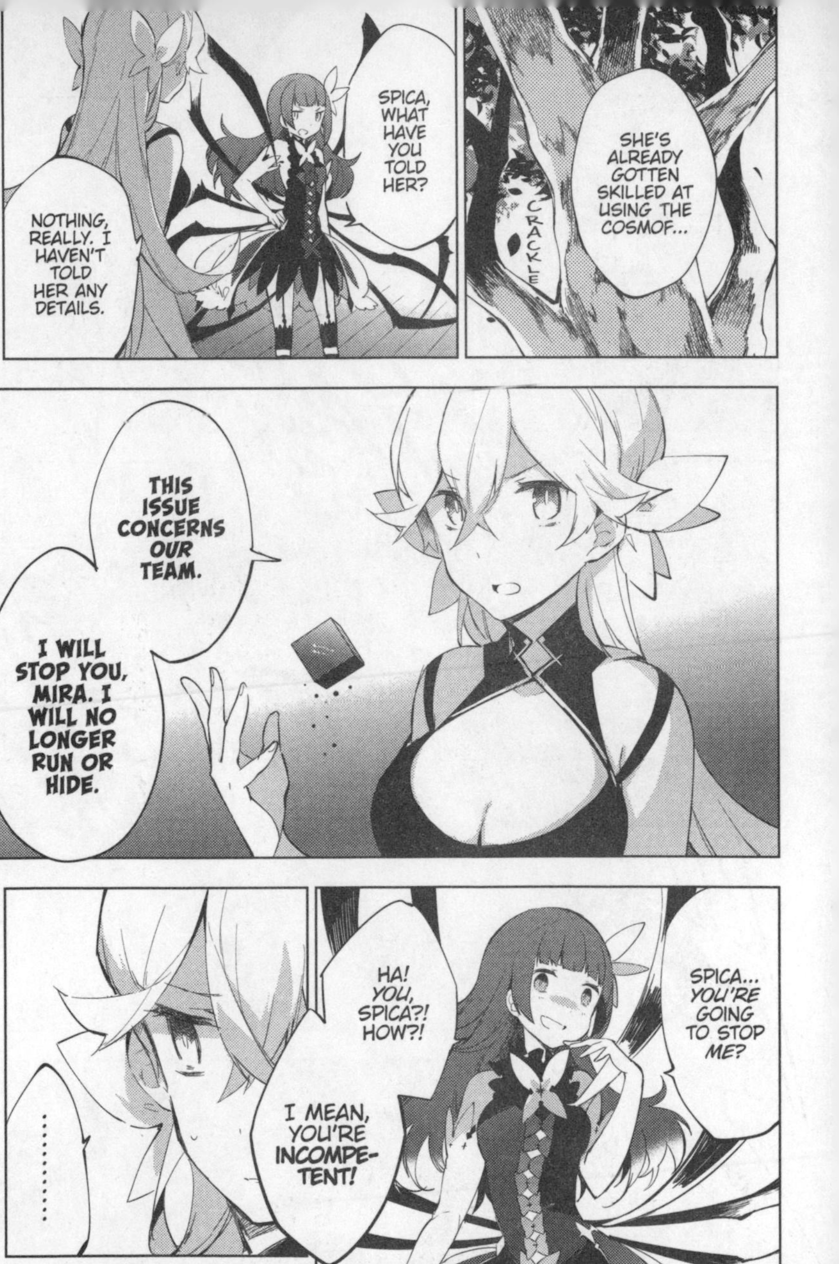
SHE'S ALREADY GOTTEN SKILLED AT USING THE COSMOF...
CRACKLE
SPICA, WHAT HAVE YOU TOLD HER?
NOTHING, REALLY. I HAVEN'T TOLD HER ANY DETAILS.
THIS ISSUE CONCERNS OUR TEAM.
I WILL STOP YOU, MIRA. I WILL NO LONGER RUN OR HIDE.
SPICA... YOU'RE GOING TO STOP ME?
HA! YOU, SPICA?! HOW?!
I MEAN, YOU'RE INCOMPETENT!
........

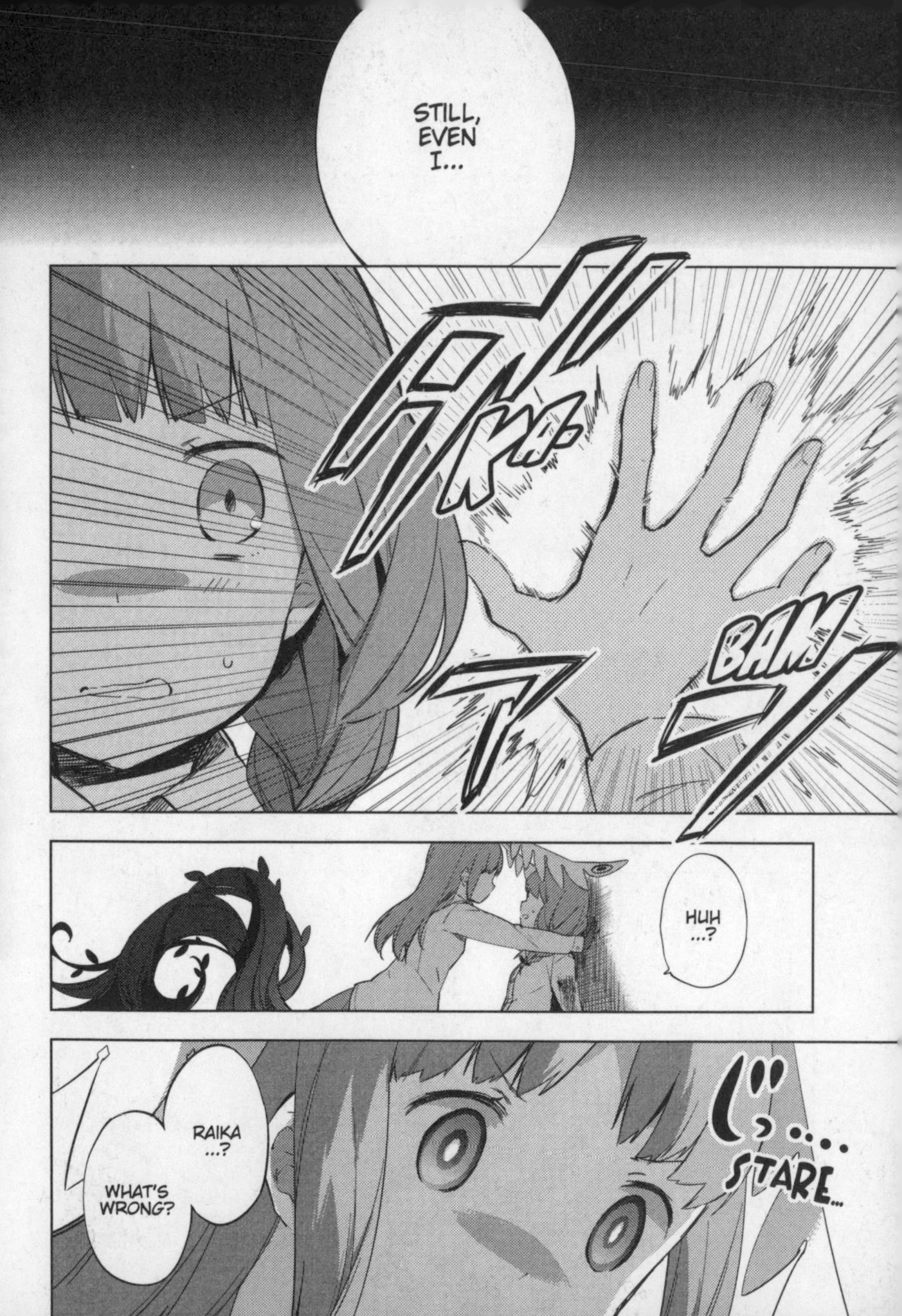
STILL, EVEN I...
BAM
HUH ...?
STARE...
RAIKA ...?
WHAT'S WRONG?

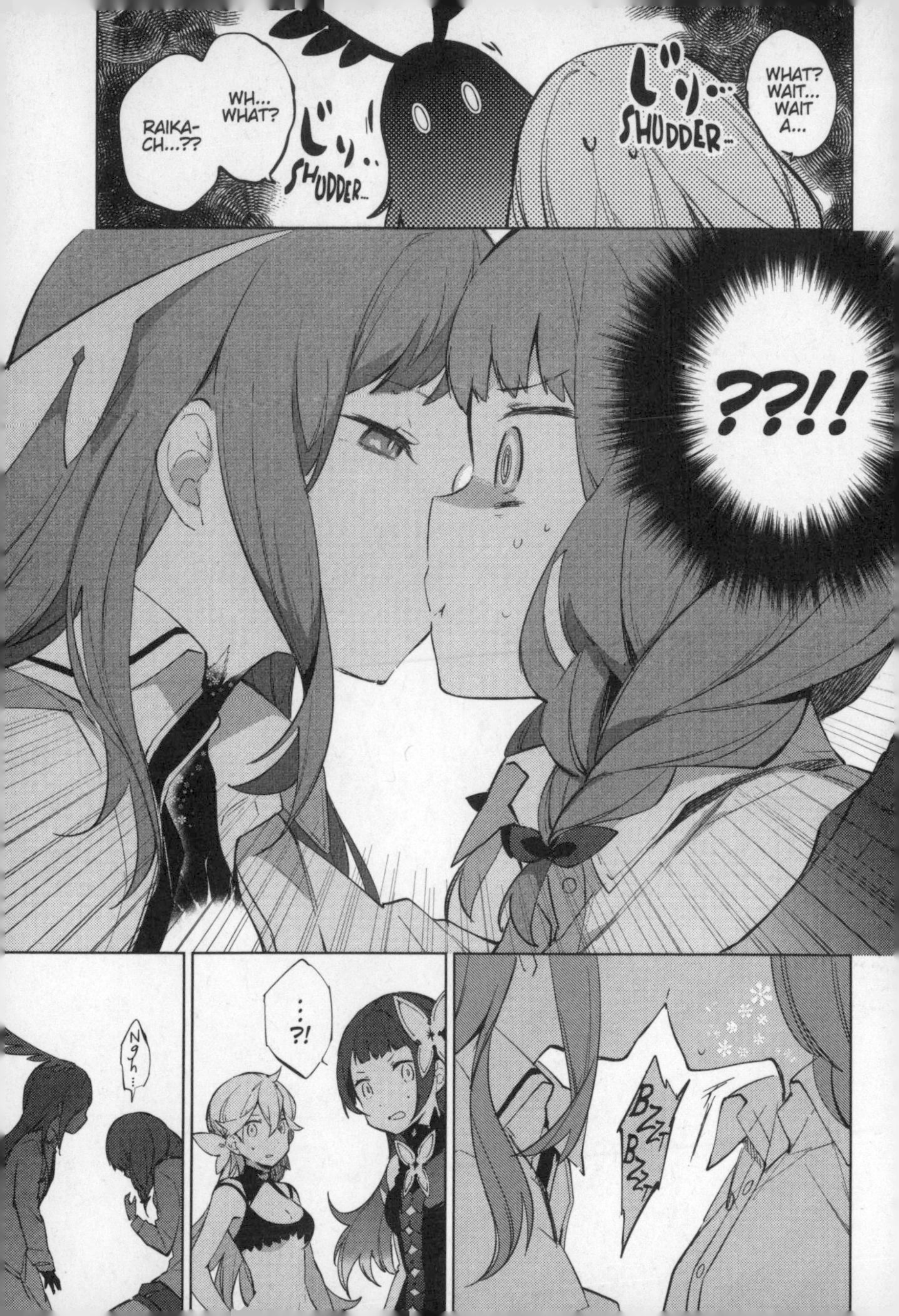
WHAT? WAIT... WAIT A...
じり.. SHUDDER..
じり.. SHUDDER..
WH... WHAT?
RAIKA-CH...??
??!!
BZZT BZZT
...?!
Ngh...

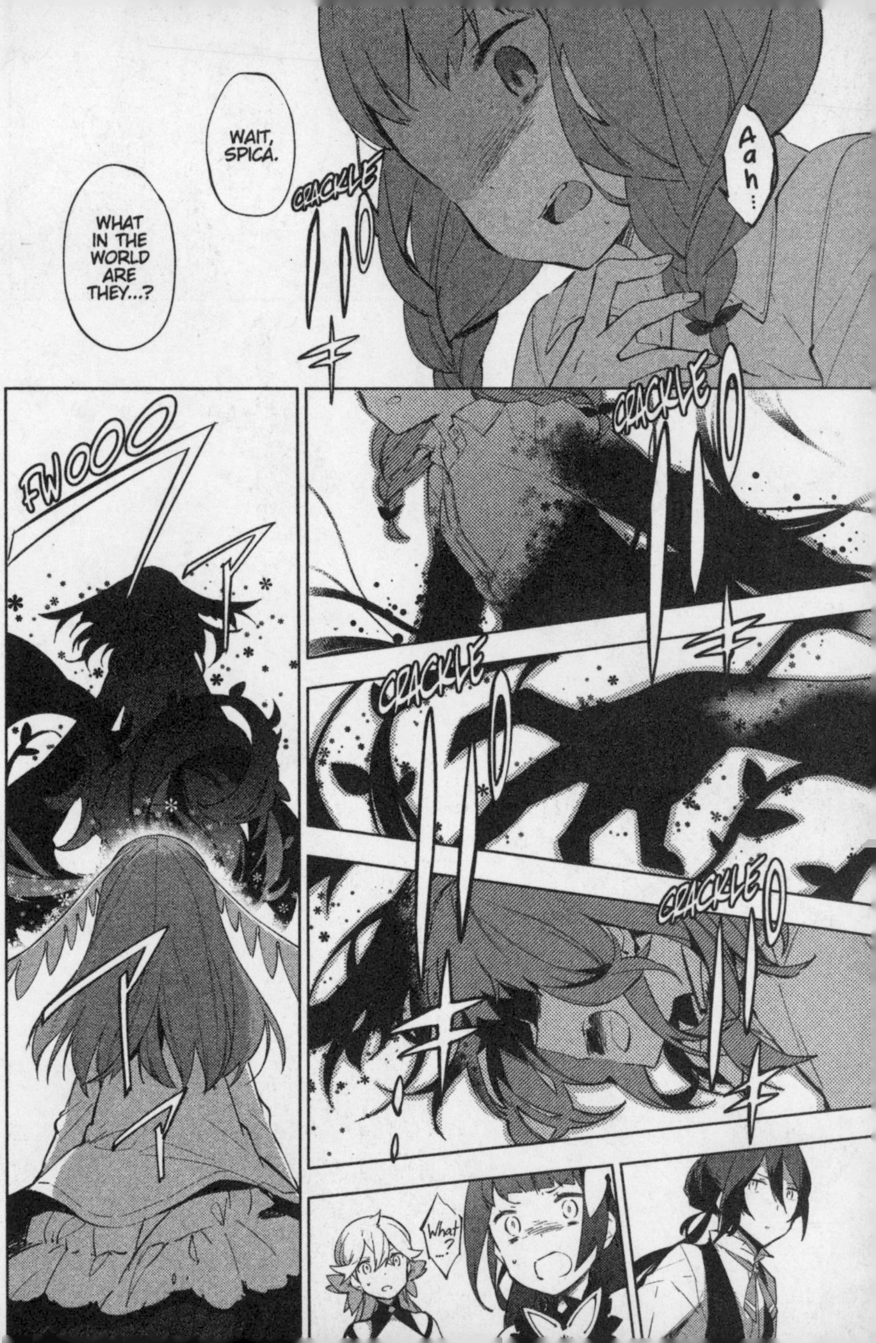
Aah...
WAIT, SPICA.
CRACKLE
WHAT IN THE WORLD ARE THEY...?
CRACKLE
CRACKLE
CRACKLE
What...?
FWOOO

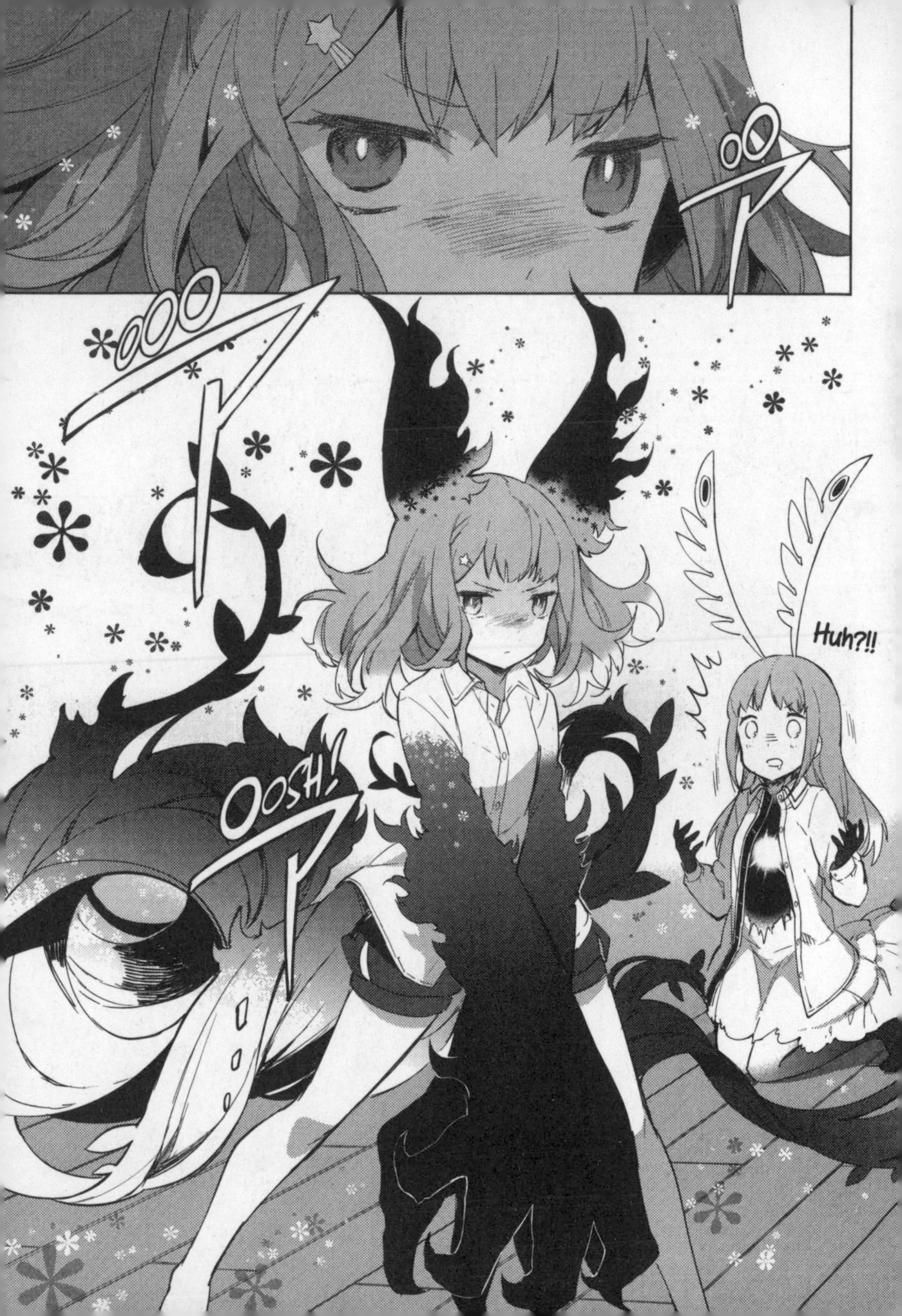
oo
OOO
Huh?!!
OOSH!

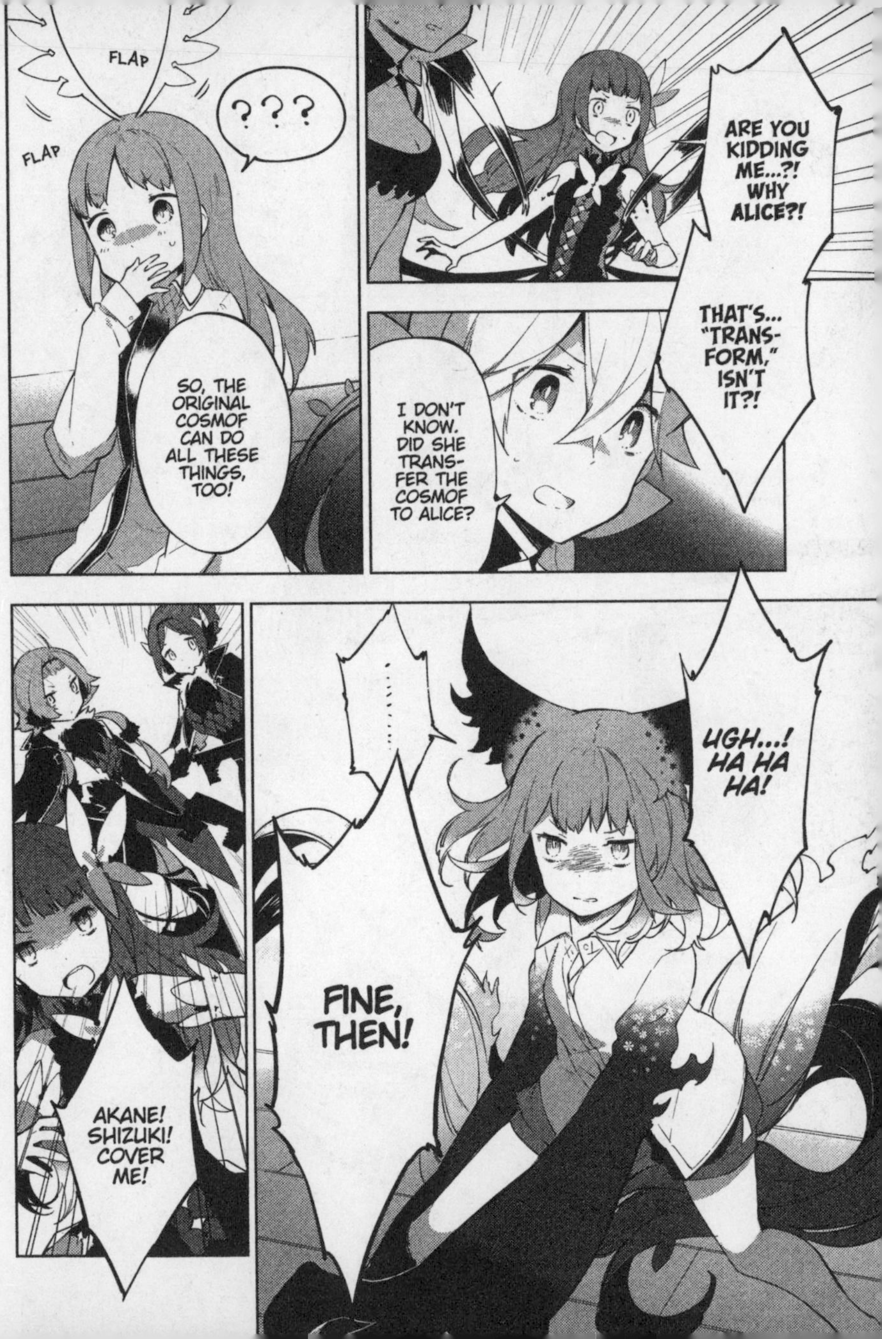

ARE YOU KIDDING ME...?! WHY ALICE?!
THAT'S... "TRANS-FORM," ISN'T IT?!
I DON'T KNOW. DID SHE TRANS-FER THE COSMOF TO ALICE?
FLAP
FLAP
???
SO, THE ORIGINAL COSMOF CAN DO ALL THESE THINGS, TOO!
UGH...! HA HA HA!
......
FINE, THEN!
AKANE! SHIZUKI! COVER ME!

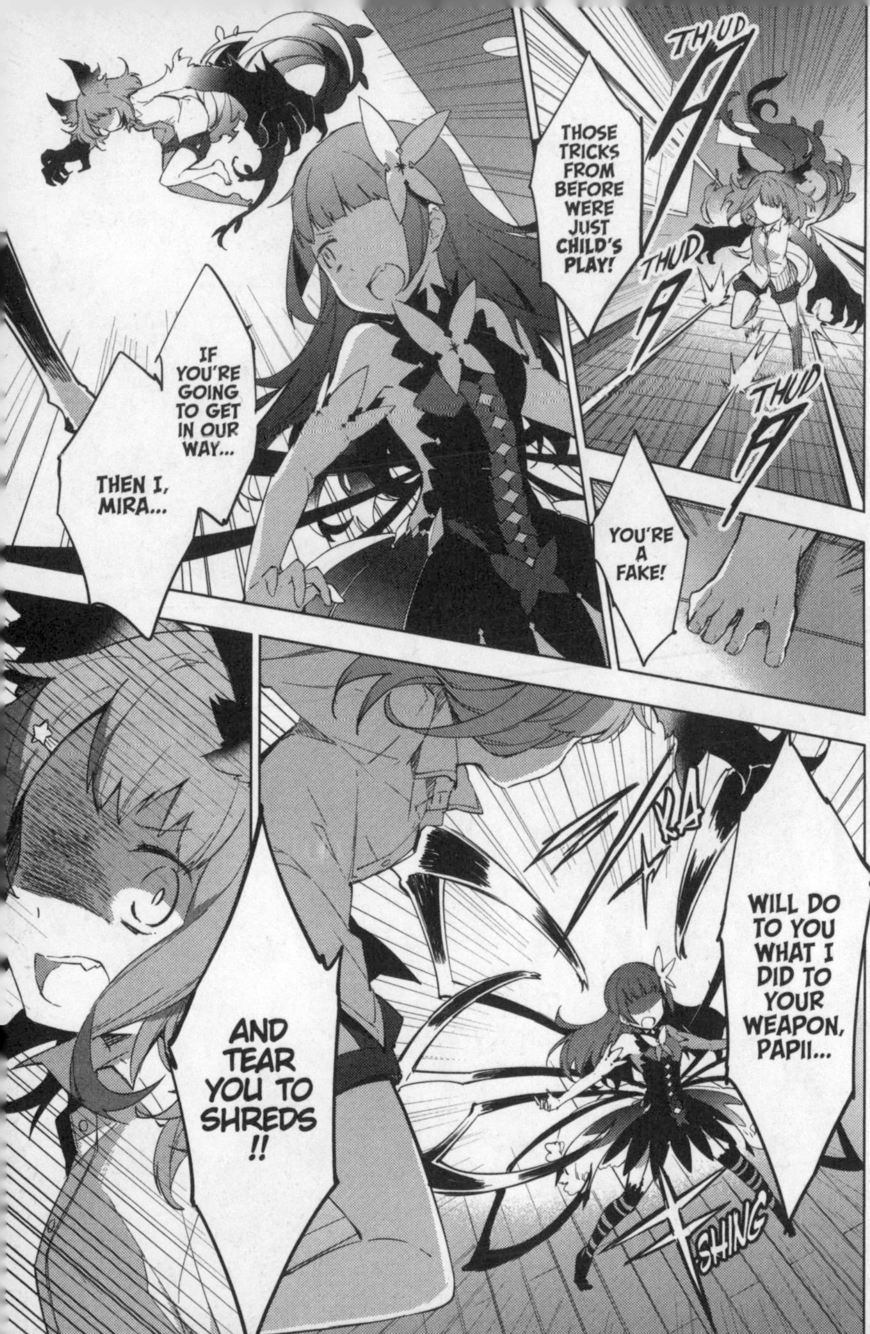

THUD
THOSE TRICKS FROM BEFORE WERE JUST CHILD'S PLAY!
THUD
THUD
YOU'RE A FAKE!
IF YOU'RE GOING TO GET IN OUR WAY...
THEN I, MIRA...
KA
WILL DO TO YOU WHAT I DID TO YOUR WEAPON, PAPII...
SHING
AND TEAR YOU TO SHREDS !!

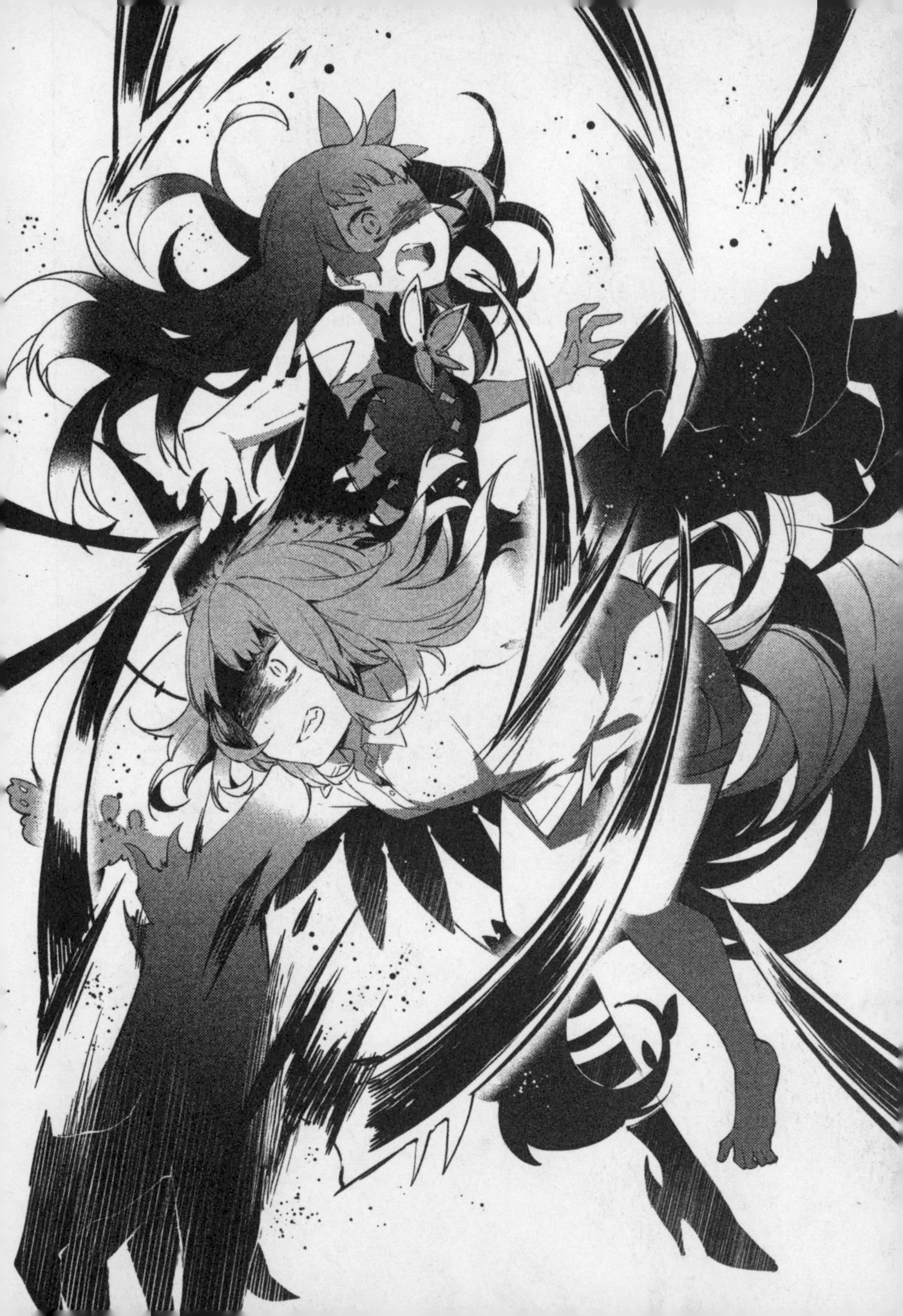

# Chapter 10 Asterisk

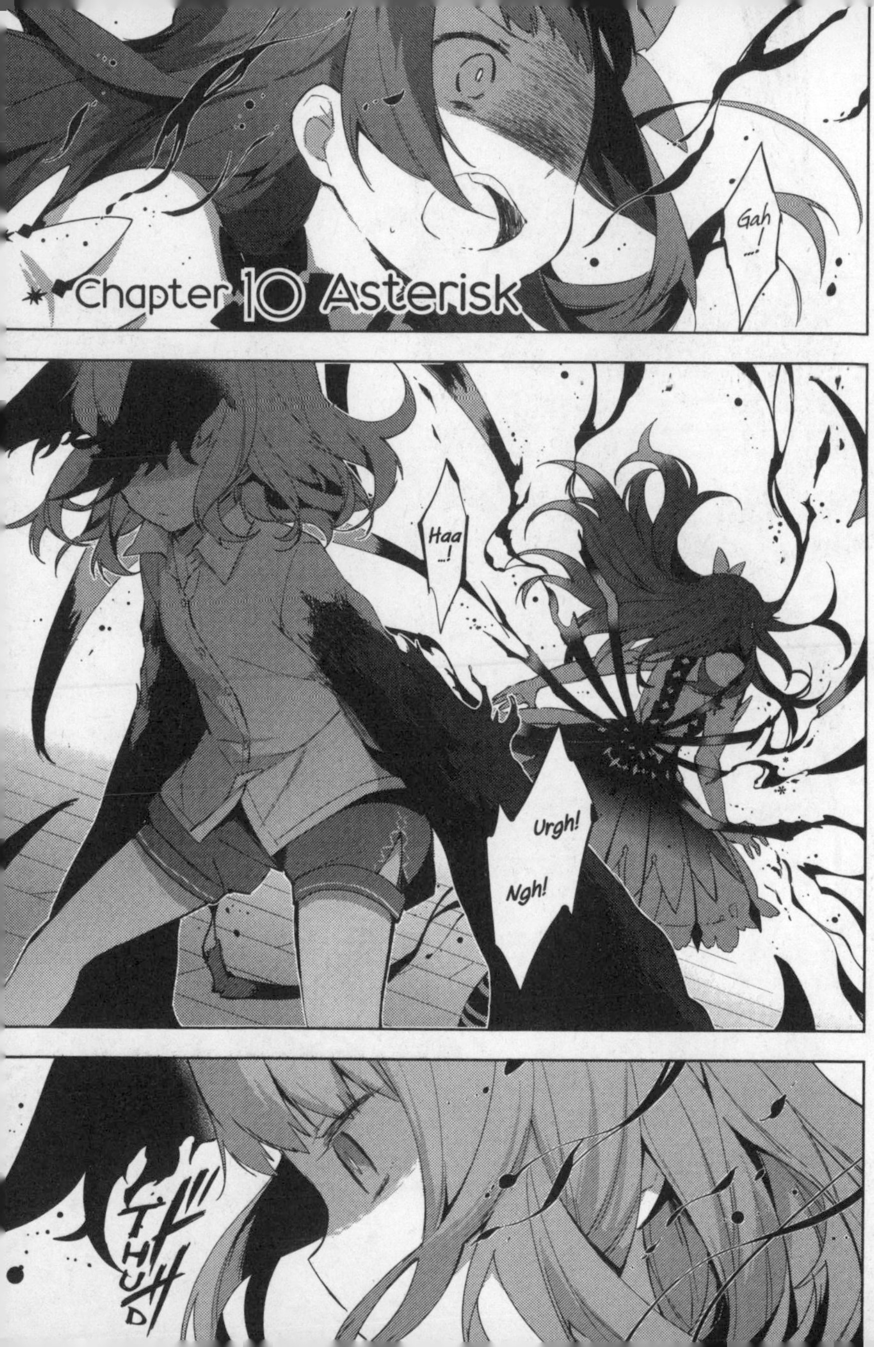
Gah ...!
Haa ...!
Urgh!
Ngh!
THUD

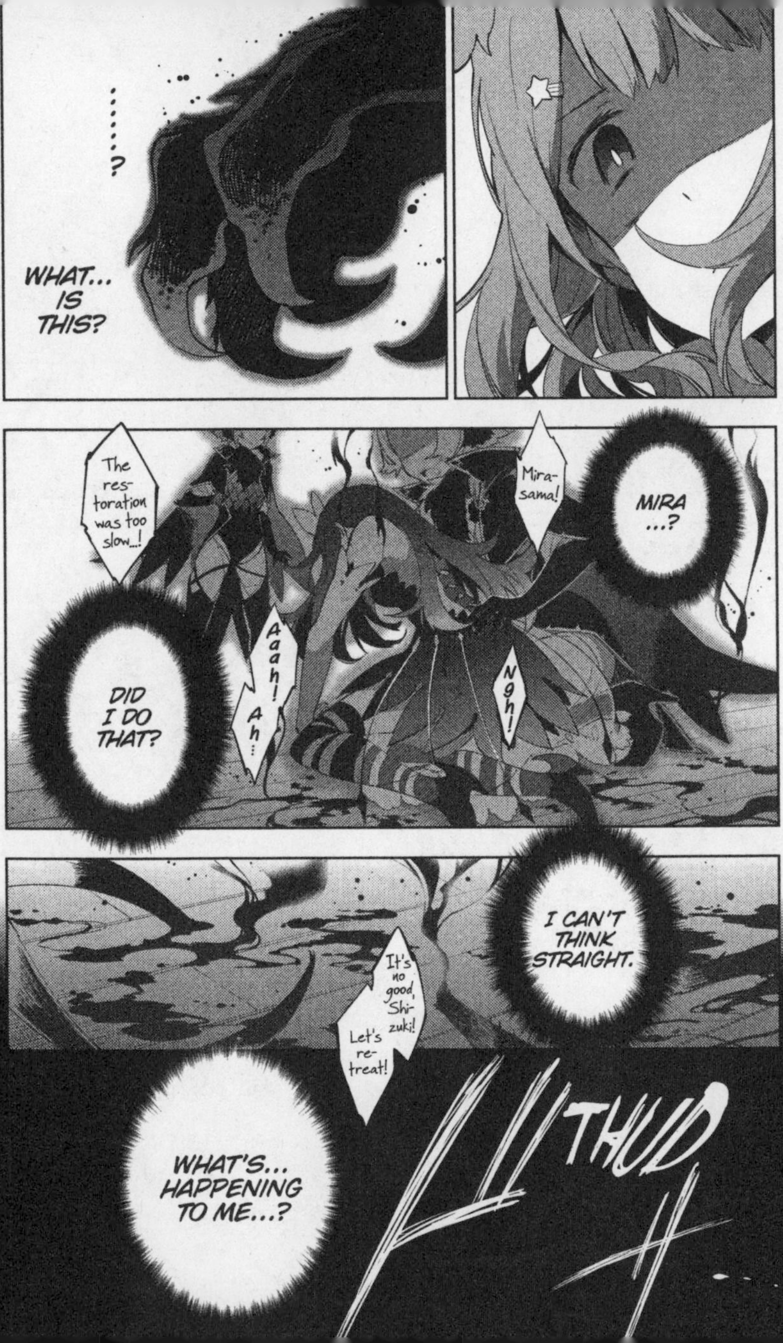
......?
WHAT... IS THIS?
MIRA...?
Mira-sama!
The restoration was too slow...!
Ngh!
Aaah! Ah...
DID I DO THAT?
I CAN'T THINK STRAIGHT.
It's no good, Shizuki!
Let's retreat!
THUD
WHAT'S... HAPPENING TO ME...?

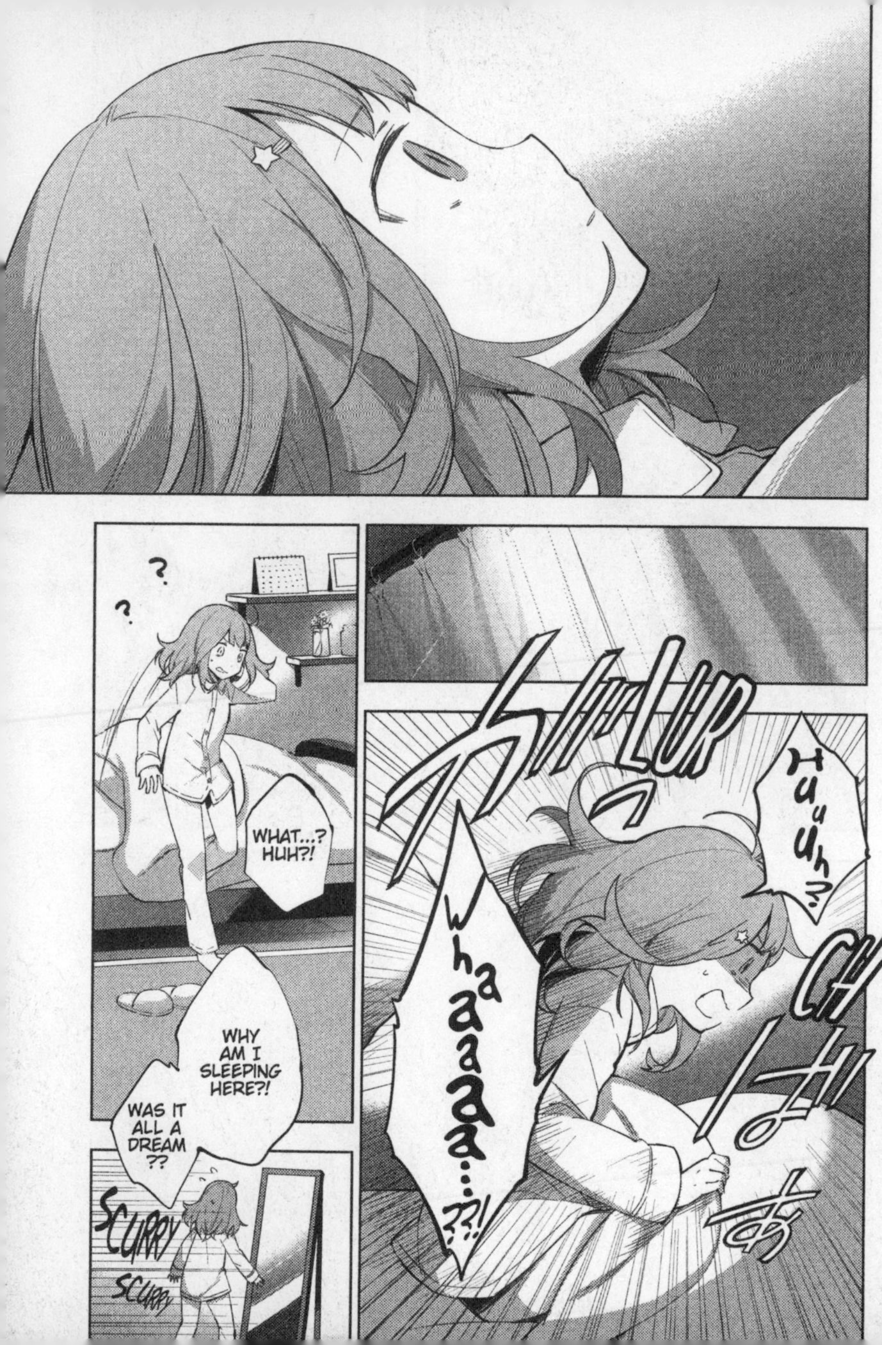
SHFLUP
Huuuuh??
Whaaaaaa...??!
??
WHAT...? HUH?!
WHY AM I SLEEPING HERE?!
WAS IT ALL A DREAM ??
SCURRY
SCURRY

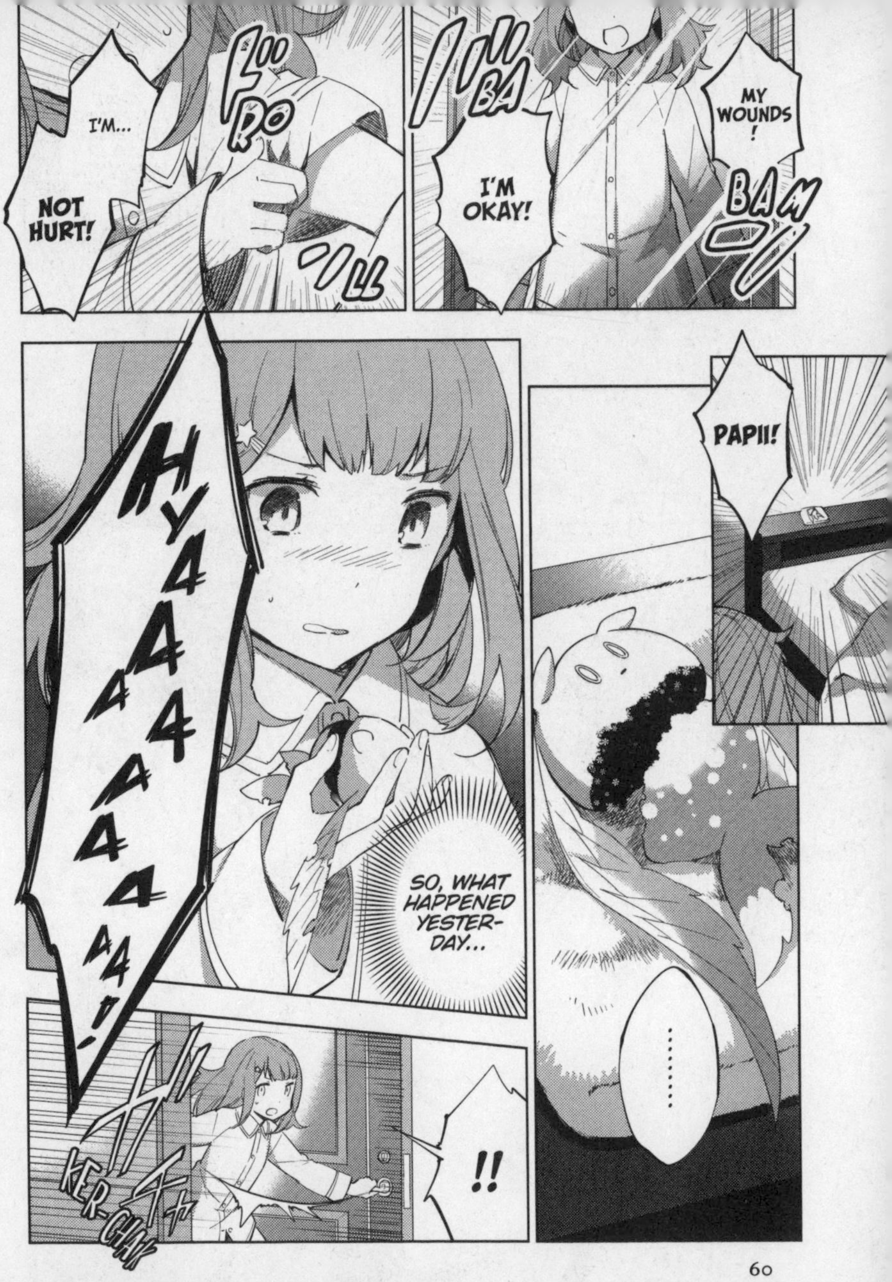
MY WOUNDS!
I'M OKAY!
BAM
I'M...
NOT HURT!
PAPII!
......
HYAAAAAAAAA!
SO, WHAT HAPPENED YESTER-DAY...
!!
KER-CHAK

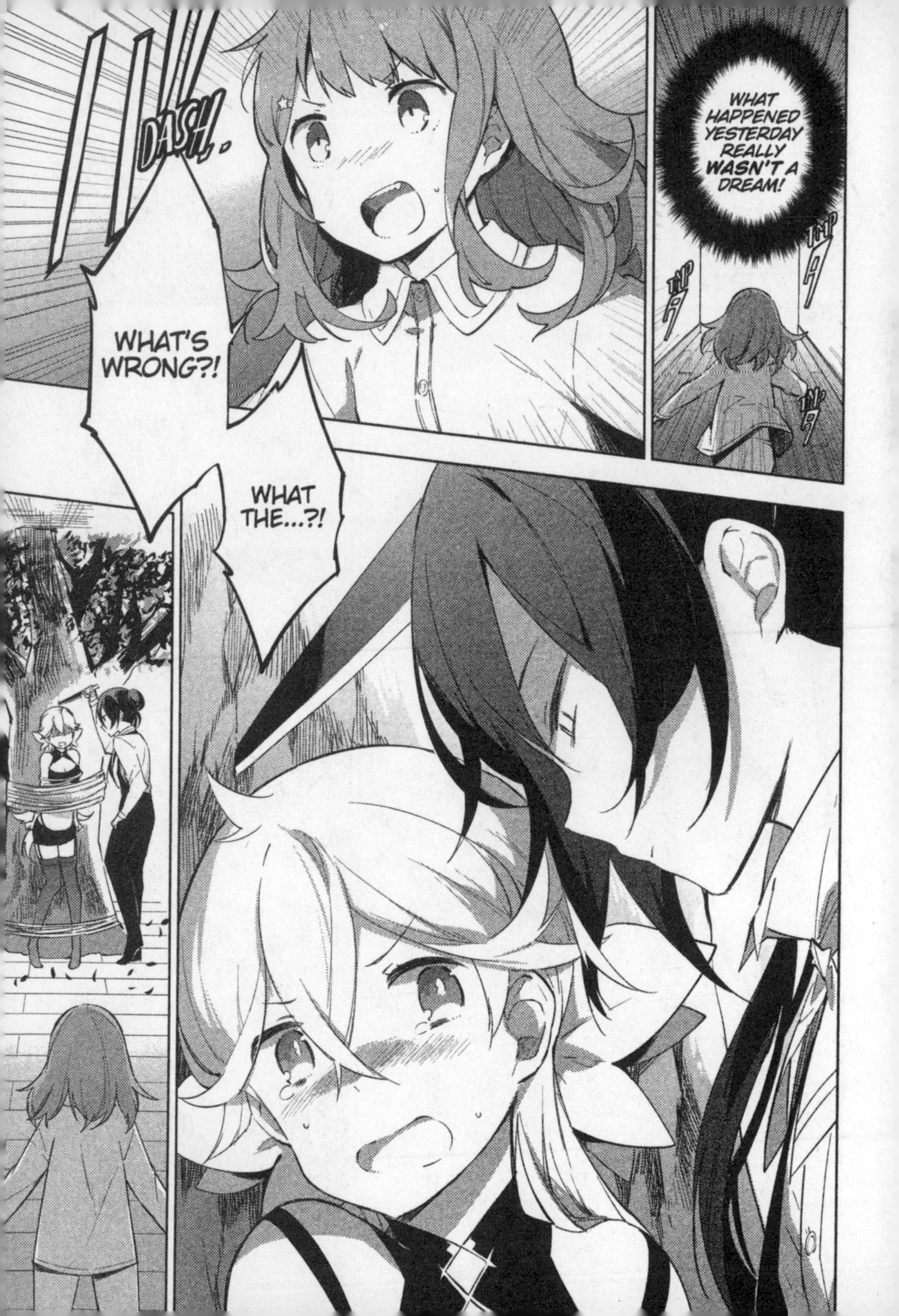
WHAT HAPPENED YESTERDAY REALLY WASN'T A DREAM!
TMP
TMP
TMP
DASH!!
WHAT'S WRONG?!
WHAT THE...?!

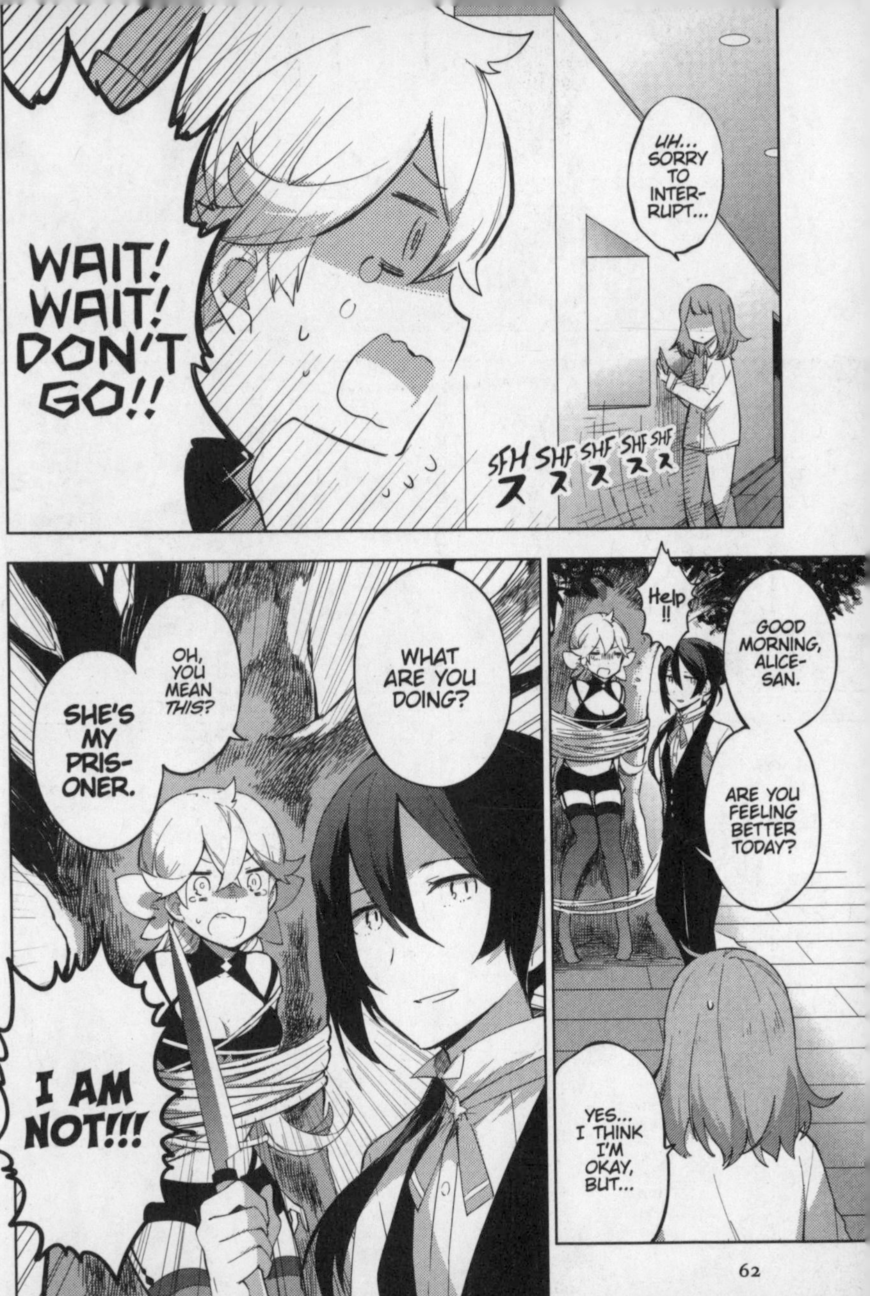
UH... SORRY TO INTERRUPT...
SFH ス SHF ス SHF ス SHF ス SHF ス
WAIT! WAIT! DON'T GO!!
Help!!
GOOD MORNING, ALICE-SAN.
ARE YOU FEELING BETTER TODAY?
YES... I THINK I'M OKAY, BUT...
WHAT ARE YOU DOING?
OH, YOU MEAN *THIS*?
SHE'S MY PRISONER.
I AM NOT!!!

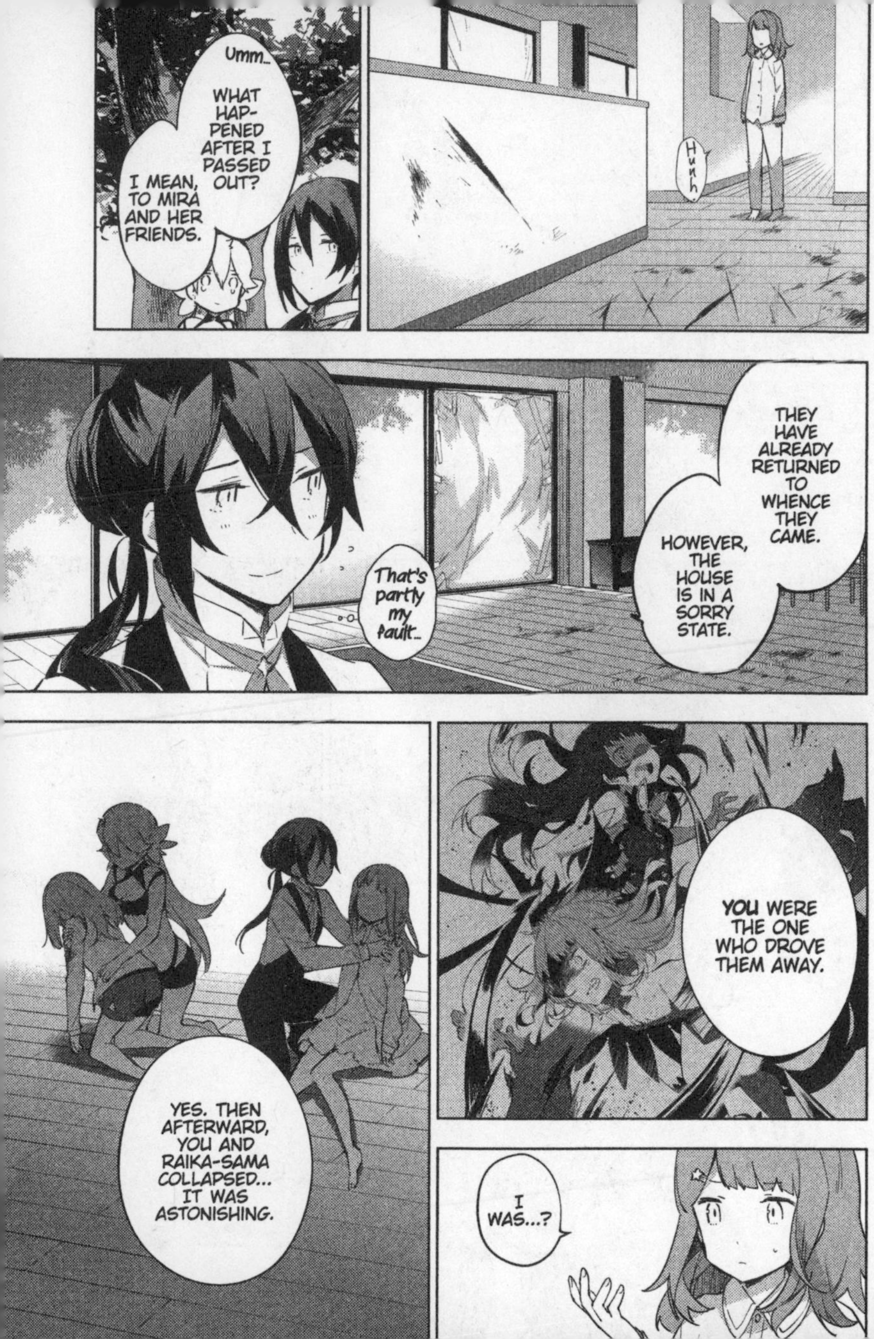
Hunh.
Umm..
WHAT HAP-PENED AFTER I PASSED OUT?
I MEAN, TO MIRA AND HER FRIENDS.
THEY HAVE ALREADY RETURNED TO WHENCE THEY CAME.
HOWEVER, THE HOUSE IS IN A SORRY STATE.
That's partly my fault..
YOU WERE THE ONE WHO DROVE THEM AWAY.
I WAS...?
YES. THEN AFTERWARD, YOU AND RAIKA-SAMA COLLAPSED... IT WAS ASTONISHING.

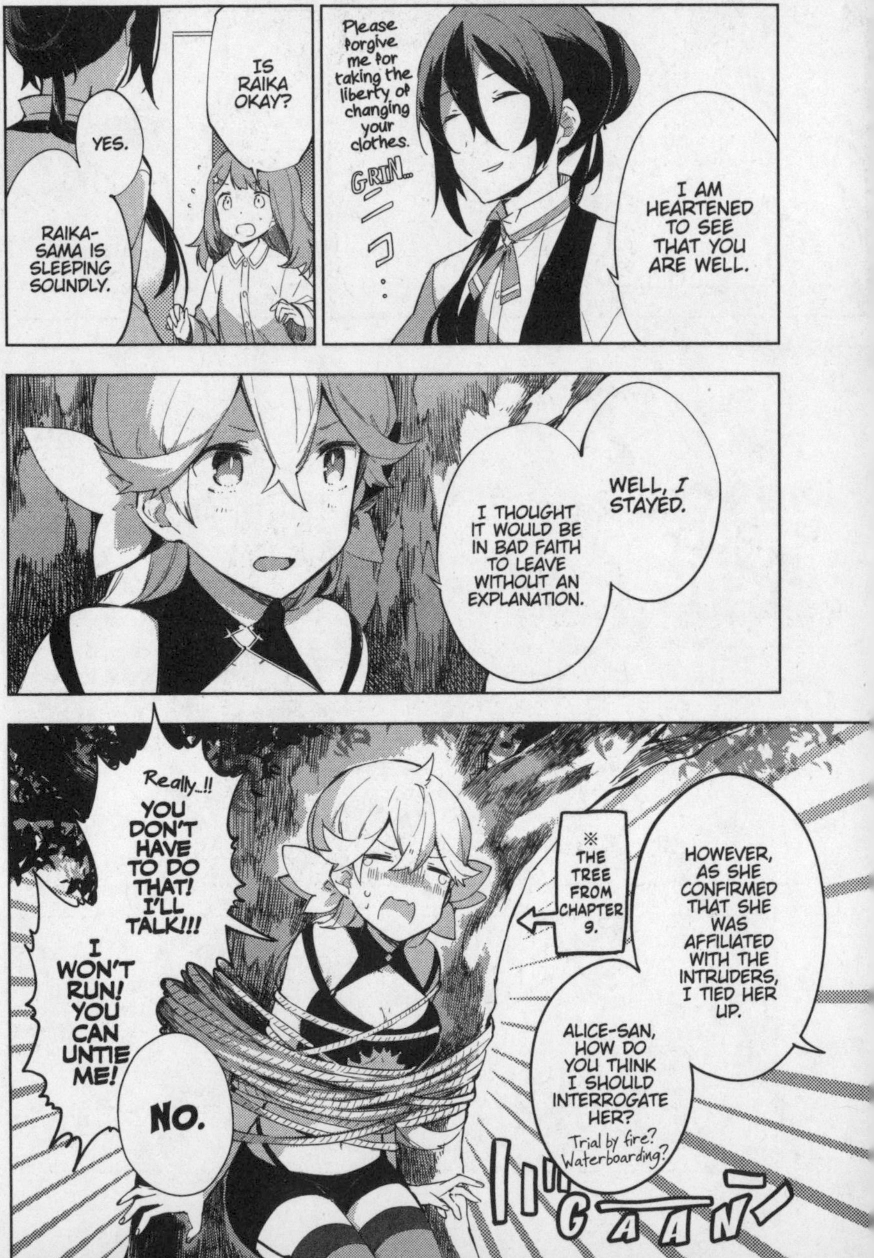
I AM HEARTENED TO SEE THAT YOU ARE WELL.
Please forgive me for taking the liberty of changing your clothes.
GRIN...
IS RAIKA OKAY?
YES.
RAIKA-SAMA IS SLEEPING SOUNDLY.
WELL, I STAYED.
I THOUGHT IT WOULD BE IN BAD FAITH TO LEAVE WITHOUT AN EXPLANATION.
HOWEVER, AS SHE CONFIRMED THAT SHE WAS AFFILIATED WITH THE INTRUDERS, I TIED HER UP.
※ THE TREE FROM CHAPTER 9.
ALICE-SAN, HOW DO YOU THINK I SHOULD INTERROGATE HER?
Trial by fire? Waterboarding?
Really...!!
YOU DON'T HAVE TO DO THAT! I'LL TALK!!!
I WON'T RUN! YOU CAN UNTIE ME!
NO.
GAAN

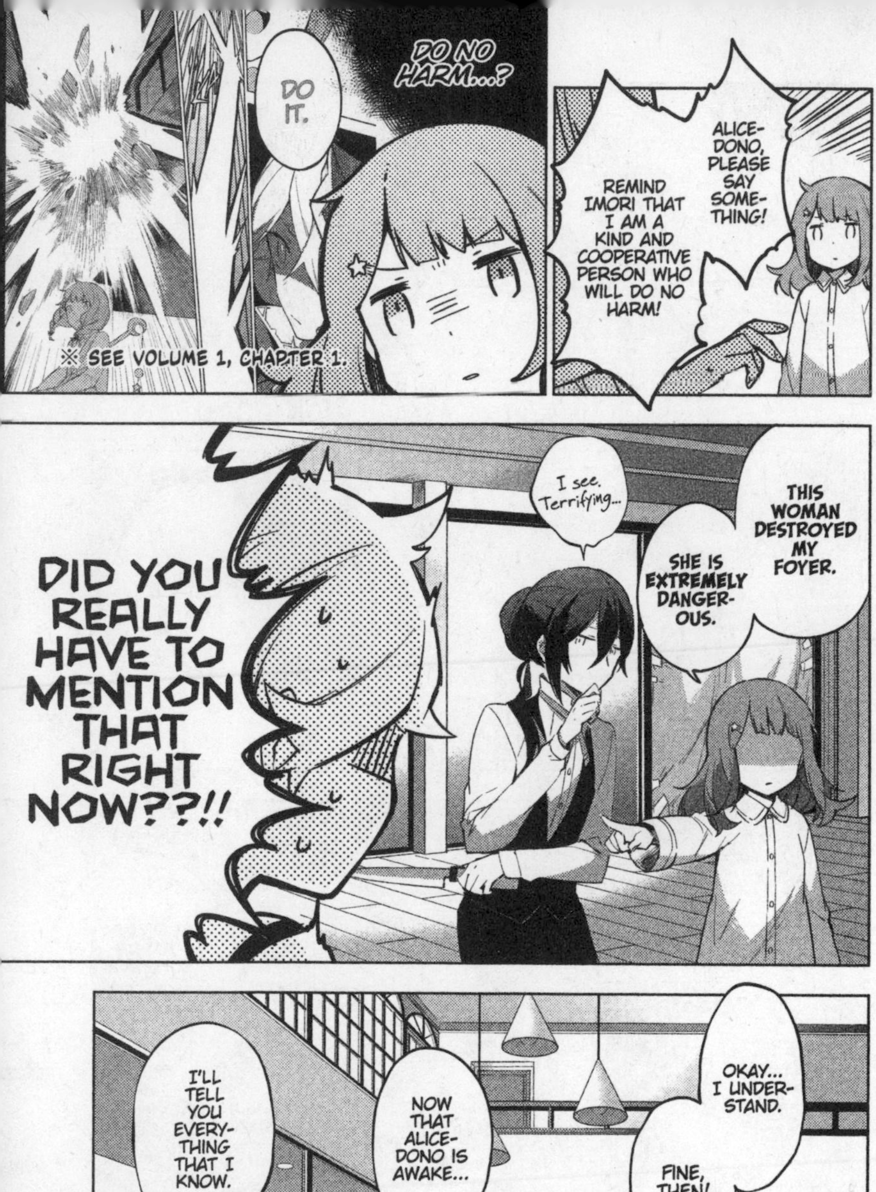
ALICE-DONO, PLEASE SAY SOMETHING!
REMIND IMORI THAT I AM A KIND AND COOPERATIVE PERSON WHO WILL DO NO HARM!
DO NO HARM...?
DO IT.
※ SEE VOLUME 1, CHAPTER 1.
THIS WOMAN DESTROYED MY FOYER.
SHE IS EXTREMELY DANGEROUS.
I see. Terrifying...
DID YOU REALLY HAVE TO MENTION THAT RIGHT NOW??!!
OKAY... I UNDERSTAND.
FINE, THEN!
NOW THAT ALICE-DONO IS AWAKE...
I'LL TELL YOU EVERYTHING THAT I KNOW.

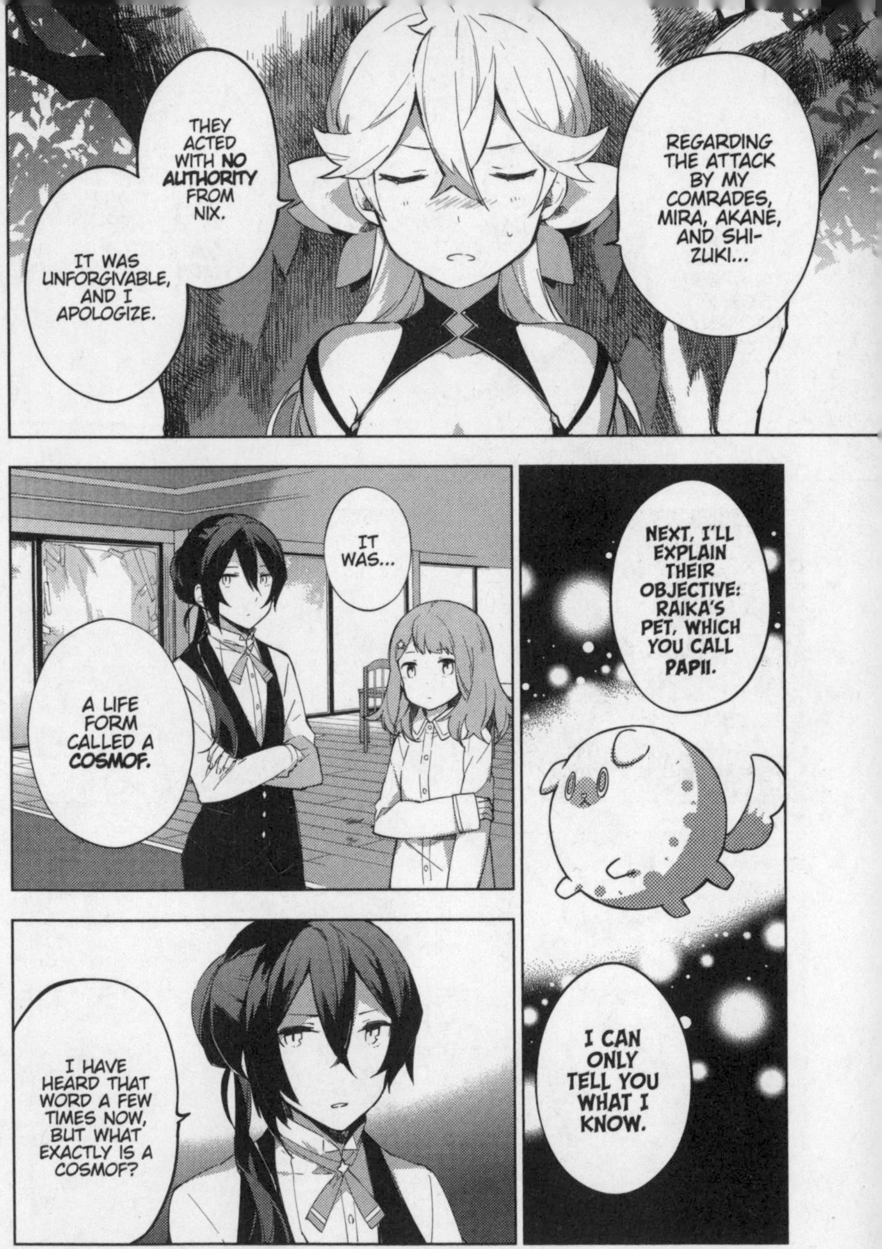
REGARDING THE ATTACK BY MY COMRADES, MIRA, AKANE, AND SHI-ZUKI...
THEY ACTED WITH **NO AUTHORITY** FROM NIX.
IT WAS UNFORGIVABLE, AND I APOLOGIZE.
NEXT, I'LL EXPLAIN THEIR OBJECTIVE: RAIKA'S PET, WHICH YOU CALL PAPII.
I CAN ONLY TELL YOU WHAT I KNOW.
IT WAS...
A LIFE FORM CALLED A **COSMOF**.
I HAVE HEARD THAT WORD A FEW TIMES NOW, BUT WHAT EXACTLY IS A COSMOF?

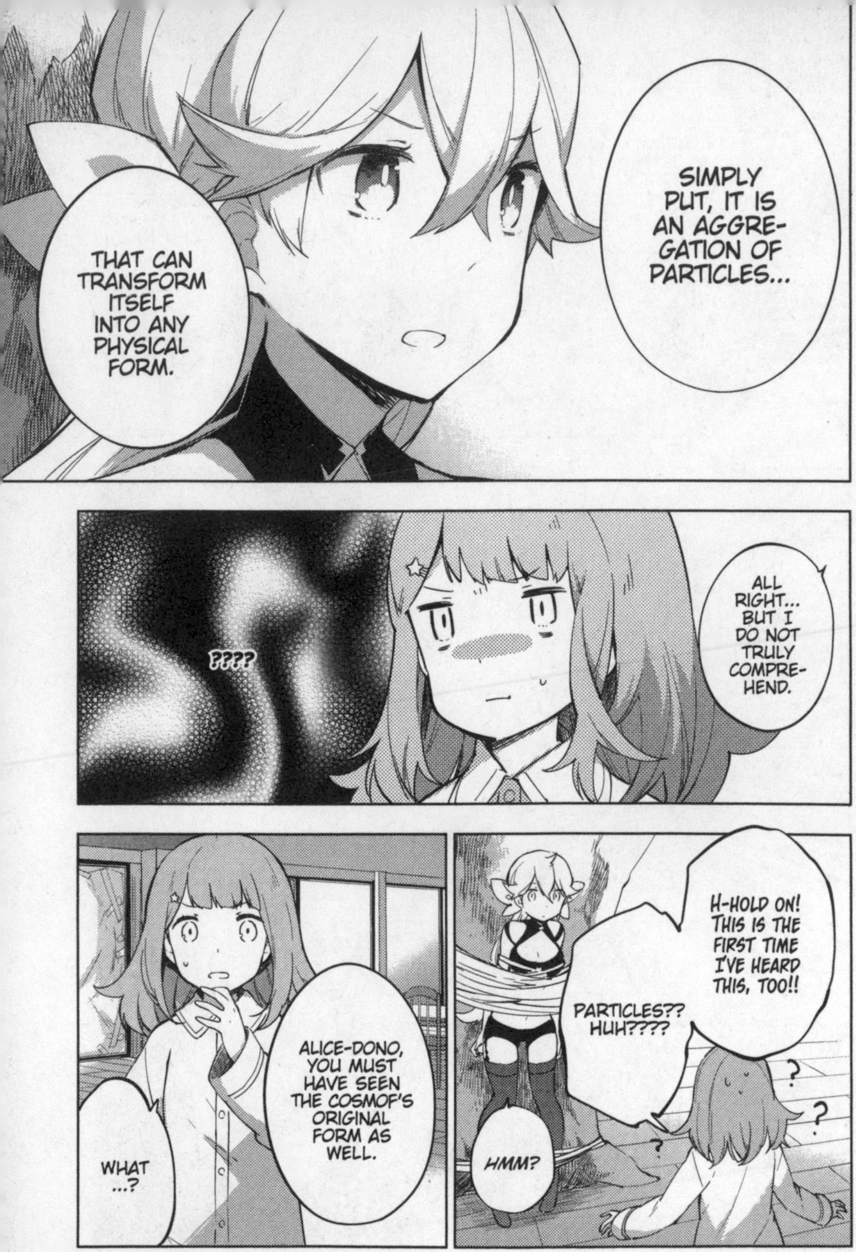
SIMPLY PUT, IT IS AN AGGREGATION OF PARTICLES...
THAT CAN TRANSFORM ITSELF INTO ANY PHYSICAL FORM.
ALL RIGHT... BUT I DO NOT TRULY COMPREHEND.
????
H-HOLD ON! THIS IS THE FIRST TIME I'VE HEARD THIS, TOO!!
PARTICLES?? HUH????
HMM?
ALICE-DONO, YOU MUST HAVE SEEN THE COSMOF'S ORIGINAL FORM AS WELL.
WHAT ...?

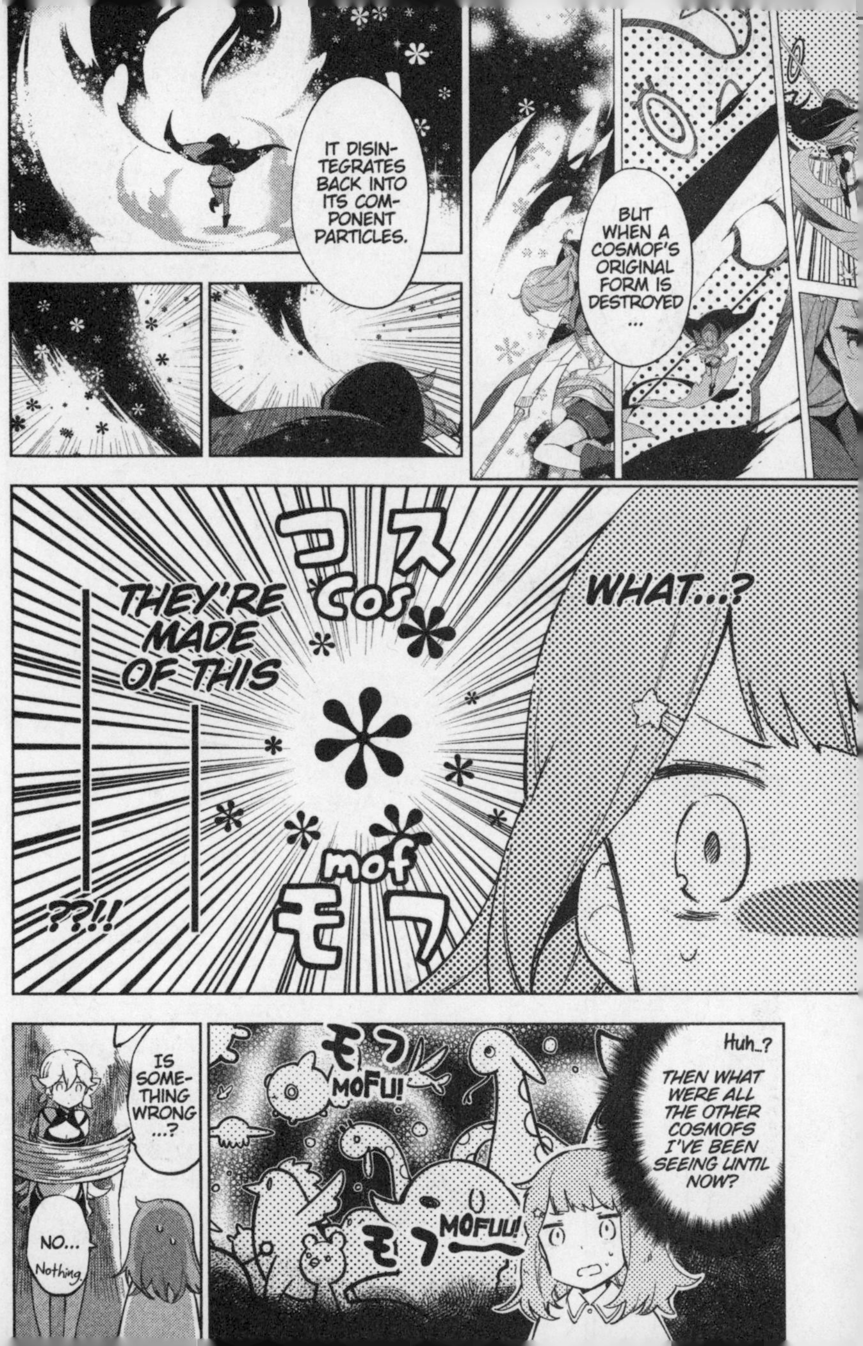
BUT WHEN A COSMOF'S ORIGINAL FORM IS DESTROYED ...
IT DISINTEGRATES BACK INTO ITS COMPONENT PARTICLES.
WHAT...?
コス
Cos
THEY'RE MADE OF THIS
mof
モフ
??!!
Huh..?
THEN WHAT WERE ALL THE OTHER COSMOFS I'VE BEEN SEEING UNTIL NOW?
モフ
MOFU!
MOFUU!
モフー
IS SOMETHING WRONG ...?
NO...
Nothing.

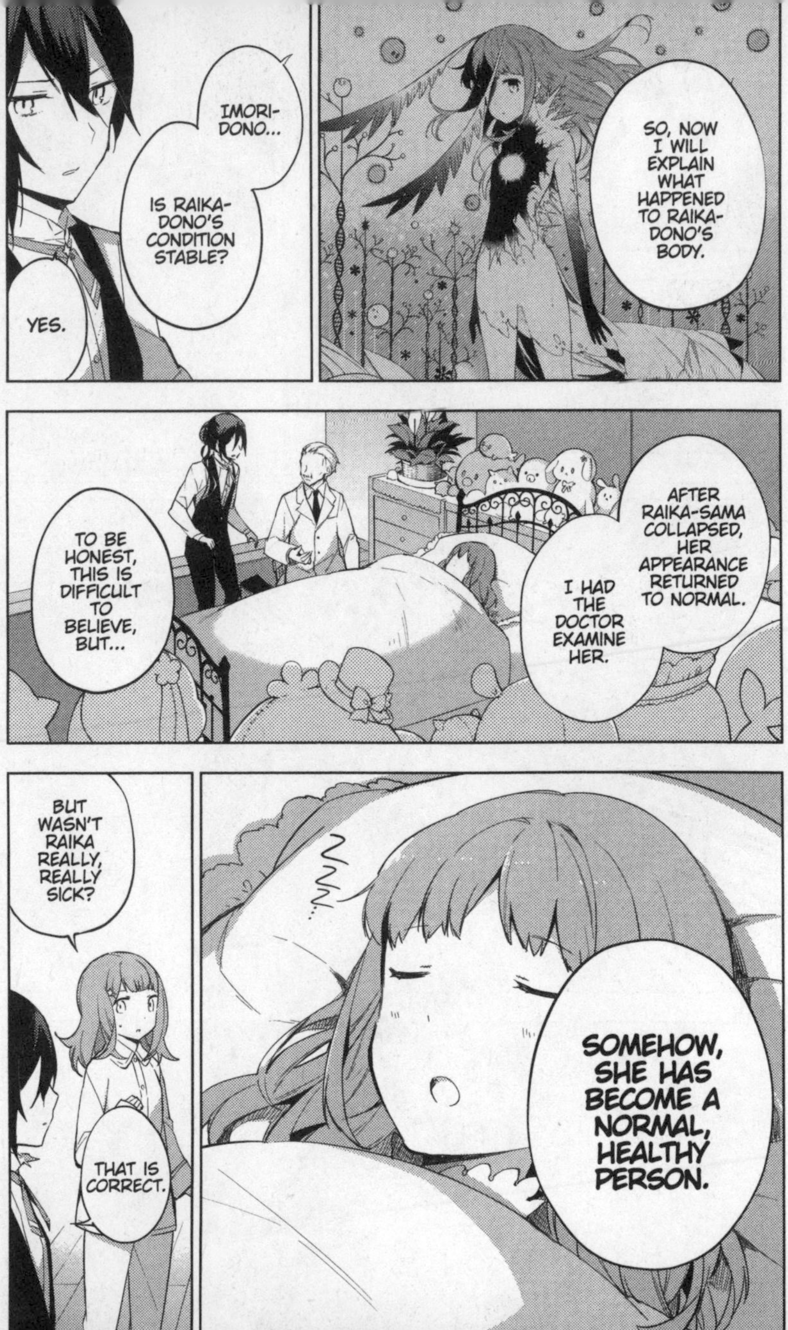
SO, NOW I WILL EXPLAIN WHAT HAPPENED TO RAIKA-DONO'S BODY.
IMORI-DONO...
IS RAIKA-DONO'S CONDITION STABLE?
YES.
AFTER RAIKA-SAMA COLLAPSED, HER APPEARANCE RETURNED TO NORMAL.
I HAD THE DOCTOR EXAMINE HER.
TO BE HONEST, THIS IS DIFFICULT TO BELIEVE, BUT...
SOMEHOW, SHE HAS BECOME A NORMAL, HEALTHY PERSON.
BUT WASN'T RAIKA REALLY, REALLY SICK?
THAT IS CORRECT.

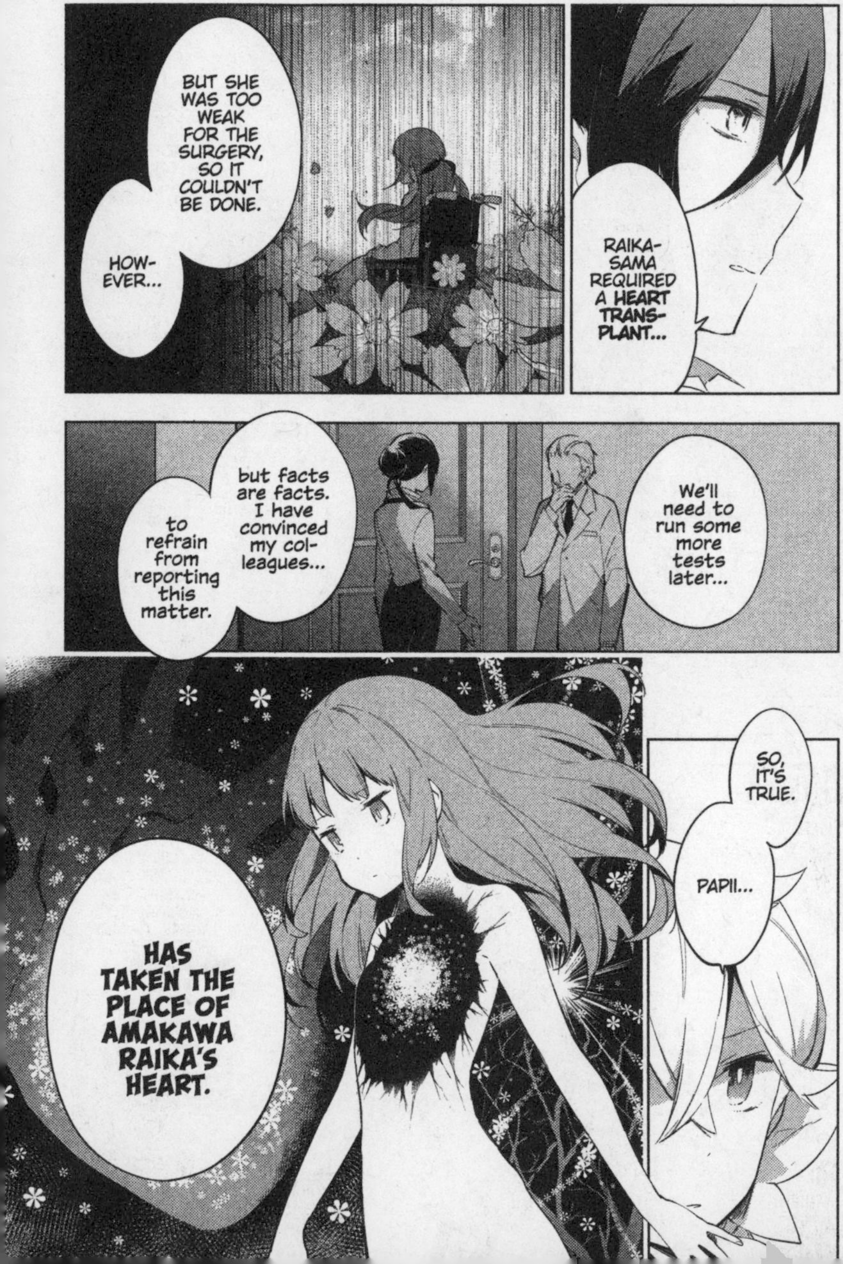
RAIKA-SAMA REQUIRED A HEART TRANS-PLANT...
BUT SHE WAS TOO WEAK FOR THE SURGERY, SO IT COULDN'T BE DONE.
HOW-EVER...
We'll need to run some more tests later...
but facts are facts. I have convinced my col-leagues...
to refrain from reporting this matter.
SO, IT'S TRUE.
PAPII...
HAS TAKEN THE PLACE OF AMAKAWA RAIKA'S HEART.

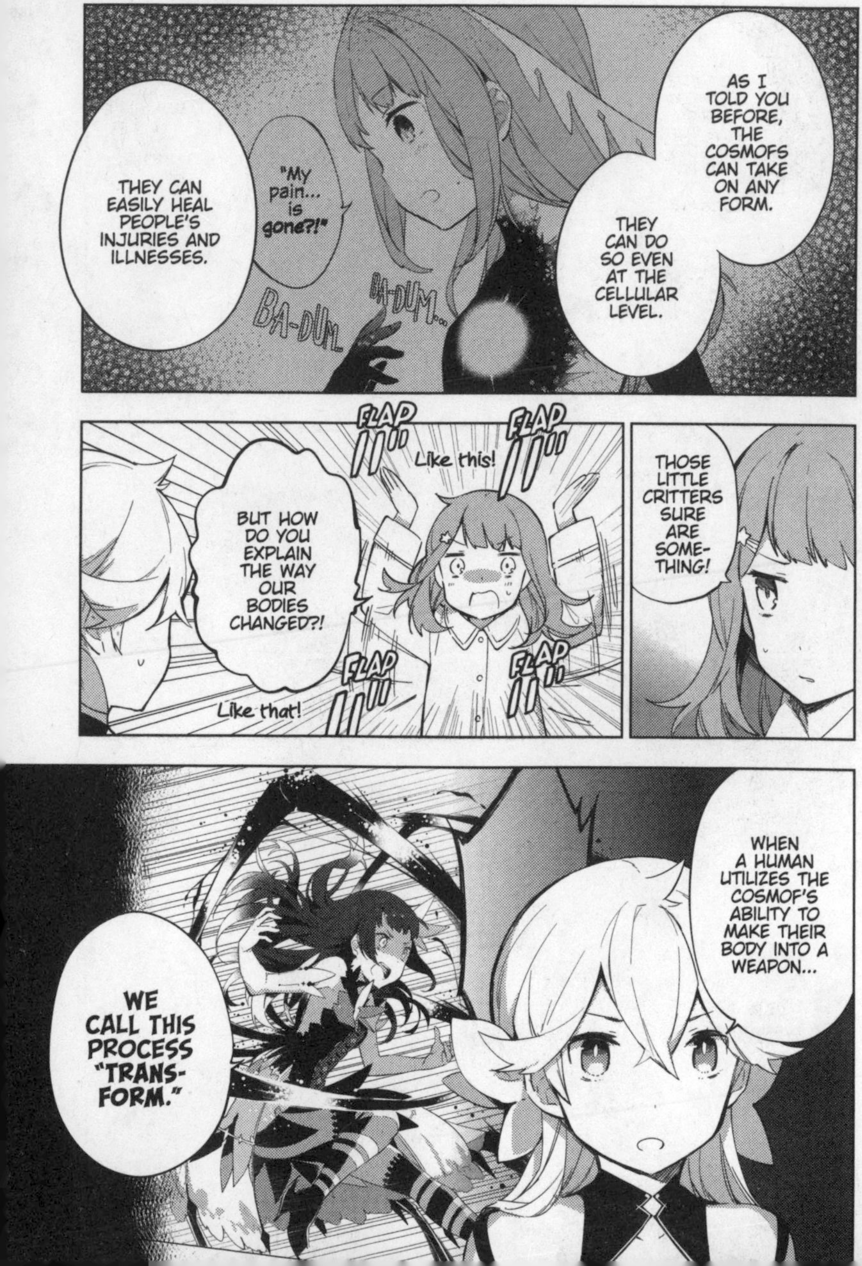
AS I TOLD YOU BEFORE, THE COSMOFS CAN TAKE ON ANY FORM.
THEY CAN DO SO EVEN AT THE CELLULAR LEVEL.
BA-DUM...
"My pain... is gone?!"
BA-DUM
THEY CAN EASILY HEAL PEOPLE'S INJURIES AND ILLNESSES.
THOSE LITTLE CRITTERS SURE ARE SOME-THING!
FLAP
FLAP
Like this!
BUT HOW DO YOU EXPLAIN THE WAY OUR BODIES CHANGED?!
FLAP
FLAP
Like that!
WHEN A HUMAN UTILIZES THE COSMOF'S ABILITY TO MAKE THEIR BODY INTO A WEAPON...
WE CALL THIS PROCESS "TRANS-FORM."

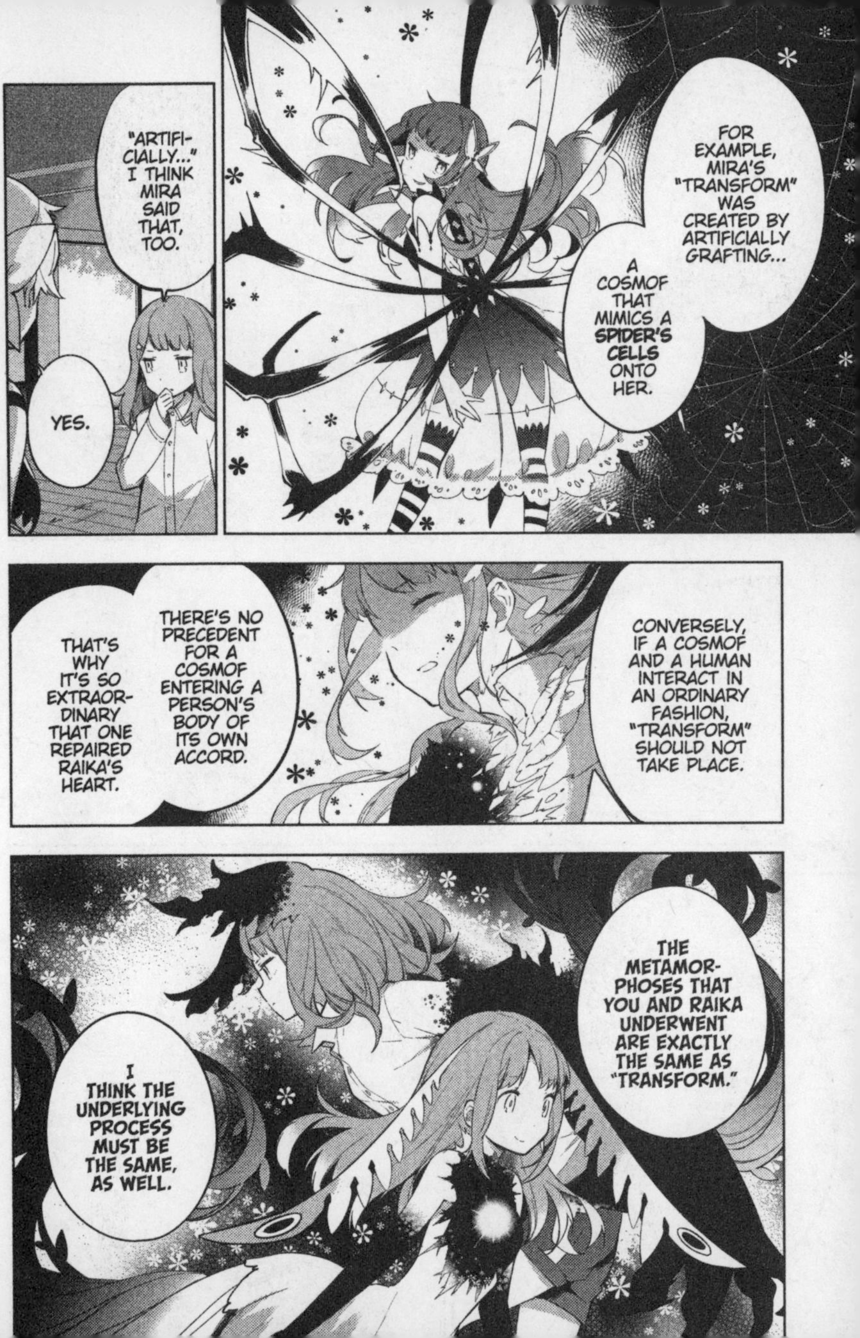
FOR EXAMPLE, MIRA'S "TRANSFORM" WAS CREATED BY ARTIFICIALLY GRAFTING...
A COSMOF THAT MIMICS A SPIDER'S CELLS ONTO HER.
"ARTIFICIALLY..." I THINK MIRA SAID THAT, TOO.
YES.
CONVERSELY, IF A COSMOF AND A HUMAN INTERACT IN AN ORDINARY FASHION, "TRANSFORM" SHOULD NOT TAKE PLACE.
THERE'S NO PRECEDENT FOR A COSMOF ENTERING A PERSON'S BODY OF ITS OWN ACCORD.
THAT'S WHY IT'S SO EXTRAORDINARY THAT ONE REPAIRED RAIKA'S HEART.
THE METAMORPHOSES THAT YOU AND RAIKA UNDERWENT ARE EXACTLY THE SAME AS "TRANSFORM."
I THINK THE UNDERLYING PROCESS MUST BE THE SAME, AS WELL.

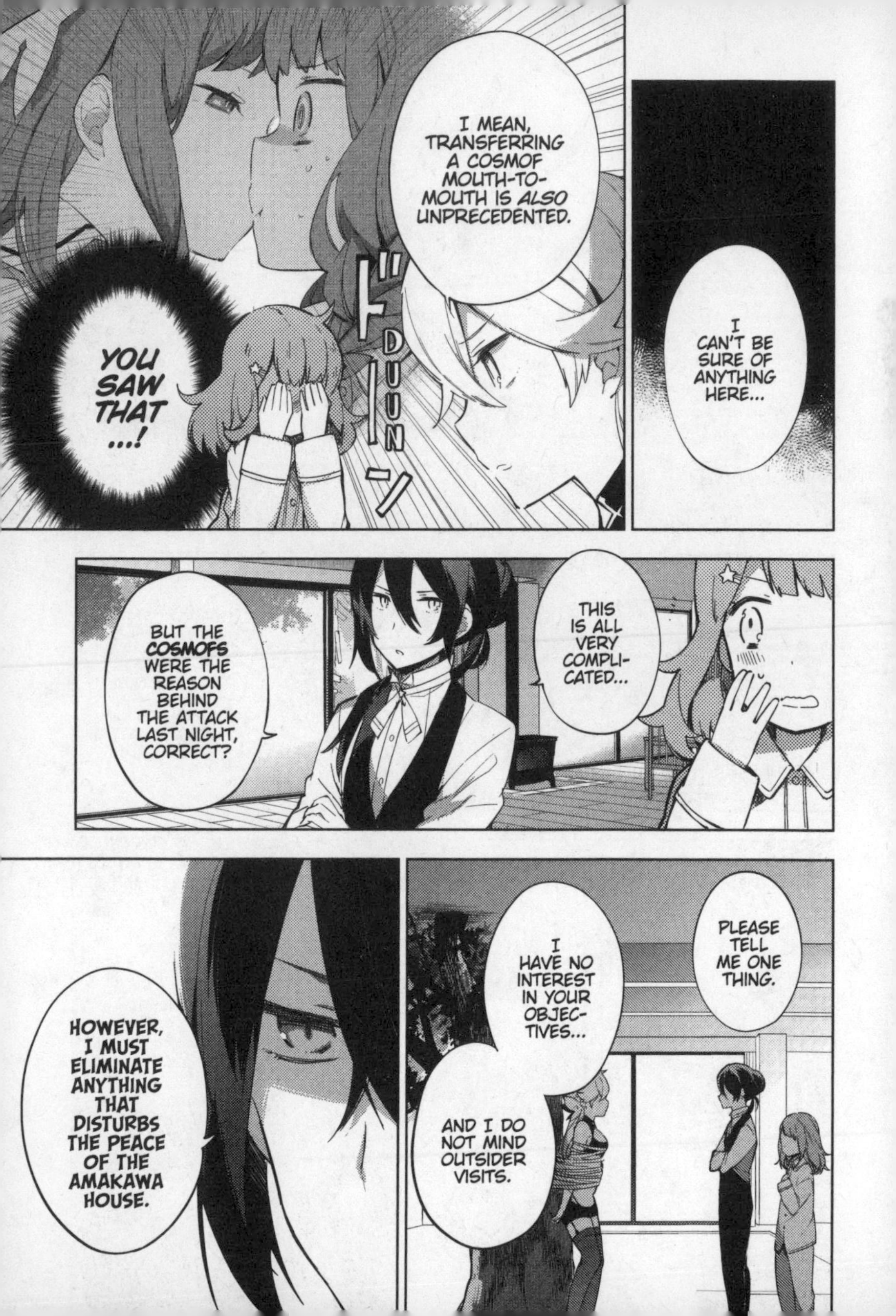
I CAN'T BE SURE OF ANYTHING HERE...
I MEAN, TRANSFERRING A COSMOF MOUTH-TO-MOUTH IS *ALSO* UNPRECEDENTED.
DUUN
YOU SAW THAT...!
THIS IS ALL VERY COMPLICATED...
BUT THE **COSMOFS** WERE THE REASON BEHIND THE ATTACK LAST NIGHT, CORRECT?
PLEASE TELL ME ONE THING.
I HAVE NO INTEREST IN YOUR OBJECTIVES...
AND I DO NOT MIND OUTSIDER VISITS.
HOWEVER, I MUST ELIMINATE ANYTHING THAT DISTURBS THE PEACE OF THE AMAKAWA HOUSE.

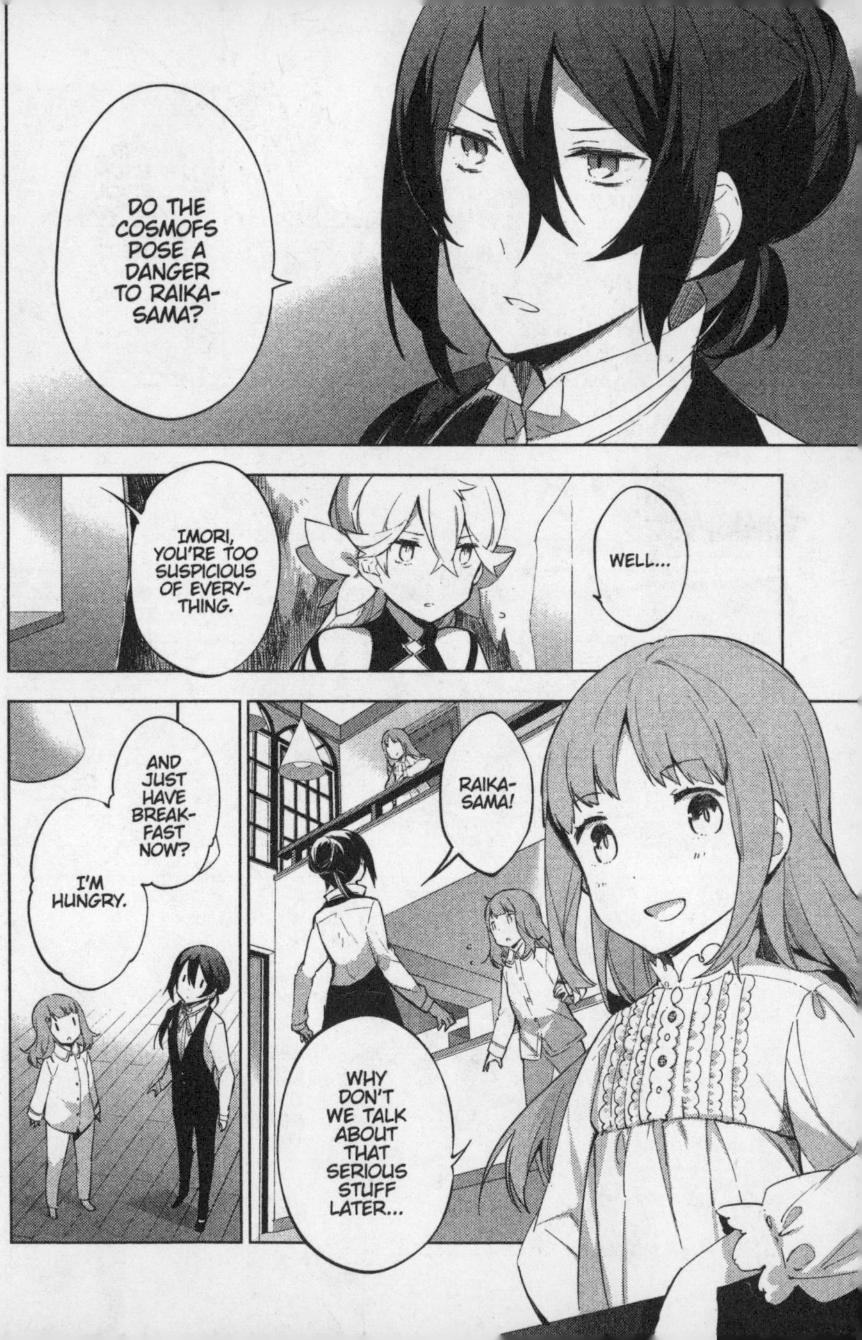
DO THE COSMOFS POSE A DANGER TO RAIKA-SAMA?
WELL...
IMORI, YOU'RE TOO SUSPICIOUS OF EVERY-THING.
RAIKA-SAMA!
WHY DON'T WE TALK ABOUT THAT SERIOUS STUFF LATER...
AND JUST HAVE BREAK-FAST NOW?
I'M HUNGRY.

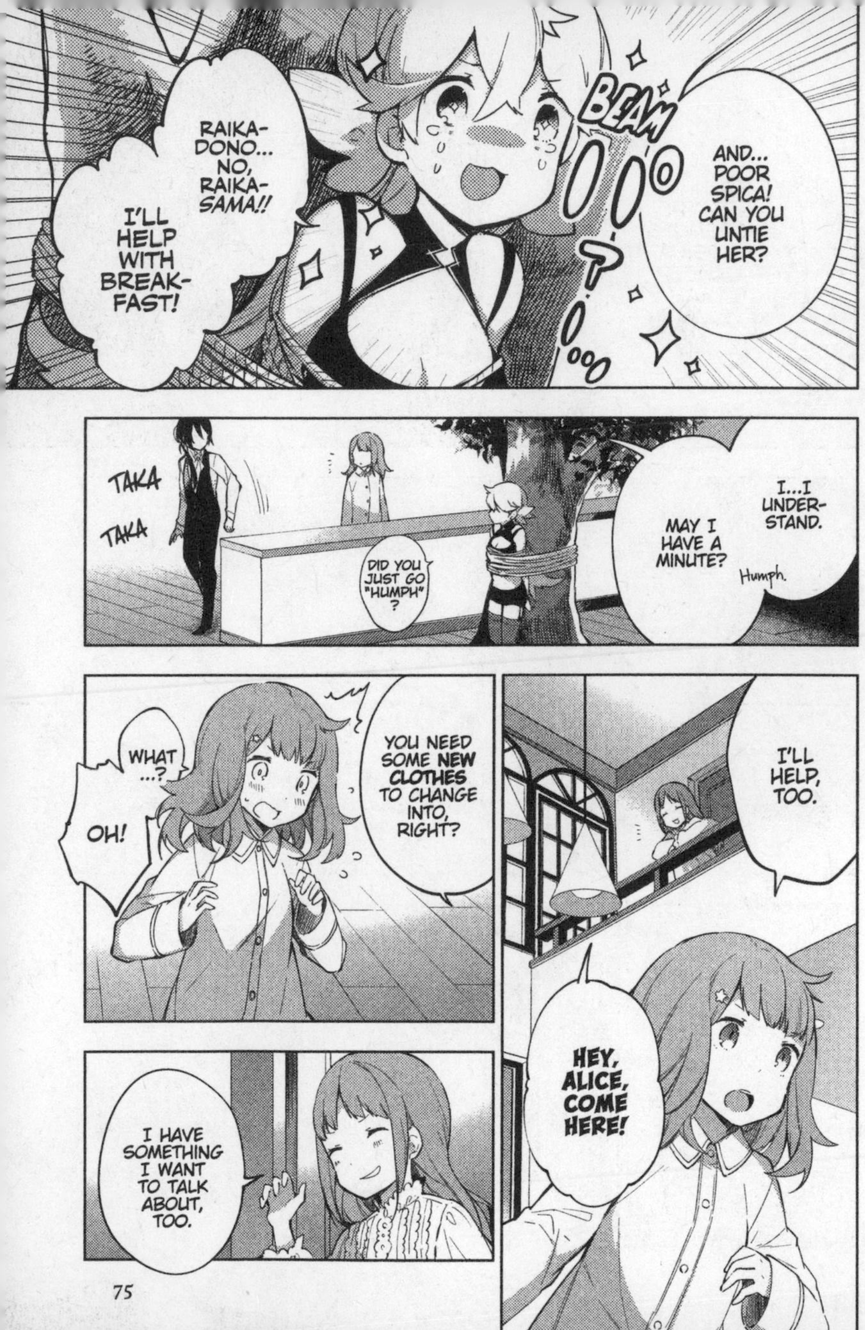
AND... POOR SPICA! CAN YOU UNTIE HER?
BEAM
OOO?...OOO
RAIKA-DONO... NO, RAIKA-SAMA!!
I'LL HELP WITH BREAK-FAST!
I...I UNDER-STAND.
MAY I HAVE A MINUTE?
Humph.
DID YOU JUST GO "HUMPH"?
TAKA
TAKA
I'LL HELP, TOO.
HEY, ALICE, COME HERE!
YOU NEED SOME NEW CLOTHES TO CHANGE INTO, RIGHT?
WHAT ...?
OH!
I HAVE SOMETHING I WANT TO TALK ABOUT, TOO.

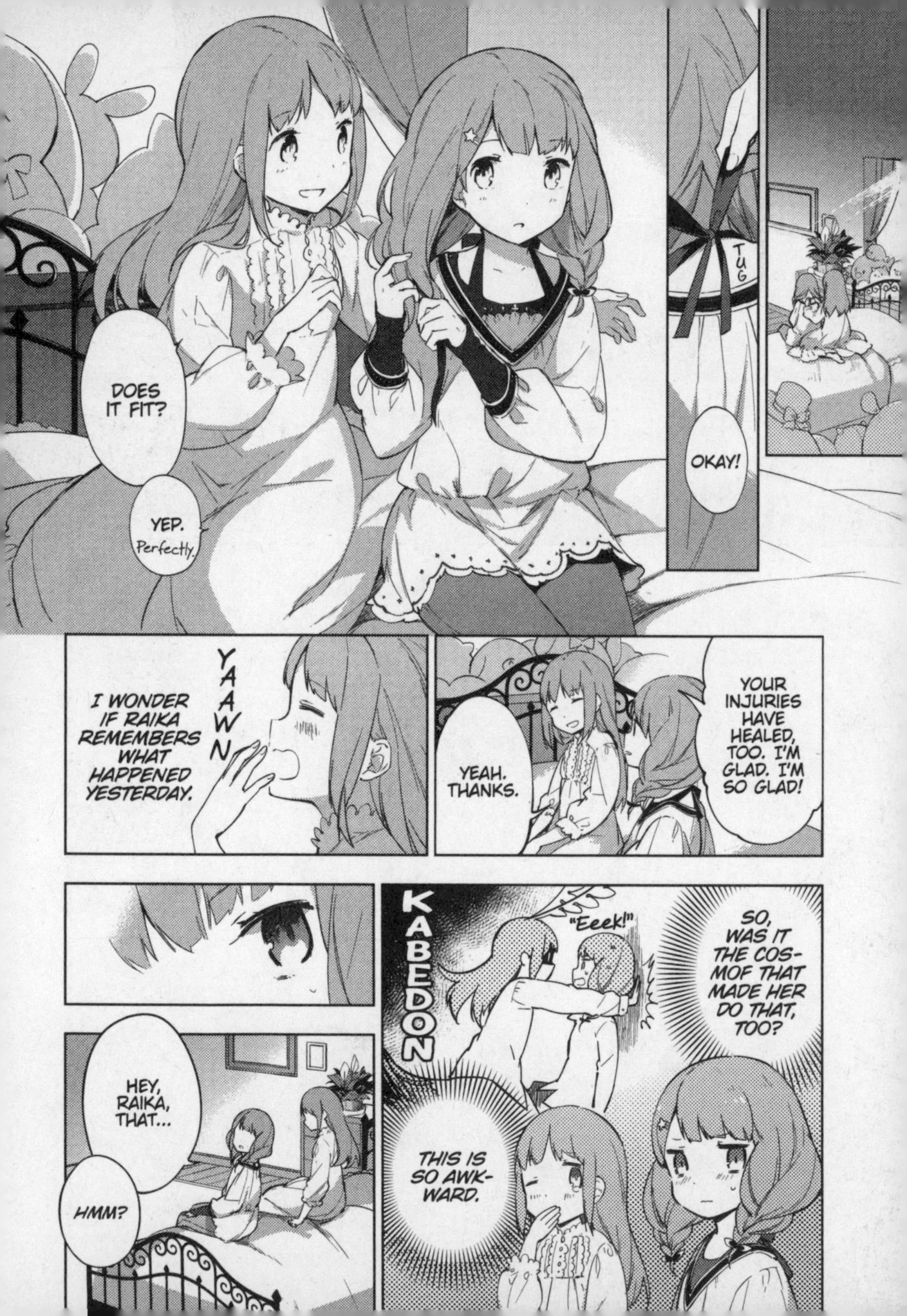
TUG
OKAY!
DOES IT FIT?
YEP.
Perfectly.
YOUR INJURIES HAVE HEALED, TOO. I'M GLAD. I'M SO GLAD!
YEAH. THANKS.
YAAWN
I WONDER IF RAIKA REMEMBERS WHAT HAPPENED YESTERDAY.
SO, WAS IT THE COS-MOF THAT MADE HER DO THAT, TOO?
KABEDON
"Eeek!"
THIS IS SO AWK-WARD.
HEY, RAIKA, THAT...
HMM?

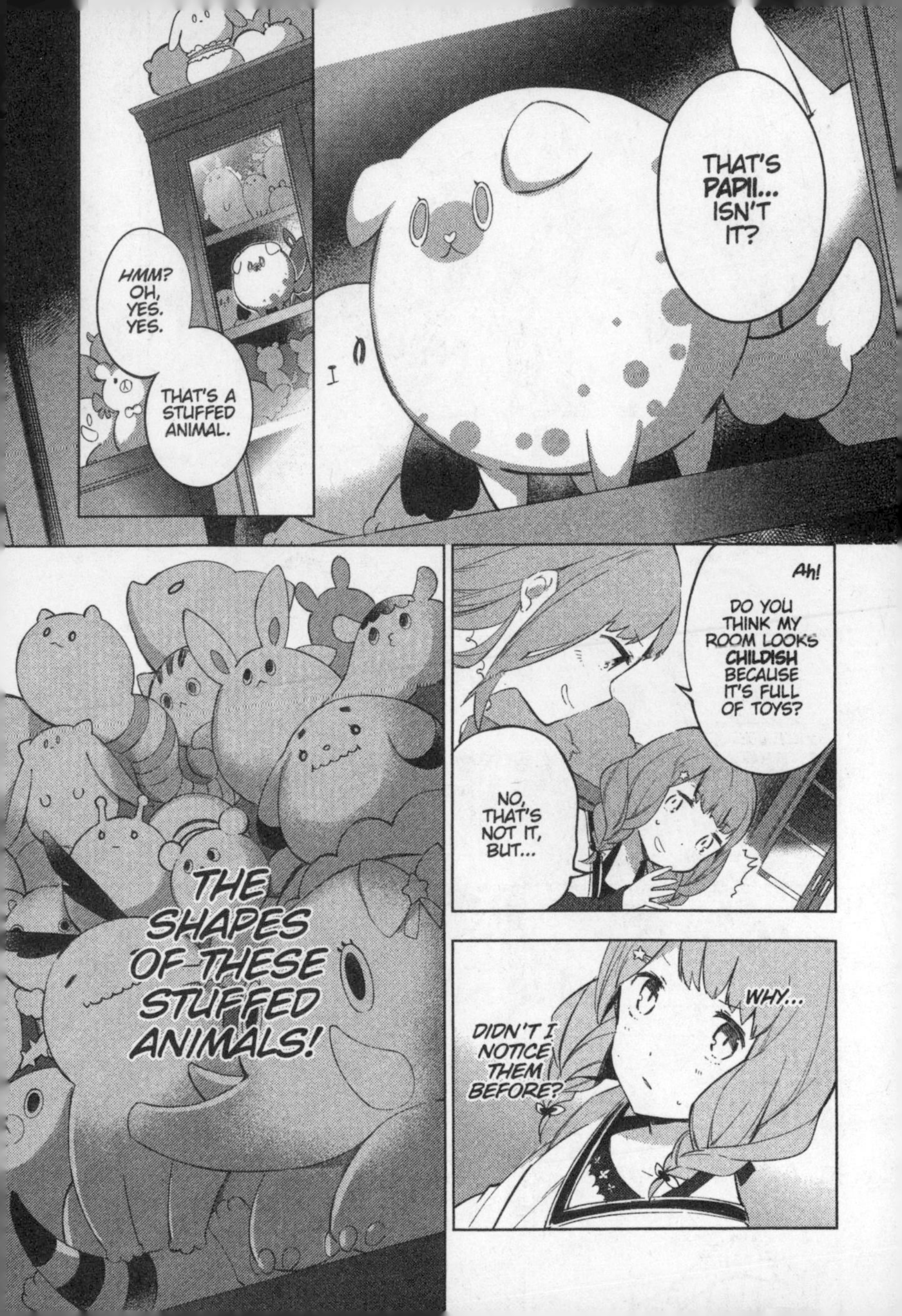
THAT'S PAPII... ISN'T IT?
HMM? OH, YES. YES.
THAT'S A STUFFED ANIMAL.
Ah!
DO YOU THINK MY ROOM LOOKS CHILDISH BECAUSE IT'S FULL OF TOYS?
NO, THAT'S NOT IT, BUT...
WHY...
DIDN'T I NOTICE THEM BEFORE?
THE SHAPES OF THESE STUFFED ANIMALS!

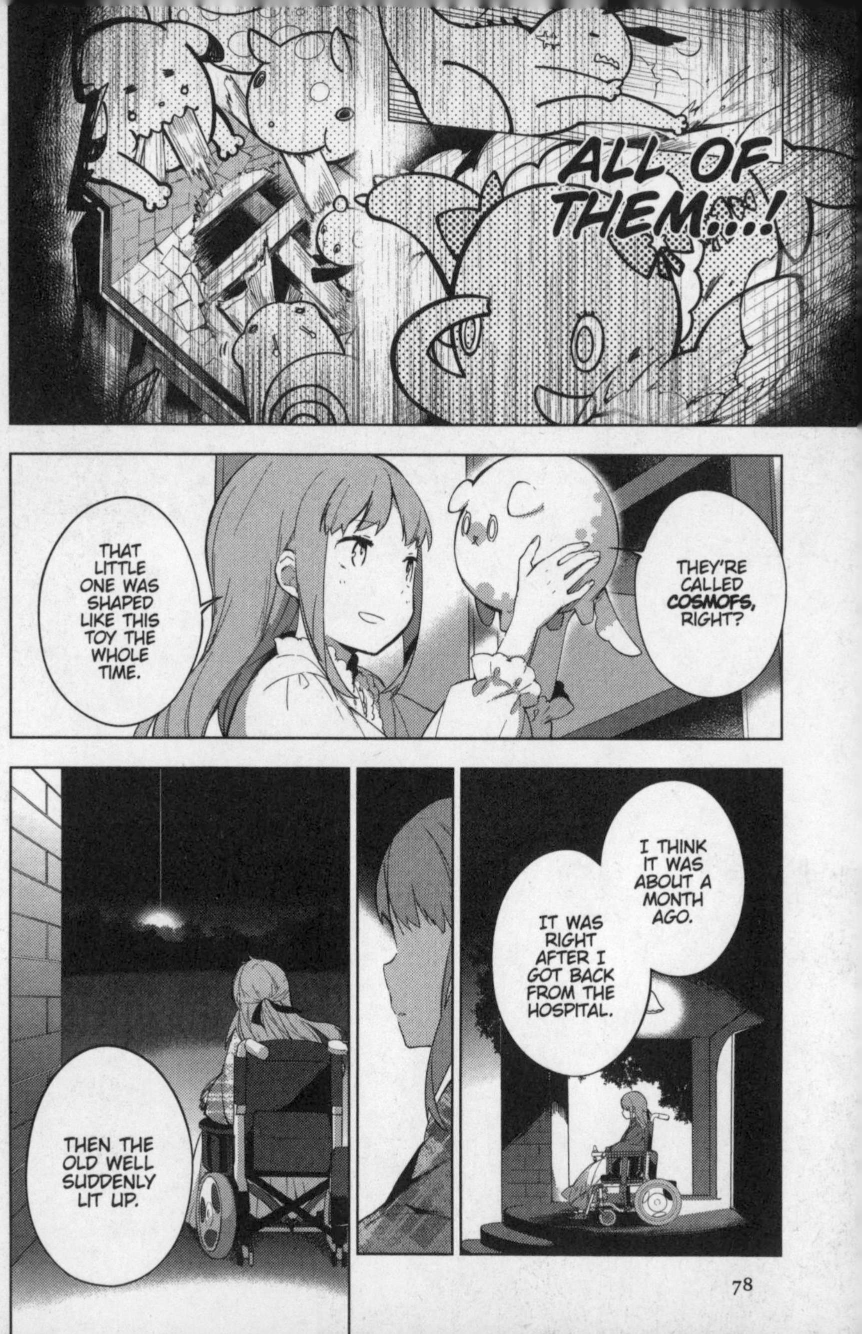
ALL OF THEM...!
THEY'RE CALLED COSMOFS, RIGHT?
THAT LITTLE ONE WAS SHAPED LIKE THIS TOY THE WHOLE TIME.
I THINK IT WAS ABOUT A MONTH AGO.
IT WAS RIGHT AFTER I GOT BACK FROM THE HOSPITAL.
THEN THE OLD WELL SUDDENLY LIT UP.

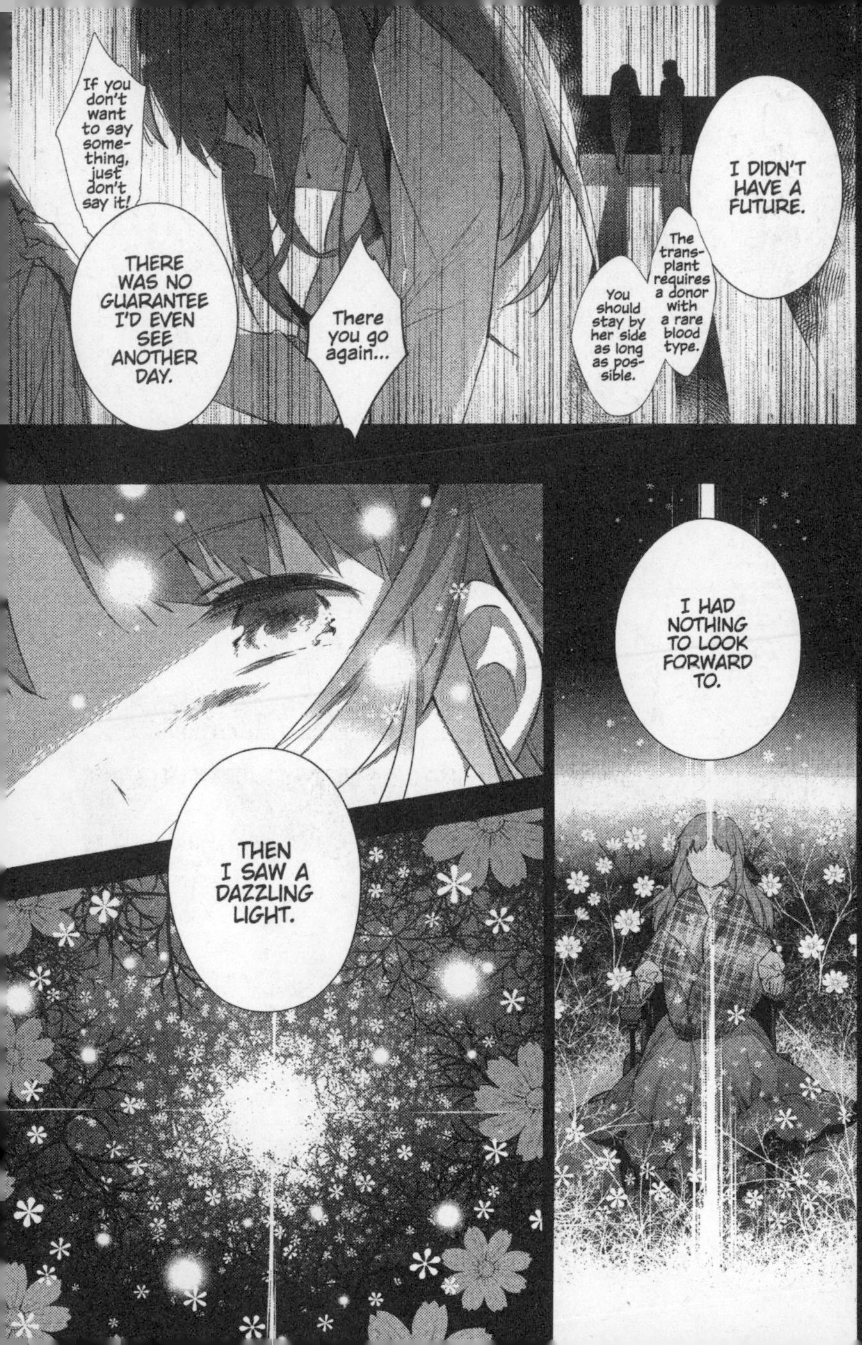
I DIDN'T HAVE A FUTURE.
The transplant requires a donor with a rare blood type.
You should stay by her side as long as possible.
THERE WAS NO GUARANTEE I'D EVEN SEE ANOTHER DAY.
There you go again...
If you don't want to say something, just don't say it!
I HAD NOTHING TO LOOK FORWARD TO.
THEN I SAW A DAZZLING LIGHT.

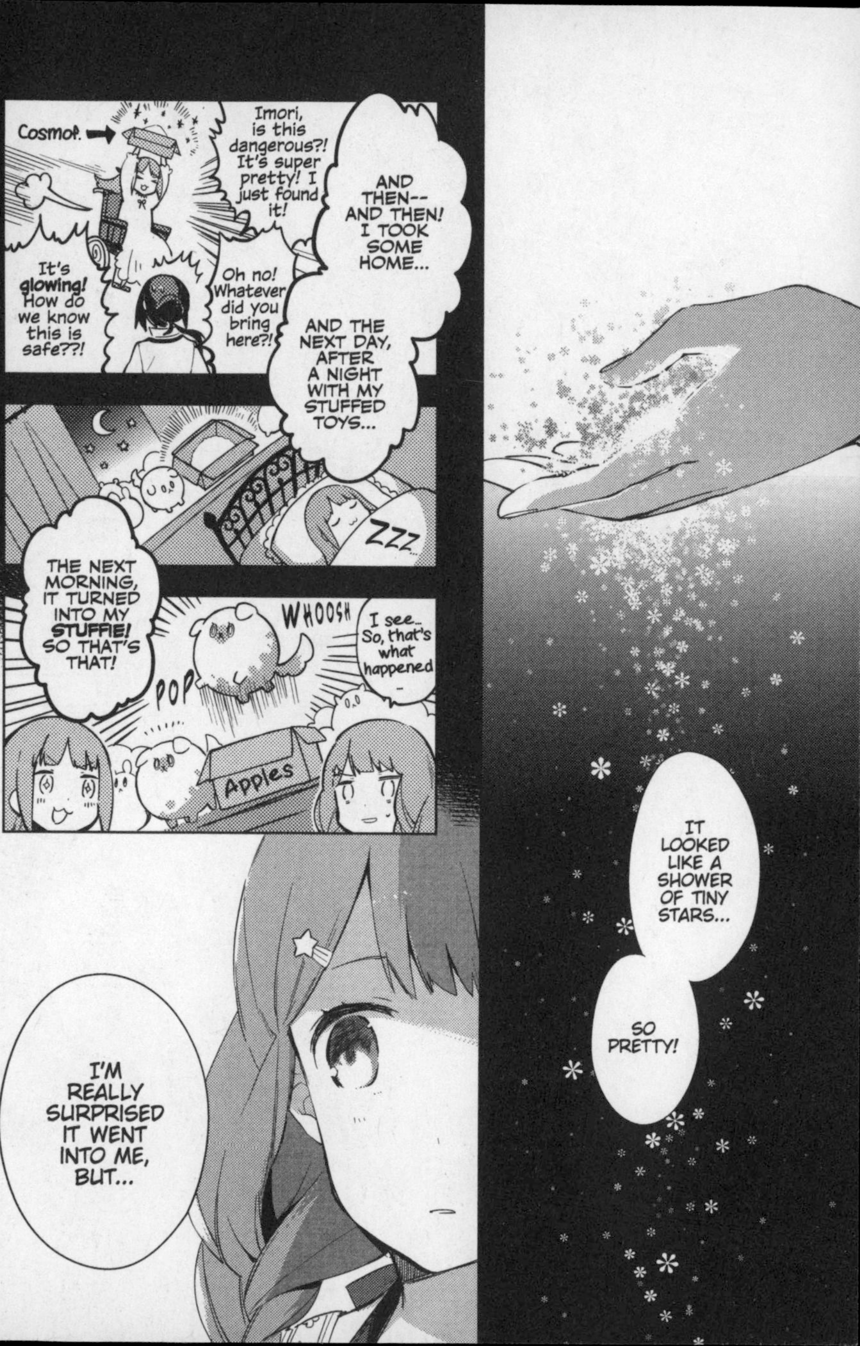
IT LOOKED LIKE A SHOWER OF TINY STARS...
SO PRETTY!
AND THEN-- AND THEN! I TOOK SOME HOME...
Imori, is this dangerous?! It's super pretty! I just found it!
Cosmo?.
Oh no! Whatever did you bring here?!
It's glowing! How do we know this is safe??!
AND THE NEXT DAY, AFTER A NIGHT WITH MY STUFFED TOYS...
ZZZ
I see... So, that's what happened
WHOOSH
THE NEXT MORNING, IT TURNED INTO MY STUFFIE! SO THAT'S THAT!
POP
Apples
I'M REALLY SURPRISED IT WENT INTO ME, BUT...

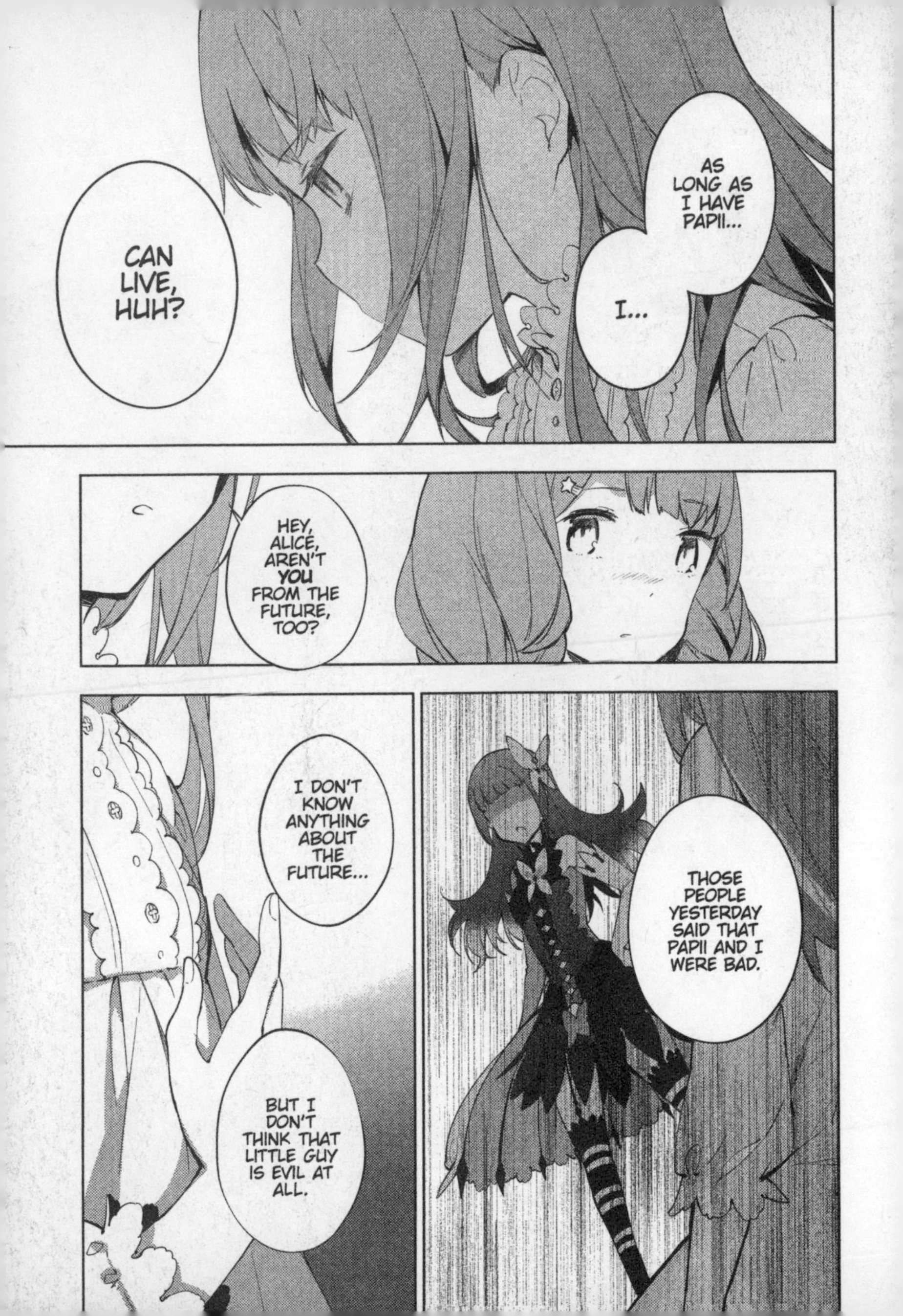
AS LONG AS I HAVE PAPII...
I...
CAN LIVE, HUH?
HEY, ALICE, AREN'T **YOU** FROM THE FUTURE, TOO?
THOSE PEOPLE YESTERDAY SAID THAT PAPII AND I WERE BAD.
I DON'T KNOW ANYTHING ABOUT THE FUTURE...
BUT I DON'T THINK THAT LITTLE GUY IS EVIL AT ALL.

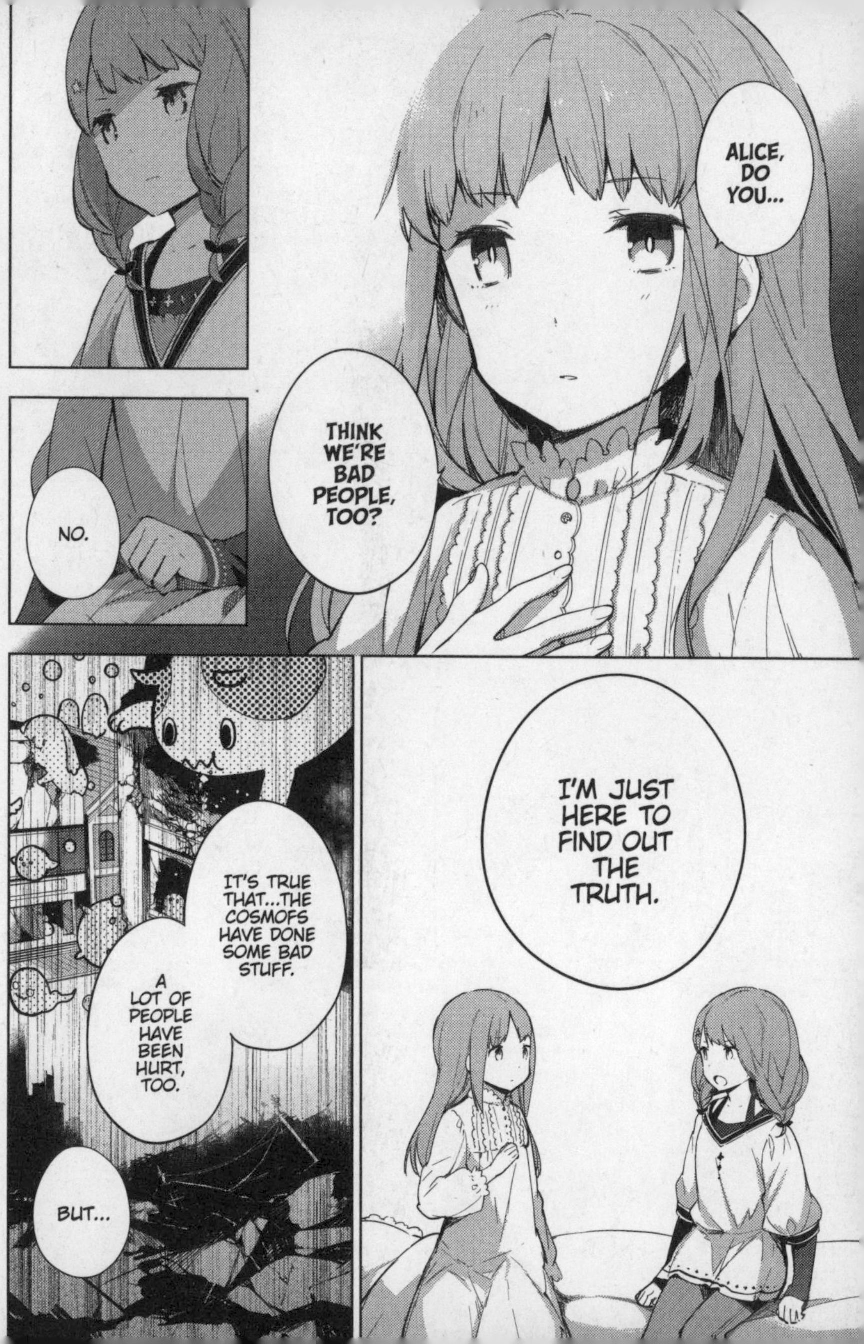
ALICE, DO YOU...
THINK WE'RE BAD PEOPLE, TOO?
NO.
I'M JUST HERE TO FIND OUT THE TRUTH.
IT'S TRUE THAT...THE COSMOFS HAVE DONE SOME BAD STUFF.
A LOT OF PEOPLE HAVE BEEN HURT, TOO.
BUT...

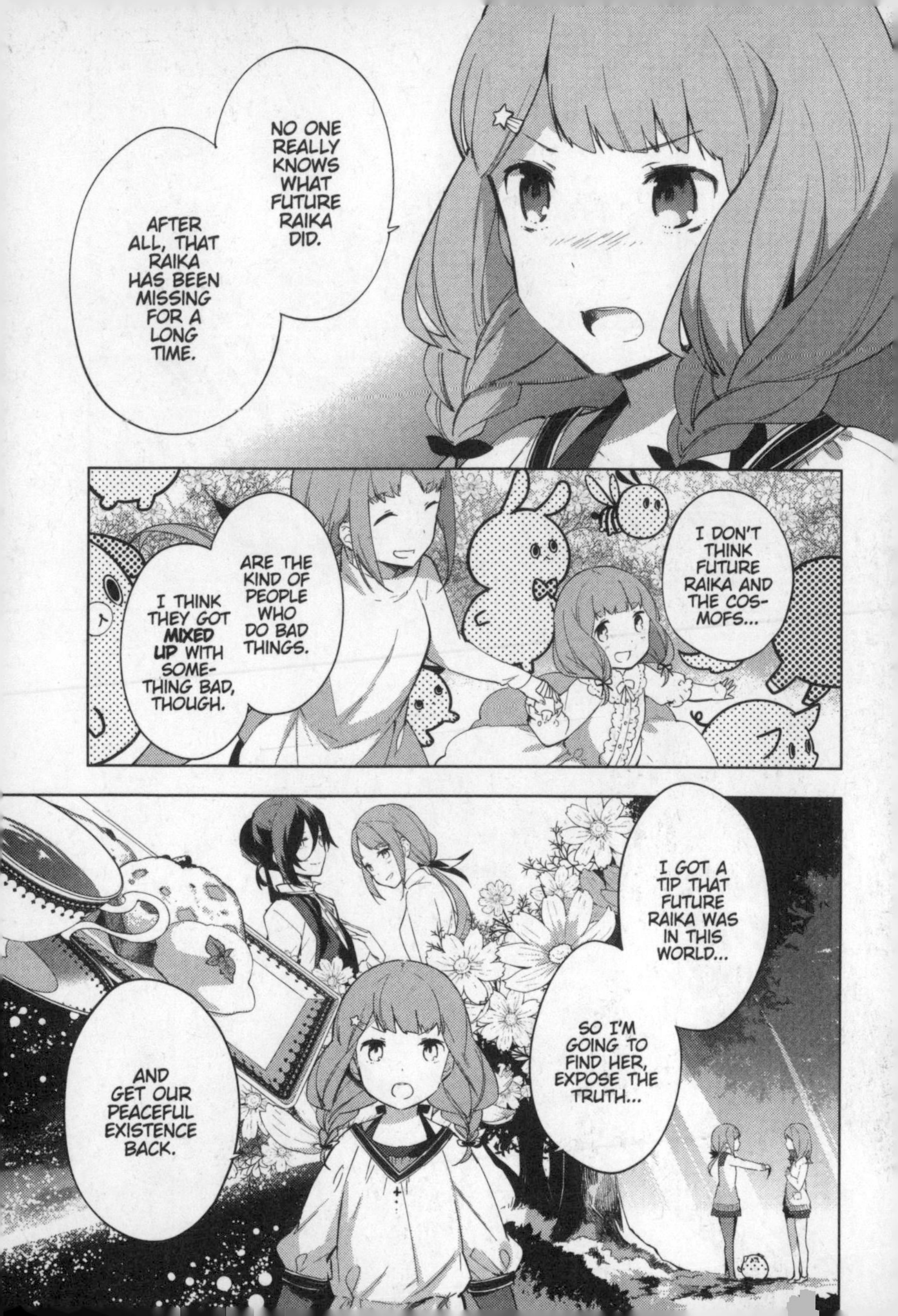
NO ONE REALLY KNOWS WHAT FUTURE RAIKA DID.
AFTER ALL, THAT RAIKA HAS BEEN MISSING FOR A LONG TIME.
I DON'T THINK FUTURE RAIKA AND THE COS-MOFS...
ARE THE KIND OF PEOPLE WHO DO BAD THINGS.
I THINK THEY GOT **MIXED UP** WITH SOME-THING BAD, THOUGH.
I GOT A TIP THAT FUTURE RAIKA WAS IN THIS WORLD...
SO I'M GOING TO FIND HER, EXPOSE THE TRUTH...
AND GET OUR PEACEFUL EXISTENCE BACK.

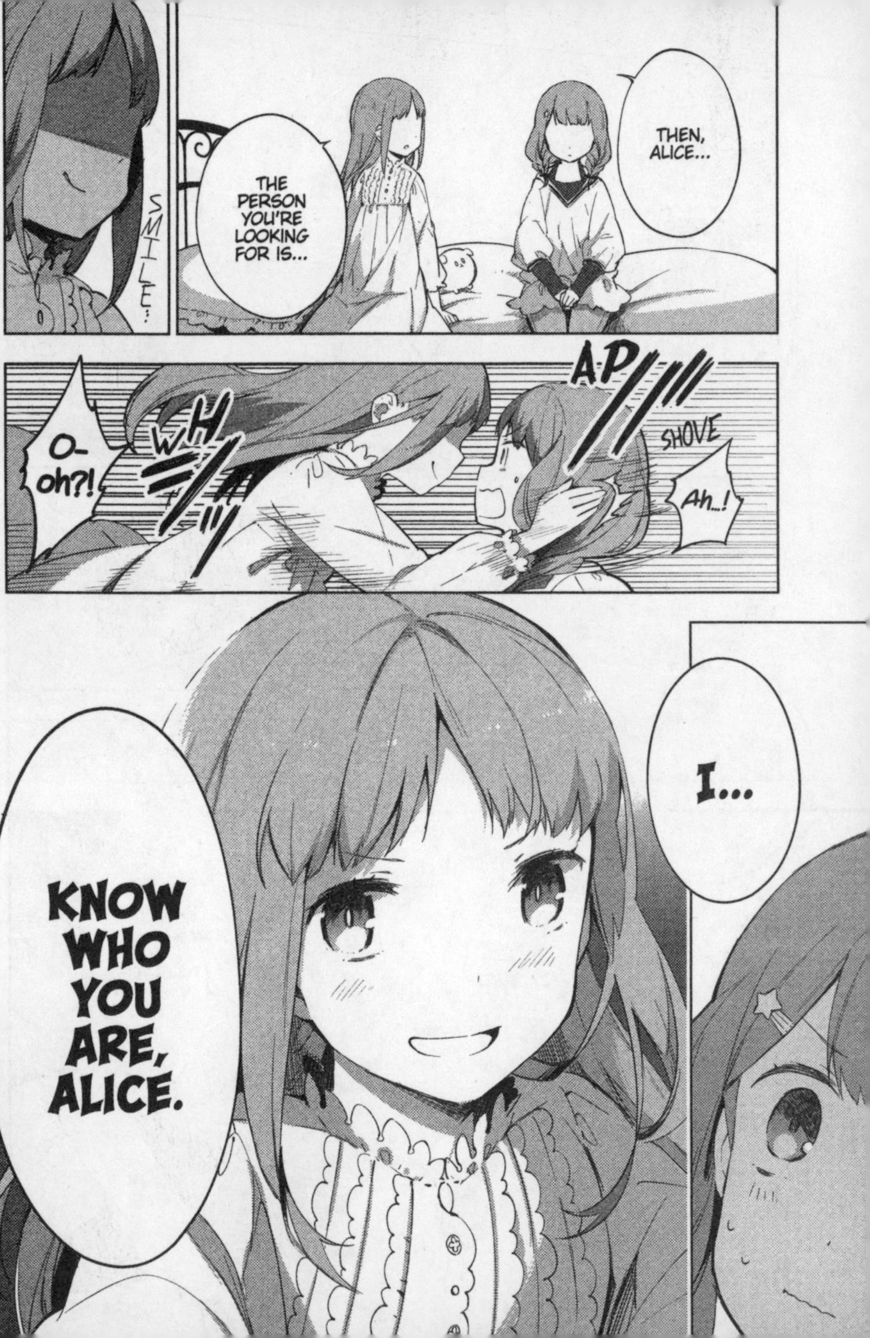
THEN, ALICE...
THE PERSON YOU'RE LOOKING FOR IS...
SMILE...
AP
SHOVE
Ah...!
WH
O-oh?!
I...
KNOW WHO YOU ARE, ALICE.

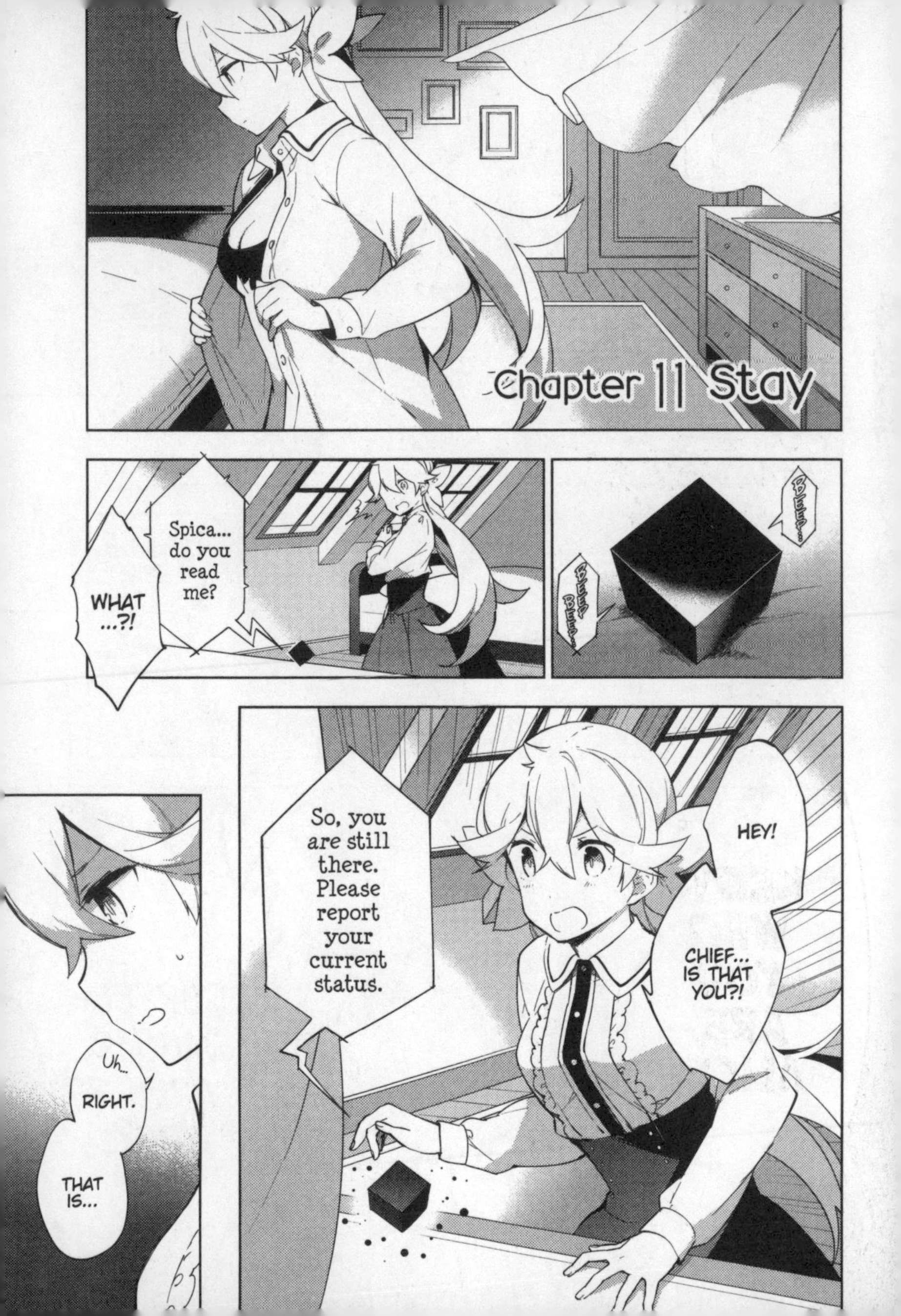
Chapter 11 Stay
Beep...
Beep Beep...
Spica... do you read me?
WHAT ...?!
HEY!
CHIEF... IS THAT YOU?!
So, you are still there. Please report your current status.
Uh...
RIGHT.
THAT IS...

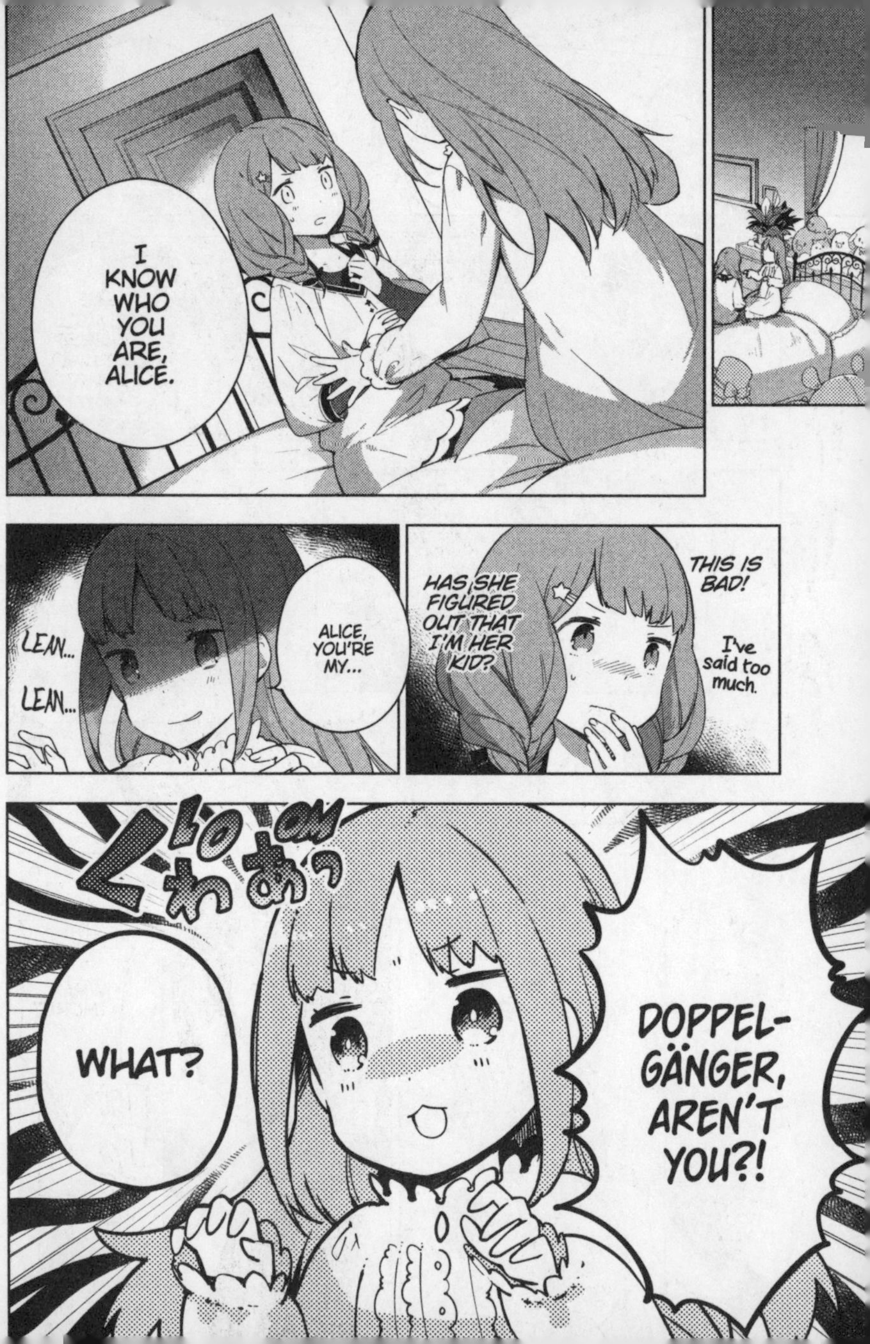
I KNOW WHO YOU ARE, ALICE.
THIS IS BAD!
HAS SHE FIGURED OUT THAT I'M HER KID?
I've said too much.
ALICE, YOU'RE MY...
LEAN... LEAN...
くわあっ
DOPPEL-GÄNGER, AREN'T YOU?!
WHAT?

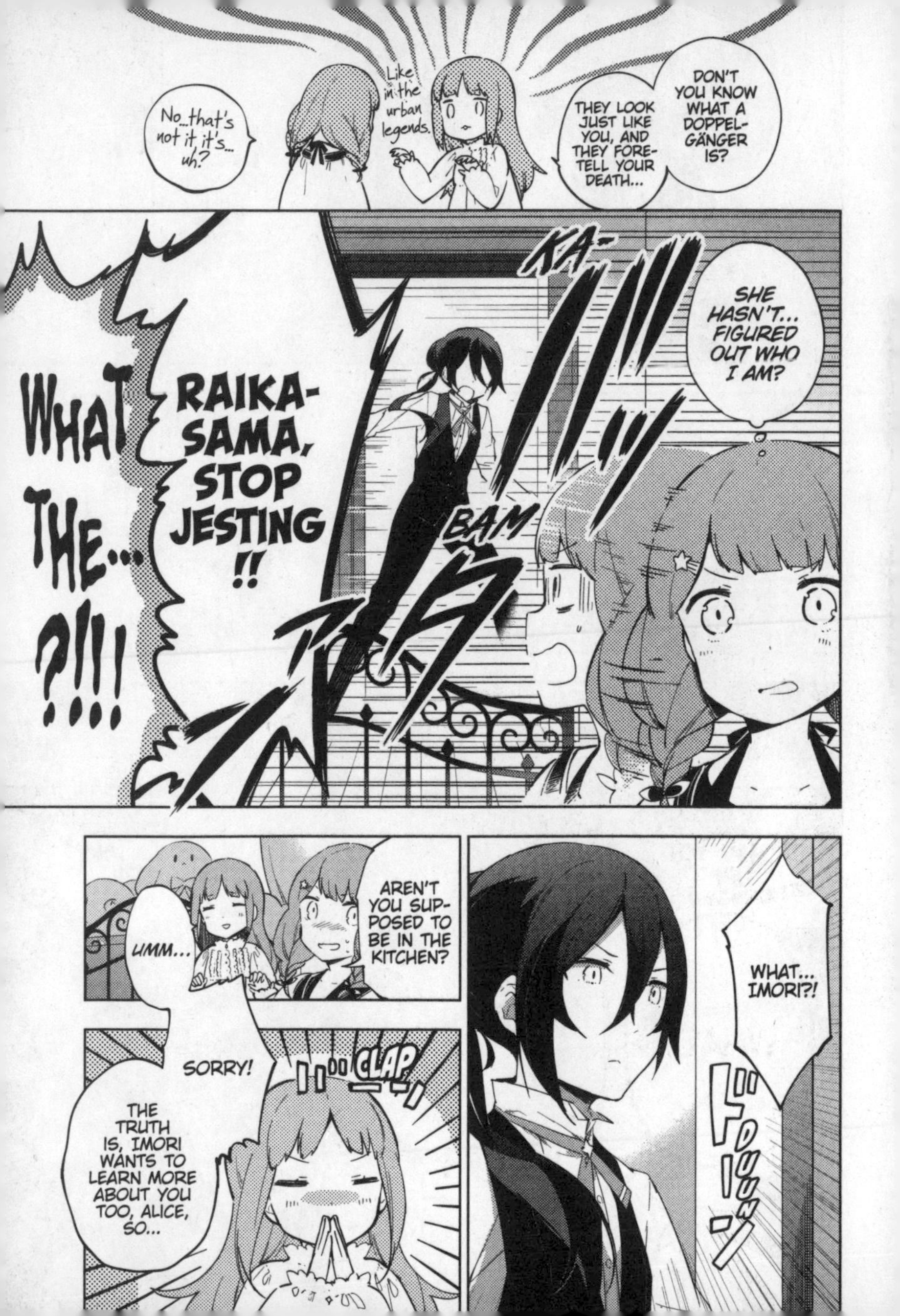
DON'T YOU KNOW WHAT A DOPPEL-GÄNGER IS?
THEY LOOK JUST LIKE YOU, AND THEY FORE-TELL YOUR DEATH...
Like in the urban legends.
No...that's not it it's... uh?
SHE HASN'T... FIGURED OUT WHO I AM?
KA-
BAM
RAIKA-SAMA, STOP JESTING !!
WHAT THE...?!!!
WHAT... IMORI?!
DUUUN
AREN'T YOU SUP-POSED TO BE IN THE KITCHEN?
UMM...
SORRY!
CLAP
THE TRUTH IS, IMORI WANTS TO LEARN MORE ABOUT YOU TOO, ALICE, SO...

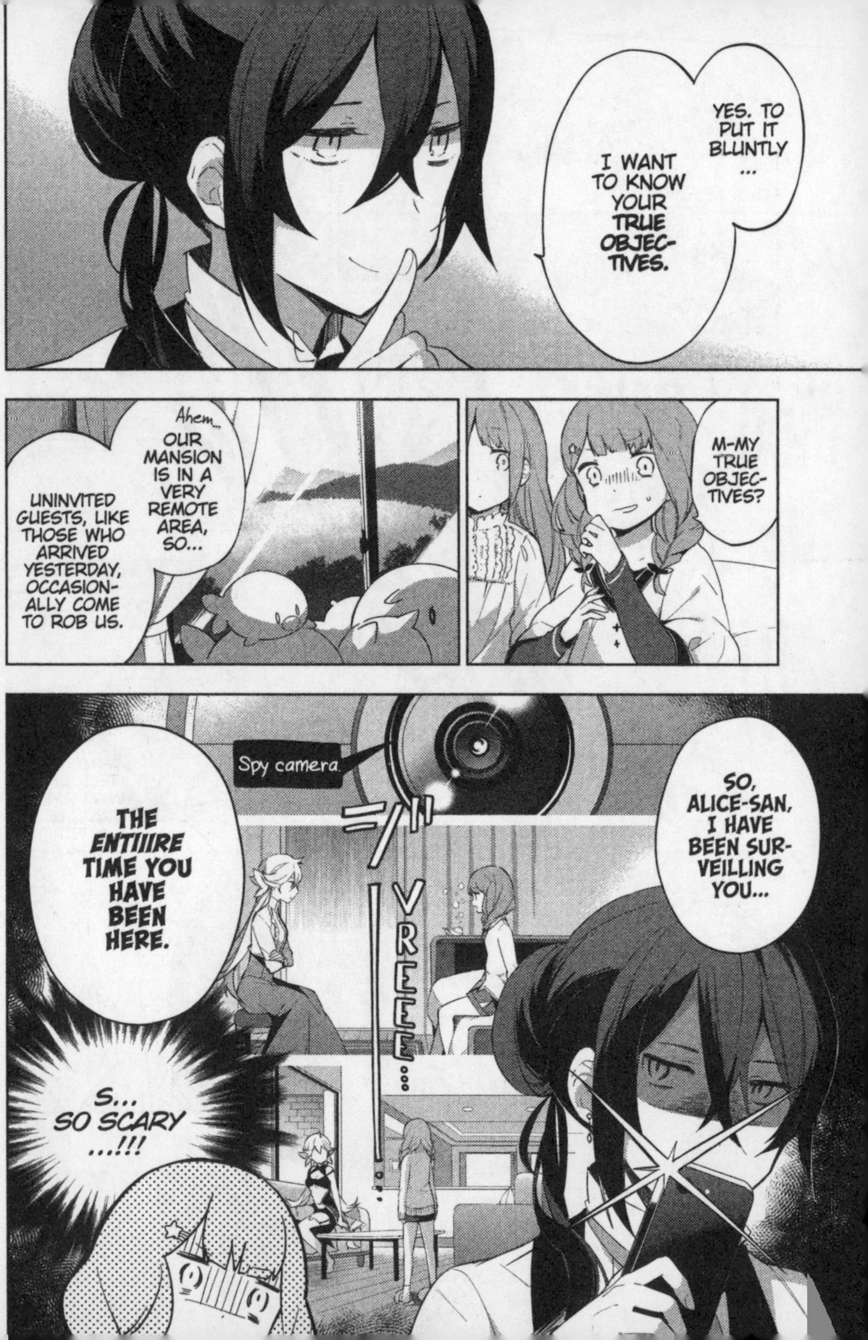
YES. TO PUT IT BLUNTLY ...
I WANT TO KNOW YOUR TRUE OBJECTIVES.
M-MY TRUE OBJECTIVES?
Ahem...
OUR MANSION IS IN A VERY REMOTE AREA, SO...
UNINVITED GUESTS, LIKE THOSE WHO ARRIVED YESTERDAY, OCCASIONALLY COME TO ROB US.
SO, ALICE-SAN, I HAVE BEEN SURVEILLING YOU...
THE ENTIIIRE TIME YOU HAVE BEEN HERE.
Spy camera.
VREEE...
S... SO SCARY ...!!!

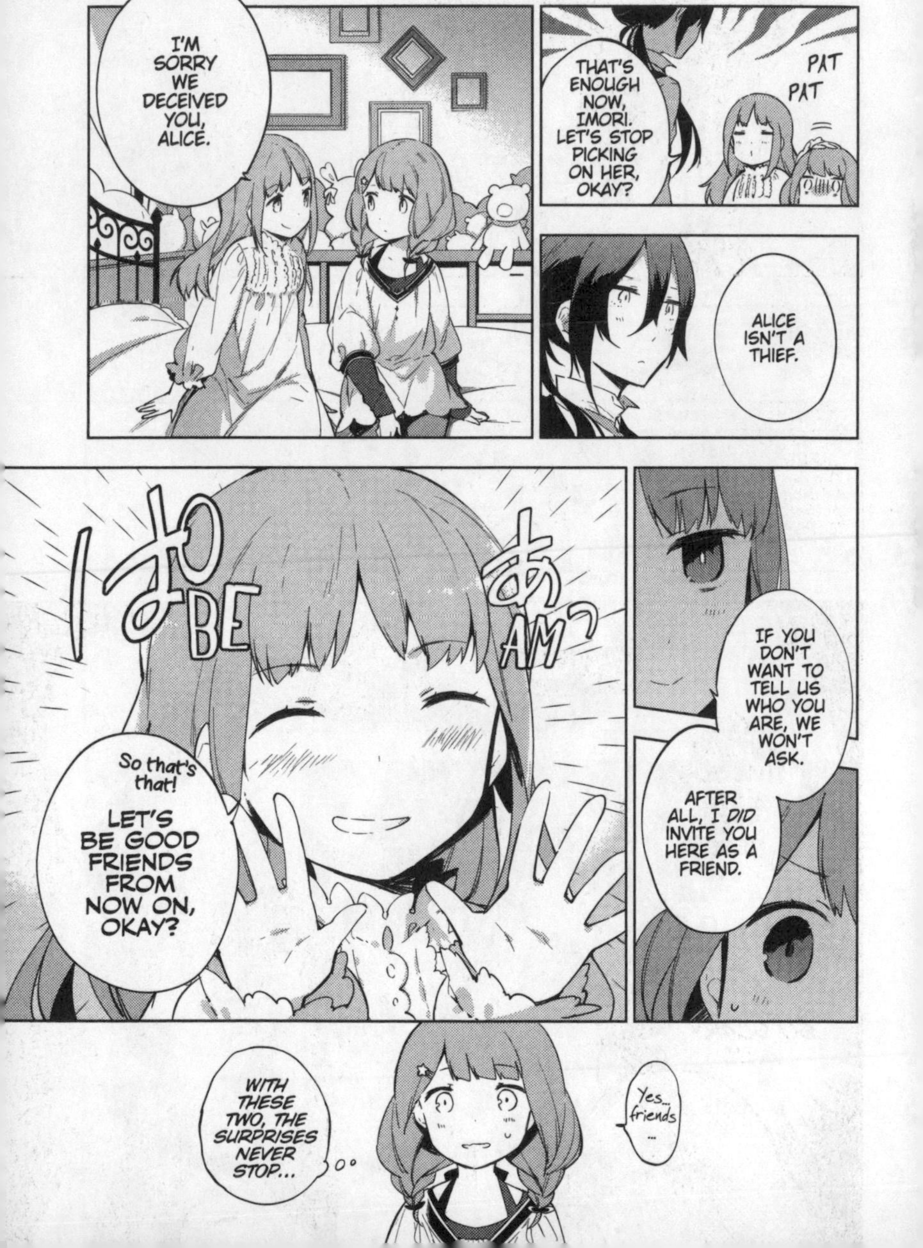
THAT'S ENOUGH NOW, IMORI. LET'S STOP PICKING ON HER, OKAY?
PAT PAT
ALICE ISN'T A THIEF.
I'M SORRY WE DECEIVED YOU, ALICE.
IF YOU DON'T WANT TO TELL US WHO YOU ARE, WE WON'T ASK.
AFTER ALL, I *DID* INVITE YOU HERE AS A FRIEND.
ぱあっ
BEAM
So that's that!
LET'S BE GOOD FRIENDS FROM NOW ON, OKAY?
Yes... friends...
WITH THESE TWO, THE SURPRISES NEVER STOP...

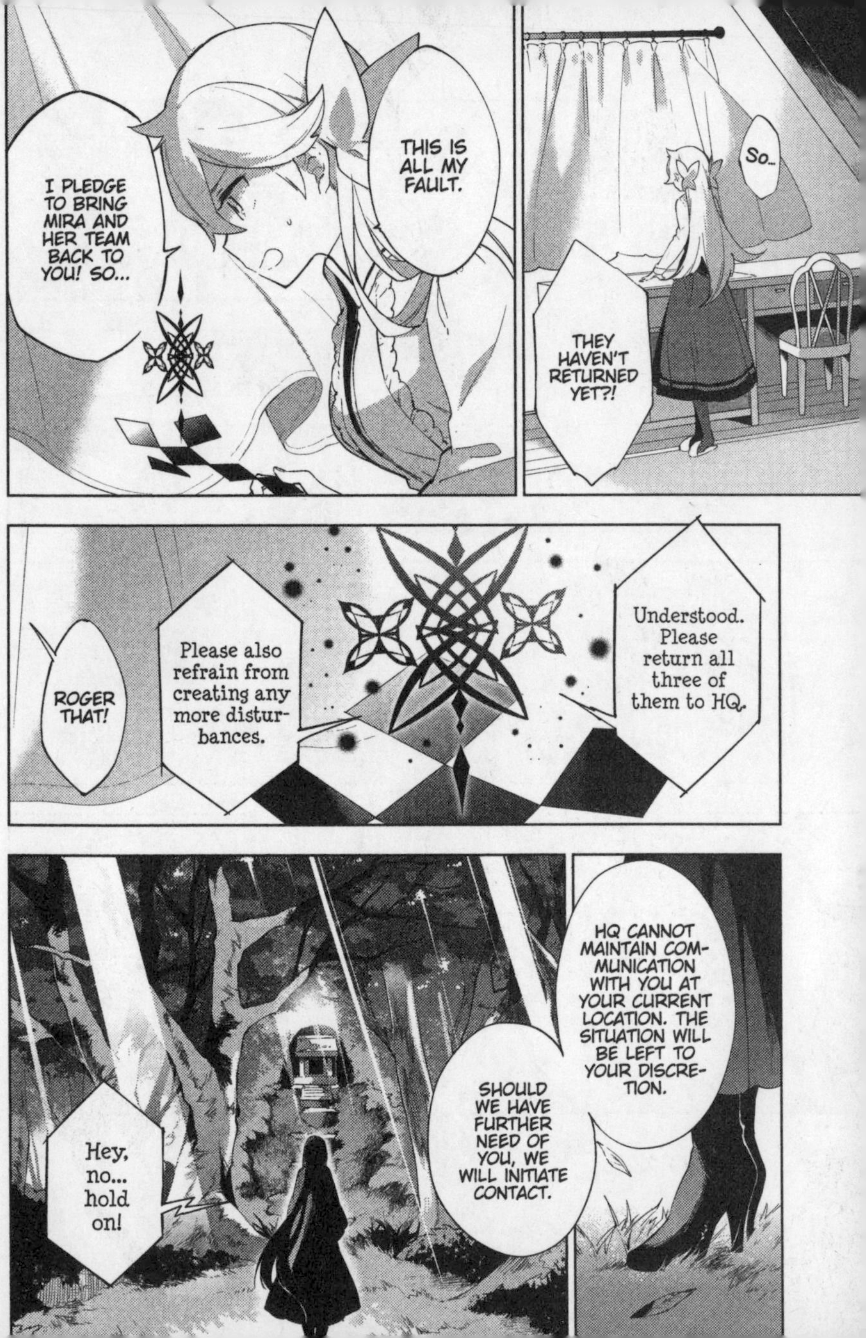
So...
THEY HAVEN'T RETURNED YET?!
THIS IS ALL MY FAULT.
I PLEDGE TO BRING MIRA AND HER TEAM BACK TO YOU! SO...
Understood. Please return all three of them to HQ.
Please also refrain from creating any more distur-bances.
ROGER THAT!
HQ CANNOT MAINTAIN COM-MUNICATION WITH YOU AT YOUR CURRENT LOCATION. THE SITUATION WILL BE LEFT TO YOUR DISCRE-TION.
SHOULD WE HAVE FURTHER NEED OF YOU, WE WILL INITIATE CONTACT.
Hey, no... hold on!

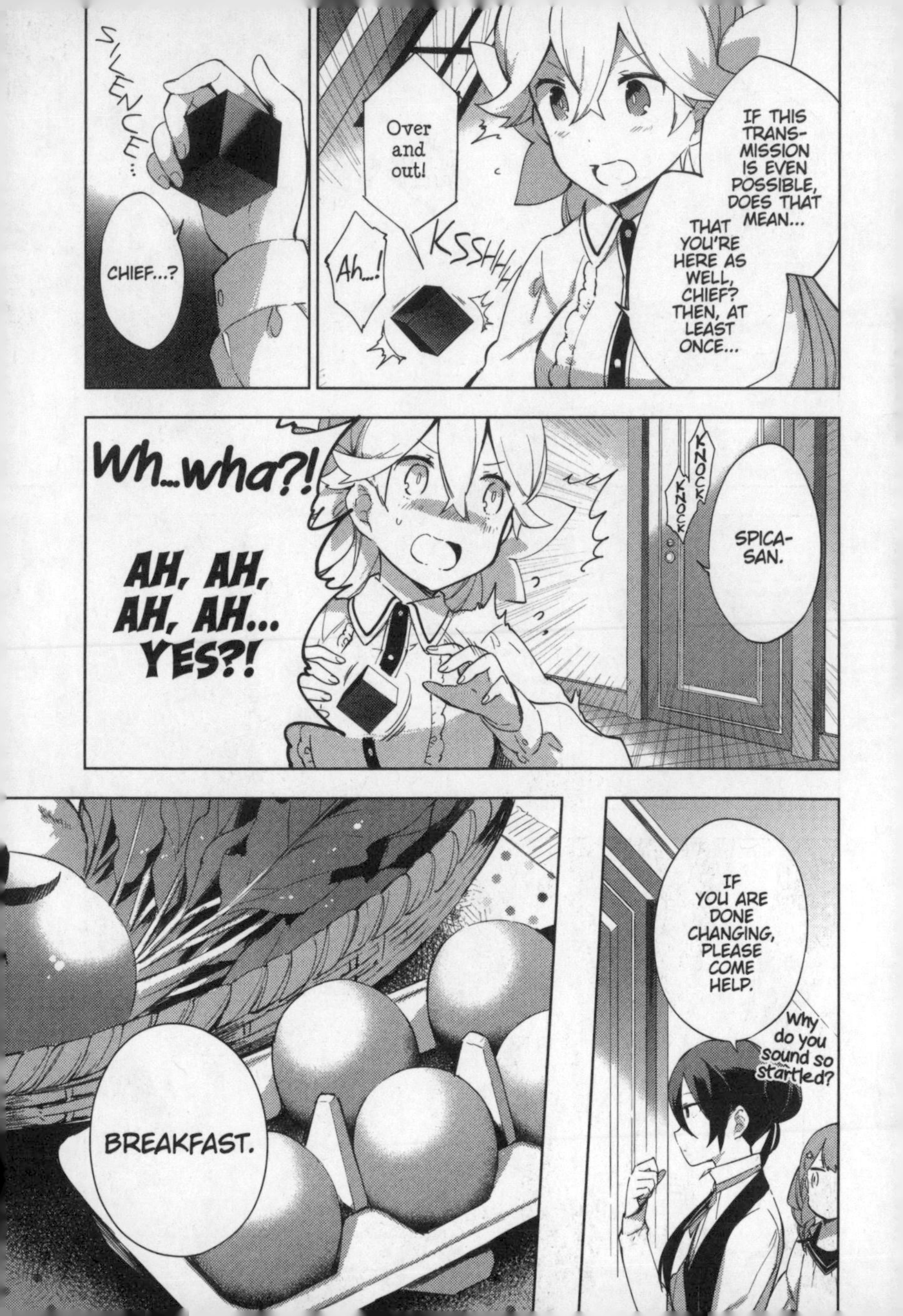
IF THIS TRANS- MISSION IS EVEN POSSIBLE, DOES THAT MEAN...
THAT YOU'RE HERE AS WELL, CHIEF? THEN, AT LEAST ONCE...
Over and out!
KSSHH
Ah...!
SILENCE...
CHIEF...?
KNOCK KNOCK
SPICA- SAN.
Wh...wha?!
AH, AH, AH, AH... YES?!
IF YOU ARE DONE CHANGING, PLEASE COME HELP.
Why do you sound so startled?
BREAKFAST.

# * IMORI'S BREAKFAST *

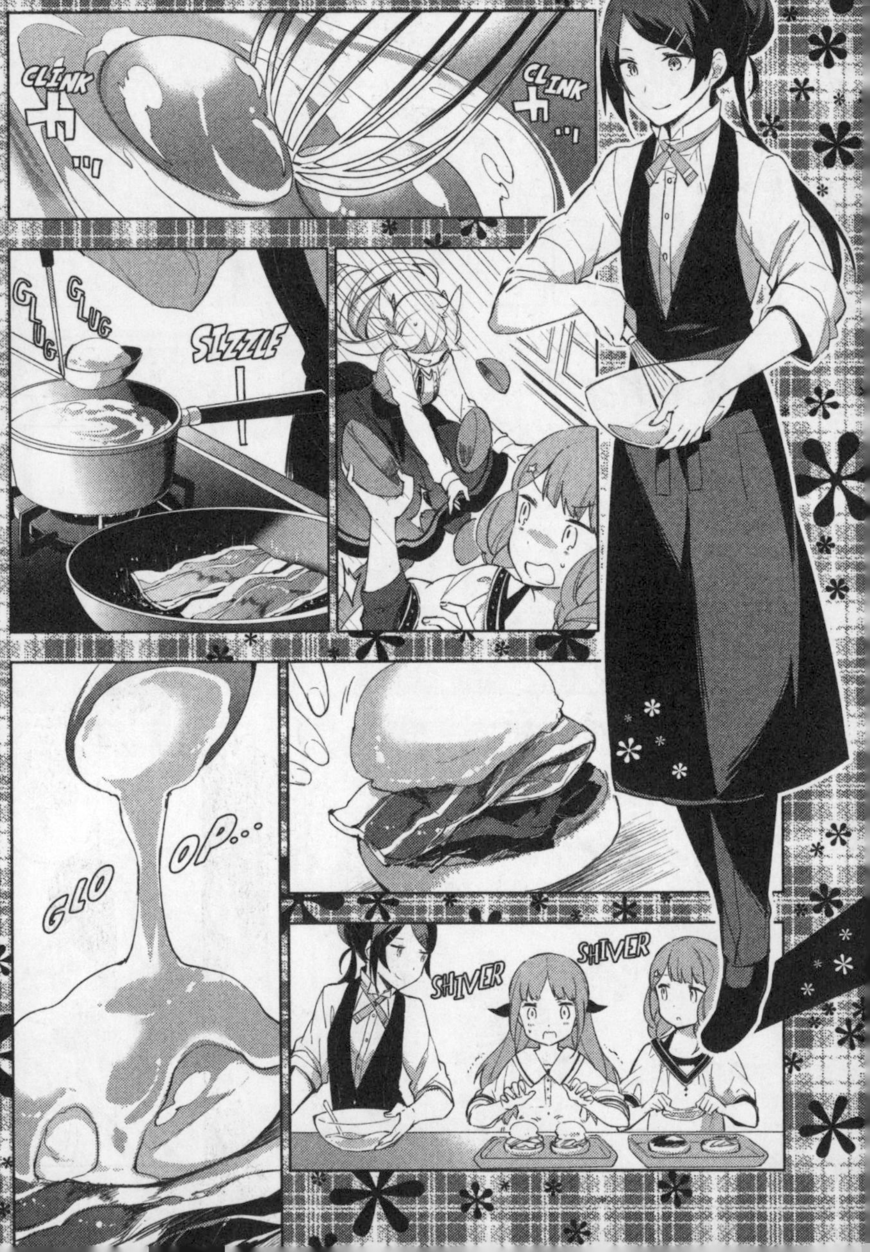
CLINK
CLINK
SIZZLE
GLUG
GLUG
SHIVER
SHIVER
GLOOP...

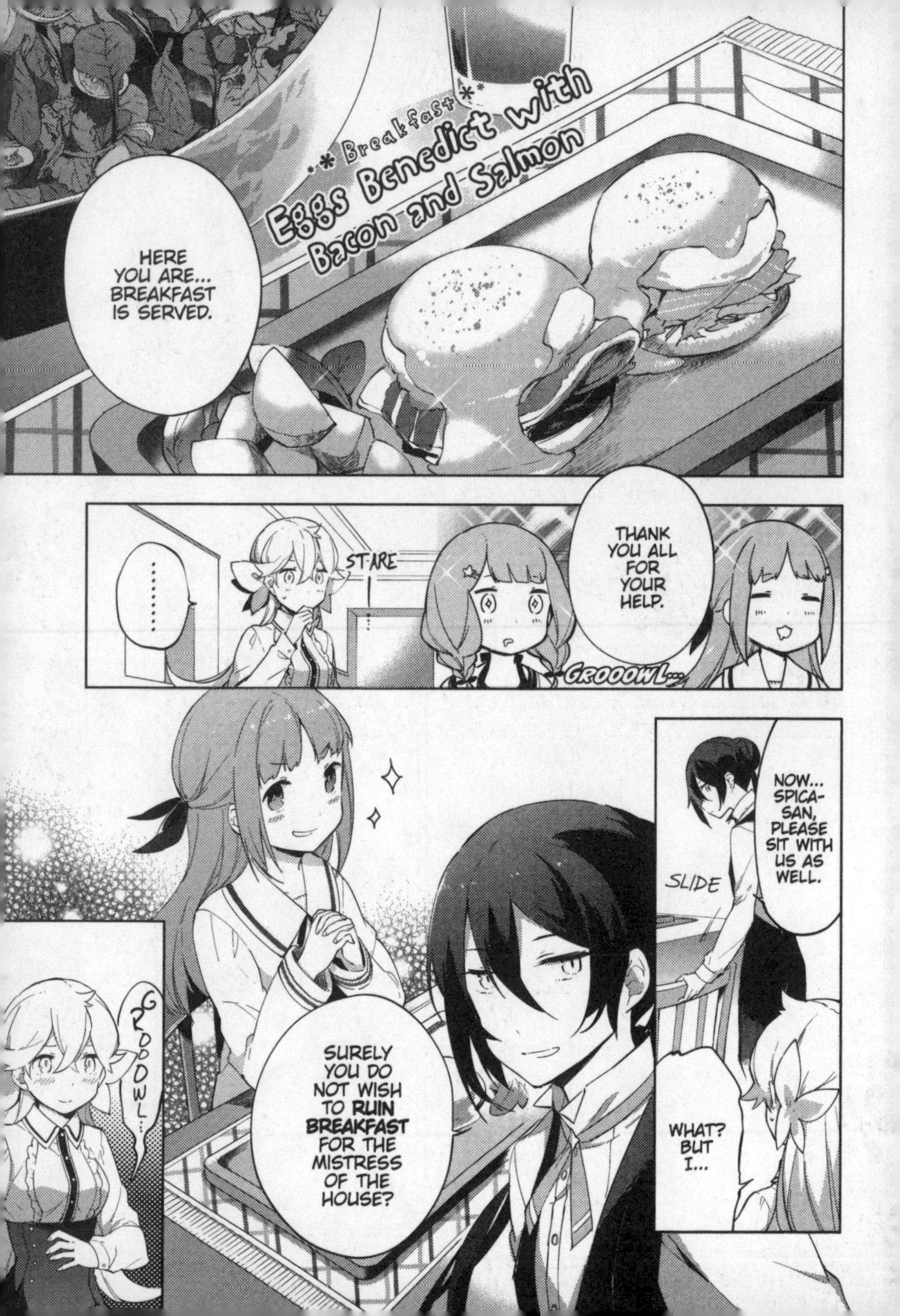
* Breakfast *
Eggs Benedict with Bacon and Salmon
HERE YOU ARE... BREAKFAST IS SERVED.
THANK YOU ALL FOR YOUR HELP.
GROOOWL...
STARE
......
NOW... SPICA-SAN, PLEASE SIT WITH US AS WELL.
SLIDE
WHAT? BUT I...
SURELY YOU DO NOT WISH TO **RUIN BREAKFAST** FOR THE MISTRESS OF THE HOUSE?
GROOOWL...

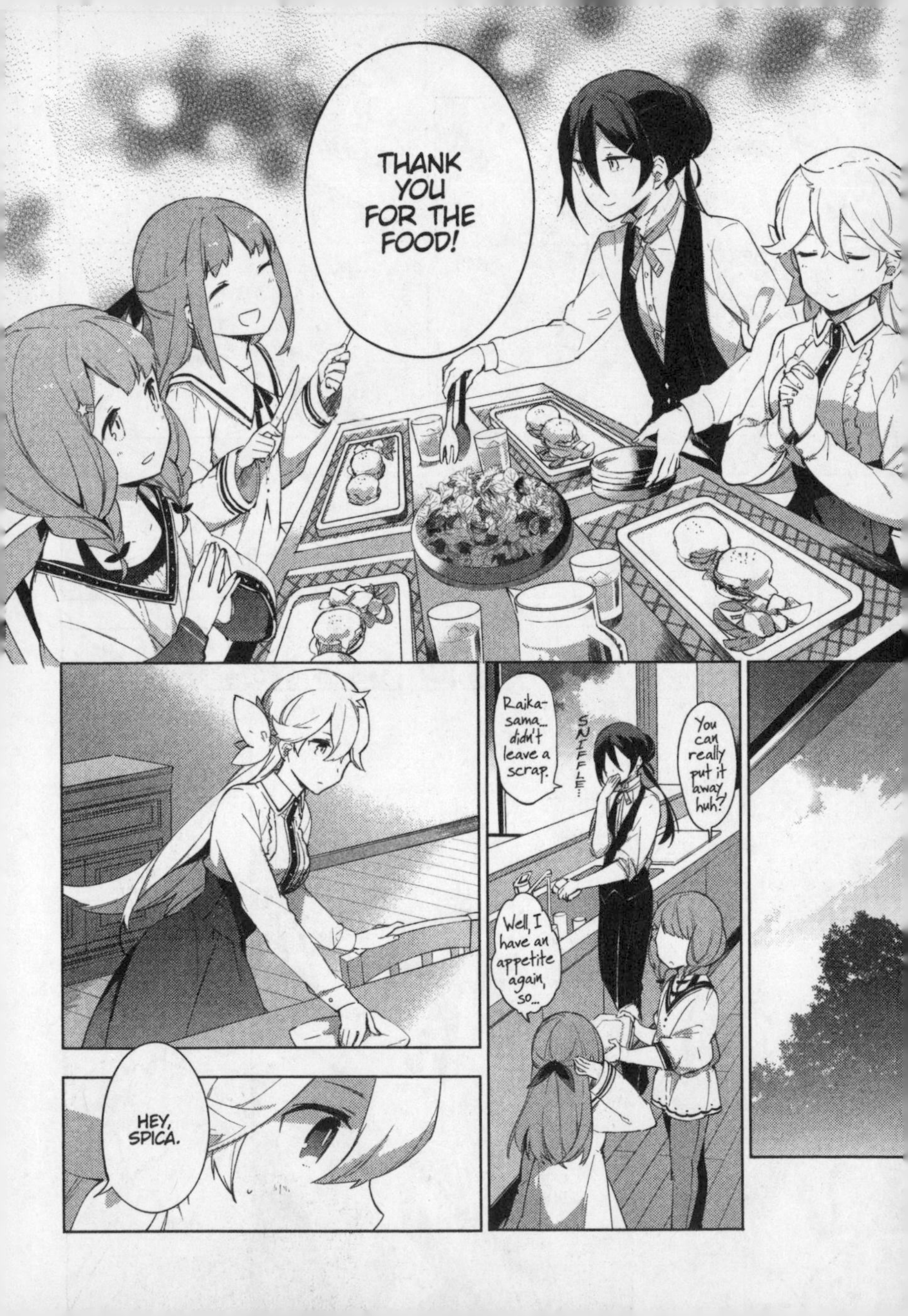
THANK YOU FOR THE FOOD!
You can really put it away, huh!?
SNIFFLE...
Raika-sama... didn't leave a scrap.
Well, I have an appetite again, so...
HEY, SPICA.

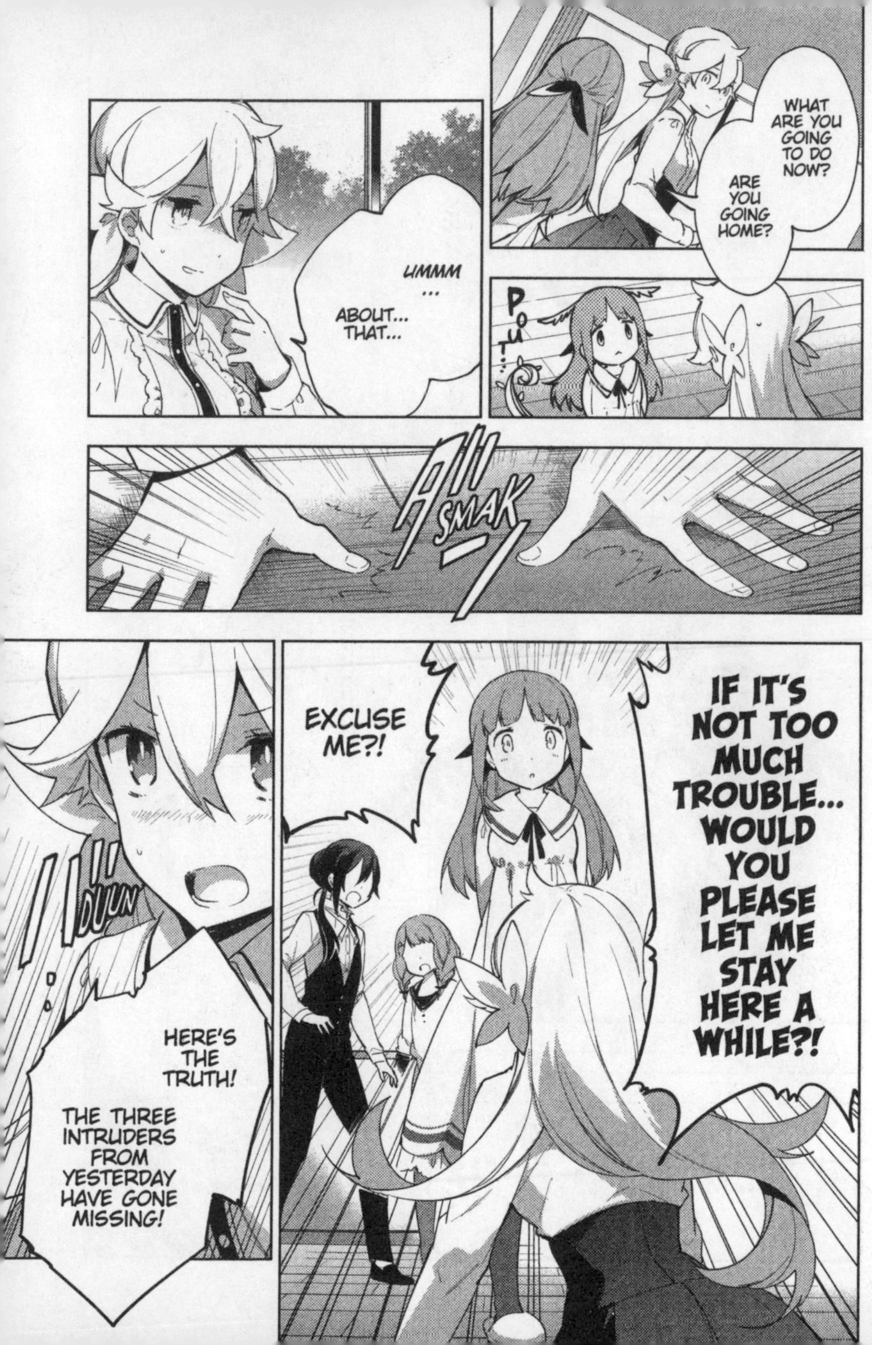
WHAT ARE YOU GOING TO DO NOW?
ARE YOU GOING HOME?
POUT...
UMMM...
ABOUT... THAT...
SMAK
IF IT'S NOT TOO MUCH TROUBLE... WOULD YOU PLEASE LET ME STAY HERE A WHILE?!
EXCUSE ME?!
DUUN
HERE'S THE TRUTH!
THE THREE INTRUDERS FROM YESTERDAY HAVE GONE MISSING!

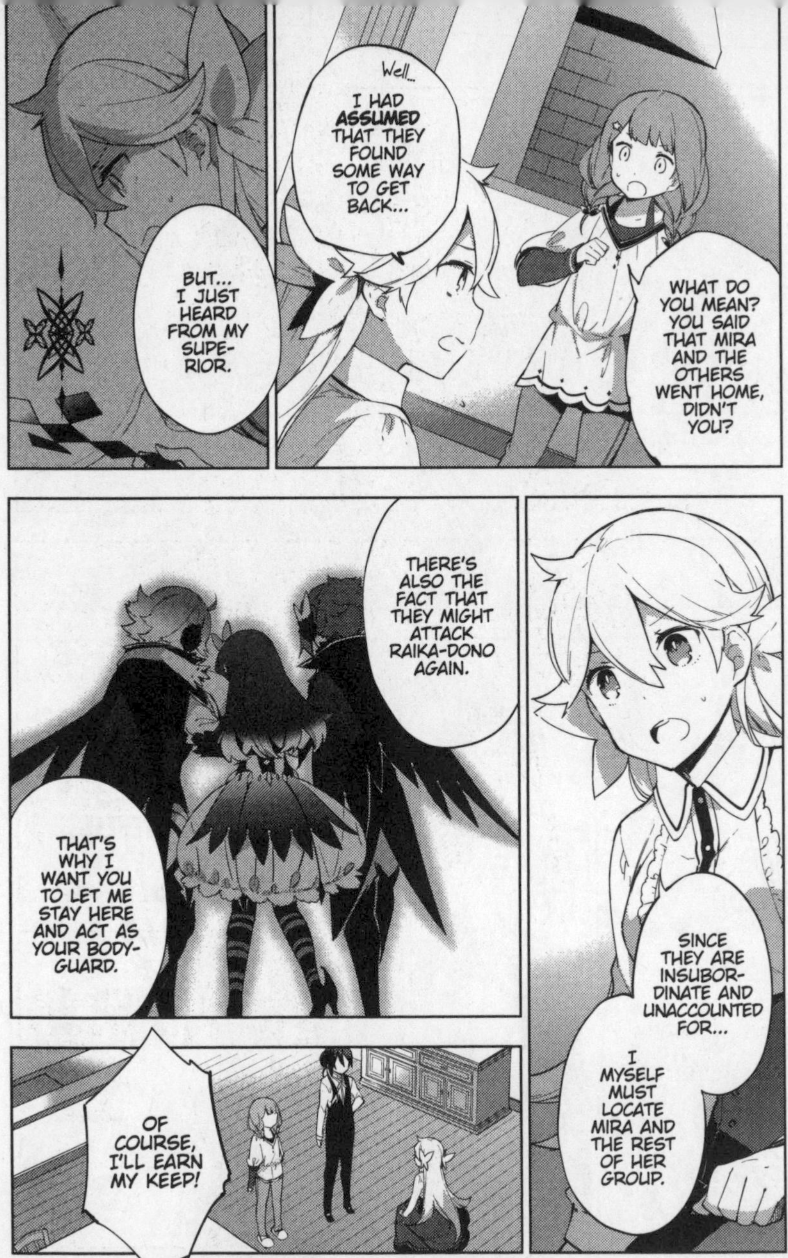
WHAT DO YOU MEAN? YOU SAID THAT MIRA AND THE OTHERS WENT HOME, DIDN'T YOU?
Well...
I HAD **ASSUMED** THAT THEY FOUND SOME WAY TO GET BACK...
BUT... I JUST HEARD FROM MY SUPER-RIOR.
SINCE THEY ARE INSUBOR-DINATE AND UNACCOUNTED FOR...
I MYSELF MUST LOCATE MIRA AND THE REST OF HER GROUP.
THERE'S ALSO THE FACT THAT THEY MIGHT ATTACK RAIKA-DONO AGAIN.
THAT'S WHY I WANT YOU TO LET ME STAY HERE AND ACT AS YOUR BODY-GUARD.
OF COURSE, I'LL EARN MY KEEP!

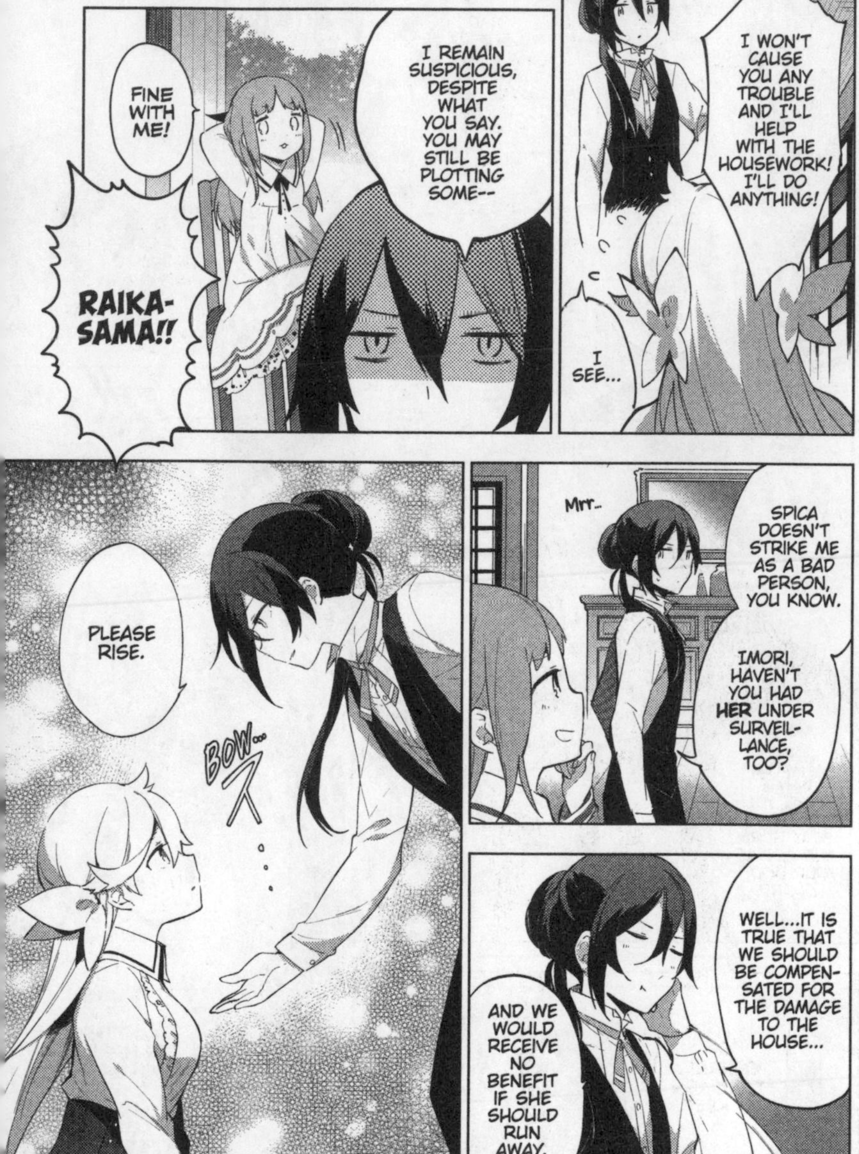
I WON'T CAUSE YOU ANY TROUBLE AND I'LL HELP WITH THE HOUSEWORK! I'LL DO ANYTHING!
I SEE...
I REMAIN SUSPICIOUS, DESPITE WHAT YOU SAY. YOU MAY STILL BE PLOTTING SOME--
FINE WITH ME!
RAIKA-SAMA!!
SPICA DOESN'T STRIKE ME AS A BAD PERSON, YOU KNOW.
Mrr..
IMORI, HAVEN'T YOU HAD HER UNDER SURVEIL-LANCE, TOO?
WELL...IT IS TRUE THAT WE SHOULD BE COMPEN-SATED FOR THE DAMAGE TO THE HOUSE...
AND WE WOULD RECEIVE NO BENEFIT IF SHE SHOULD RUN AWAY.
PLEASE RISE.
BOW...

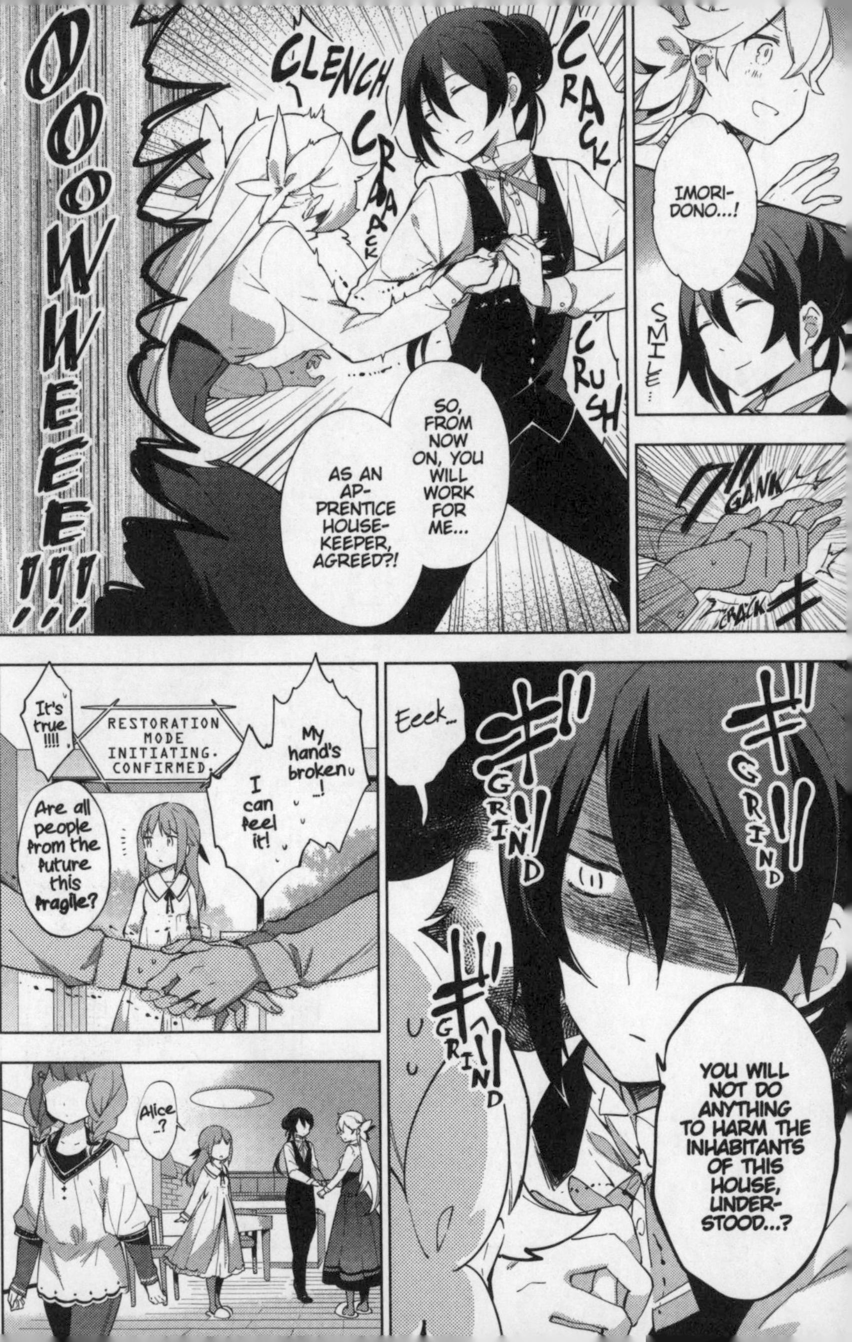
IMORI-DONO...!
SMILE...
GANK
CRACK
CRACK
CLENCH
CRACK
CRACK
CRUSH
SO, FROM NOW ON, YOU WILL WORK FOR ME...
AS AN APPRENTICE HOUSEKEEPER, AGREED?!
OOOWWEEE!!!!
GRIND
GRIND
Eeek...
GRIND
YOU WILL NOT DO ANYTHING TO HARM THE INHABITANTS OF THIS HOUSE, UNDERSTOOD...?
My hand's broken...!
I can feel it!
RESTORATION MODE INITIATING. CONFIRMED.
It's true!!!!
Are all people from the future this fragile?
Alice...?

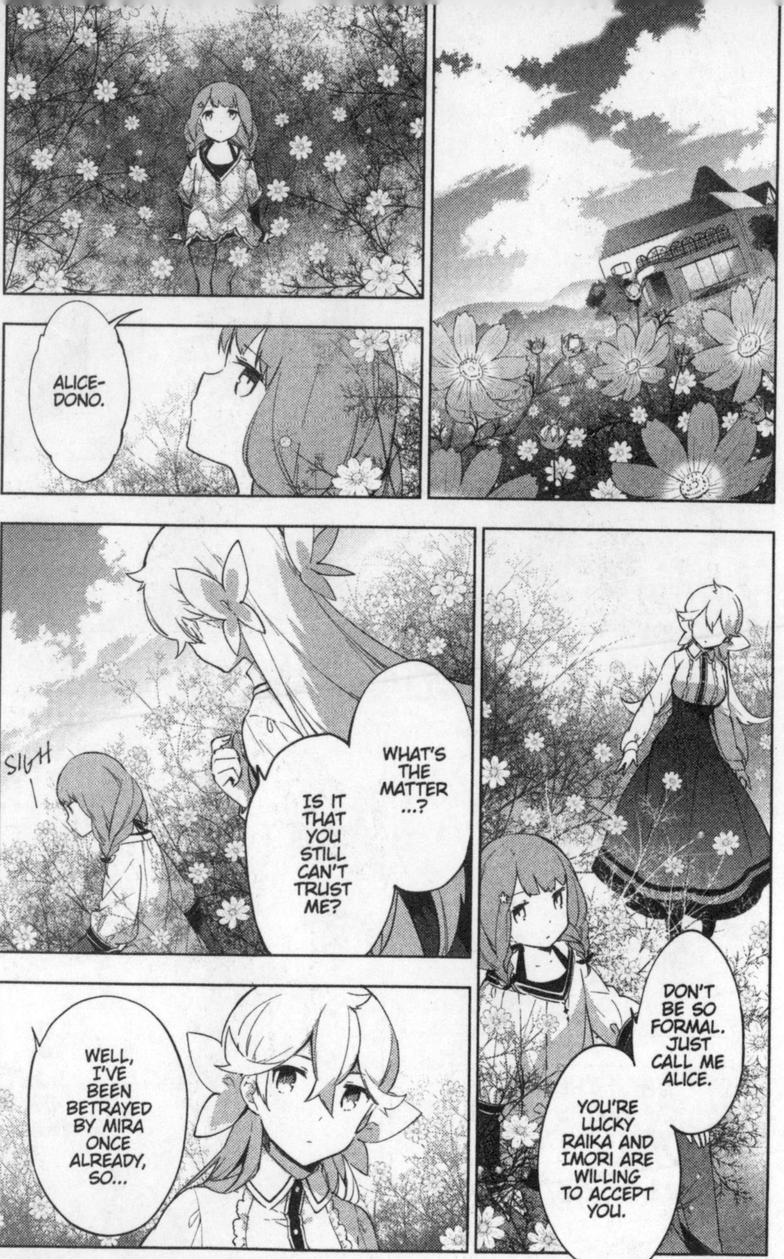
ALICE-DONO.
WHAT'S THE MATTER ...?
IS IT THAT YOU STILL CAN'T TRUST ME?
SIGH
DON'T BE SO FORMAL. JUST CALL ME ALICE.
YOU'RE LUCKY RAIKA AND IMORI ARE WILLING TO ACCEPT YOU.
WELL, I'VE BEEN BETRAYED BY MIRA ONCE ALREADY, SO...

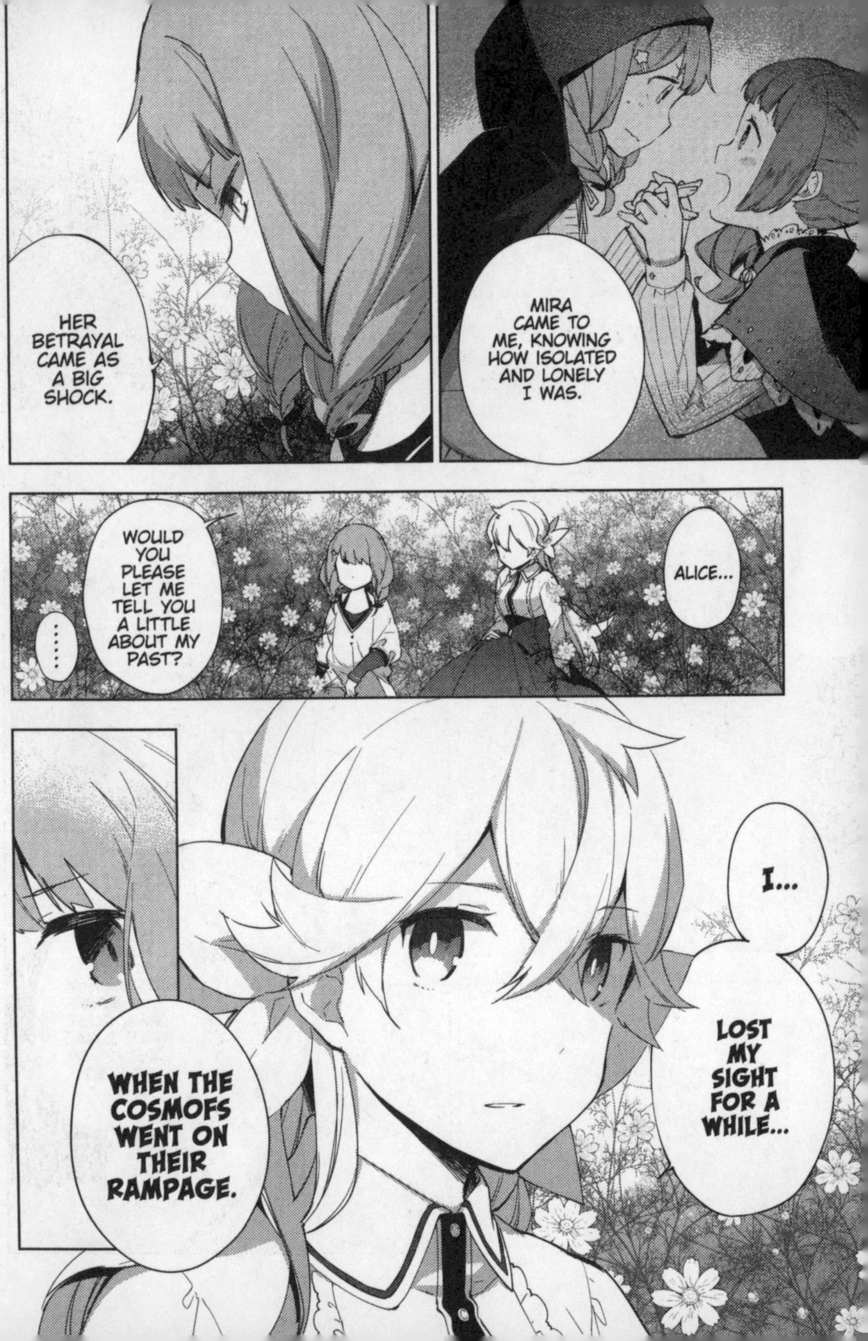
MIRA CAME TO ME, KNOWING HOW ISOLATED AND LONELY I WAS.
HER BETRAYAL CAME AS A BIG SHOCK.
ALICE...
WOULD YOU PLEASE LET ME TELL YOU A LITTLE ABOUT MY PAST?
......
I...
LOST MY SIGHT FOR A WHILE...
WHEN THE COSMOFS WENT ON THEIR RAMPAGE.

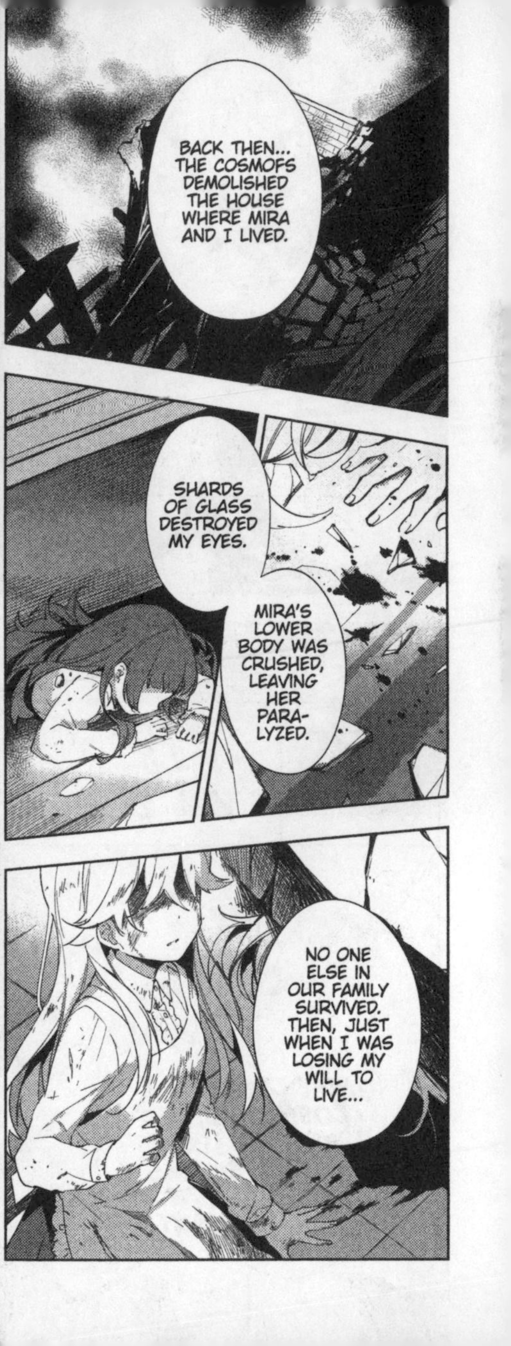
BACK THEN... THE COSMOFS DEMOLISHED THE HOUSE WHERE MIRA AND I LIVED.
SHARDS OF GLASS DESTROYED MY EYES.
MIRA'S LOWER BODY WAS CRUSHED, LEAVING HER PARA-LYZED.
NO ONE ELSE IN OUR FAMILY SURVIVED. THEN, JUST WHEN I WAS LOSING MY WILL TO LIVE...

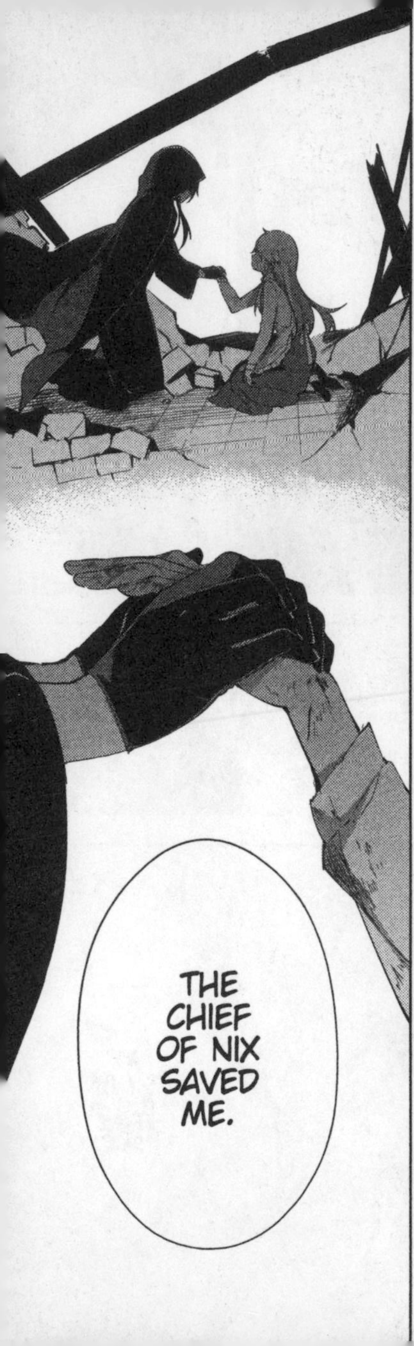
THE CHIEF OF NIX SAVED ME.

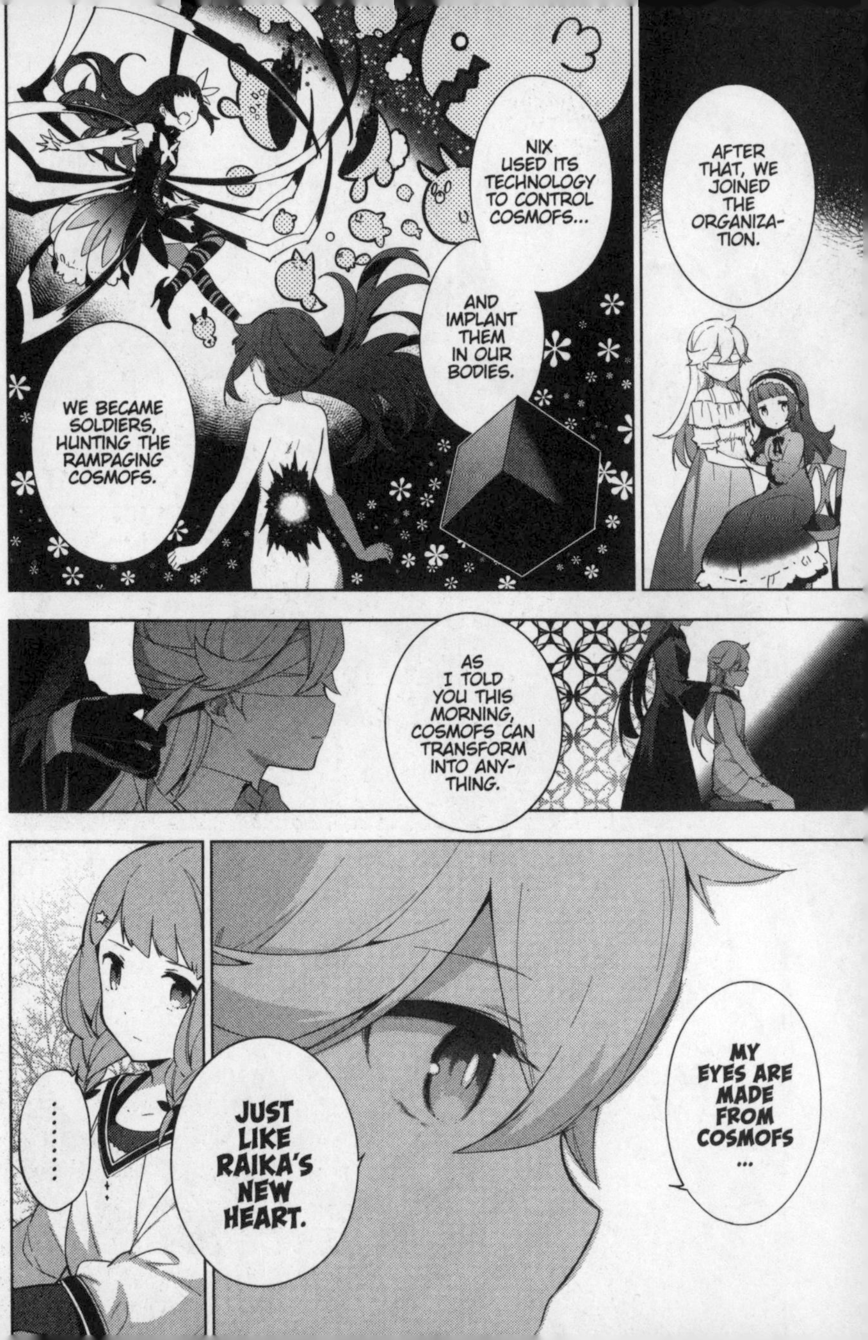
AFTER THAT, WE JOINED THE ORGANIZATION.
NIX USED ITS TECHNOLOGY TO CONTROL COSMOFS...
AND IMPLANT THEM IN OUR BODIES.
WE BECAME SOLDIERS, HUNTING THE RAMPAGING COSMOFS.
AS I TOLD YOU THIS MORNING, COSMOFS CAN TRANSFORM INTO ANYTHING.
MY EYES ARE MADE FROM COSMOFS...
JUST LIKE RAIKA'S NEW HEART.
......

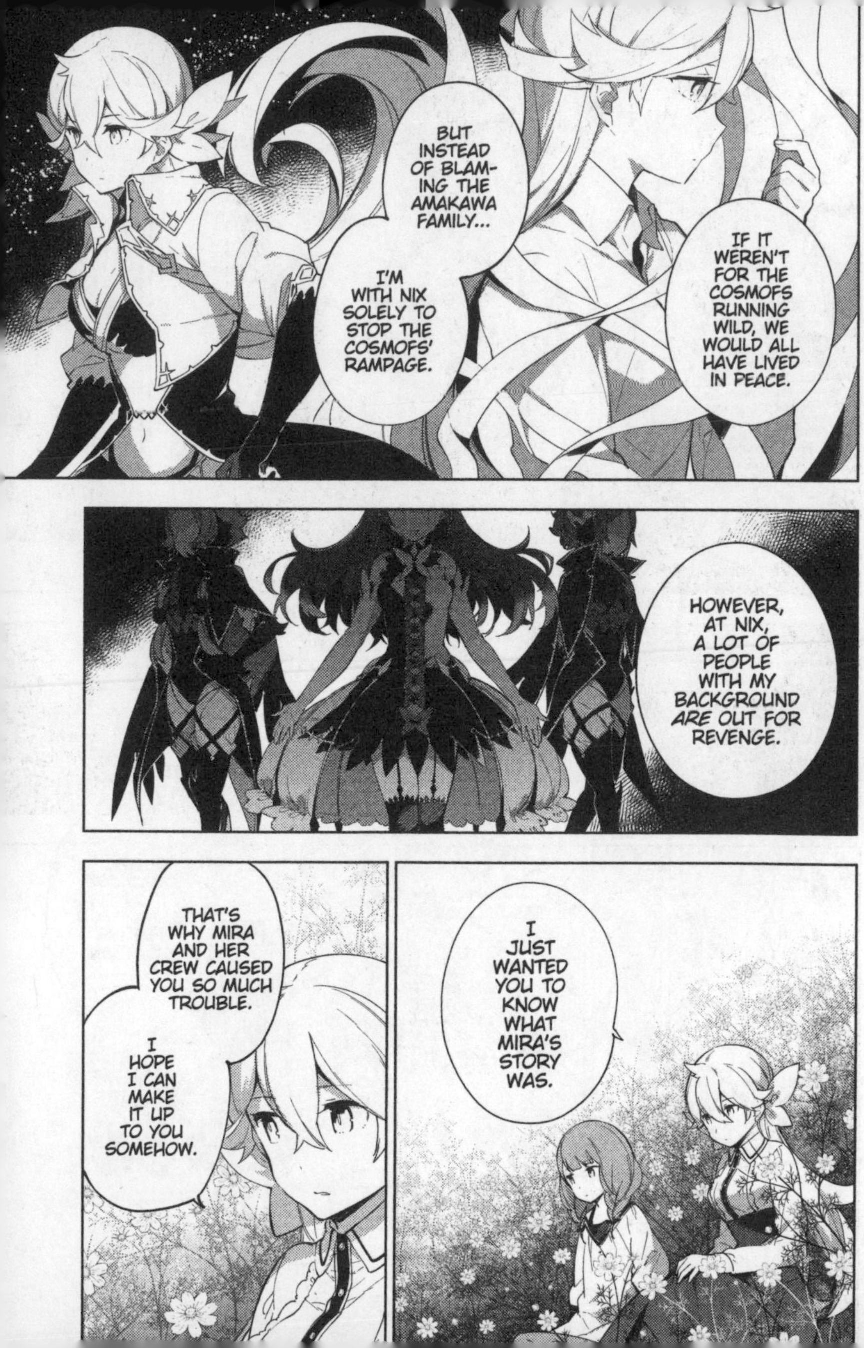
IF IT WEREN'T FOR THE COSMOFS RUNNING WILD, WE WOULD ALL HAVE LIVED IN PEACE.
BUT INSTEAD OF BLAM-ING THE AMAKAWA FAMILY...
I'M WITH NIX SOLELY TO STOP THE COSMOFS' RAMPAGE.
HOWEVER, AT NIX, A LOT OF PEOPLE WITH MY BACKGROUND *ARE* OUT FOR REVENGE.
I JUST WANTED YOU TO KNOW WHAT MIRA'S STORY WAS.
THAT'S WHY MIRA AND HER CREW CAUSED YOU SO MUCH TROUBLE.
I HOPE I CAN MAKE IT UP TO YOU SOMEHOW.

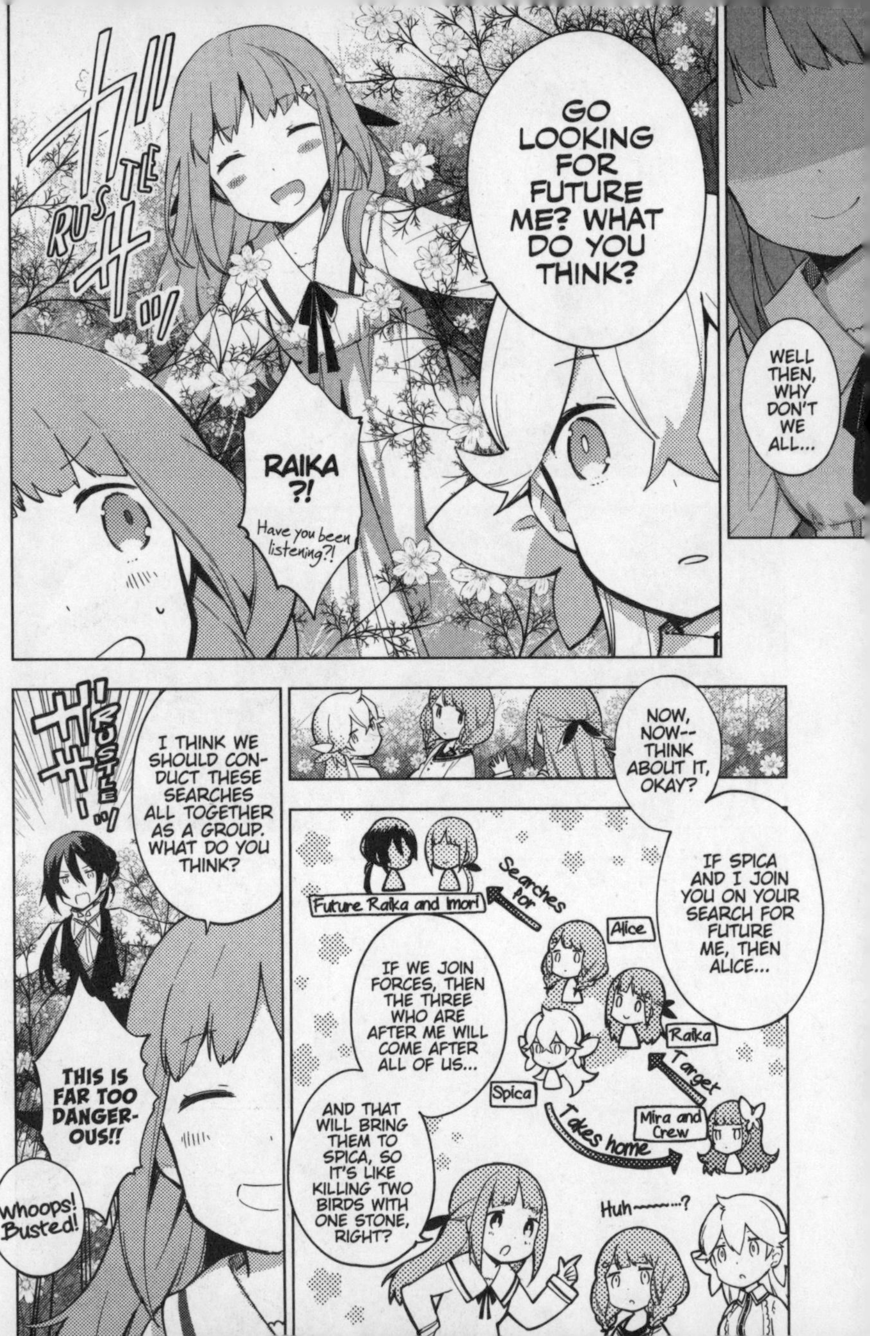
WELL THEN, WHY DON'T WE ALL...
RUSTLE
GO LOOKING FOR FUTURE ME? WHAT DO YOU THINK?
RAIKA ?!
Have you been listening?!
NOW, NOW-- THINK ABOUT IT, OKAY?
IF SPICA AND I JOIN YOU ON YOUR SEARCH FOR FUTURE ME, THEN ALICE...
Future Raika and Imori
Searches for
Alice
Raika
Target
Mira and Crew
Takes home
Spica
IF WE JOIN FORCES, THEN THE THREE WHO ARE AFTER ME WILL COME AFTER ALL OF US...
AND THAT WILL BRING THEM TO SPICA, SO IT'S LIKE KILLING TWO BIRDS WITH ONE STONE, RIGHT?
Huh~~~~~?
RUSTLE
I THINK WE SHOULD CONDUCT THESE SEARCHES ALL TOGETHER AS A GROUP. WHAT DO YOU THINK?
THIS IS FAR TOO DANGEROUS!!
Whoops! Busted!

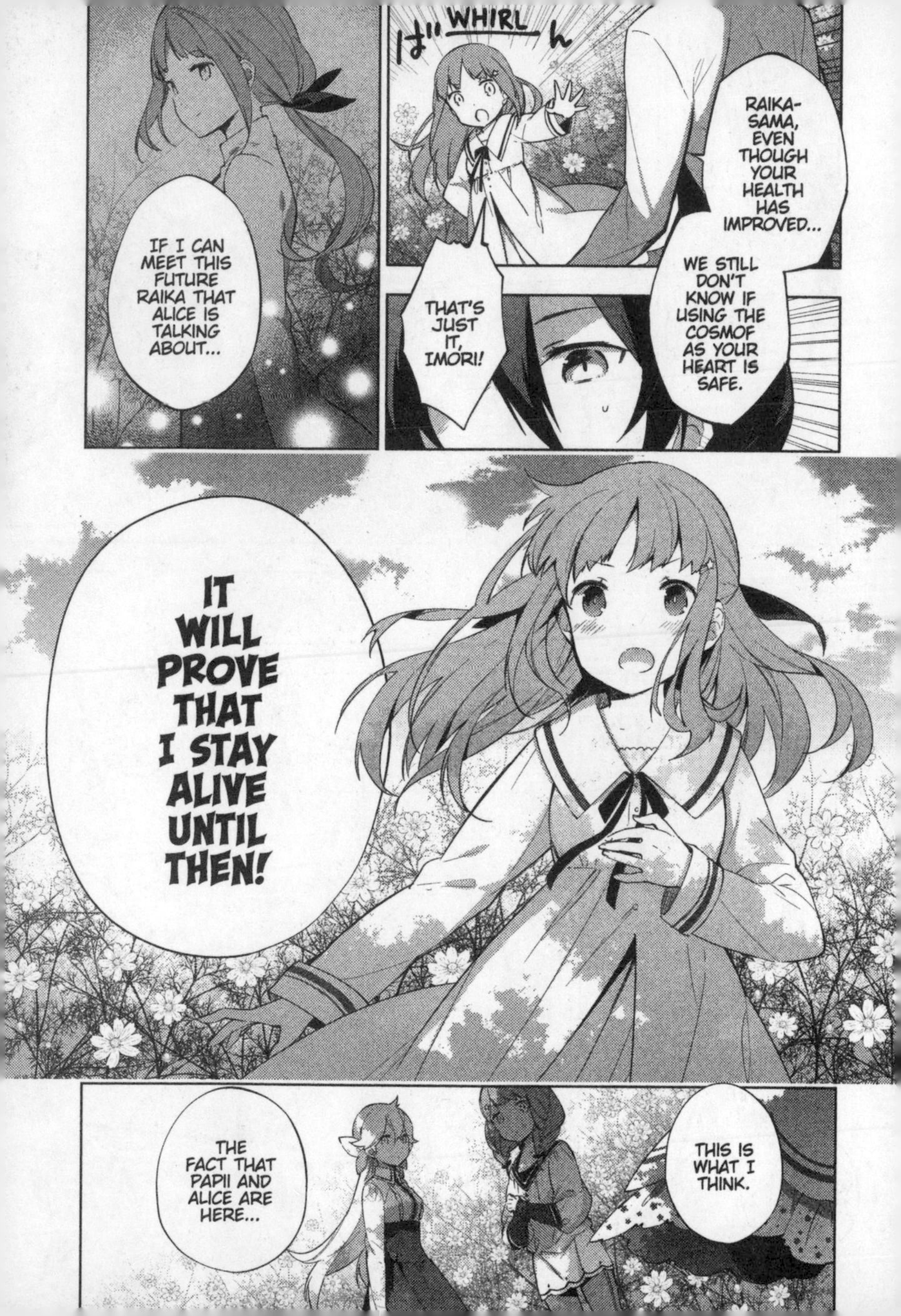
ば WHIRL ん
RAIKA-SAMA, EVEN THOUGH YOUR HEALTH HAS IMPROVED...
WE STILL DON'T KNOW IF USING THE COSMOF AS YOUR HEART IS SAFE.
THAT'S JUST IT, IMORI!
IF I CAN MEET THIS FUTURE RAIKA THAT ALICE IS TALKING ABOUT...
IT WILL PROVE THAT I STAY ALIVE UNTIL THEN!
THIS IS WHAT I THINK.
THE FACT THAT PAPII AND ALICE ARE HERE...

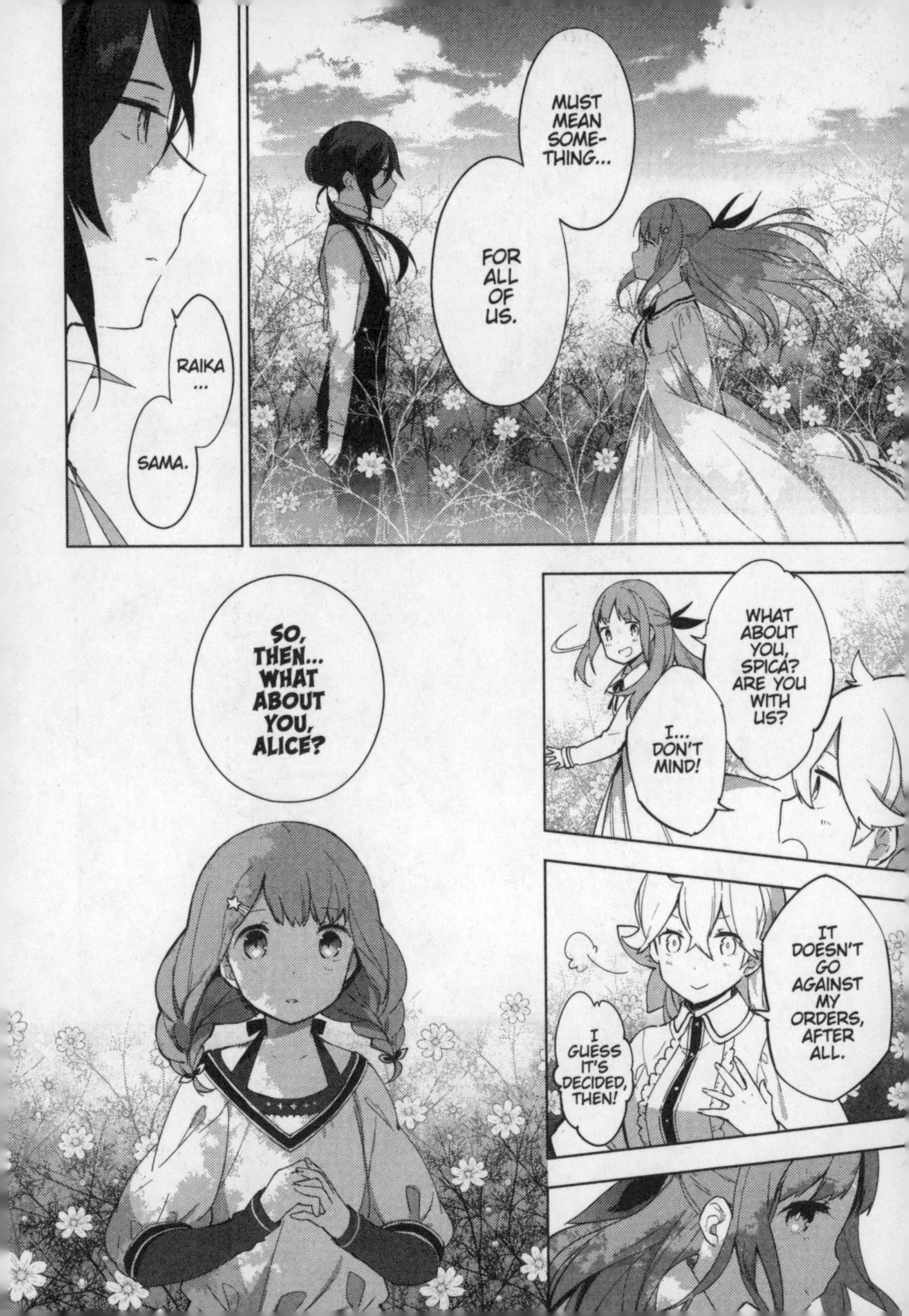
MUST MEAN SOME-THING...
FOR ALL OF US.
RAIKA ...
SAMA.
WHAT ABOUT YOU, SPICA? ARE YOU WITH US?
I... DON'T MIND!
IT DOESN'T GO AGAINST MY ORDERS, AFTER ALL.
I GUESS IT'S DECIDED, THEN!
SO, THEN... WHAT ABOUT YOU, ALICE?

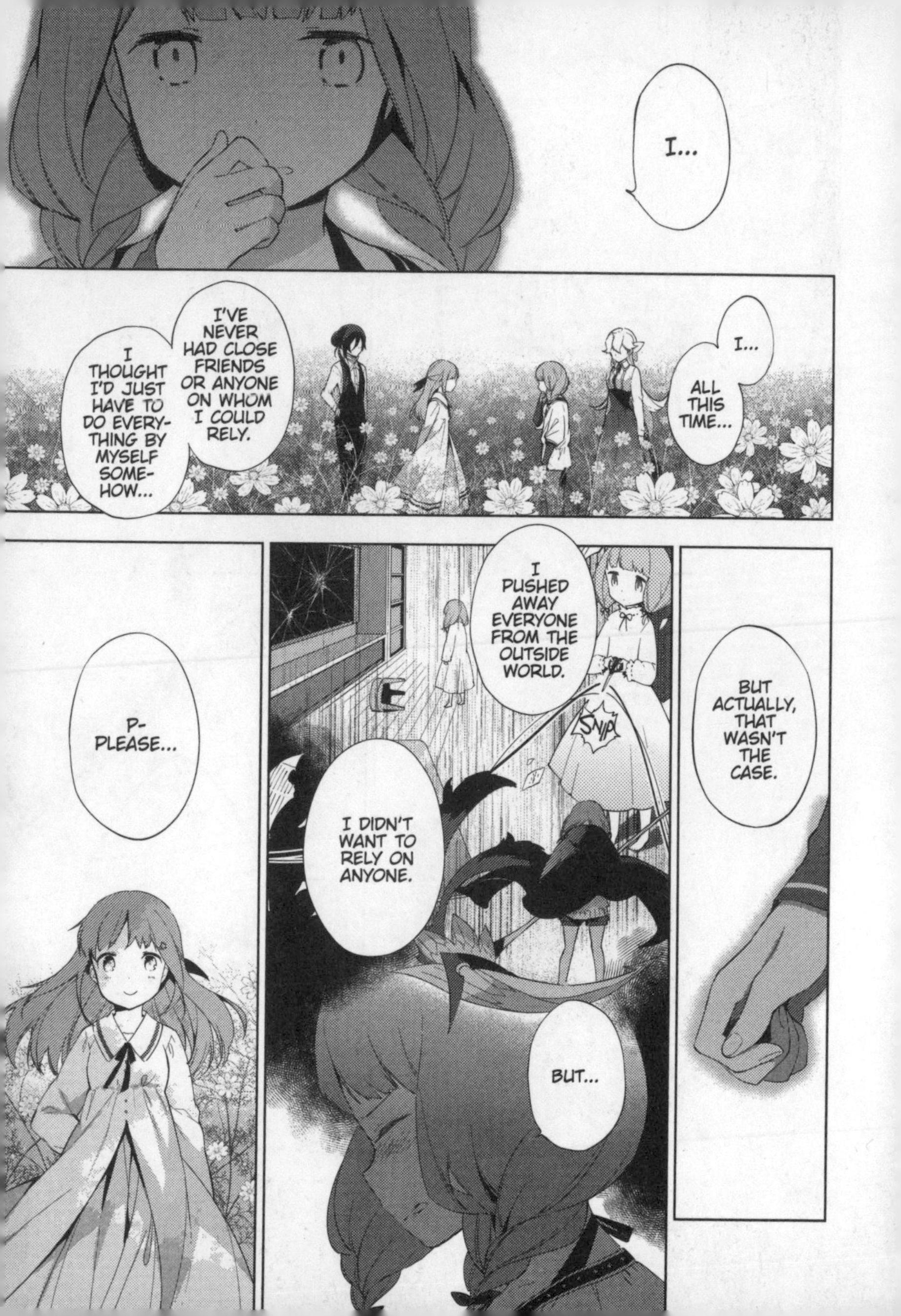
I...
I... ALL THIS TIME...
I'VE NEVER HAD CLOSE FRIENDS OR ANYONE ON WHOM I COULD RELY.
I THOUGHT I'D JUST HAVE TO DO EVERY-THING BY MYSELF SOME-HOW...
BUT ACTUALLY, THAT WASN'T THE CASE.
I PUSHED AWAY EVERYONE FROM THE OUTSIDE WORLD.
SNIP
I DIDN'T WANT TO RELY ON ANYONE.
BUT...
P-PLEASE...

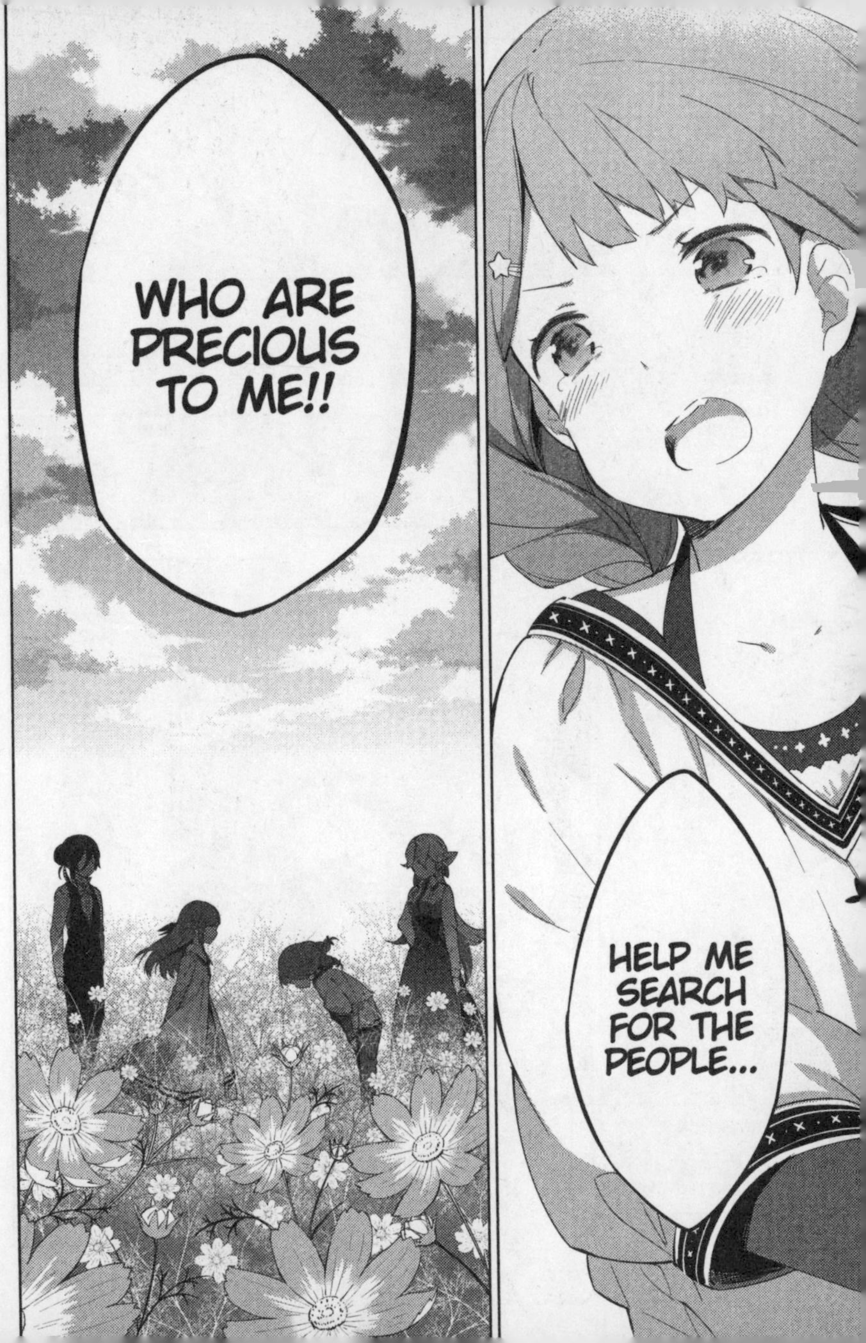
HELP ME SEARCH FOR THE PEOPLE...
WHO ARE PRECIOUS TO ME!!

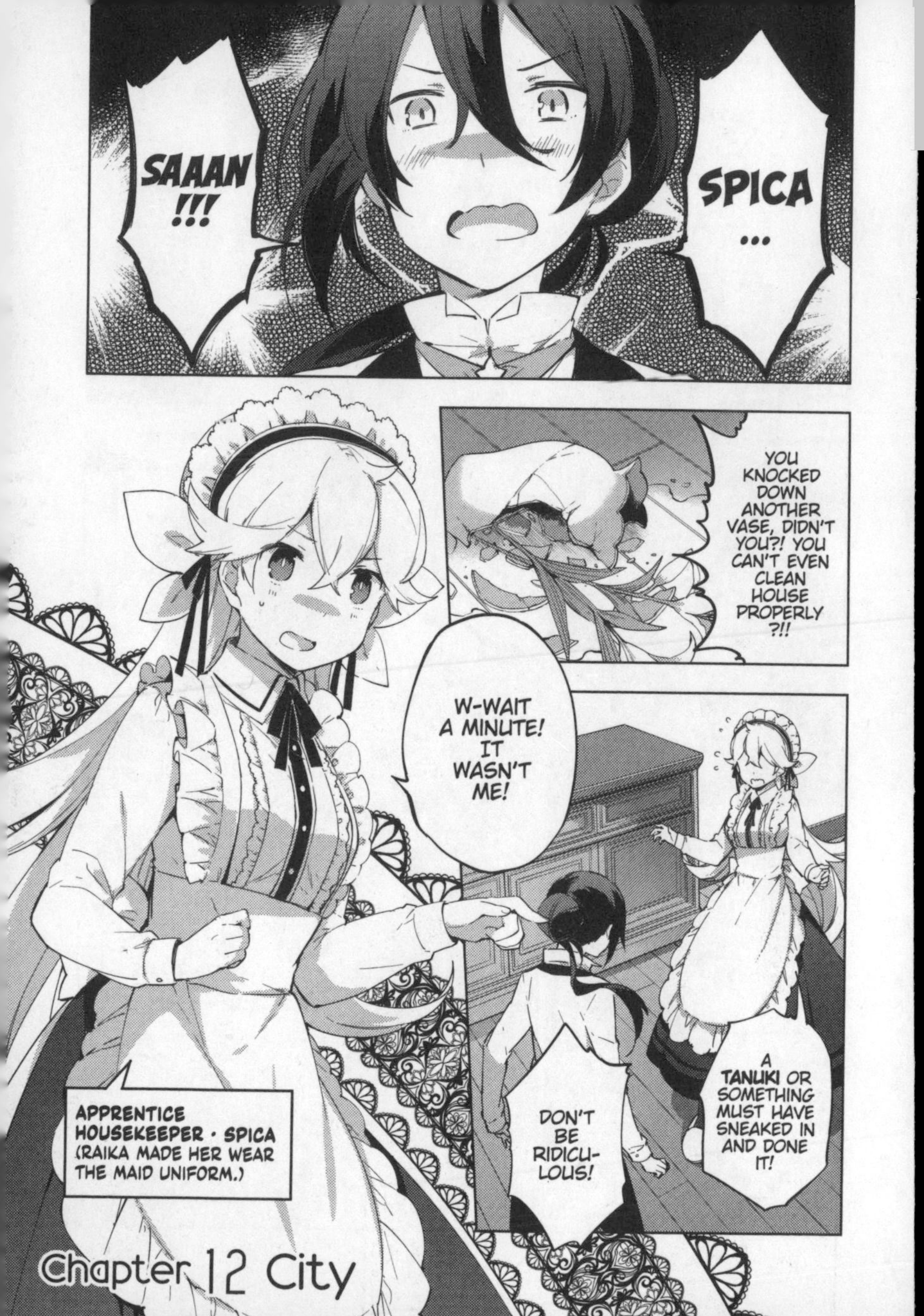
SPICA ...
SAAAN !!!
YOU KNOCKED DOWN ANOTHER VASE, DIDN'T YOU?! YOU CAN'T EVEN CLEAN HOUSE PROPERLY ?!!
W-WAIT A MINUTE! IT WASN'T ME!
A TANUKI OR SOMETHING MUST HAVE SNEAKED IN AND DONE IT!
DON'T BE RIDICU-LOUS!
APPRENTICE HOUSEKEEPER · SPICA (RAIKA MADE HER WEAR THE MAID UNIFORM.)
Chapter 12 City

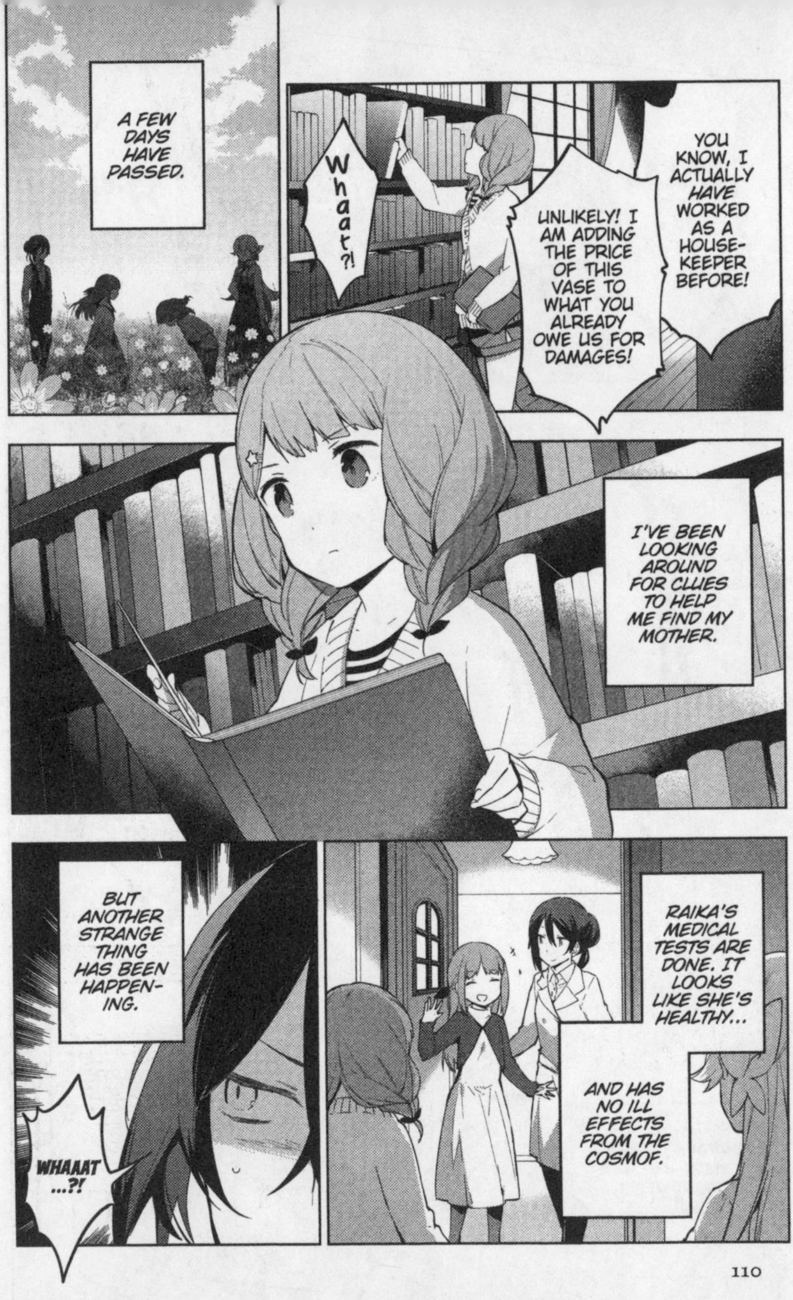
YOU KNOW, I ACTUALLY HAVE WORKED AS A HOUSE-KEEPER BEFORE!
UNLIKELY! I AM ADDING THE PRICE OF THIS VASE TO WHAT YOU ALREADY OWE US FOR DAMAGES!
Whaat?!
A FEW DAYS HAVE PASSED.
I'VE BEEN LOOKING AROUND FOR CLUES TO HELP ME FIND MY MOTHER.
RAIKA'S MEDICAL TESTS ARE DONE. IT LOOKS LIKE SHE'S HEALTHY...
AND HAS NO ILL EFFECTS FROM THE COSMOF.
BUT ANOTHER STRANGE THING HAS BEEN HAPPEN-ING.
WHAAAT ...?!

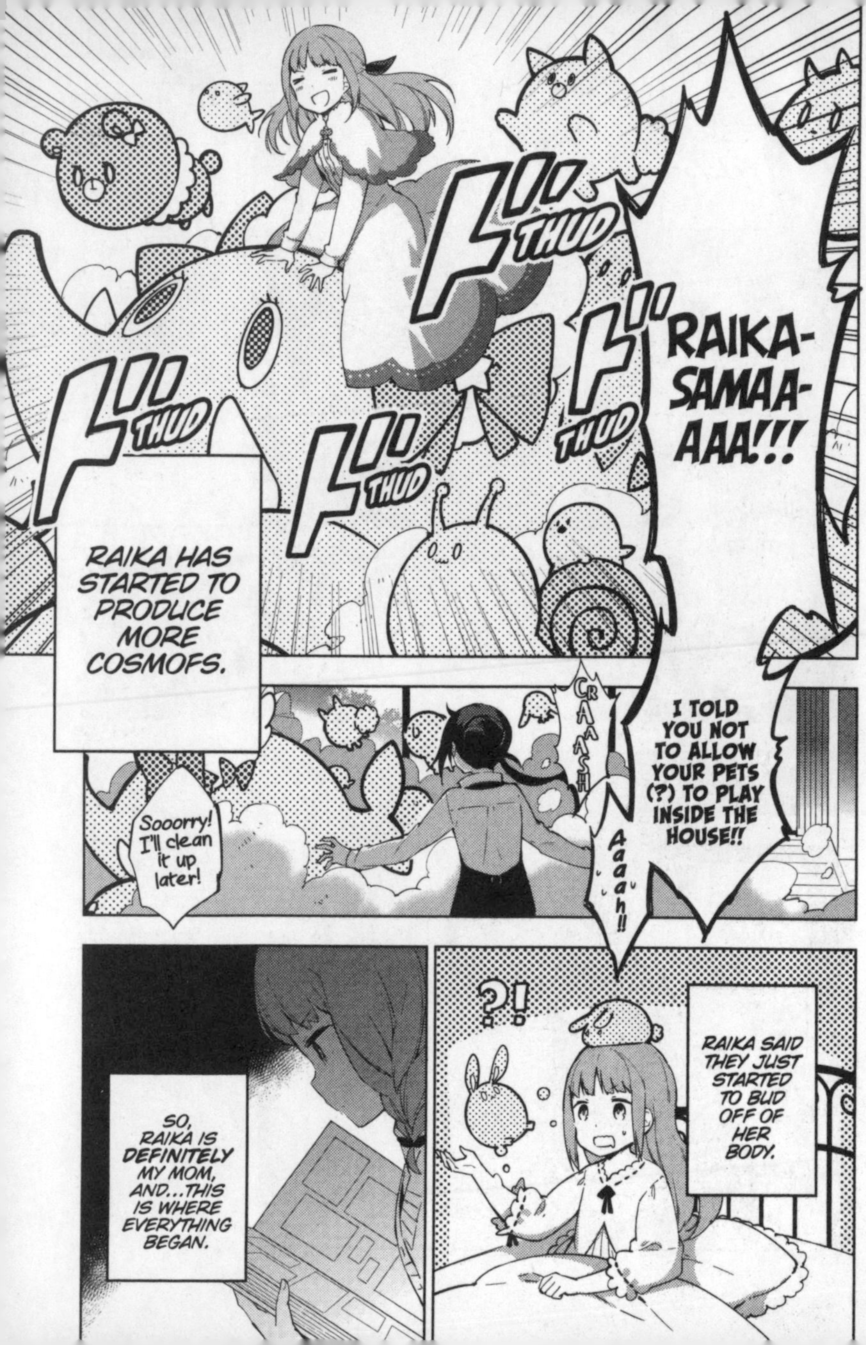
RAIKA-SAMAAA-AAA!!!
THUD
THUD
THUD
THUD
RAIKA HAS STARTED TO PRODUCE MORE COSMOFS.
I TOLD YOU NOT TO ALLOW YOUR PETS (?) TO PLAY INSIDE THE HOUSE!!
CRAAASH
Aaaah!!
Sooorry! I'll clean it up later!
?!
RAIKA SAID THEY JUST STARTED TO BUD OFF OF HER BODY.
SO, RAIKA IS DEFINITELY MY MOM, AND...THIS IS WHERE EVERYTHING BEGAN.

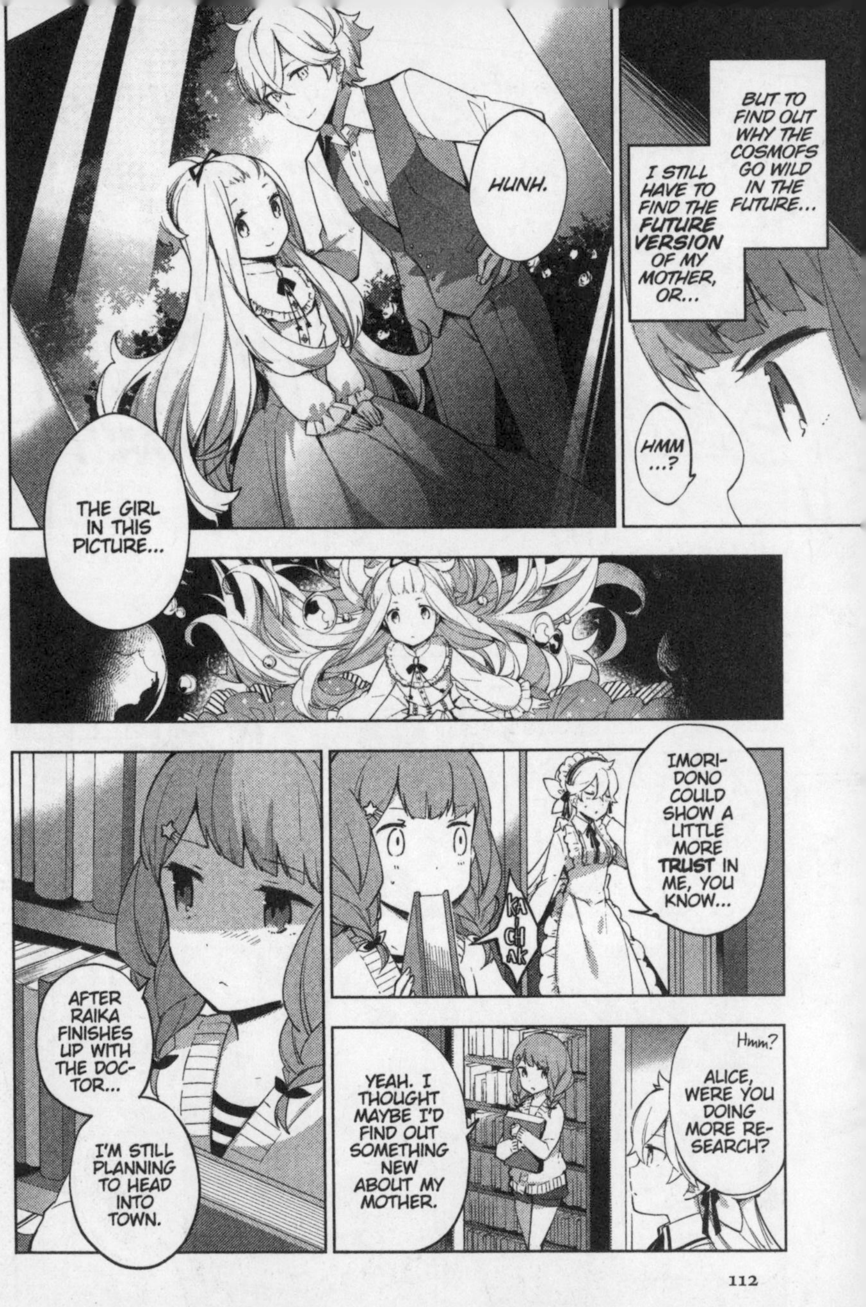
BUT TO FIND OUT WHY THE COSMOFS GO WILD IN THE FUTURE...
I STILL HAVE TO FIND THE **FUTURE VERSION** OF MY MOTHER, OR...
HMM ...?
HUNH.
THE GIRL IN THIS PICTURE...
IMORI-DONO COULD SHOW A LITTLE MORE **TRUST** IN ME, YOU KNOW...
KA CHAK
Hmm?
ALICE, WERE YOU DOING MORE RE-SEARCH?
YEAH. I THOUGHT MAYBE I'D FIND OUT SOMETHING NEW ABOUT MY MOTHER.
AFTER RAIKA FINISHES UP WITH THE DOC-TOR...
I'M STILL PLANNING TO HEAD INTO TOWN.

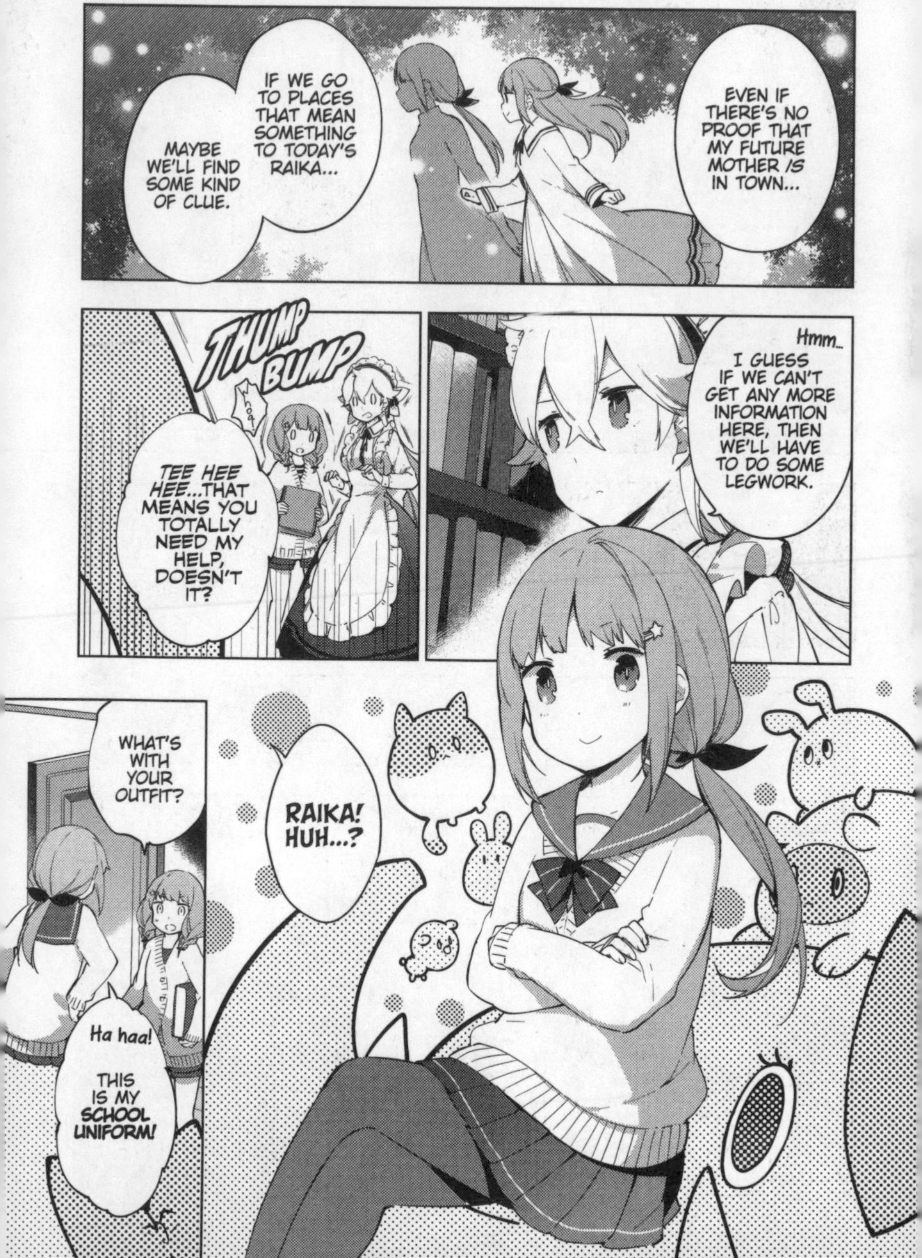
EVEN IF THERE'S NO PROOF THAT MY FUTURE MOTHER *IS* IN TOWN...
IF WE GO TO PLACES THAT MEAN SOMETHING TO TODAY'S RAIKA...
MAYBE WE'LL FIND SOME KIND OF CLUE.
Hmm... I GUESS IF WE CAN'T GET ANY MORE INFORMATION HERE, THEN WE'LL HAVE TO DO SOME LEGWORK.
THUMP BUMP
*TEE HEE HEE*...THAT MEANS YOU TOTALLY NEED MY HELP, DOESN'T IT?
RAIKA! HUH...?
WHAT'S WITH YOUR OUTFIT?
Ha haa!
THIS IS MY **SCHOOL UNIFORM!**

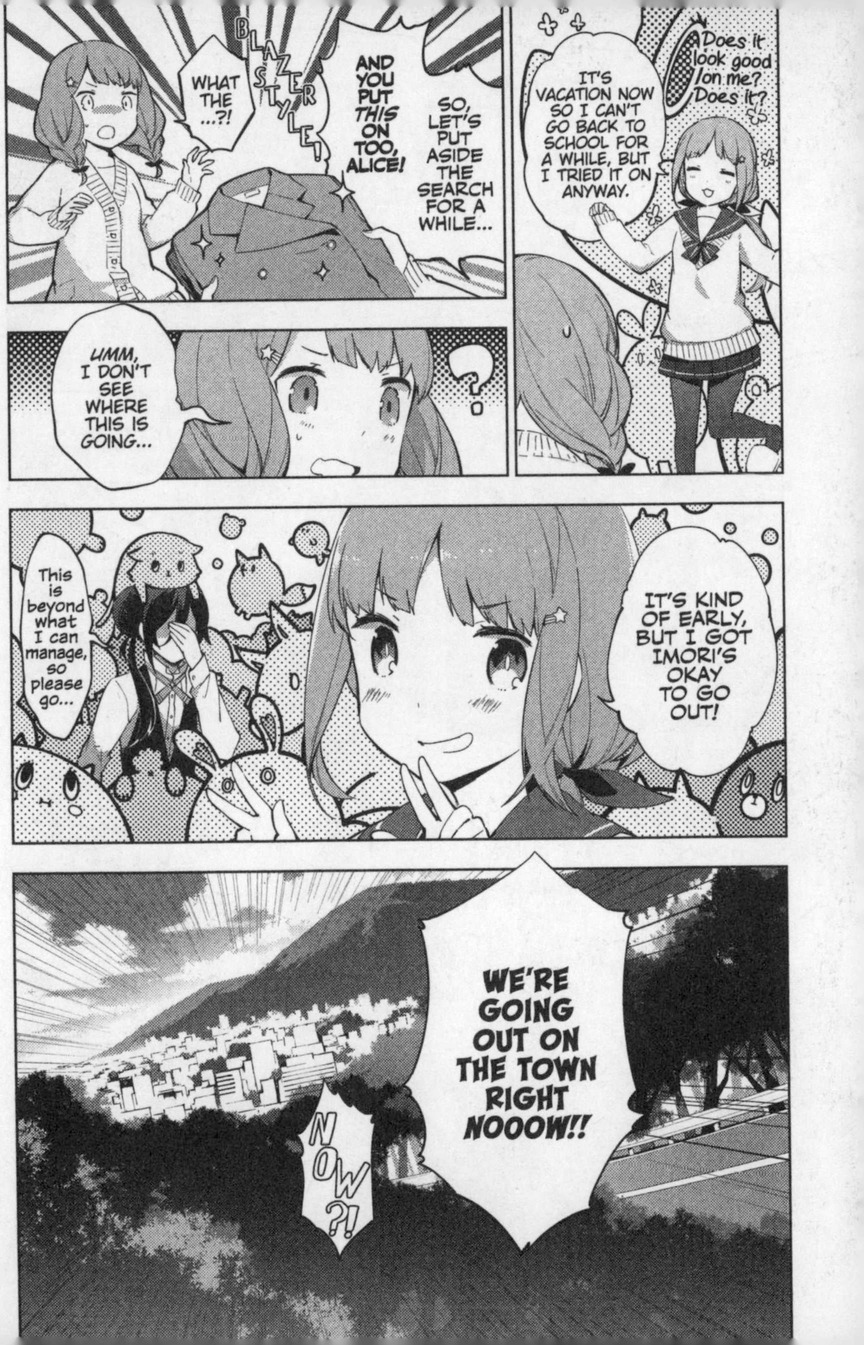
IT'S VACATION NOW SO I CAN'T GO BACK TO SCHOOL FOR A WHILE, BUT I TRIED IT ON ANYWAY.
Does it look good on me? Does it?
SO, LET'S PUT ASIDE THE SEARCH FOR A WHILE...
AND YOU PUT *THIS* ON TOO, ALICE!
BLAZER STYLE!
WHAT THE ...?!
?
UMM, I DON'T SEE WHERE THIS IS GOING...
IT'S KIND OF EARLY, BUT I GOT IMORI'S OKAY TO GO OUT!
This is beyond what I can manage, so please go...
WE'RE GOING OUT ON THE TOWN RIGHT *NOOOW!!*
NOW?!

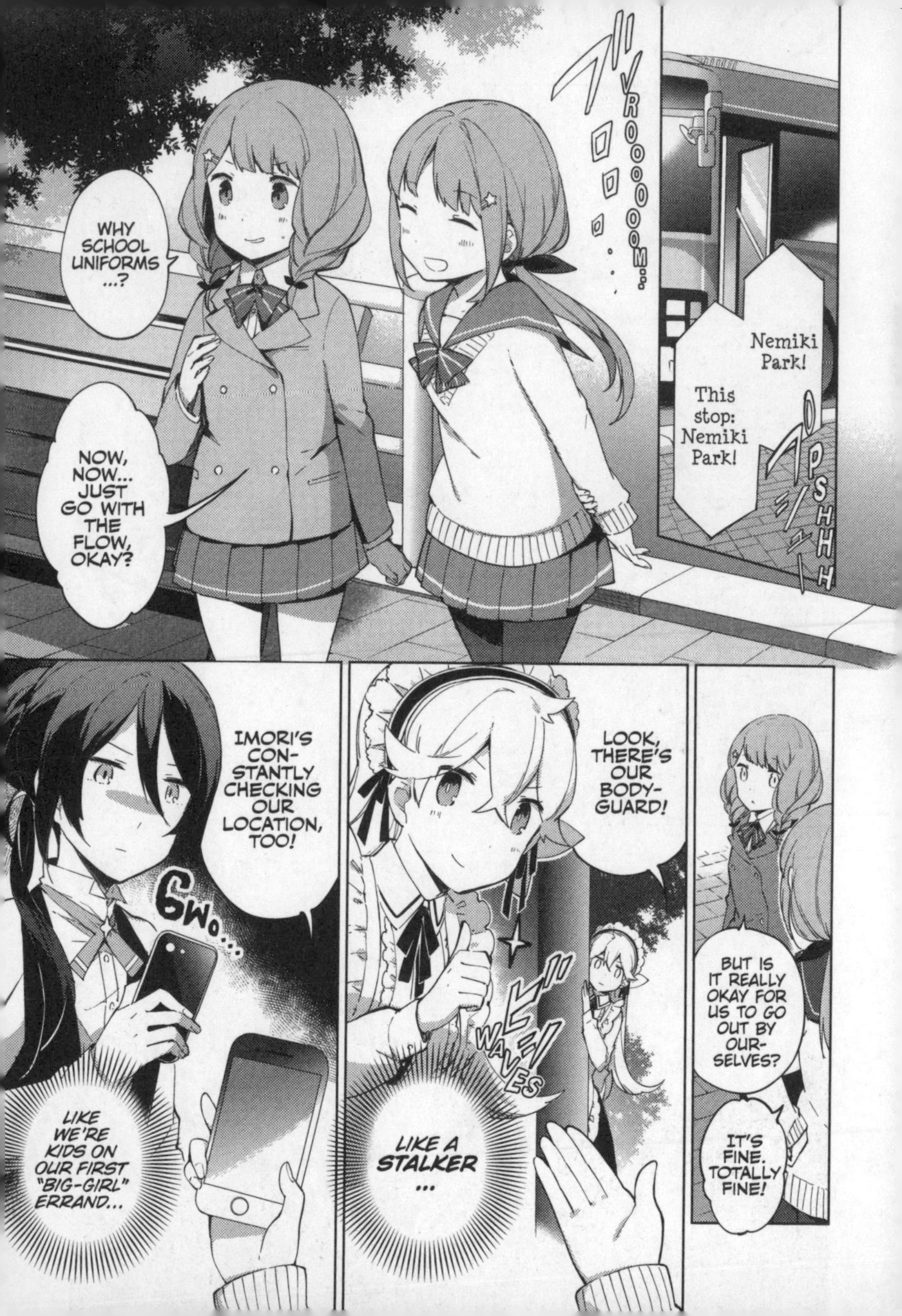
This stop: Nemiki Park!
Nemiki Park!
PSHHH
VROOOOOOOM...
WHY SCHOOL UNIFORMS ...?
NOW, NOW... JUST GO WITH THE FLOW, OKAY?
BUT IS IT REALLY OKAY FOR US TO GO OUT BY OUR-SELVES?
IT'S FINE. TOTALLY FINE!
LOOK, THERE'S OUR BODY-GUARD!
WAVES
LIKE A STALKER ...
IMORI'S CON-STANTLY CHECKING OUR LOCATION, TOO!
GWO...
LIKE WE'RE KIDS ON OUR FIRST "BIG-GIRL" ERRAND...

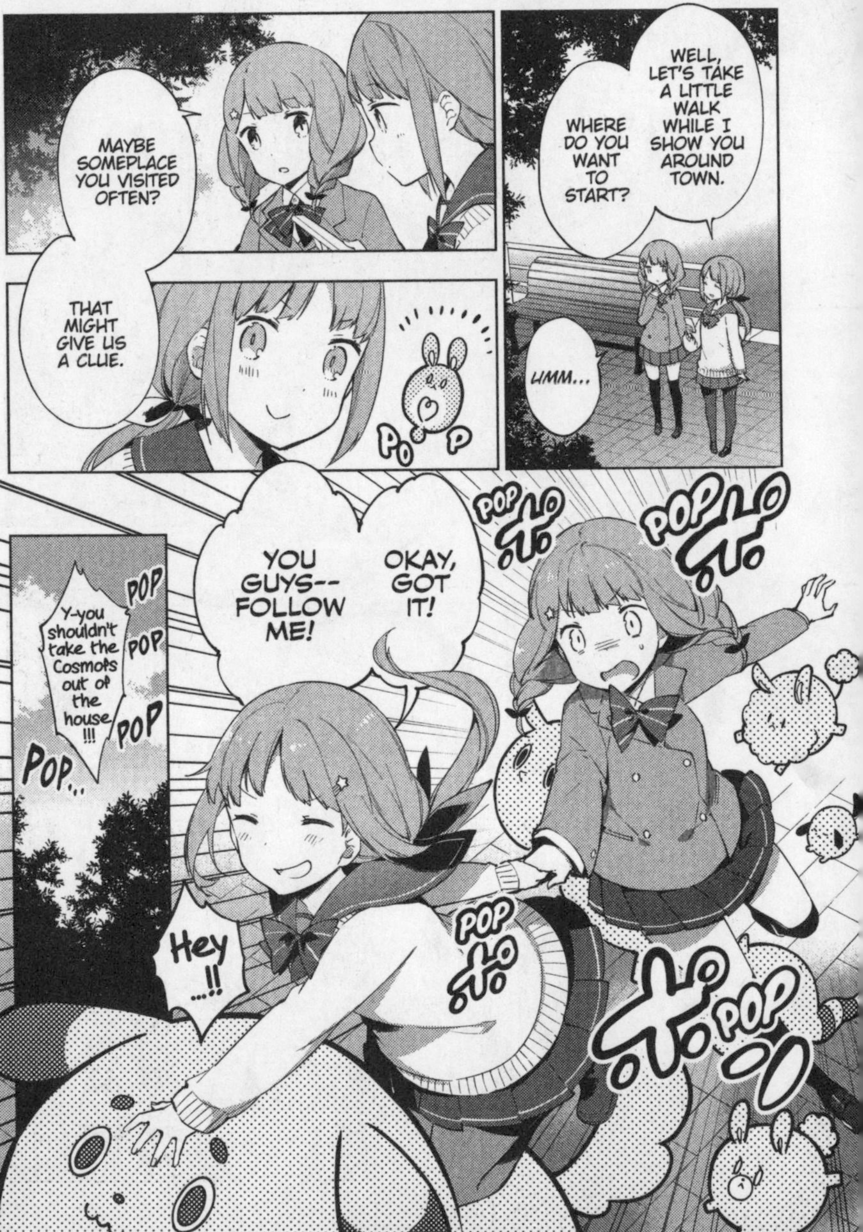
WELL, LET'S TAKE A LITTLE WALK WHILE I SHOW YOU AROUND TOWN.
WHERE DO YOU WANT TO START?
UMM...
MAYBE SOMEPLACE YOU VISITED OFTEN?
THAT MIGHT GIVE US A CLUE.
POP
OKAY, GOT IT!
YOU GUYS-- FOLLOW ME!
POP
POP
POP
POP
Y-you shouldn't take the Cosmos out of the house!!!
POP
POP
POP
POP...
Hey ...!!
POP
POP

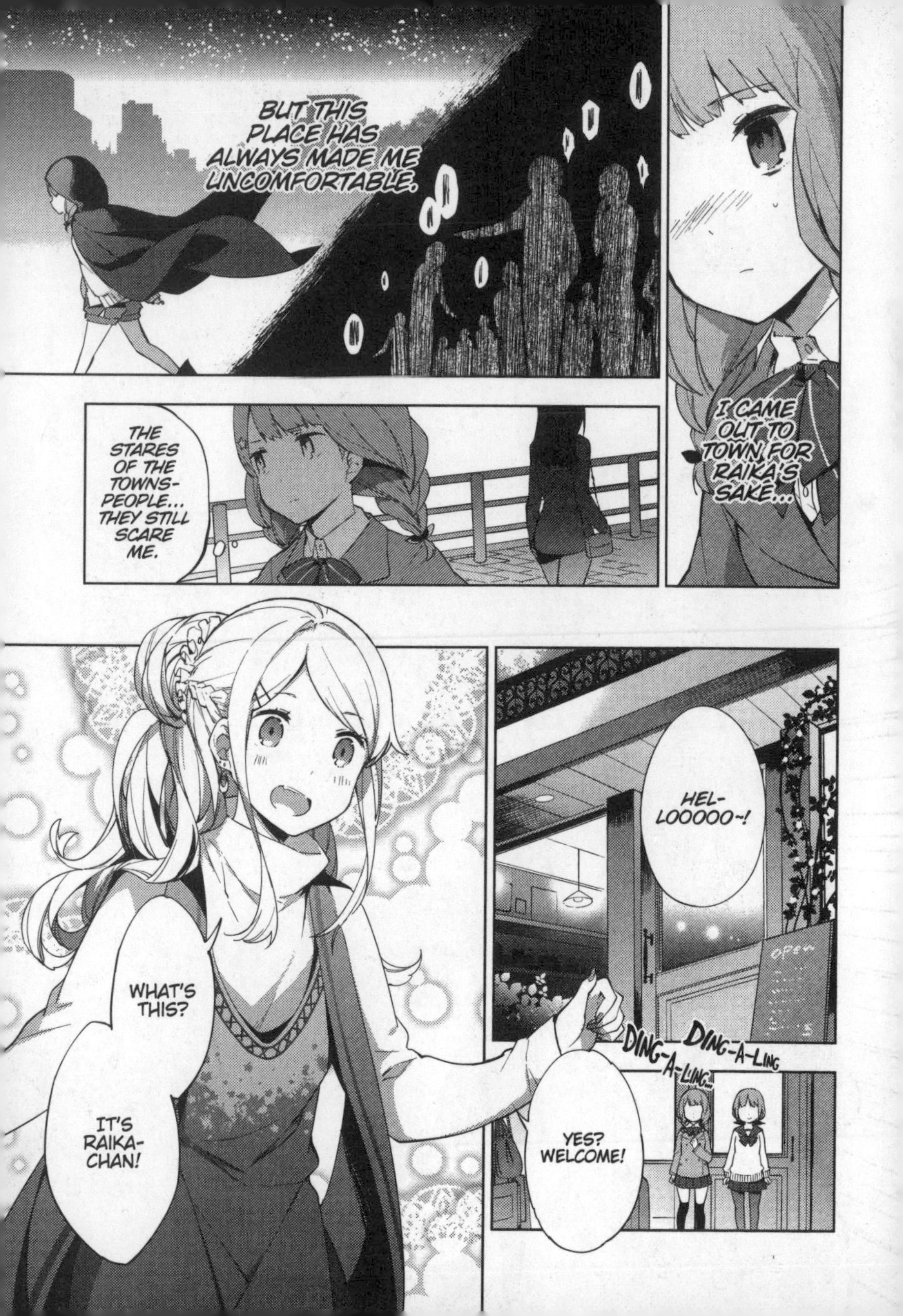
I CAME OUT TO TOWN FOR RAIKA'S SAKE...
BUT THIS PLACE HAS ALWAYS MADE ME UNCOMFORTABLE.
THE STARES OF THE TOWNS-PEOPLE... THEY STILL SCARE ME.
HEL-LOOOOO~!
DING-A-LING
DING-A-LING...
YES? WELCOME!
WHAT'S THIS?
IT'S RAIKA-CHAN!

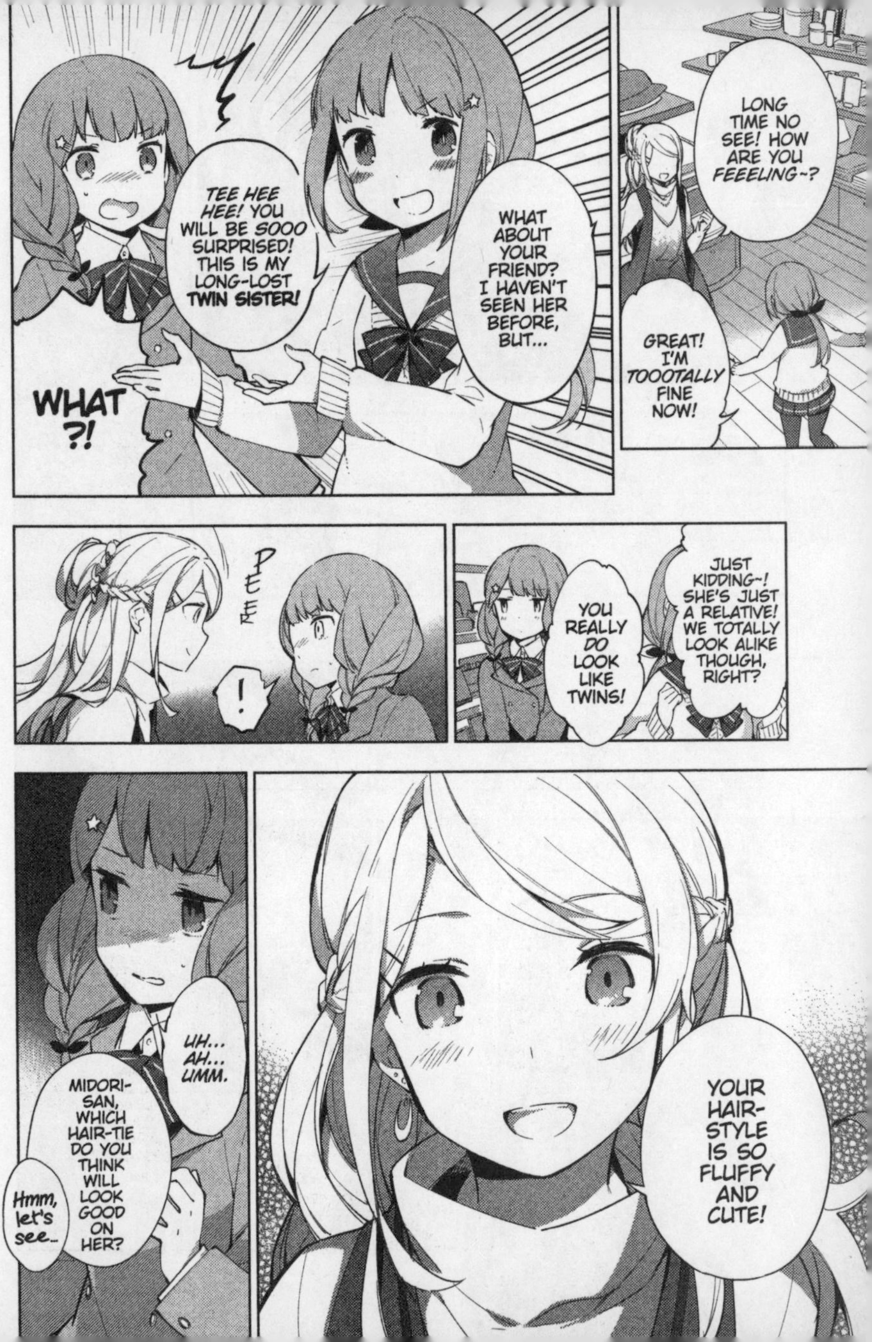
LONG TIME NO SEE! HOW ARE YOU FEEELING~?
GREAT! I'M TOOOTALLY FINE NOW!
WHAT ABOUT YOUR FRIEND? I HAVEN'T SEEN HER BEFORE, BUT...
TEE HEE HEE! YOU WILL BE SOOO SURPRISED! THIS IS MY LONG-LOST TWIN SISTER!
WHAT?!
JUST KIDDING~! SHE'S JUST A RELATIVE! WE TOTALLY LOOK ALIKE THOUGH, RIGHT?
YOU REALLY DO LOOK LIKE TWINS!
PEER
!
YOUR HAIR-STYLE IS SO FLUFFY AND CUTE!
UH... AH... UMM.
MIDORI-SAN, WHICH HAIR-TIE DO YOU THINK WILL LOOK GOOD ON HER?
Hmm, let's see...

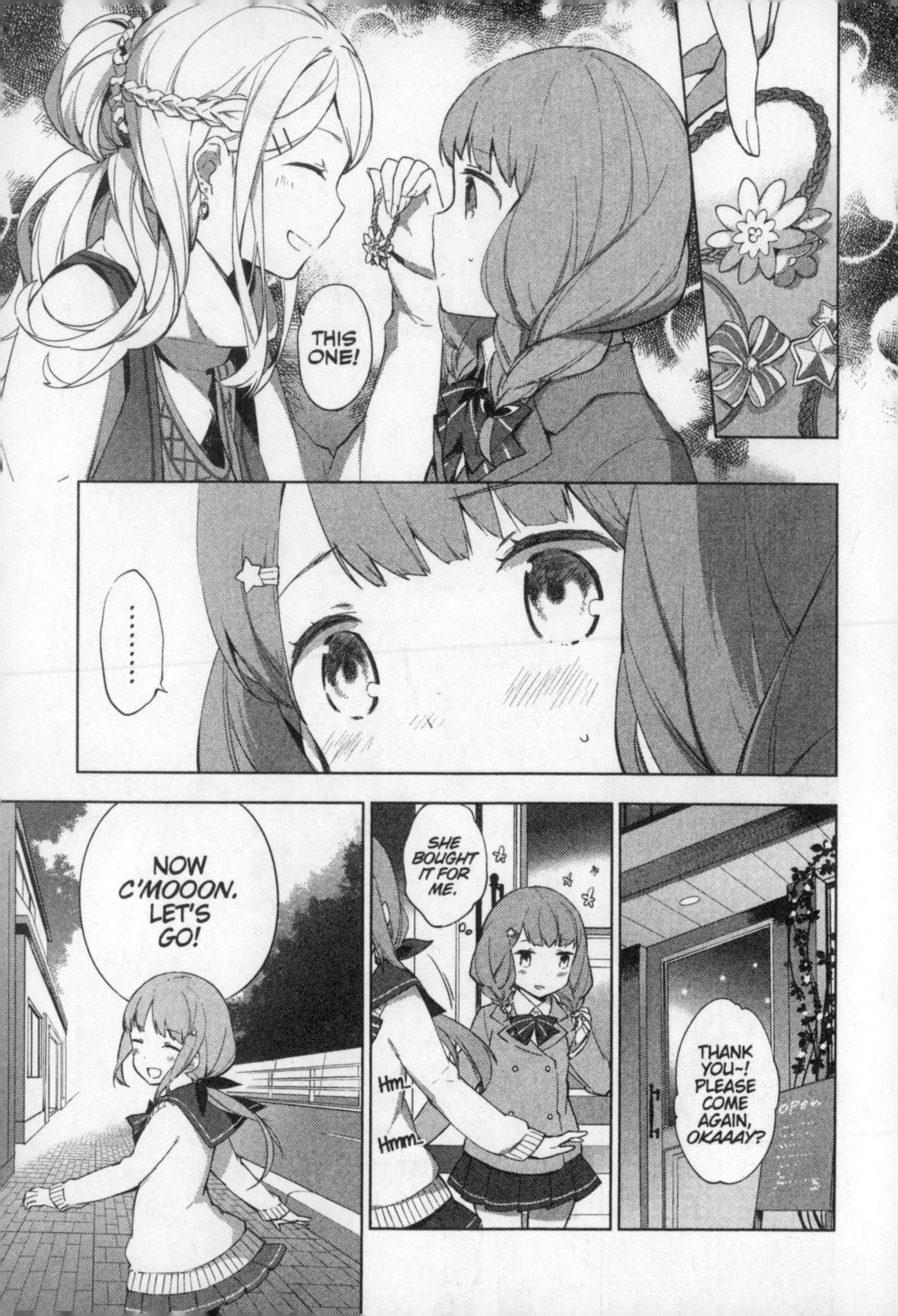
THIS ONE!
……
THANK YOU~! PLEASE COME AGAIN, OKAAAY?
SHE BOUGHT IT FOR ME.
Hm...
Hmm...
NOW C'MOOON. LET'S GO!

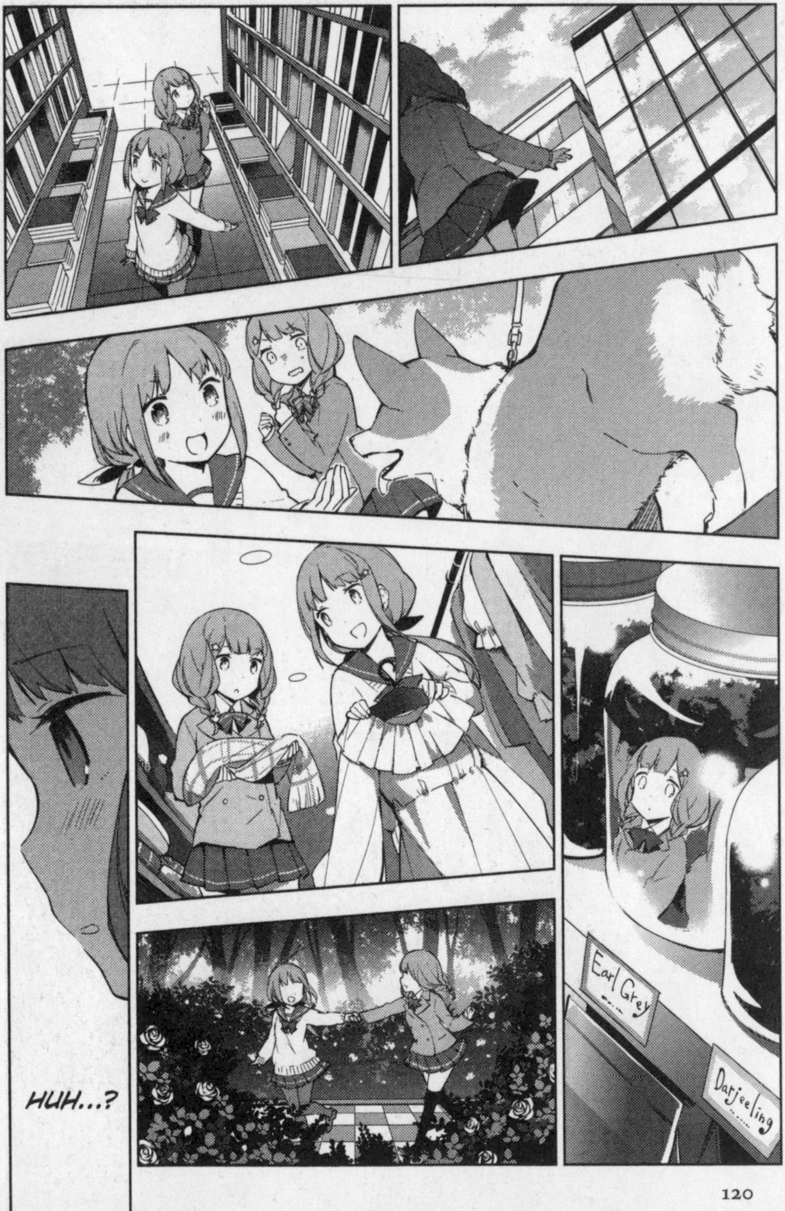
Earl Grey
Darjeeling
HUH...?

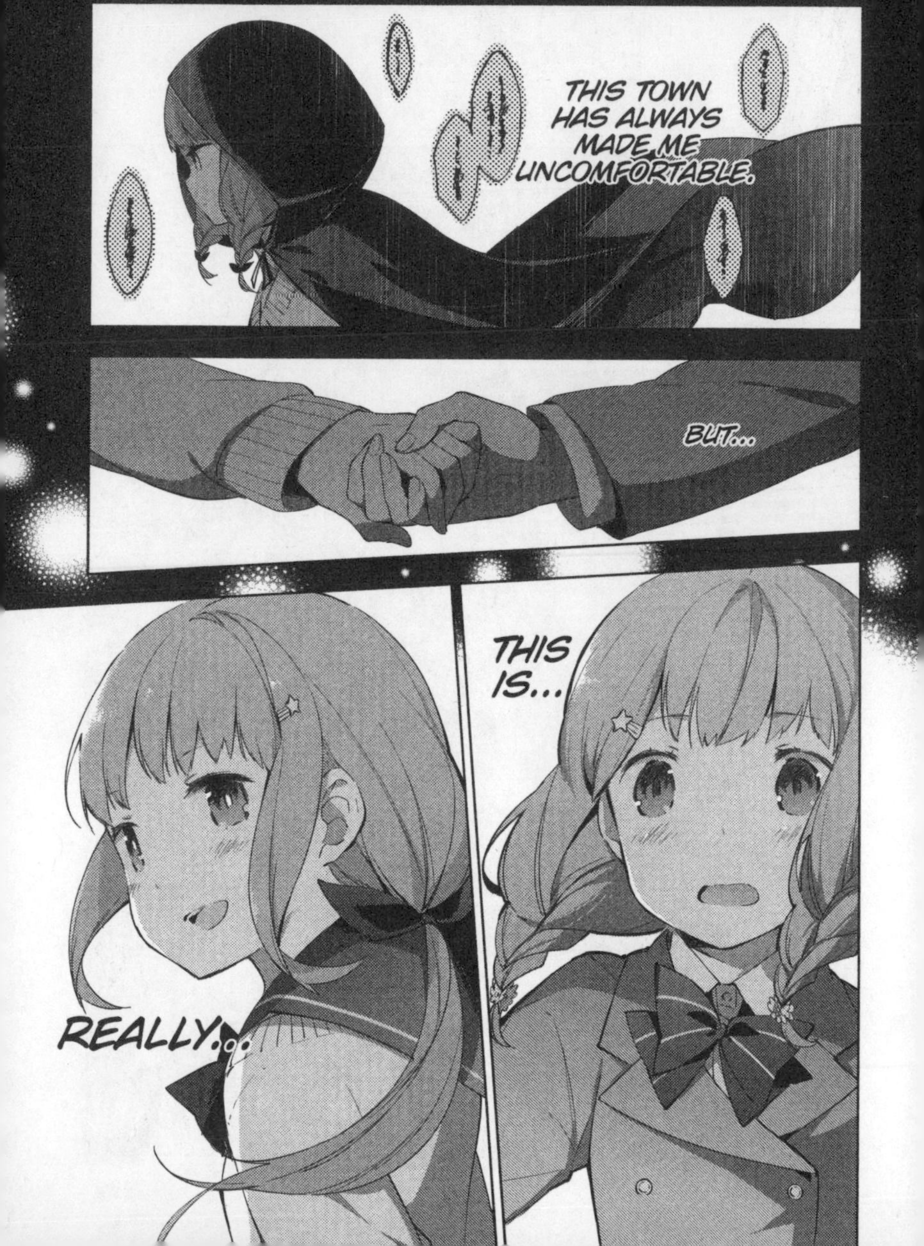
THIS TOWN HAS ALWAYS MADE ME UNCOMFORTABLE.
BUT...
THIS IS...
REALLY...

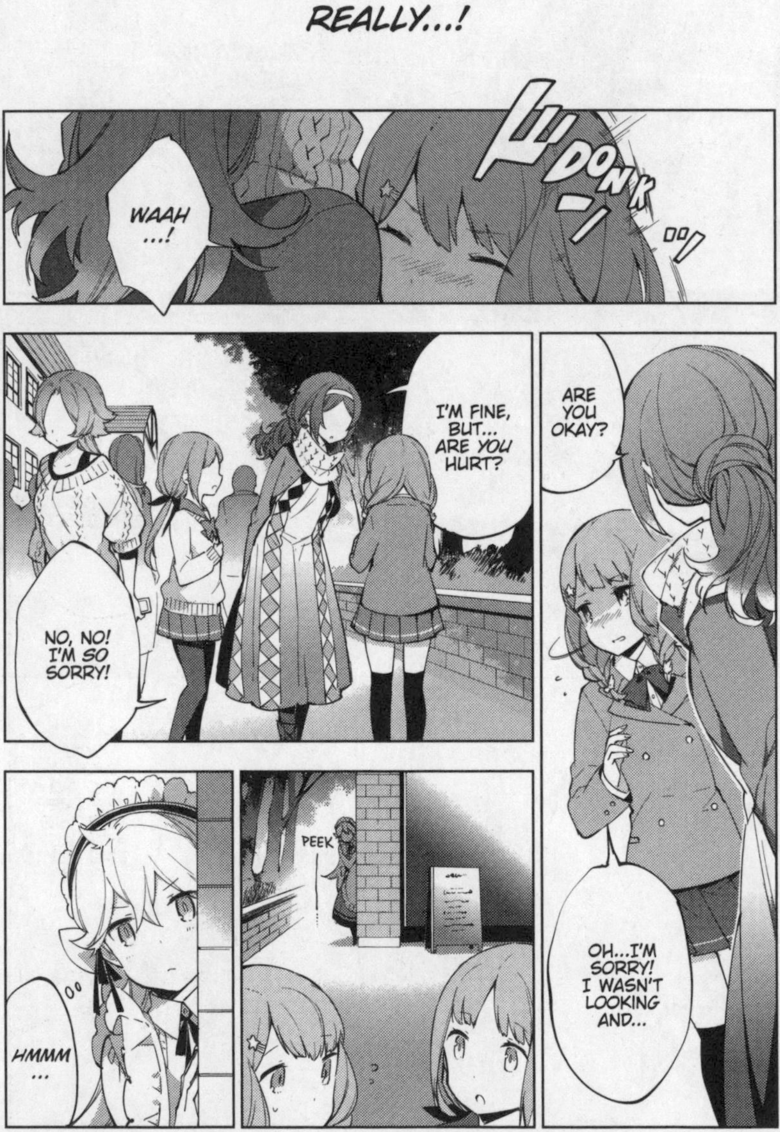
REALLY...!
DONK
WAAH ...!
ARE YOU OKAY?
OH...I'M SORRY! I WASN'T LOOKING AND...
I'M FINE, BUT... ARE *YOU* HURT?
NO, NO! I'M SO SORRY!
PEEK
HMMM ...

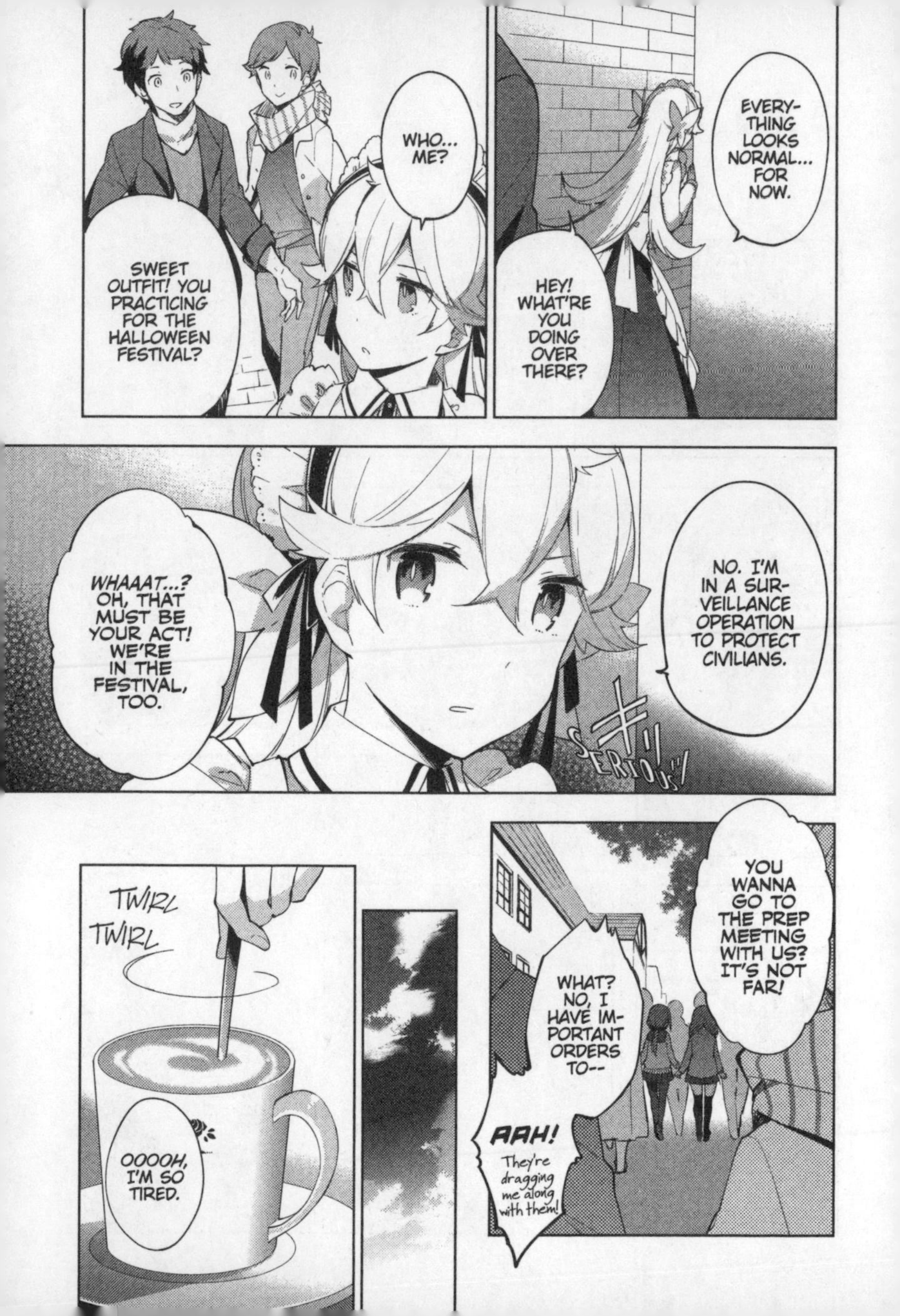
EVERY-THING LOOKS NORMAL... FOR NOW.
HEY! WHAT'RE YOU DOING OVER THERE?
WHO... ME?
SWEET OUTFIT! YOU PRACTICING FOR THE HALLOWEEN FESTIVAL?
NO. I'M IN A SUR-VEILLANCE OPERATION TO PROTECT CIVILIANS.
SERIOUS!!
WHAAAT...? OH, THAT MUST BE YOUR ACT! WE'RE IN THE FESTIVAL, TOO.
YOU WANNA GO TO THE PREP MEETING WITH US? IT'S NOT FAR!
WHAT? NO, I HAVE IM-PORTANT ORDERS TO--
AAH!
They're dragging me along with them!
TWIRL
TWIRL
OOOOH, I'M SO TIRED.

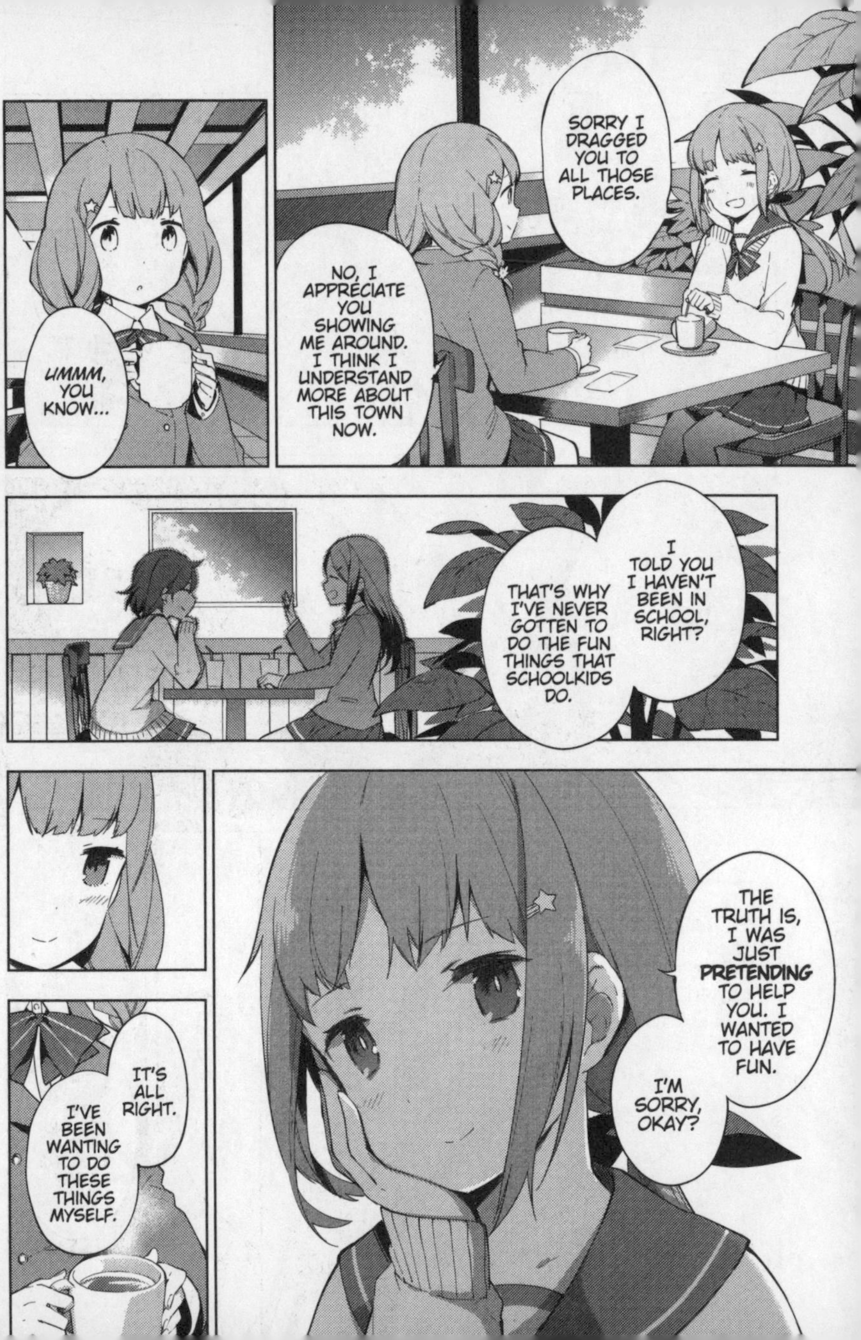
SORRY I DRAGGED YOU TO ALL THOSE PLACES.
NO, I APPRECIATE YOU SHOWING ME AROUND. I THINK I UNDERSTAND MORE ABOUT THIS TOWN NOW.
UMMM, YOU KNOW...
I TOLD YOU I HAVEN'T BEEN IN SCHOOL, RIGHT?
THAT'S WHY I'VE NEVER GOTTEN TO DO THE FUN THINGS THAT SCHOOLKIDS DO.
THE TRUTH IS, I WAS JUST **PRETENDING** TO HELP YOU. I WANTED TO HAVE FUN.
I'M SORRY, OKAY?
IT'S ALL RIGHT.
I'VE BEEN WANTING TO DO THESE THINGS MYSELF.

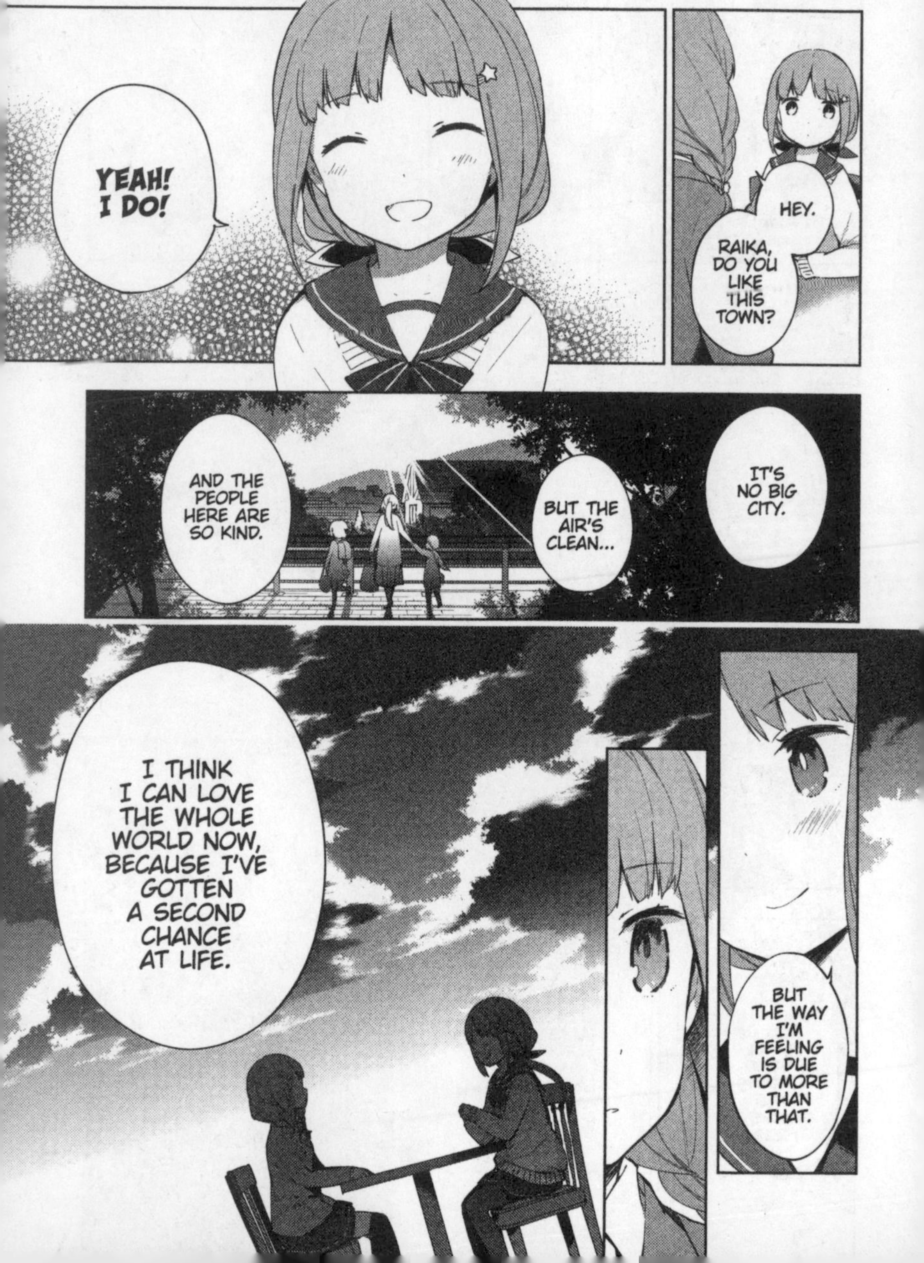
HEY.
RAIKA, DO YOU LIKE THIS TOWN?
YEAH! I DO!
IT'S NO BIG CITY.
BUT THE AIR'S CLEAN...
AND THE PEOPLE HERE ARE SO KIND.
BUT THE WAY I'M FEELING IS DUE TO MORE THAN THAT.
I THINK I CAN LOVE THE WHOLE WORLD NOW, BECAUSE I'VE GOTTEN A SECOND CHANCE AT LIFE.

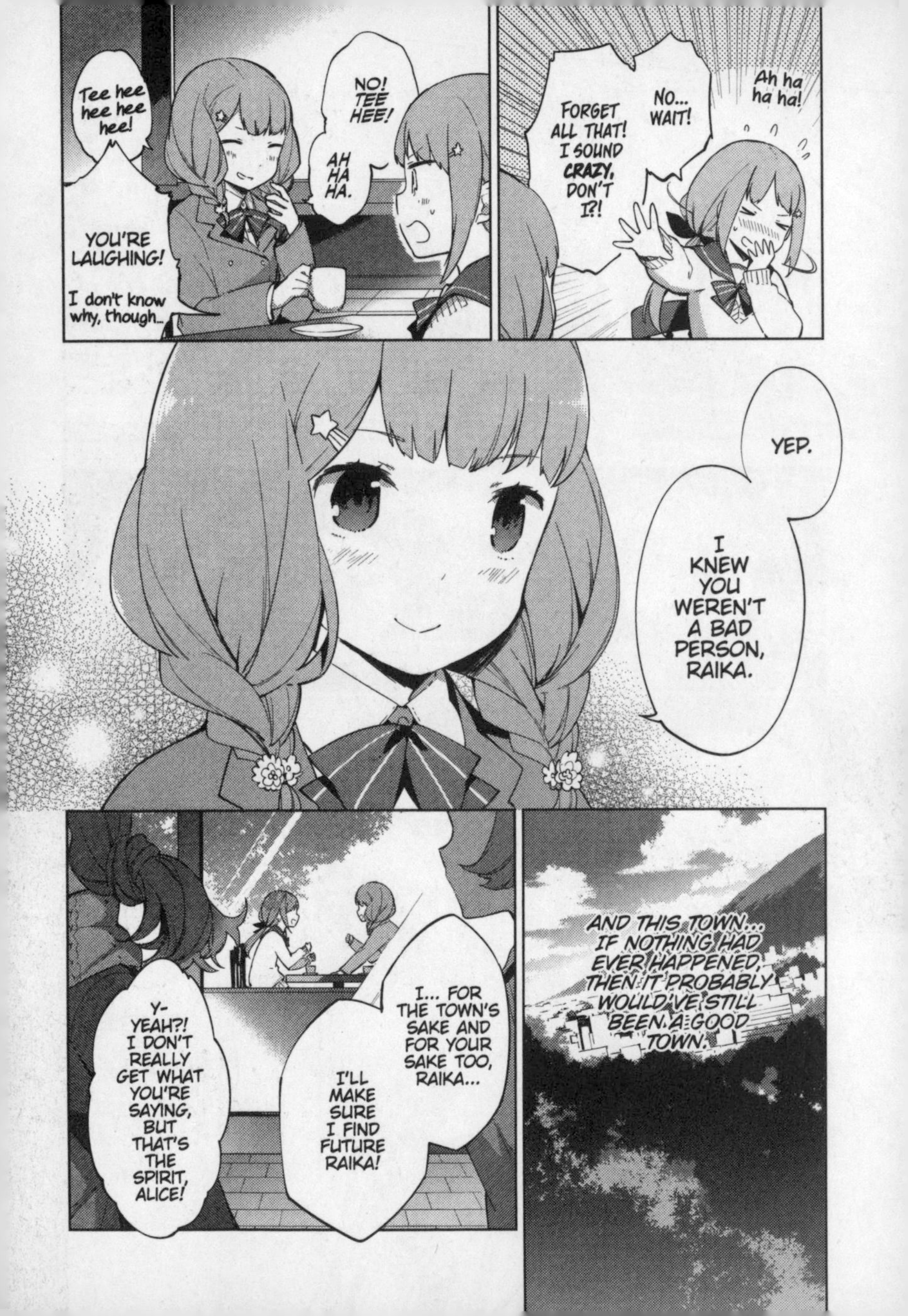
Ah ha ha ha!
NO... WAIT!
FORGET ALL THAT! I SOUND CRAZY, DON'T I?!
NO! TEE HEE!
AH HA HA.
Tee hee hee hee hee!
YOU'RE LAUGHING!
I don't know why, though...
YEP.
I KNEW YOU WEREN'T A BAD PERSON, RAIKA.
AND THIS TOWN... IF NOTHING HAD EVER HAPPENED, THEN IT PROBABLY WOULD'VE STILL BEEN A GOOD TOWN.
I... FOR THE TOWN'S SAKE AND FOR YOUR SAKE TOO, RAIKA...
I'LL MAKE SURE I FIND FUTURE RAIKA!
Y-YEAH?! I DON'T REALLY GET WHAT YOU'RE SAYING, BUT THAT'S THE SPIRIT, ALICE!

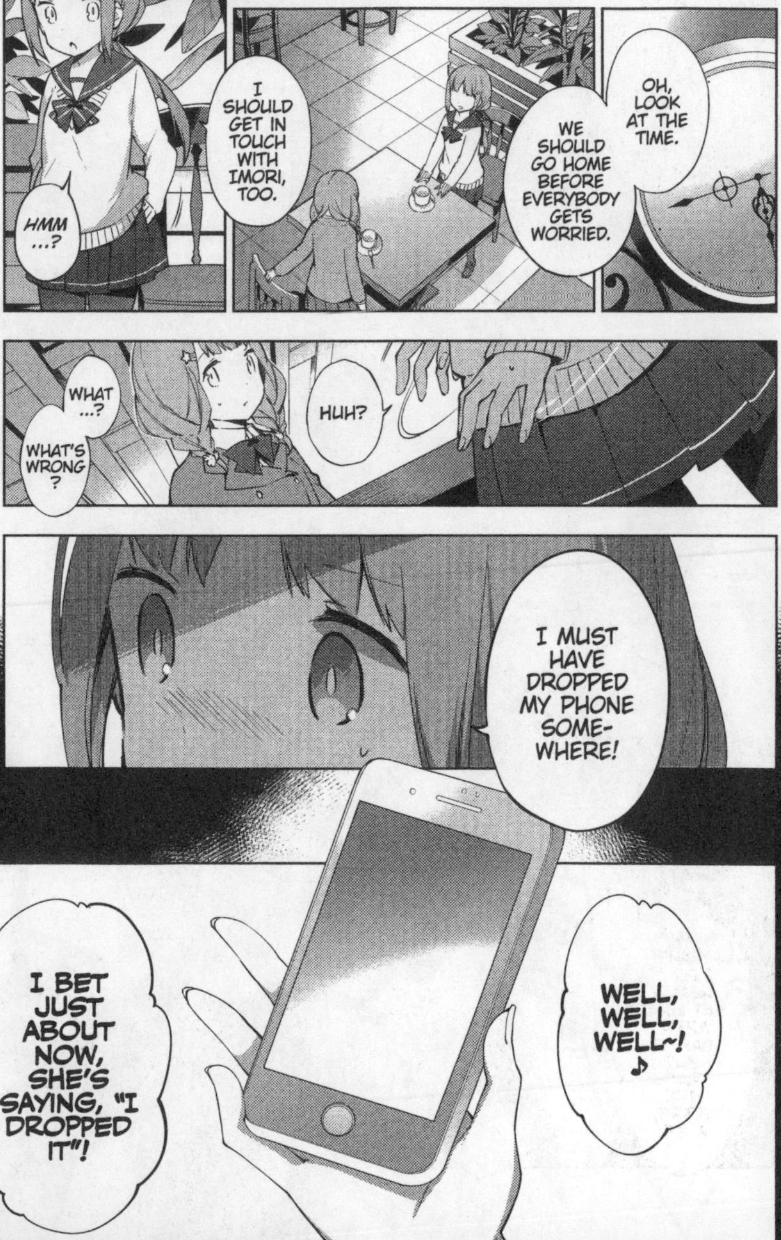
OH, LOOK AT THE TIME.
WE SHOULD GO HOME BEFORE EVERYBODY GETS WORRIED.
I SHOULD GET IN TOUCH WITH IMORI, TOO.
HMM ...?
HUH?
WHAT ...?
WHAT'S WRONG ?
I MUST HAVE DROPPED MY PHONE SOME-WHERE!
WELL, WELL, WELL~! ♪
I BET JUST ABOUT NOW, SHE'S SAYING, "I DROPPED IT"!

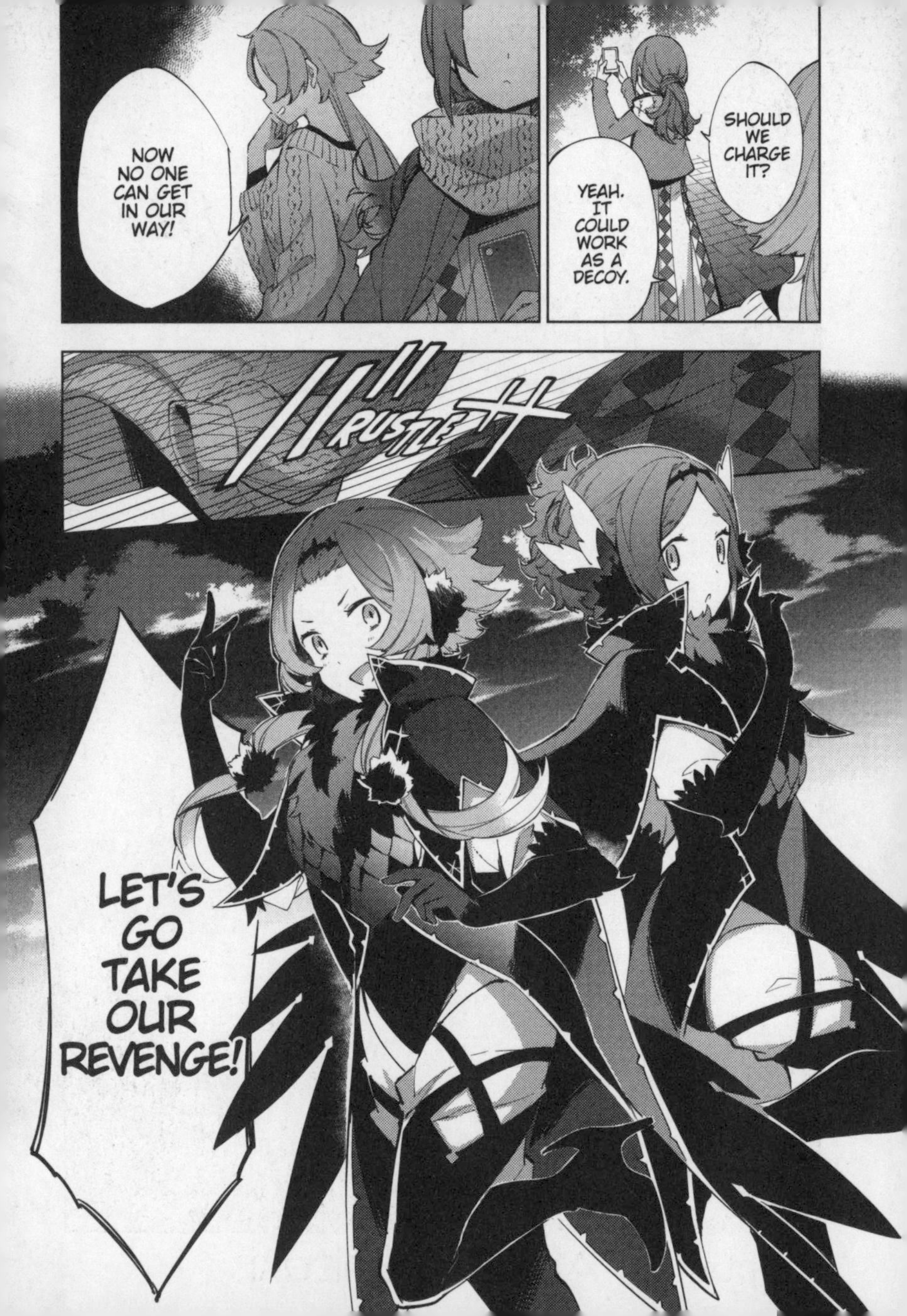
SHOULD WE CHARGE IT?
YEAH. IT COULD WORK AS A DECOY.
NOW NO ONE CAN GET IN OUR WAY!
RUSTLE
LET'S GO TAKE OUR REVENGE!

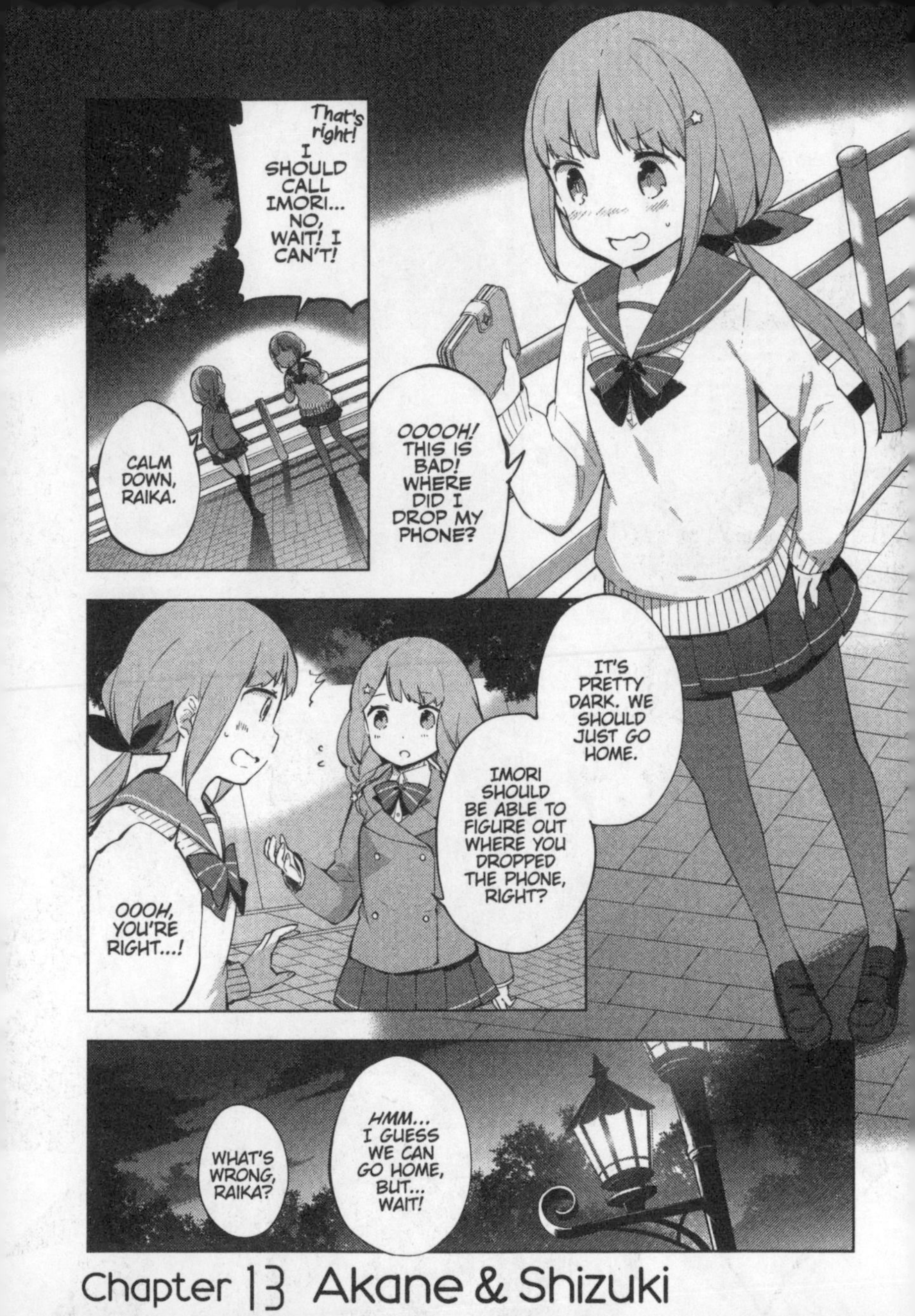
OOOOH! THIS IS BAD! WHERE DID I DROP MY PHONE?
That's right! I SHOULD CALL IMORI... NO, WAIT! I CAN'T!
CALM DOWN, RAIKA.
IT'S PRETTY DARK. WE SHOULD JUST GO HOME.
IMORI SHOULD BE ABLE TO FIGURE OUT WHERE YOU DROPPED THE PHONE, RIGHT?
OOOH, YOU'RE RIGHT...!
HMM... I GUESS WE CAN GO HOME, BUT... WAIT!
WHAT'S WRONG, RAIKA?

# Chapter 13 Akane & Shizuki

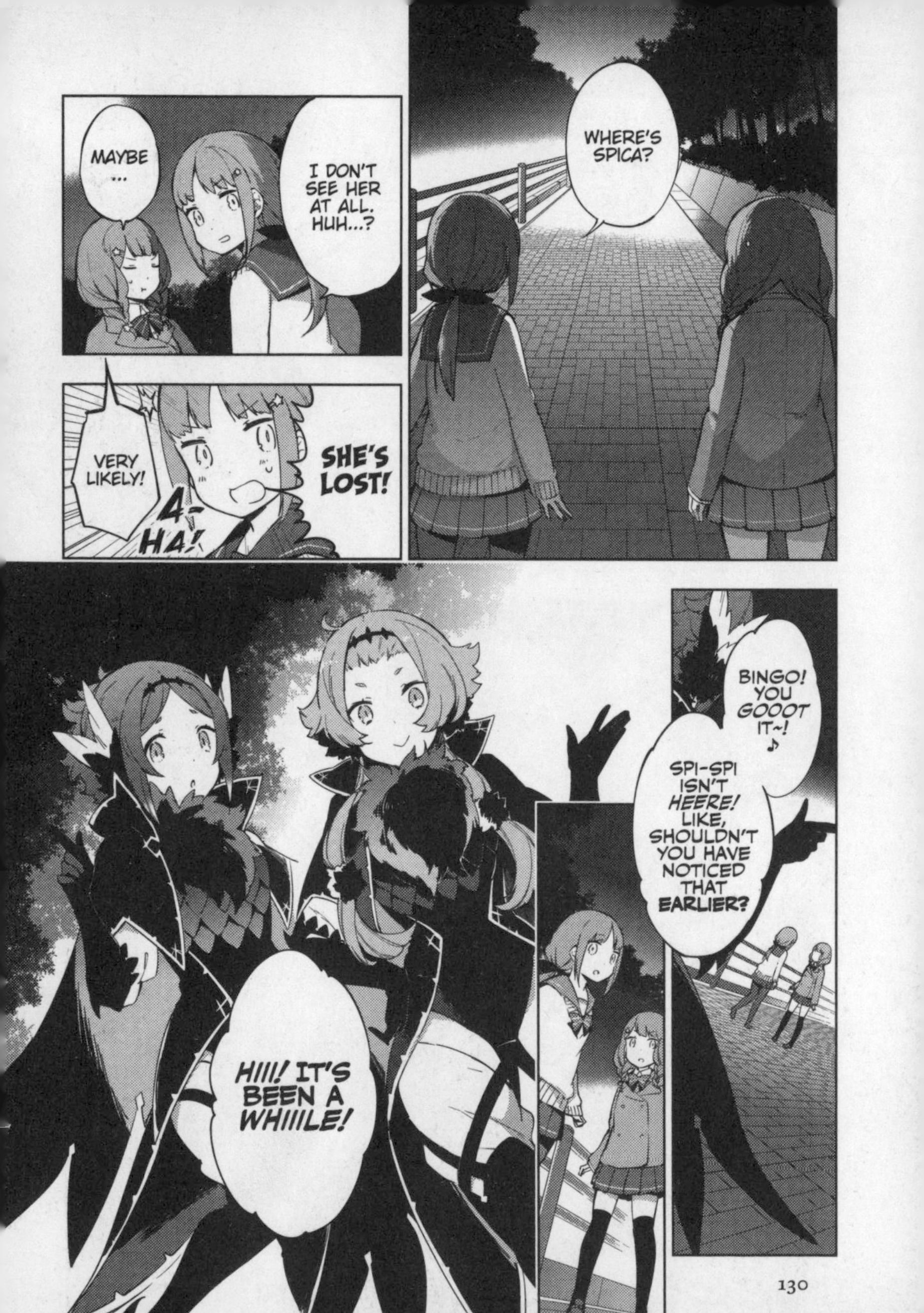
WHERE'S SPICA?
I DON'T SEE HER AT ALL. HUH...?
MAYBE ...
SHE'S LOST!
VERY LIKELY!
A-HA!
BINGO! YOU GOOOT IT~! ♪
SPI-SPI ISN'T HEERE! LIKE, SHOULDN'T YOU HAVE NOTICED THAT EARLIER?
HIIII! IT'S BEEN A WHIIILE!

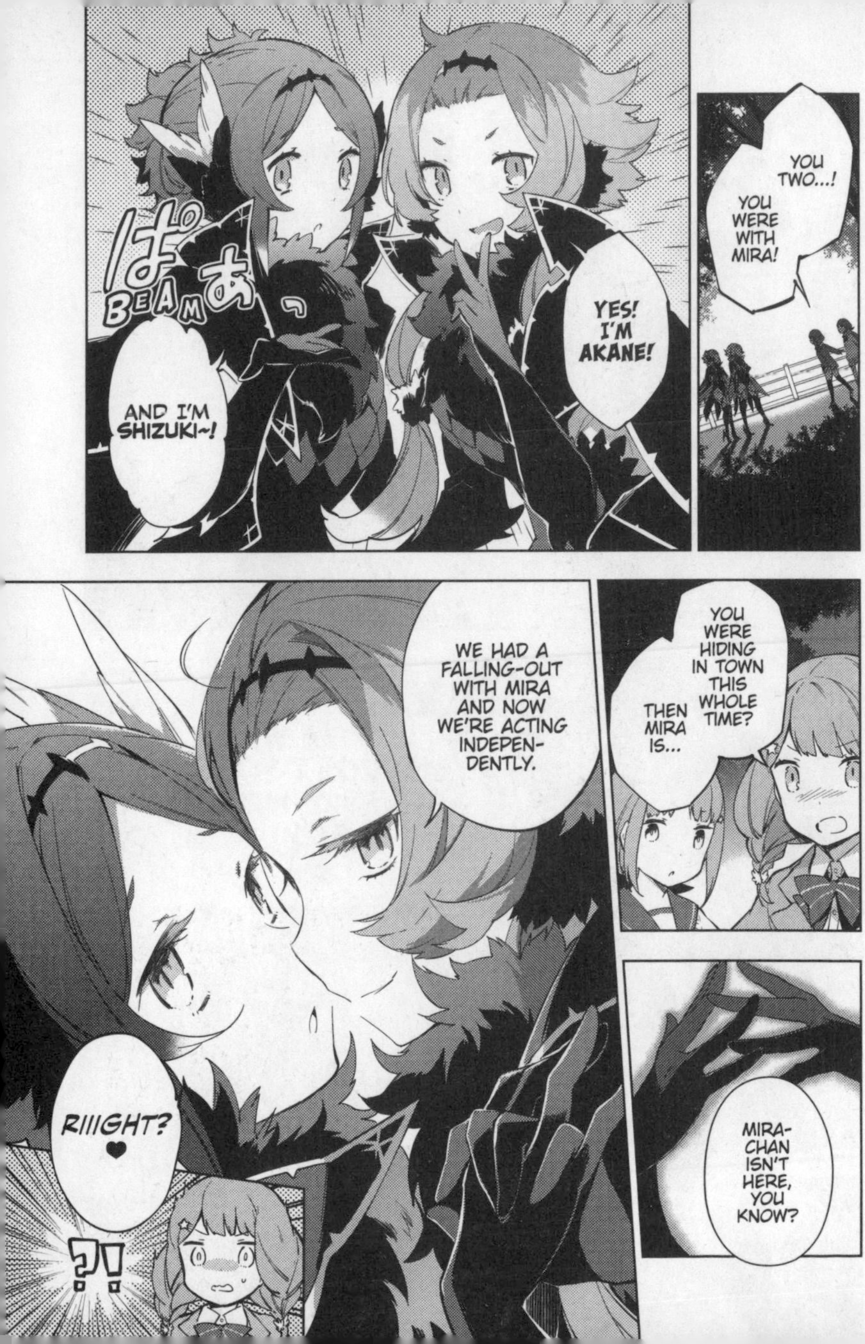
YOU TWO...!
YOU WERE WITH MIRA!
YES! I'M AKANE!
ぱぁっ
BEAM
AND I'M SHIZUKI~!
YOU WERE HIDING IN TOWN THIS WHOLE TIME?
THEN MIRA IS...
MIRA-CHAN ISN'T HERE, YOU KNOW?
WE HAD A FALLING-OUT WITH MIRA AND NOW WE'RE ACTING INDEPEN-DENTLY.
RIIIGHT? ♥
?!

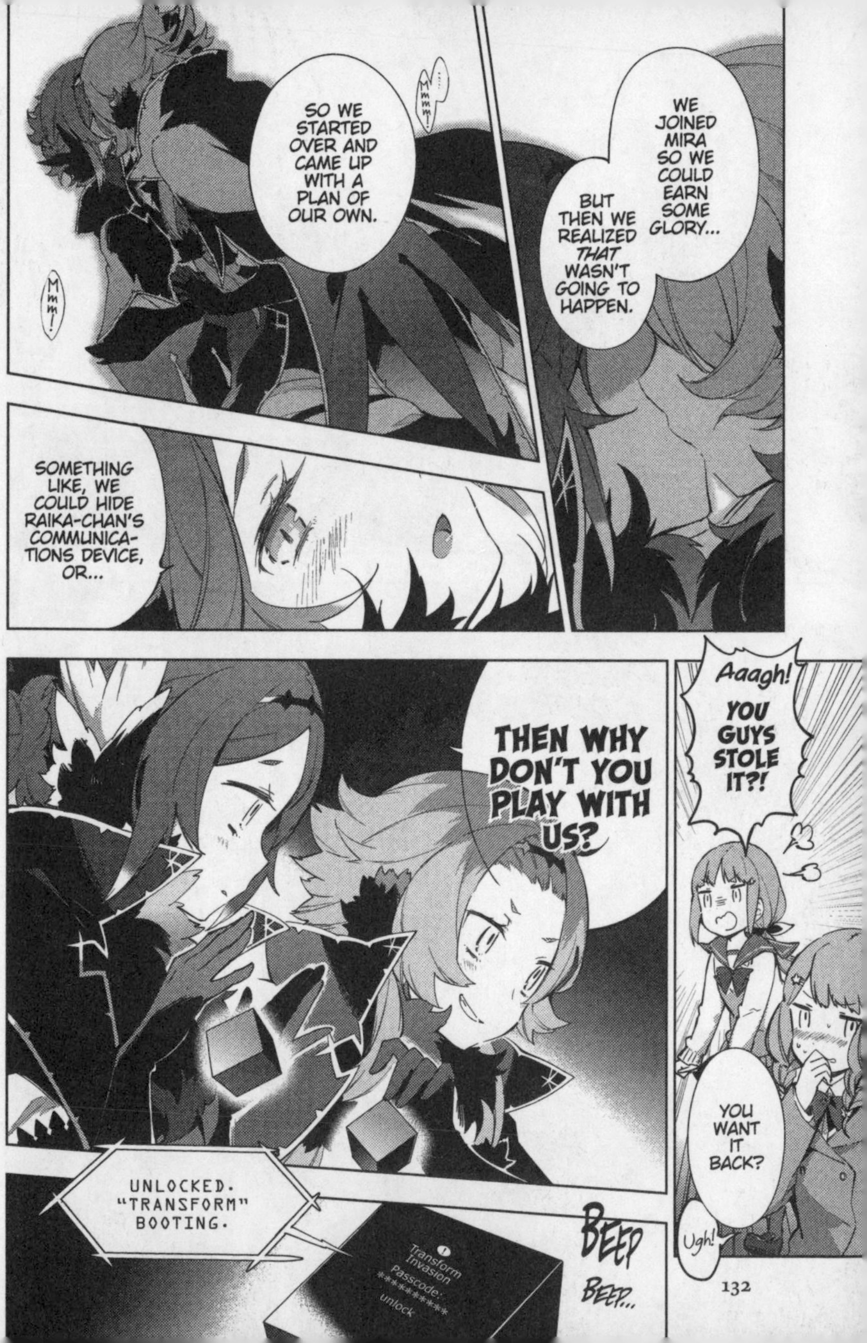
WE JOINED MIRA SO WE COULD EARN SOME GLORY...
BUT THEN WE REALIZED *THAT* WASN'T GOING TO HAPPEN.
...Mmmm!
SO WE STARTED OVER AND CAME UP WITH A PLAN OF OUR OWN.
Mmm!
SOMETHING LIKE, WE COULD HIDE RAIKA-CHAN'S COMMUNICA-TIONS DEVICE, OR...
Aaagh!
YOU GUYS STOLE IT?!
YOU WANT IT BACK?
Ugh!
THEN WHY DON'T YOU PLAY WITH US?
UNLOCKED. "TRANSFORM" BOOTING.
BEEP
BEEP...
Transform Invasion Passcode: ********* unlock

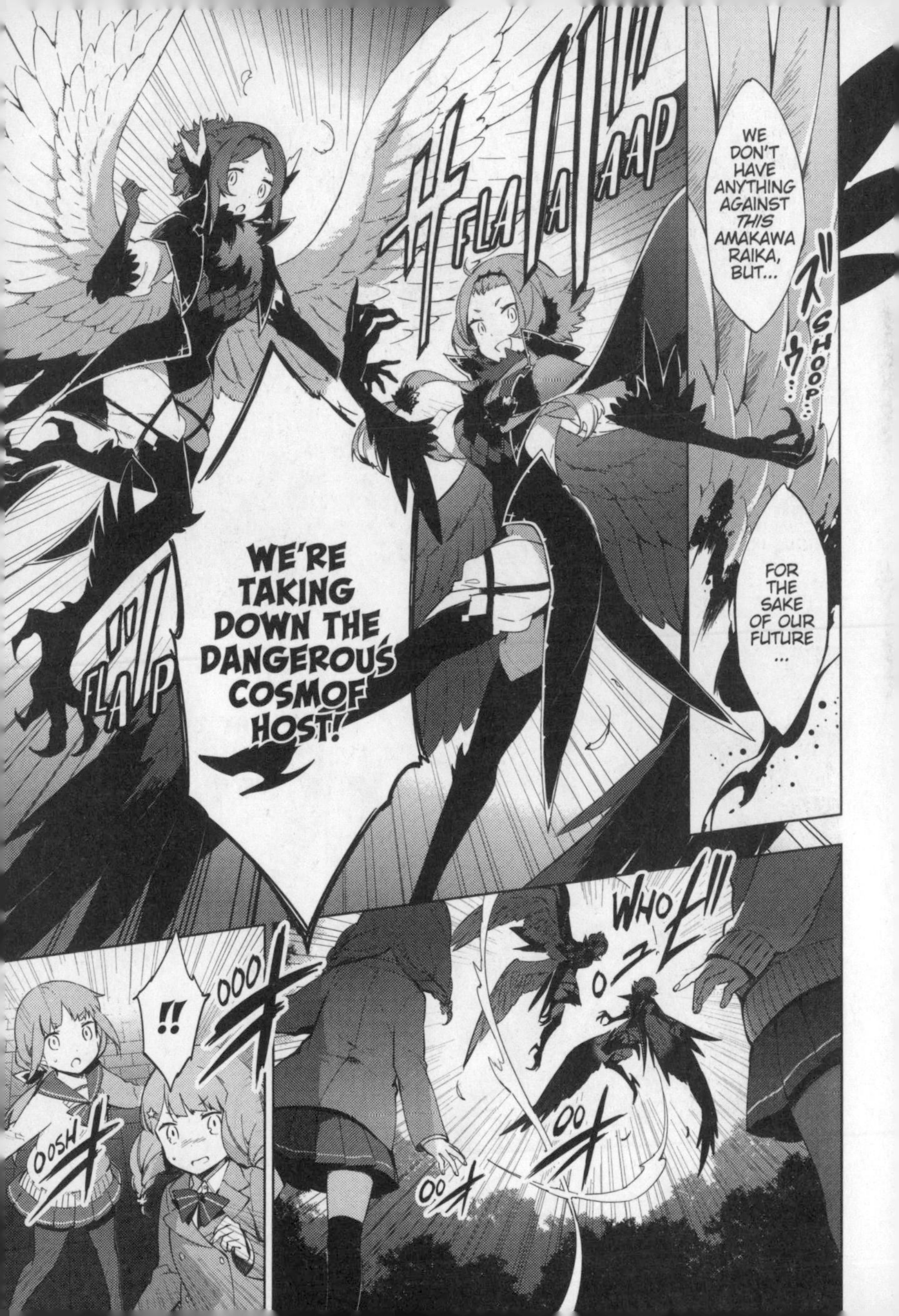
WE DON'T HAVE ANYTHING AGAINST *THIS* AMAKAWA RAIKA, BUT...
SHOOP...
FOR THE SAKE OF OUR FUTURE ...
FLAAAAP
WE'RE TAKING DOWN THE DANGEROUS COSMOF HOST!
FLAP
WHOOM
OOOSH
!!
OOSH
OOSH

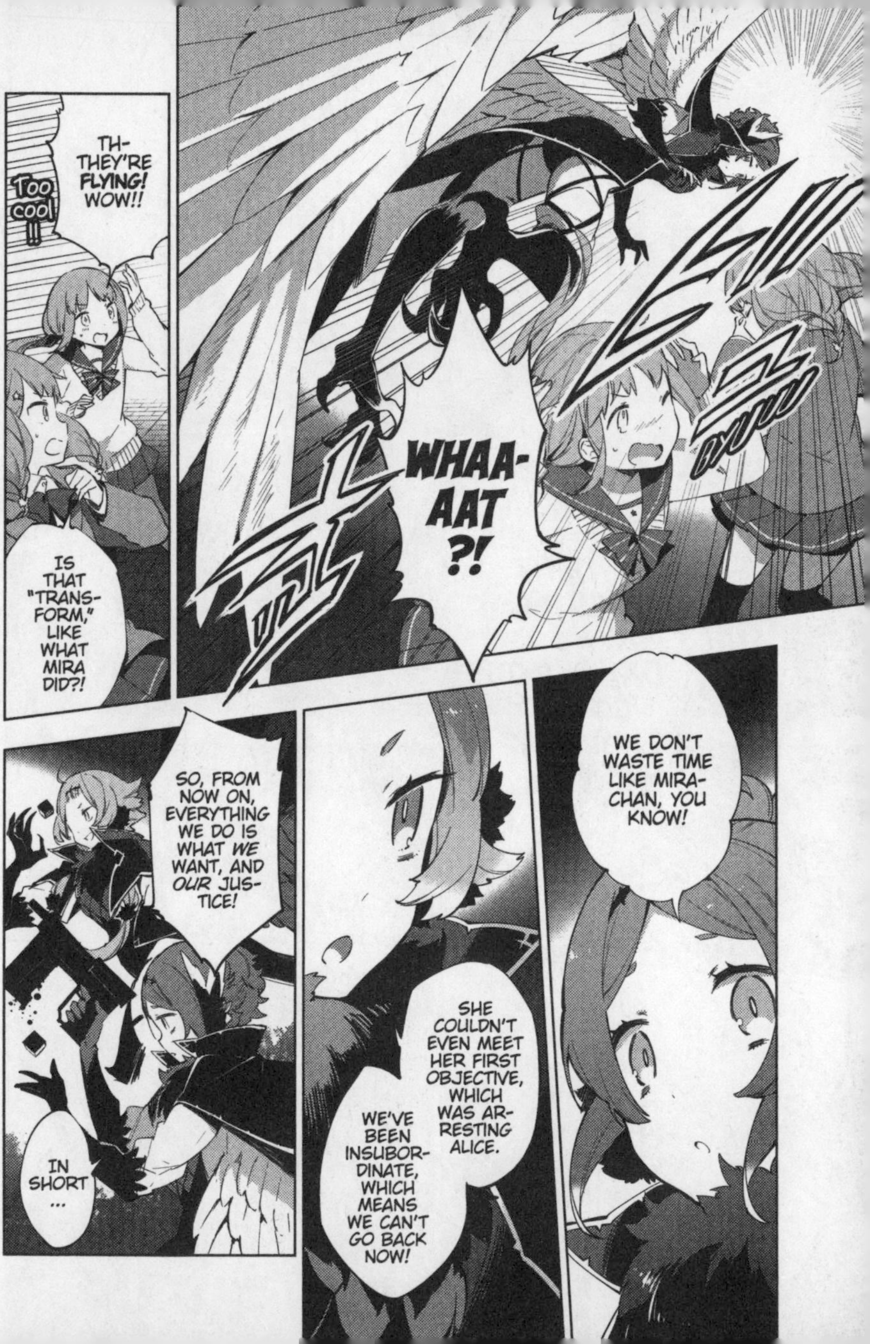
WHAA-AAT?!
TH-THEY'RE FLYING! WOW!!
Too cool!!
IS THAT "TRANSFORM," LIKE WHAT MIRA DID?!
WE DON'T WASTE TIME LIKE MIRA-CHAN, YOU KNOW!
SHE COULDN'T EVEN MEET HER FIRST OBJECTIVE, WHICH WAS ARRESTING ALICE.
WE'VE BEEN INSUBORDINATE, WHICH MEANS WE CAN'T GO BACK NOW!
SO, FROM NOW ON, EVERYTHING WE DO IS WHAT WE WANT, AND OUR JUSTICE!
IN SHORT...

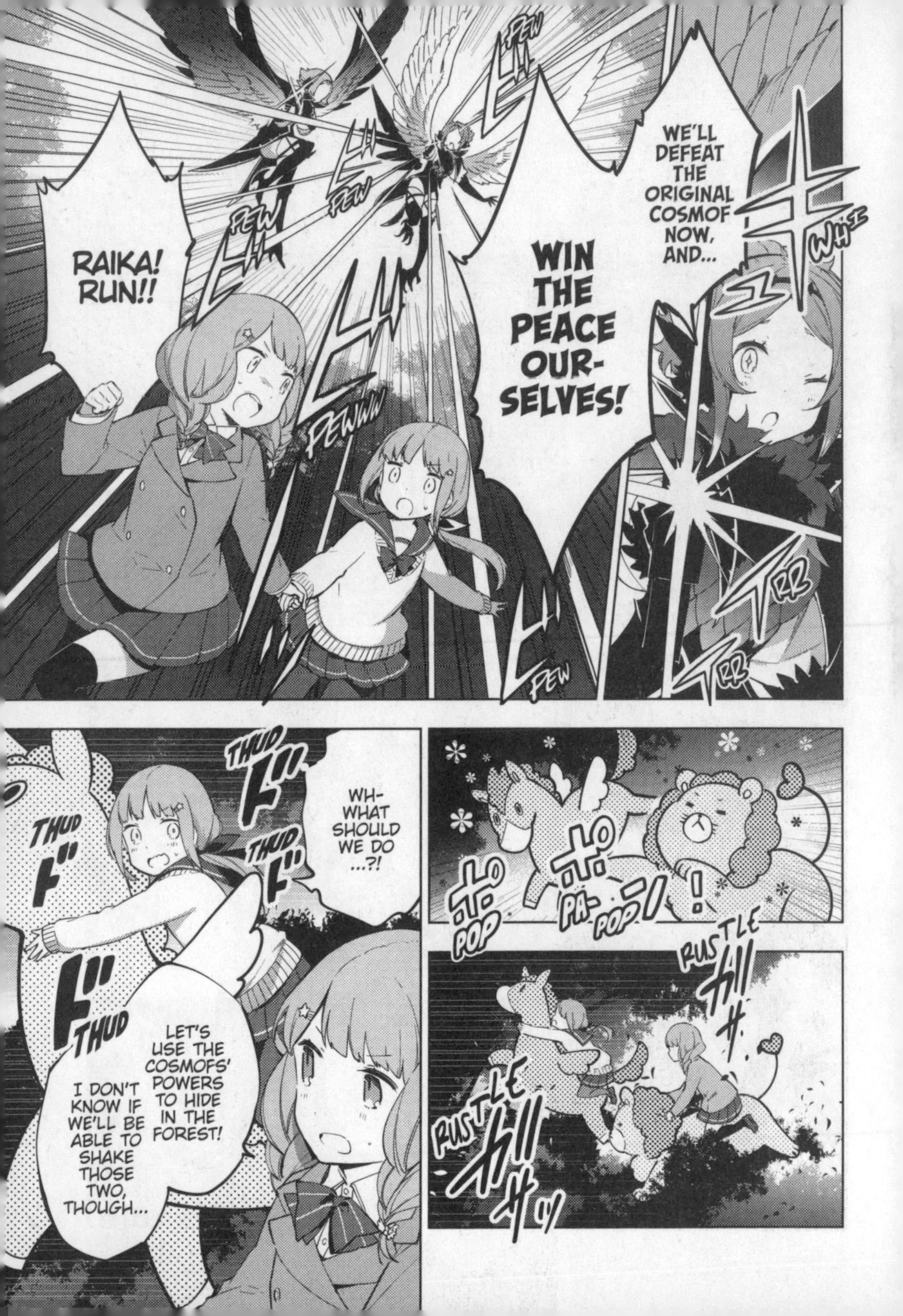
PEW
PEW
PEW
WHI
ZZ
WE'LL DEFEAT THE ORIGINAL COSMOF NOW, AND...
WIN THE PEACE OURSELVES!
TRR
TRR
PEW
PEWWW
PEW
RAIKA! RUN!!
POP
PA-POP
!
RUSTLE
RUSTLE
THUD
THUD
THUD
WH-WHAT SHOULD WE DO ...?!
THUD
LET'S USE THE COSMOFS' POWERS TO HIDE IN THE FOREST!
I DON'T KNOW IF WE'LL BE ABLE TO SHAKE THOSE TWO, THOUGH...

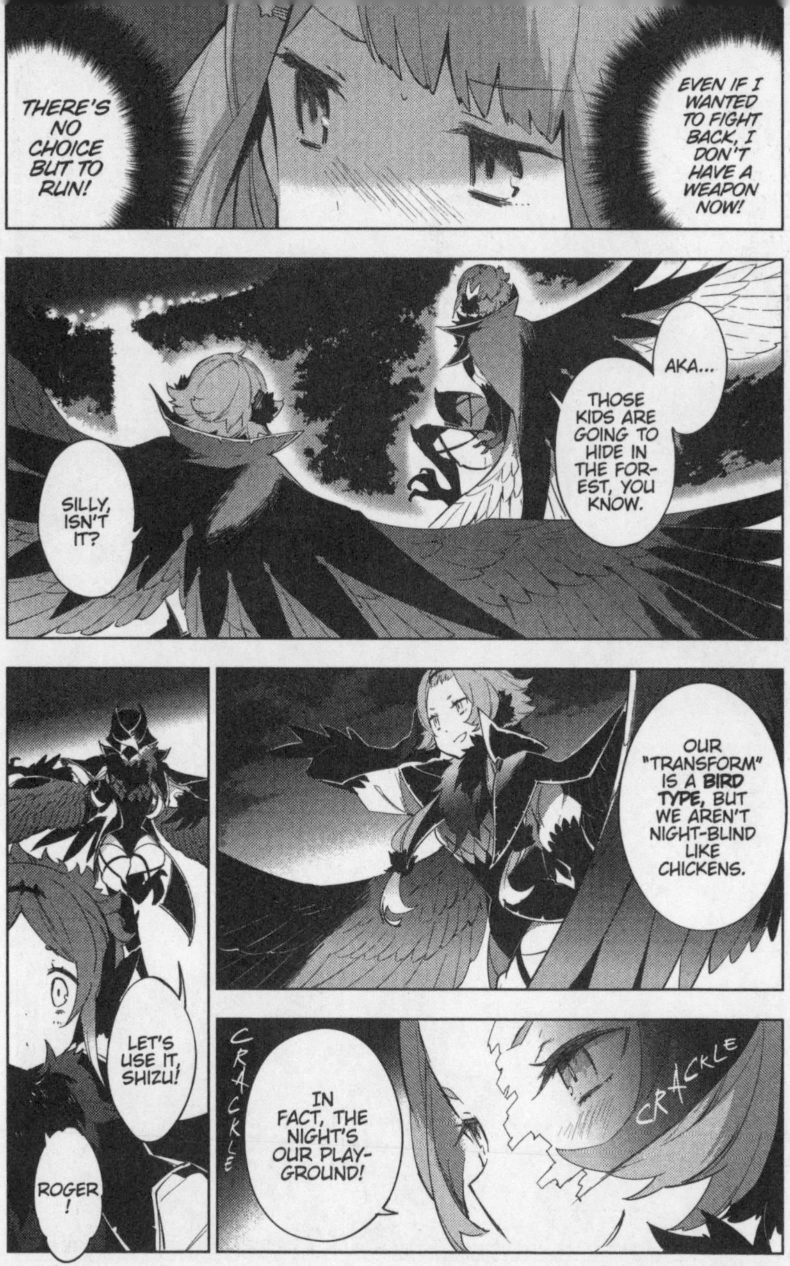
EVEN IF I WANTED TO FIGHT BACK, I DON'T HAVE A WEAPON NOW!
THERE'S NO CHOICE BUT TO RUN!
AKA...
THOSE KIDS ARE GOING TO HIDE IN THE FOR-EST, YOU KNOW.
SILLY, ISN'T IT?
OUR "TRANSFORM" IS A **BIRD TYPE,** BUT WE AREN'T NIGHT-BLIND LIKE CHICKENS.
CRACKLE
IN FACT, THE NIGHT'S OUR PLAY-GROUND!
CRACKLE
LET'S USE IT, SHIZU!
ROGER!

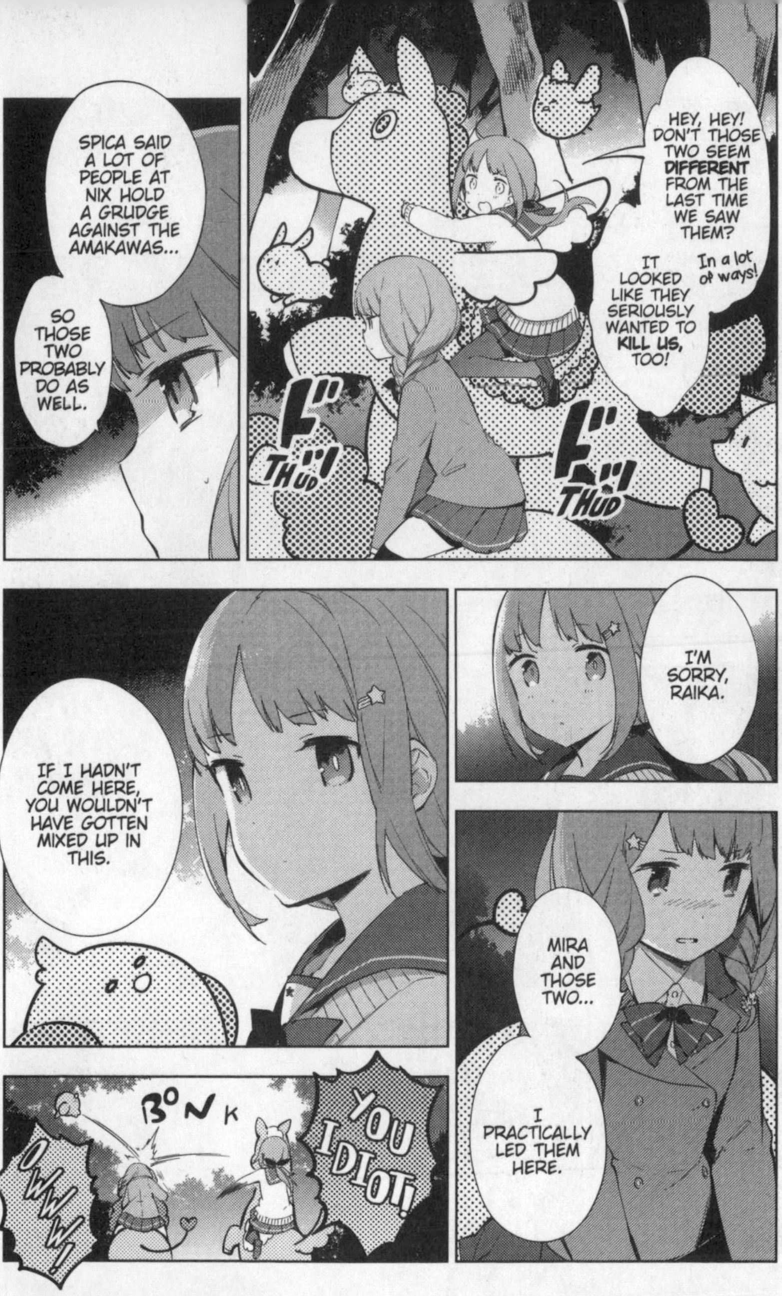
HEY, HEY! DON'T THOSE TWO SEEM **DIFFERENT** FROM THE LAST TIME WE SAW THEM?
In a lot of ways!
IT LOOKED LIKE THEY SERIOUSLY WANTED TO **KILL US,** TOO!
ドッ THUD
ドッ THUD
SPICA SAID A LOT OF PEOPLE AT NIX HOLD A GRUDGE AGAINST THE AMAKAWAS...
SO THOSE TWO PROBABLY DO AS WELL.
I'M SORRY, RAIKA.
MIRA AND THOSE TWO...
I PRACTICALLY LED THEM HERE.
IF I HADN'T COME HERE, YOU WOULDN'T HAVE GOTTEN MIXED UP IN THIS.
YOU IDIOT!
BONK
OWWW!

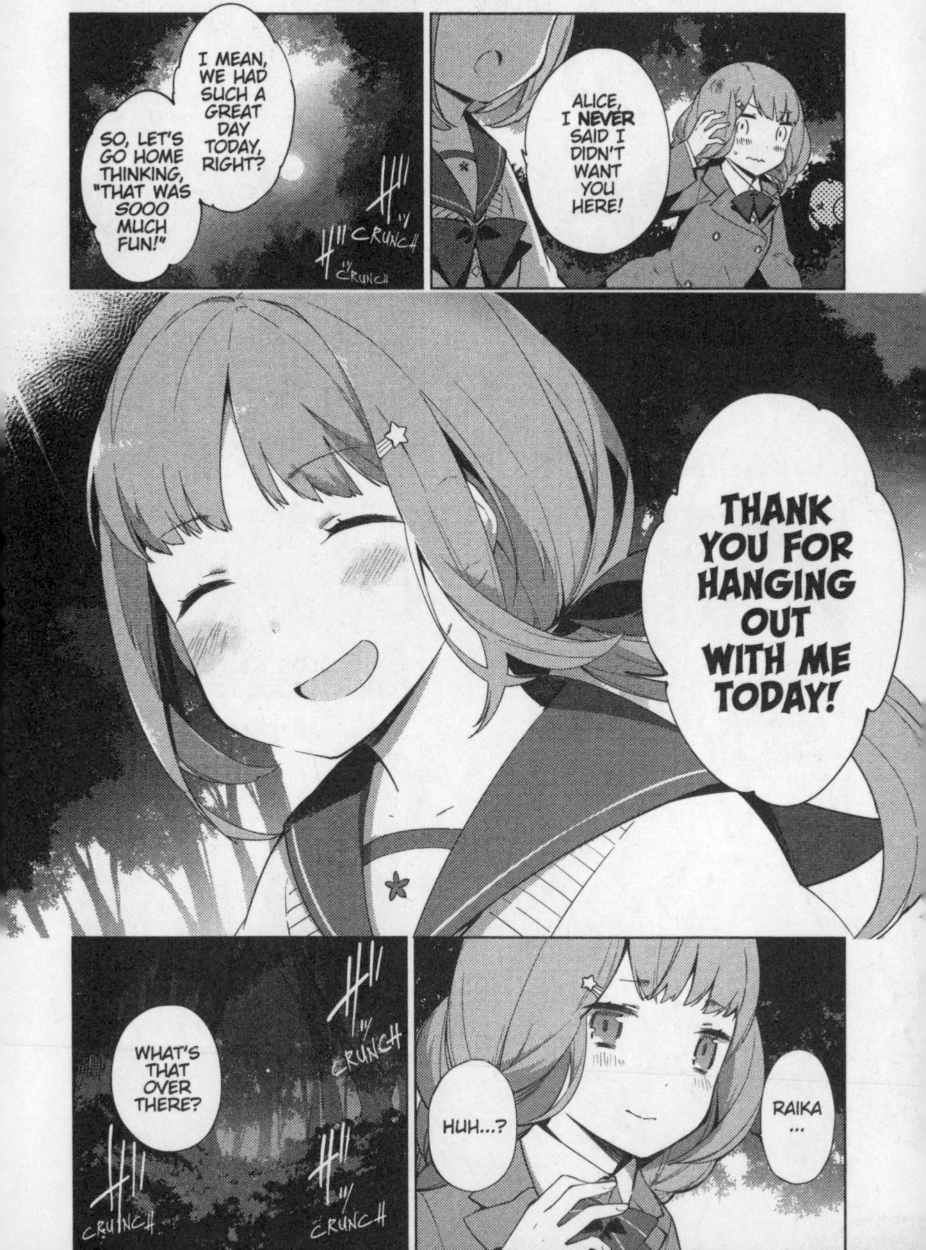
ALICE, I **NEVER** SAID I DIDN'T WANT YOU HERE!
I MEAN, WE HAD SUCH A GREAT DAY TODAY, RIGHT?
SO, LET'S GO HOME THINKING, "THAT WAS SOOO MUCH FUN!"
CRUNCH
CRUNCH
THANK YOU FOR HANGING OUT WITH ME TODAY!
RAIKA ...
HUH...?
CRUNCH
WHAT'S THAT OVER THERE?
CRUNCH
CRUNCH

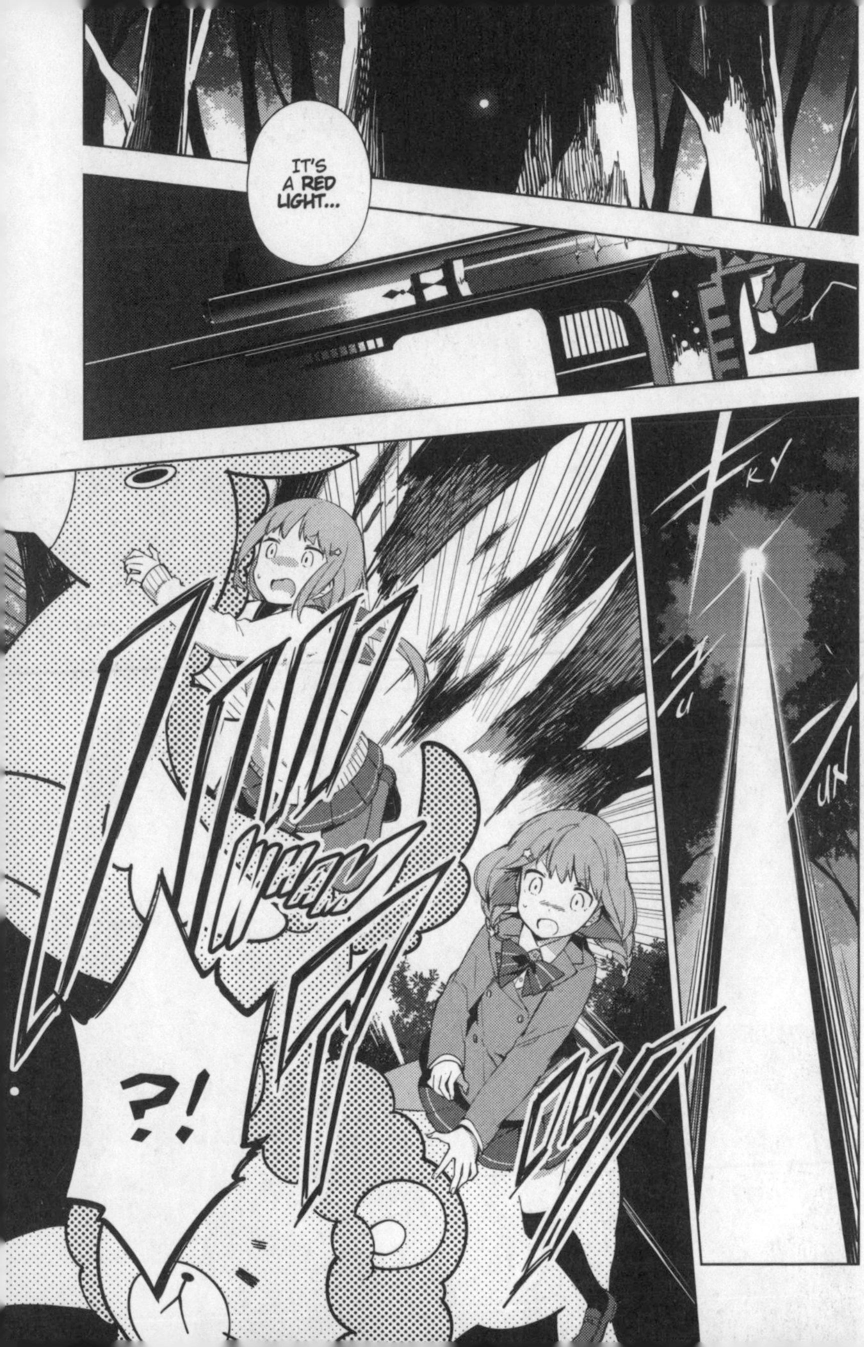
IT'S A RED LIGHT...
KY
U
UN
?!

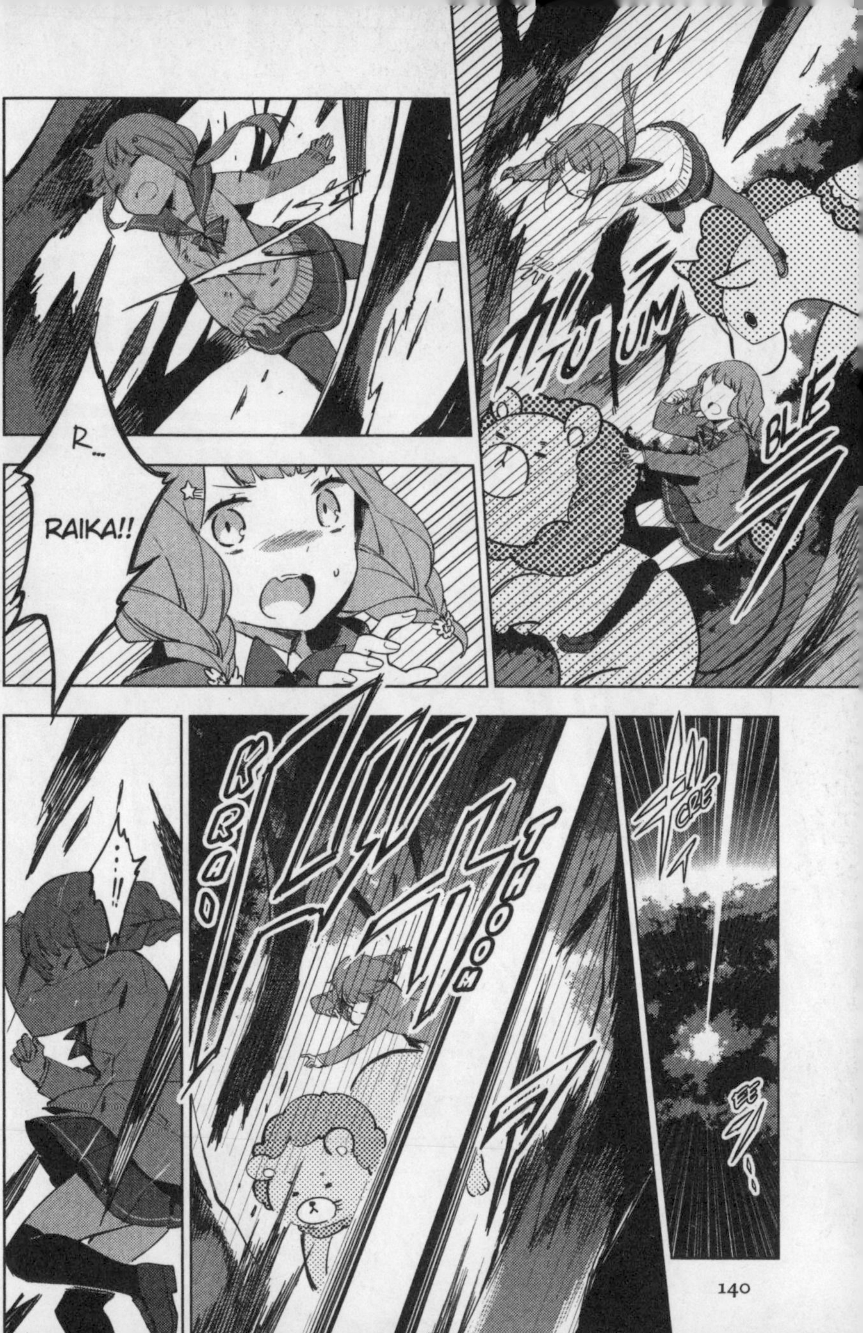
TUTUM
BLIE
R...
RAIKA!!
CRE
EE
KRRAO
THOOOM
...!!

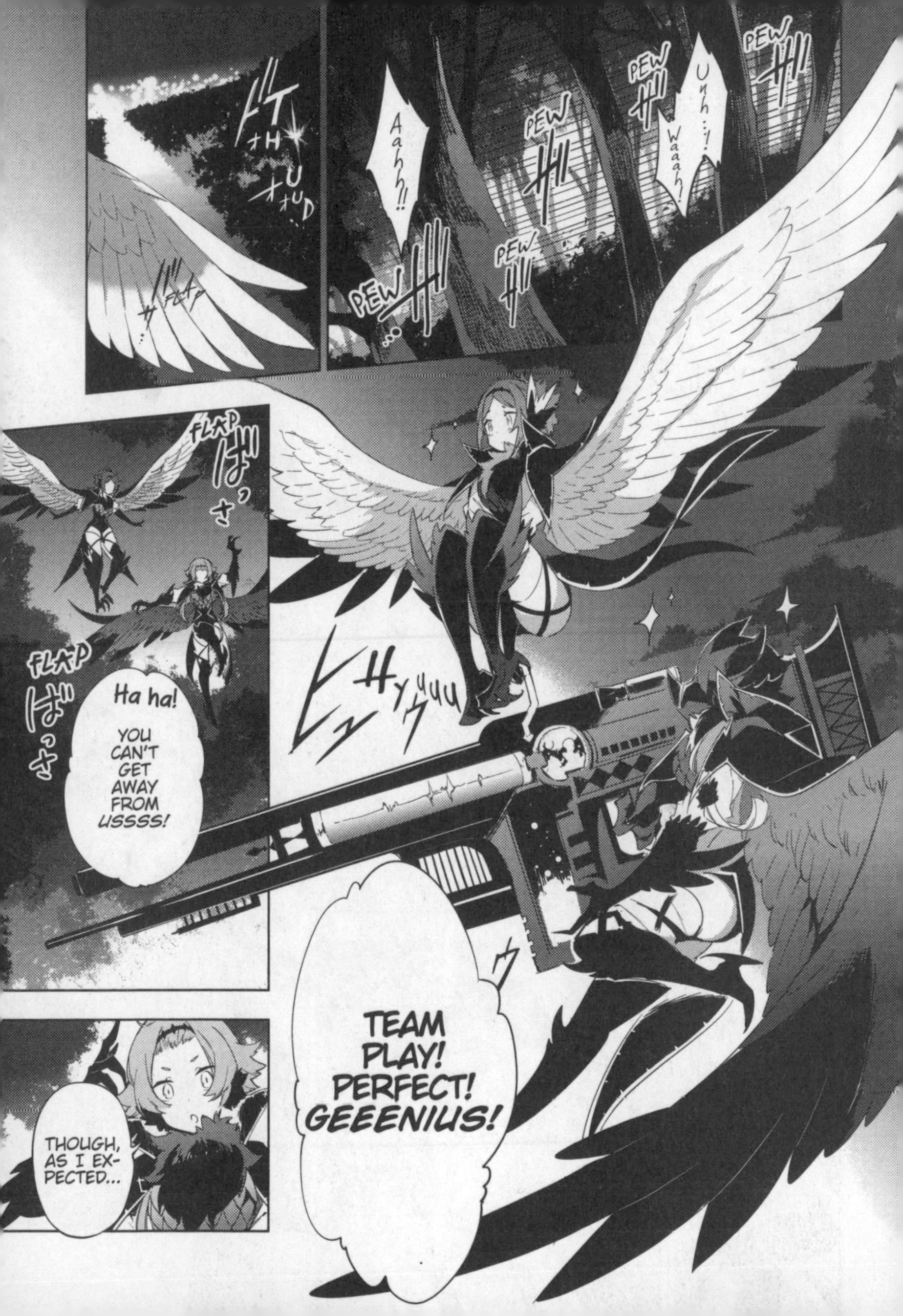
PEW
Unh...!
Waaah!
PEW
Aahh!!
PEW
PEW
PEW
...
THUD
FLAP
HYUUU
TEAM PLAY! PERFECT! GEEENIUS!
FLAP
ばっさ
FLAP
ばっさ
Ha ha!
YOU CAN'T GET AWAY FROM USSSS!
THOUGH, AS I EXPECTED...

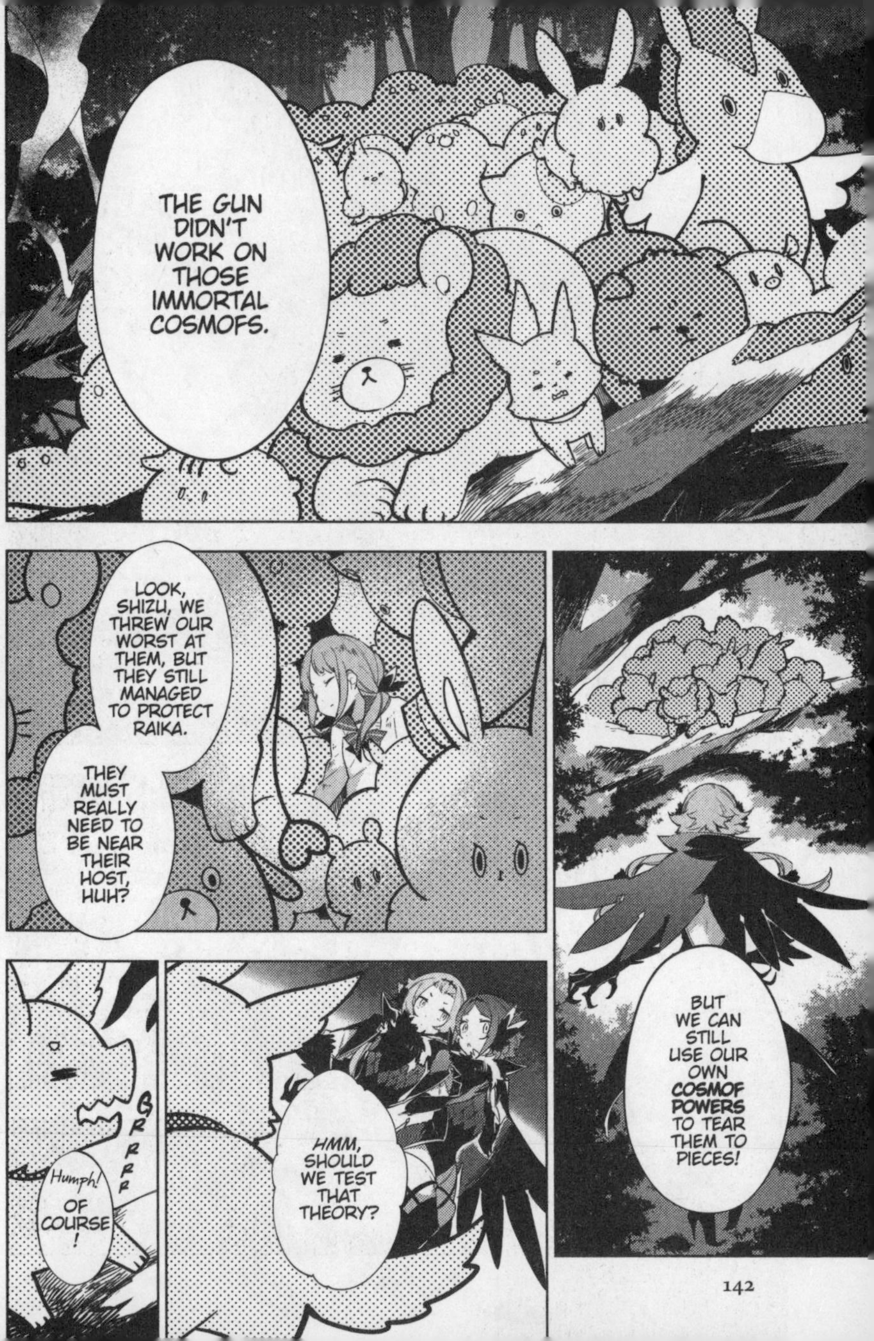
THE GUN DIDN'T WORK ON THOSE IMMORTAL COSMOFS.
BUT WE CAN STILL USE OUR OWN **COSMOF POWERS** TO TEAR THEM TO PIECES!
LOOK, SHIZU, WE THREW OUR WORST AT THEM, BUT THEY STILL MANAGED TO PROTECT RAIKA.
THEY MUST REALLY NEED TO BE NEAR THEIR HOST, HUH?
HMM, SHOULD WE TEST THAT THEORY?
BRRRR
Humph! OF COURSE!

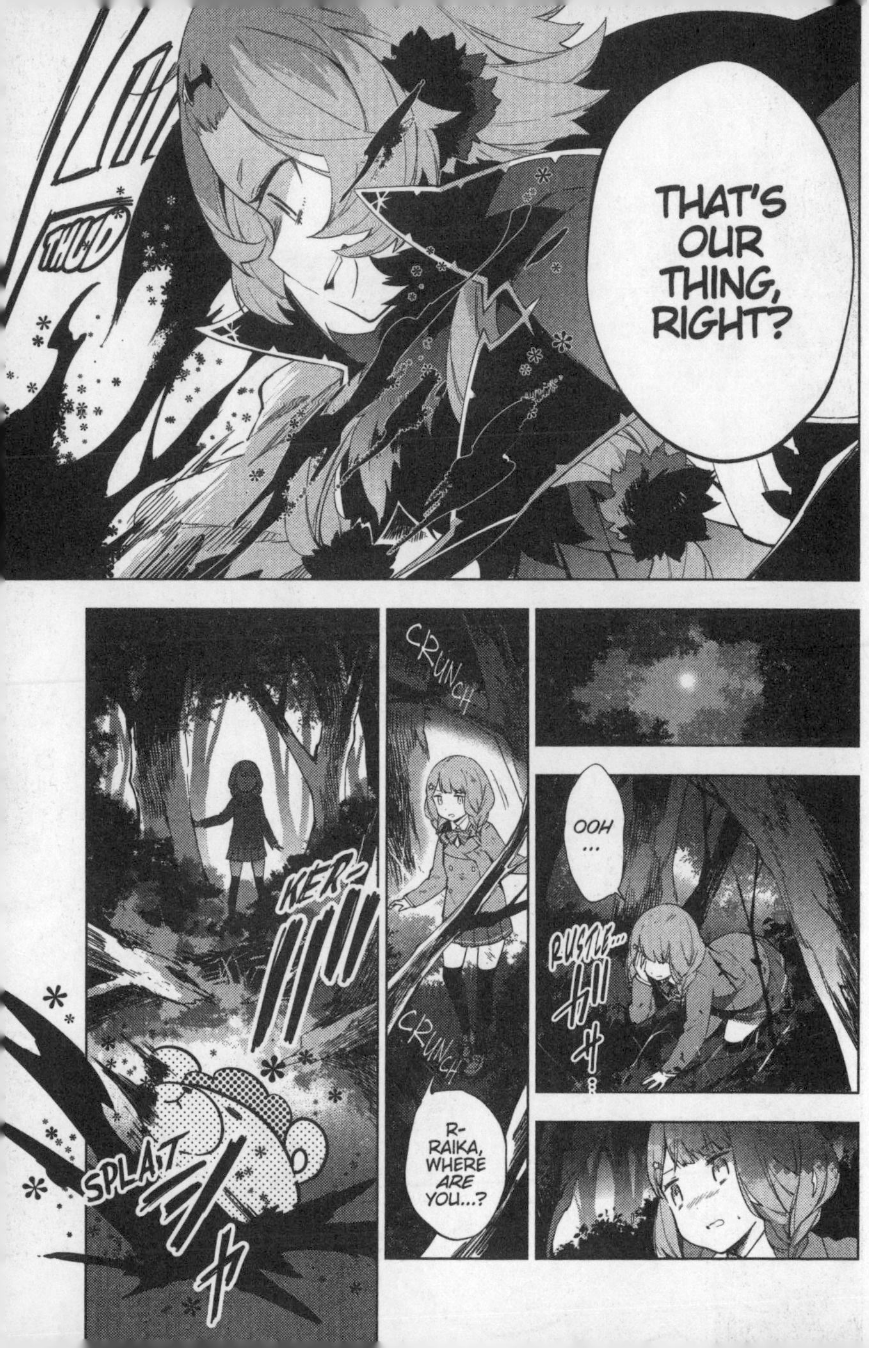
THAT'S OUR THING, RIGHT?
THUD
OOH...
RUSTLE...
CRUNCH
CRUNCH
R-RAIKA, WHERE ARE YOU...?
KER-
SPLAT

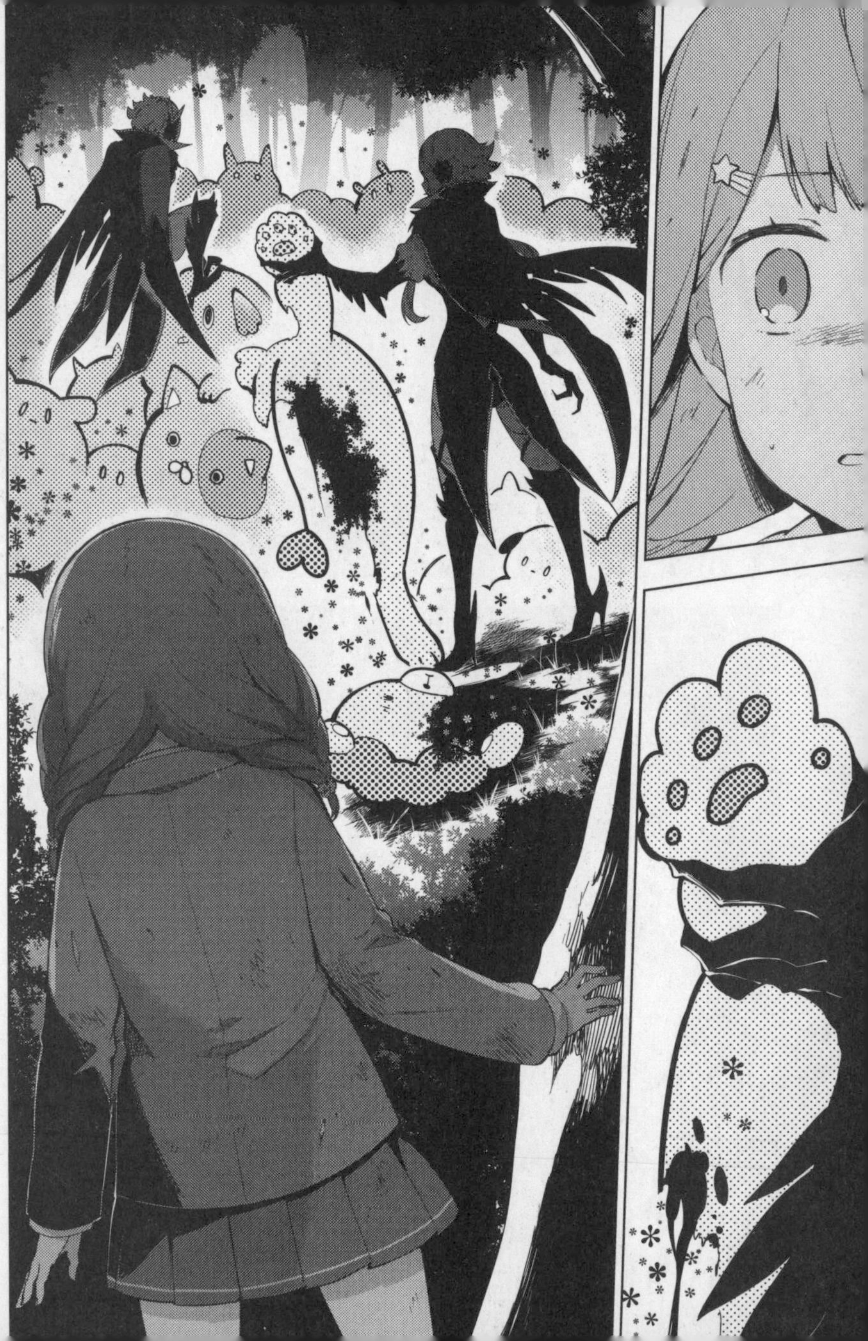

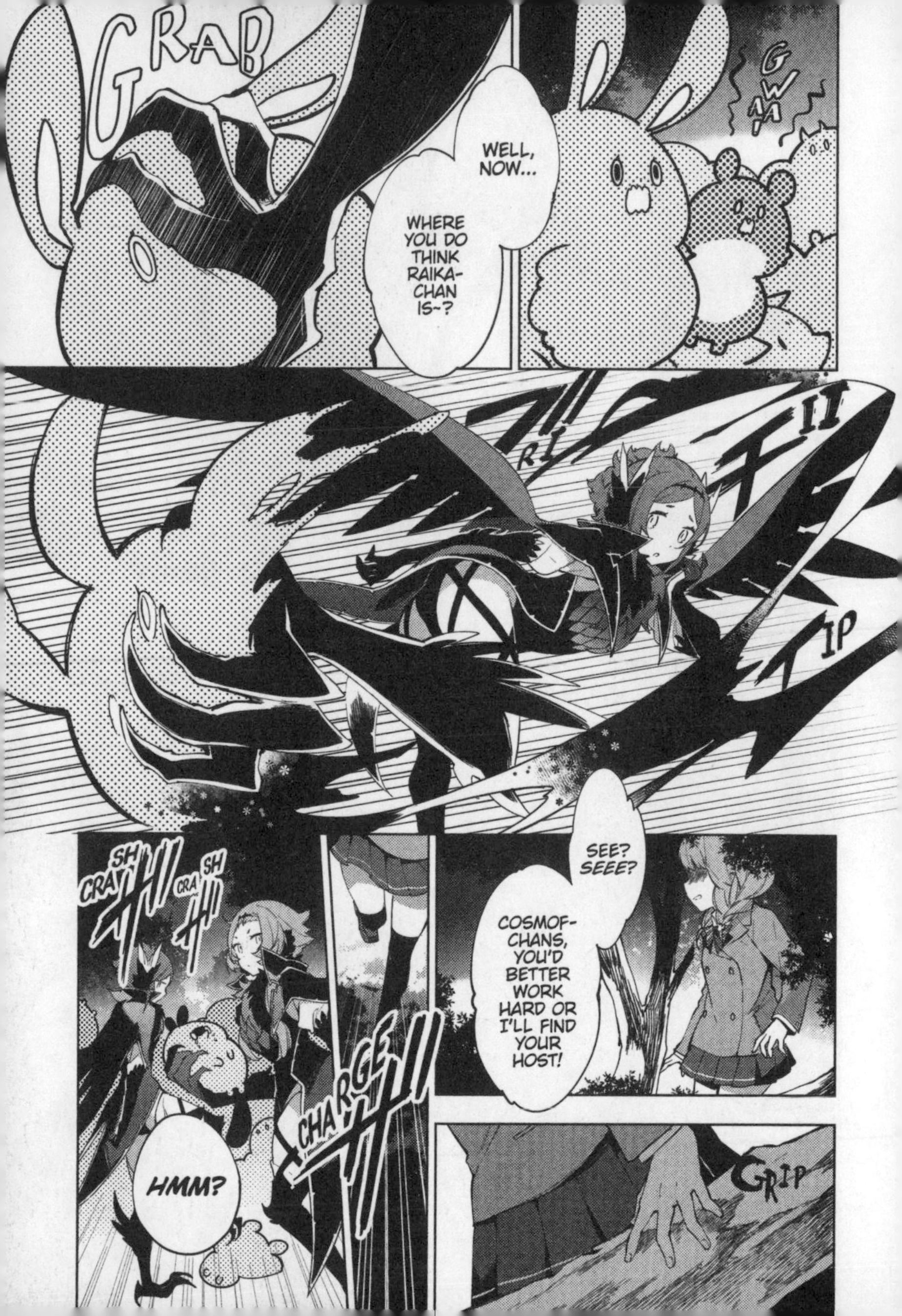
GWAAA
WELL, NOW...
WHERE YOU DO THINK RAIKA-CHAN IS~?
GRAB
RIIIIP
SEE? SEEE?
COSMOF-CHANS, YOU'D BETTER WORK HARD OR I'LL FIND YOUR HOST!
GRIP
CHARGE
CRASH
CRASH
HMM?

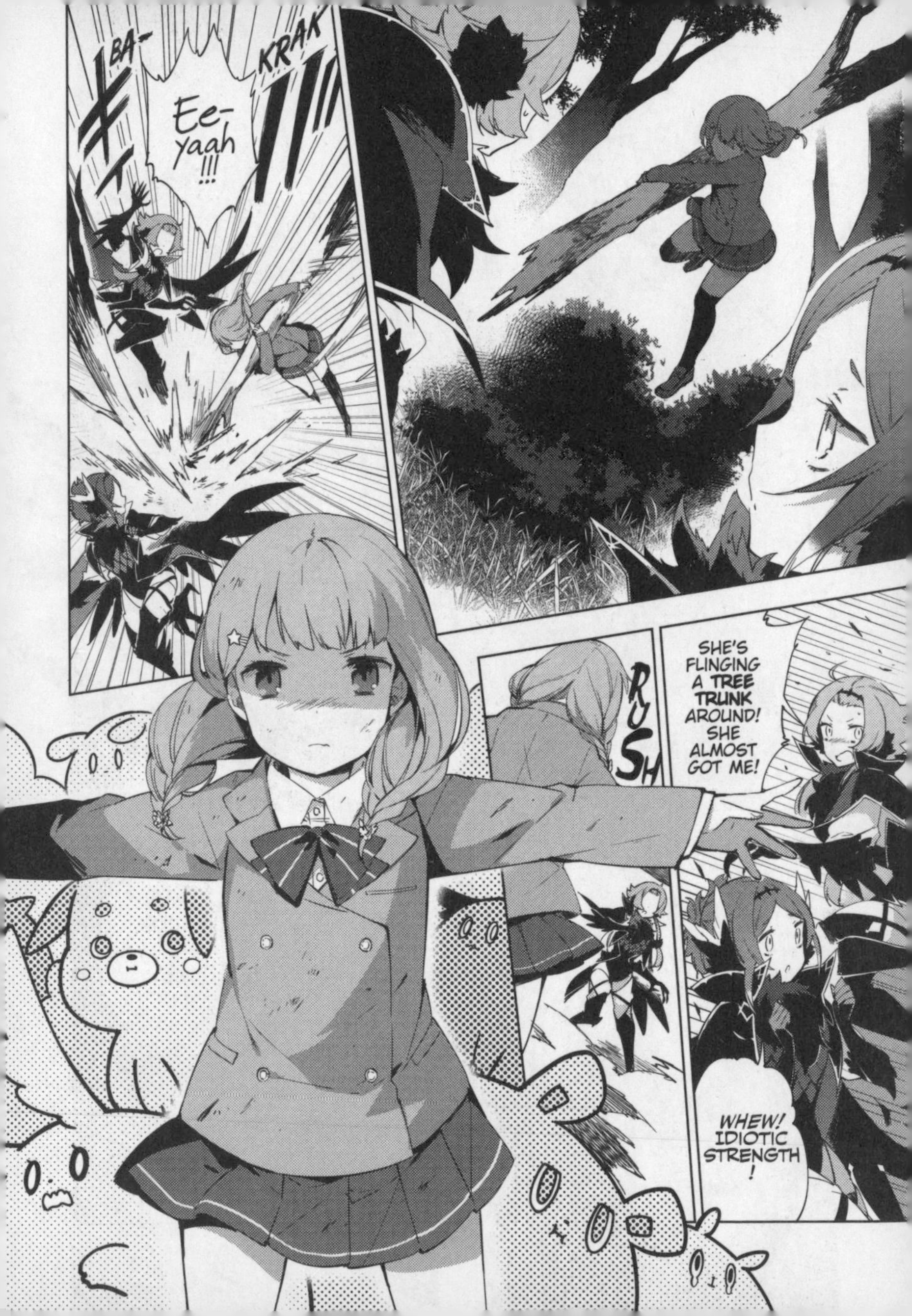
BA-KRAK
Ee-yaah!!!
SHE'S FLINGING A TREE TRUNK AROUND! SHE ALMOST GOT ME!
RUSH
WHEW! IDIOTIC STRENGTH!

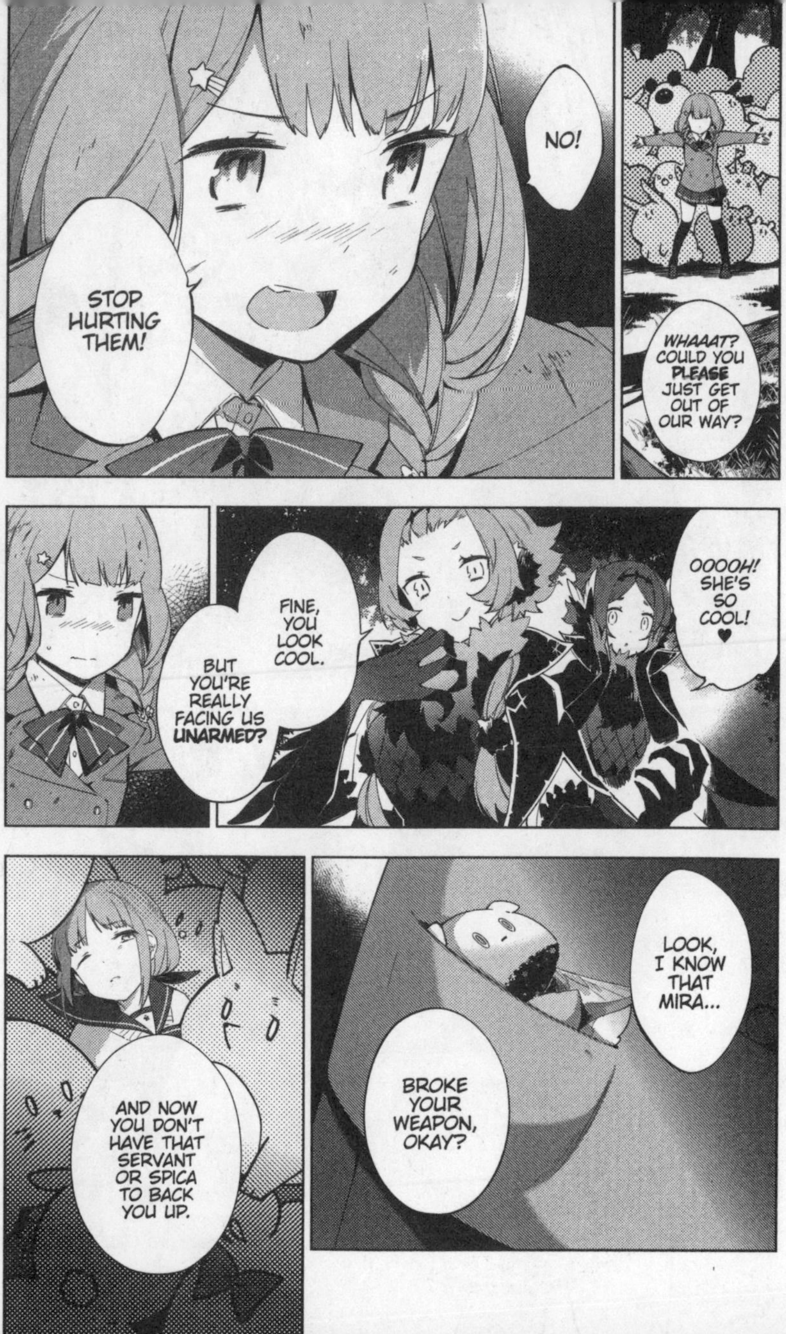
WHAAAT? COULD YOU PLEASE JUST GET OUT OF OUR WAY?
NO!
STOP HURTING THEM!
OOOOH! SHE'S SO COOL! ♥
FINE, YOU LOOK COOL.
BUT YOU'RE REALLY FACING US UNARMED?
LOOK, I KNOW THAT MIRA...
BROKE YOUR WEAPON, OKAY?
AND NOW YOU DON'T HAVE THAT SERVANT OR SPICA TO BACK YOU UP.

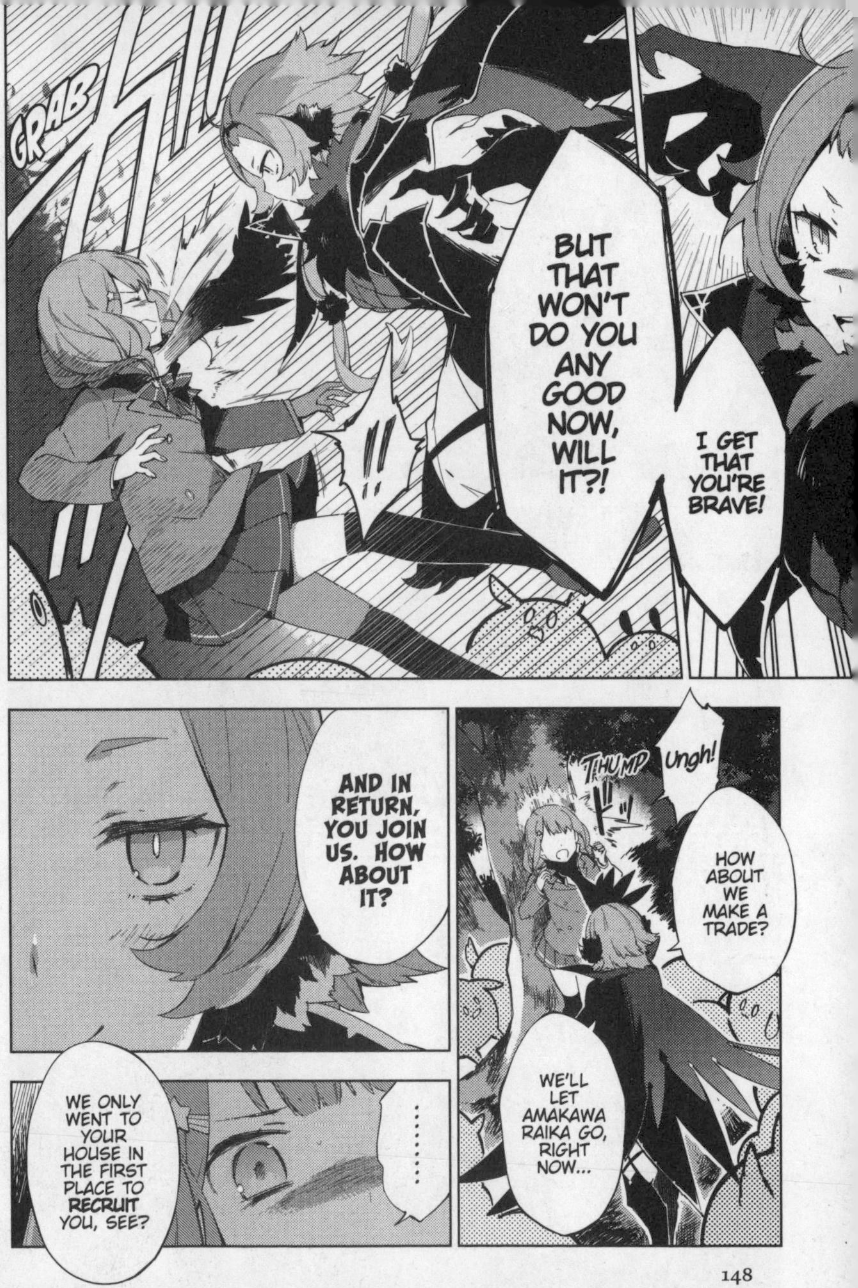

I GET THAT YOU'RE BRAVE!
BUT THAT WON'T DO YOU ANY GOOD NOW, WILL IT?!
GRAB
!!
THUMP
Ungh!
HOW ABOUT WE MAKE A TRADE?
WE'LL LET AMAKAWA RAIKA GO, RIGHT NOW...
AND IN RETURN, YOU JOIN US. HOW ABOUT IT?
......
WE ONLY WENT TO YOUR HOUSE IN THE FIRST PLACE TO RECRUIT YOU, SEE?

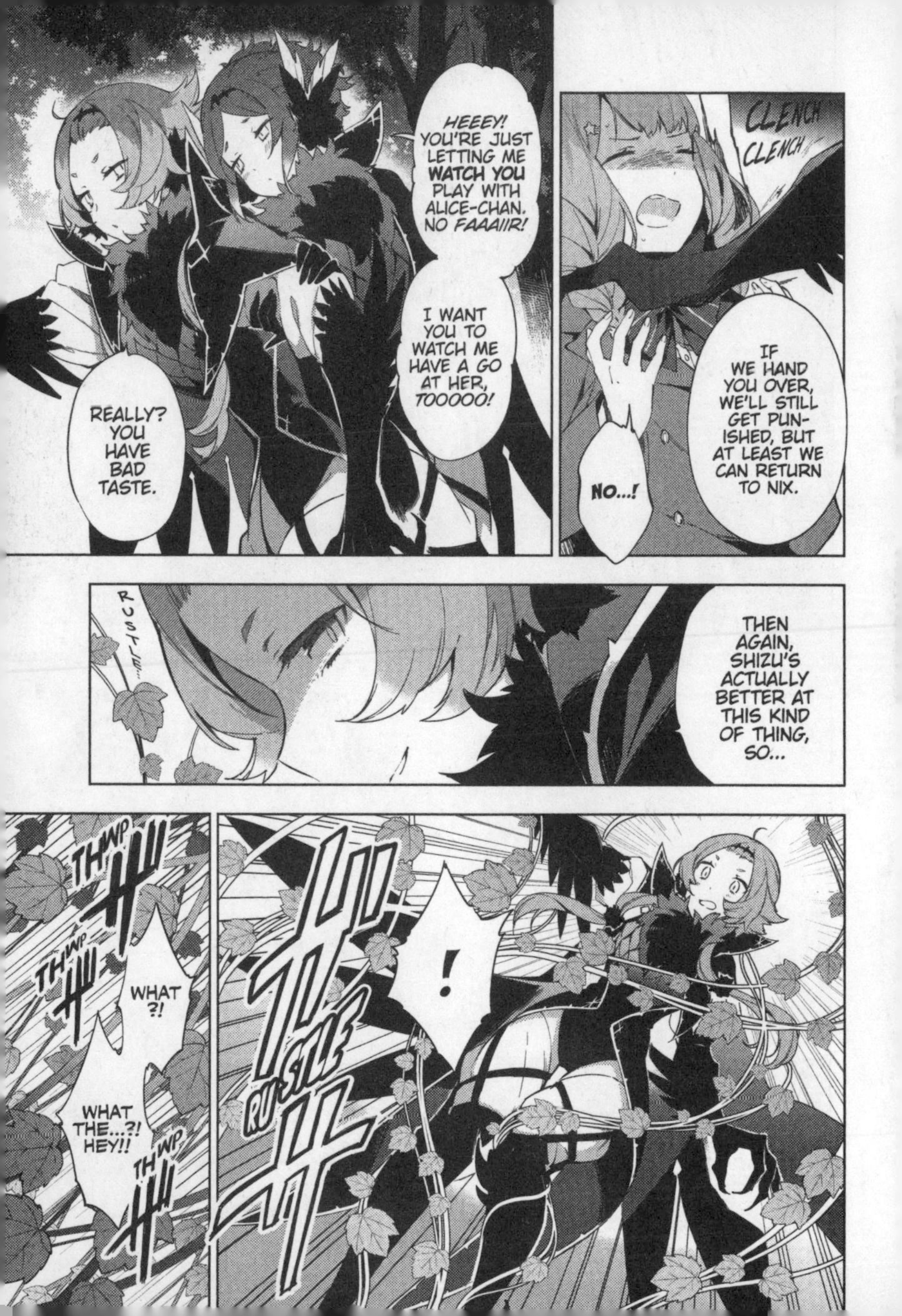
CLENCH
CLENCH
IF WE HAND YOU OVER, WE'LL STILL GET PUN-ISHED, BUT AT LEAST WE CAN RETURN TO NIX.
NO...!
HEEEY! YOU'RE JUST LETTING ME **WATCH YOU** PLAY WITH ALICE-CHAN. NO *FAAAIIR!*
I WANT YOU TO WATCH ME HAVE A GO AT HER, *TOOOOO!*
REALLY? YOU HAVE BAD TASTE.
THEN AGAIN, SHIZU'S ACTUALLY BETTER AT THIS KIND OF THING, SO...
RUSTLE...
!
RUSTLE
THWP
THWP
WHAT?!
WHAT THE...?! HEY!!
THWP

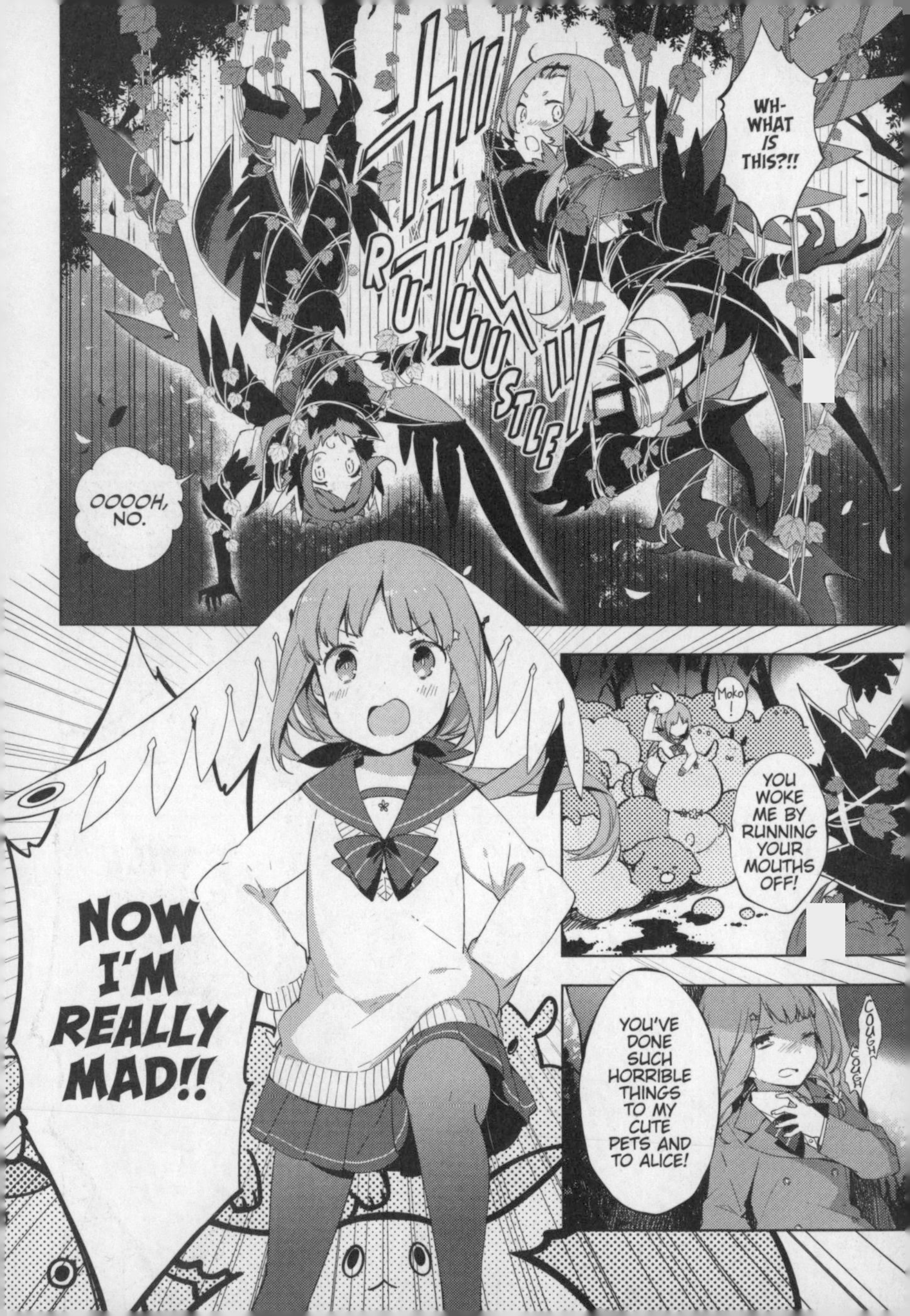
WH-WHAT IS THIS?!!
RUUUUSTLE
OOOOH, NO.
Moko!
YOU WOKE ME BY RUNNING YOUR MOUTHS OFF!
COUGH COUGH
YOU'VE DONE SUCH HORRIBLE THINGS TO MY CUTE PETS AND TO ALICE!
NOW I'M REALLY MAD!!

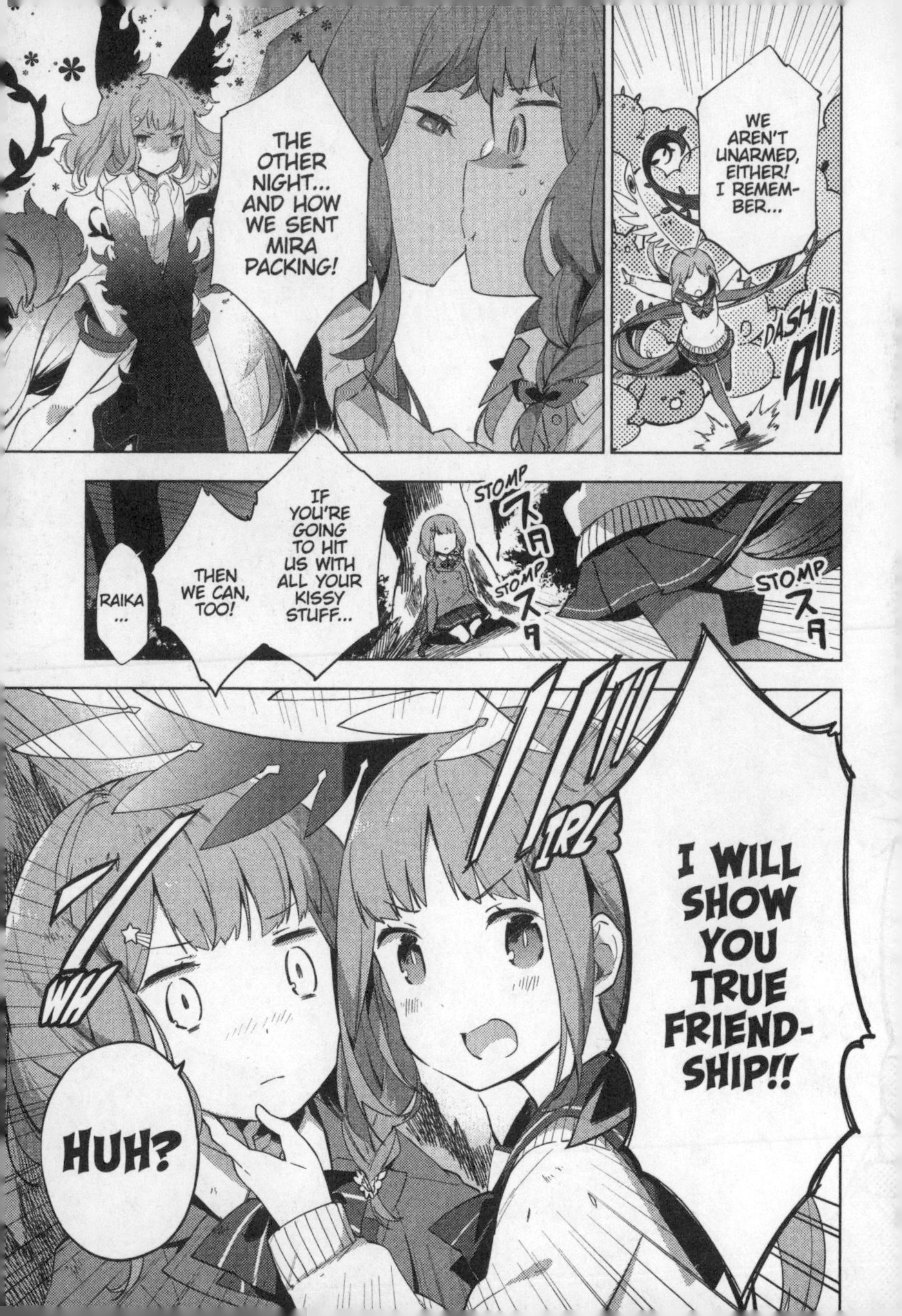
WE AREN'T UNARMED, EITHER! I REMEMBER...
DASH
THE OTHER NIGHT... AND HOW WE SENT MIRA PACKING!
STOMP
STOMP
STOMP
IF YOU'RE GOING TO HIT US WITH ALL YOUR KISSY STUFF...
THEN WE CAN, TOO!
RAIKA...
I WILL SHOW YOU TRUE FRIEND-SHIP!!
HUH?

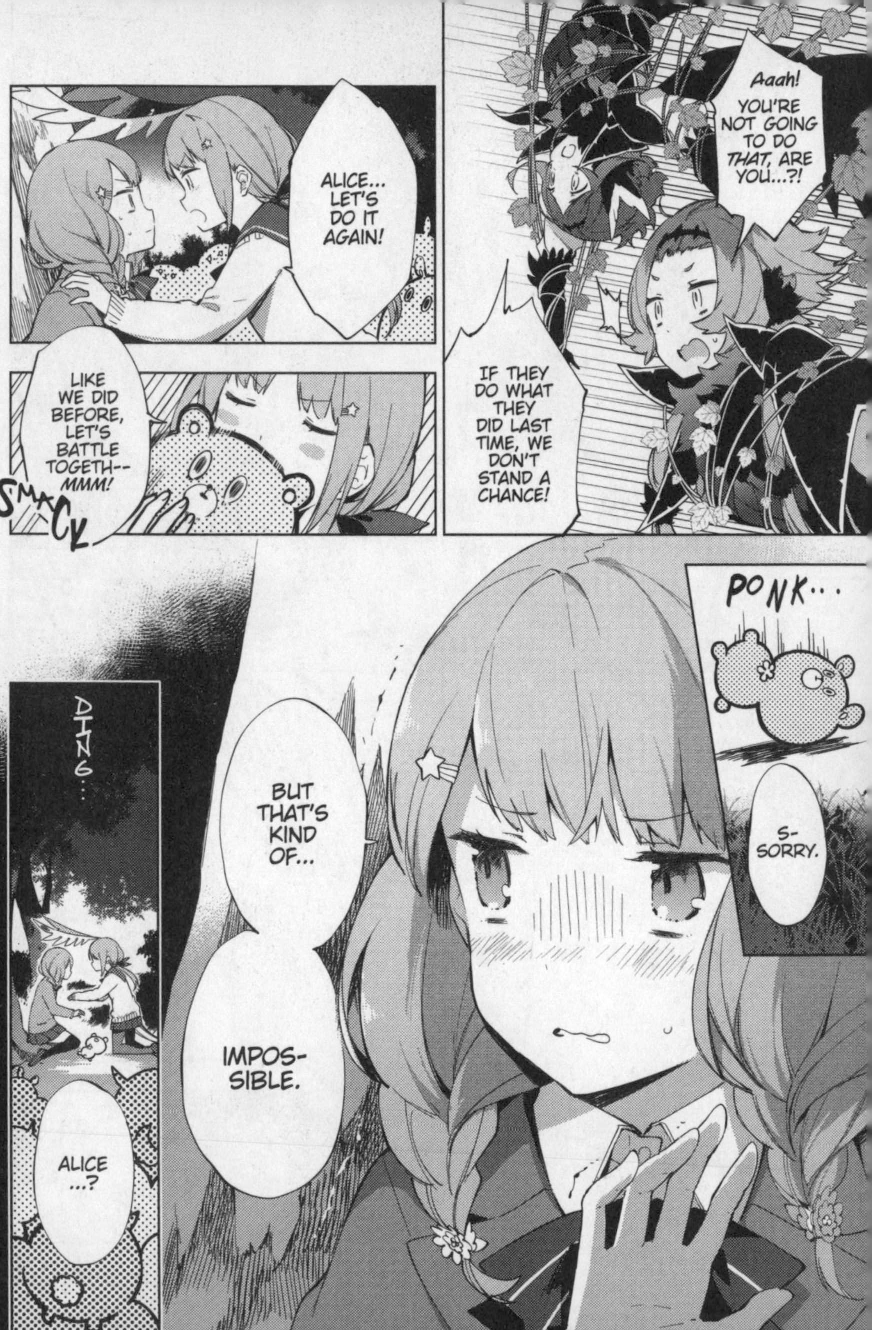
Aaah!
YOU'RE NOT GOING TO DO *THAT*, ARE YOU...?!
IF THEY DO WHAT THEY DID LAST TIME, WE DON'T STAND A CHANCE!
ALICE... LET'S DO IT AGAIN!
LIKE WE DID BEFORE, LET'S BATTLE TOGETH--MMM!
SMACK
PONK...
S-SORRY.
BUT THAT'S KIND OF...
IMPOSSIBLE.
DING...
ALICE ...?

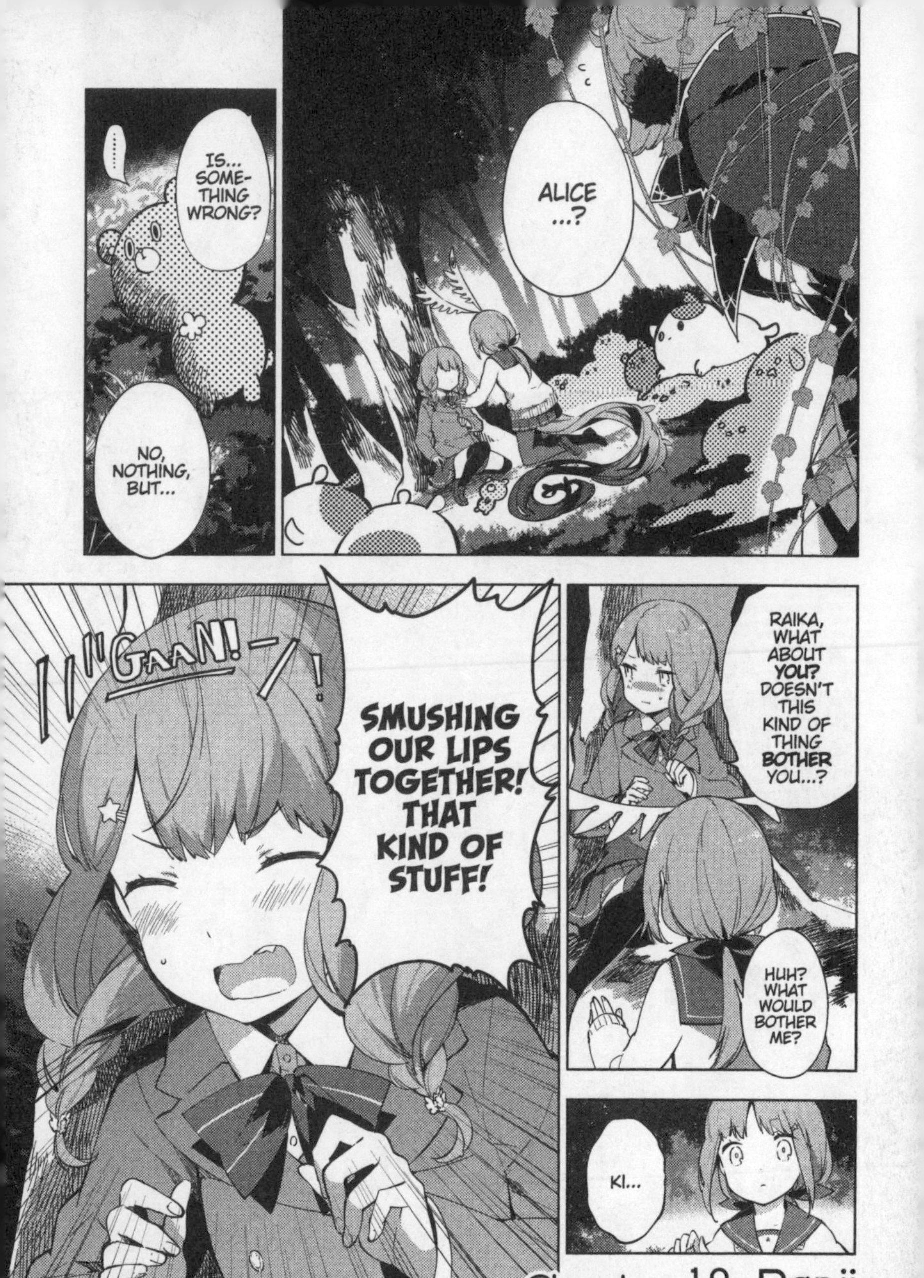
ALICE ...?
......
IS... SOMETHING WRONG?
NO, NOTHING, BUT...
RAIKA, WHAT ABOUT YOU? DOESN'T THIS KIND OF THING BOTHER YOU...?
HUH? WHAT WOULD BOTHER ME?
KI...
GAAN!
SMUSHING OUR LIPS TOGETHER! THAT KIND OF STUFF!

## Chapter 19 Papii

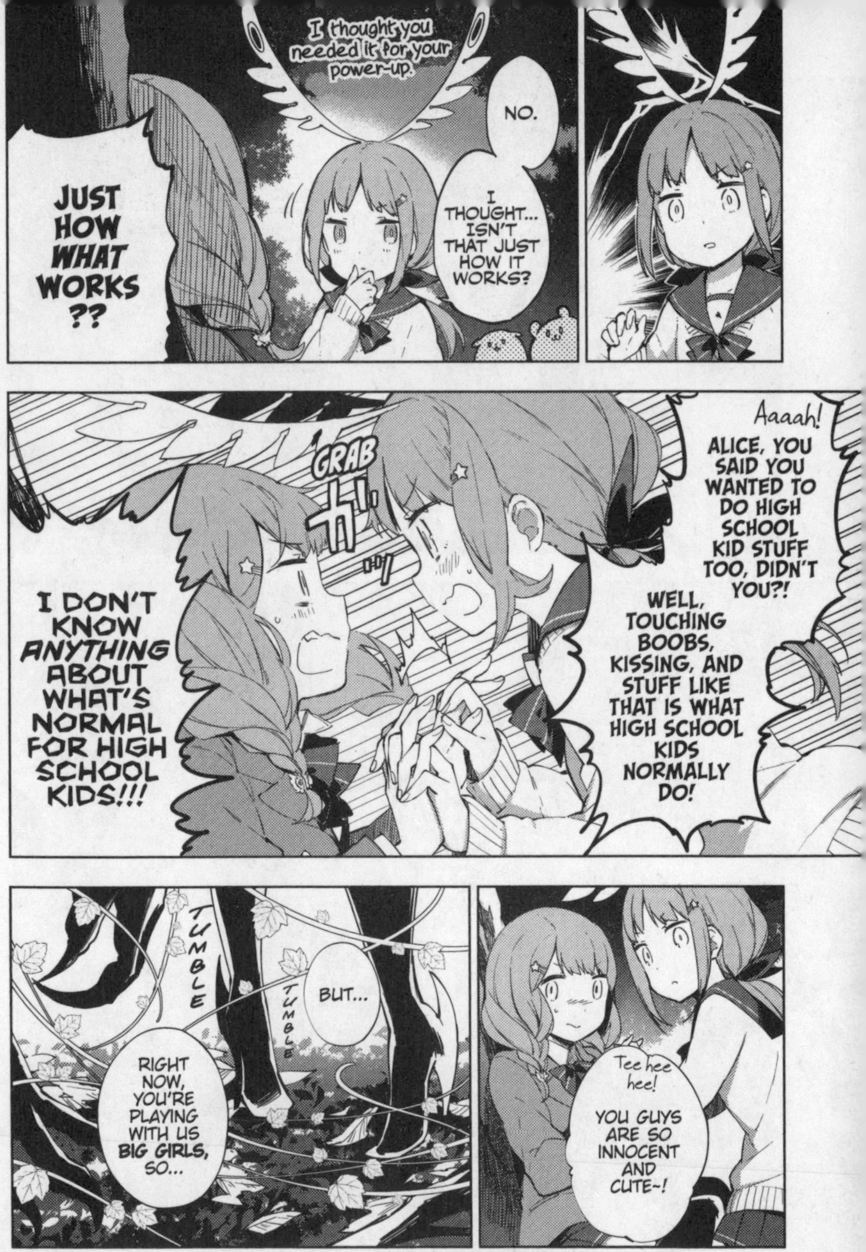
I thought you needed it for your power-up.
NO.
I THOUGHT... ISN'T THAT JUST HOW IT WORKS?
JUST HOW WHAT WORKS??
Aaaah!
ALICE, YOU SAID YOU WANTED TO DO HIGH SCHOOL KID STUFF TOO, DIDN'T YOU?!
WELL, TOUCHING BOOBS, KISSING, AND STUFF LIKE THAT IS WHAT HIGH SCHOOL KIDS NORMALLY DO!
GRAB
ガッ
I DON'T KNOW ANYTHING ABOUT WHAT'S NORMAL FOR HIGH SCHOOL KIDS!!!
Tee hee hee!
YOU GUYS ARE SO INNOCENT AND CUTE~!
TUMBLE
BUT...
TUMBLE
RIGHT NOW, YOU'RE PLAYING WITH US BIG GIRLS, SO...

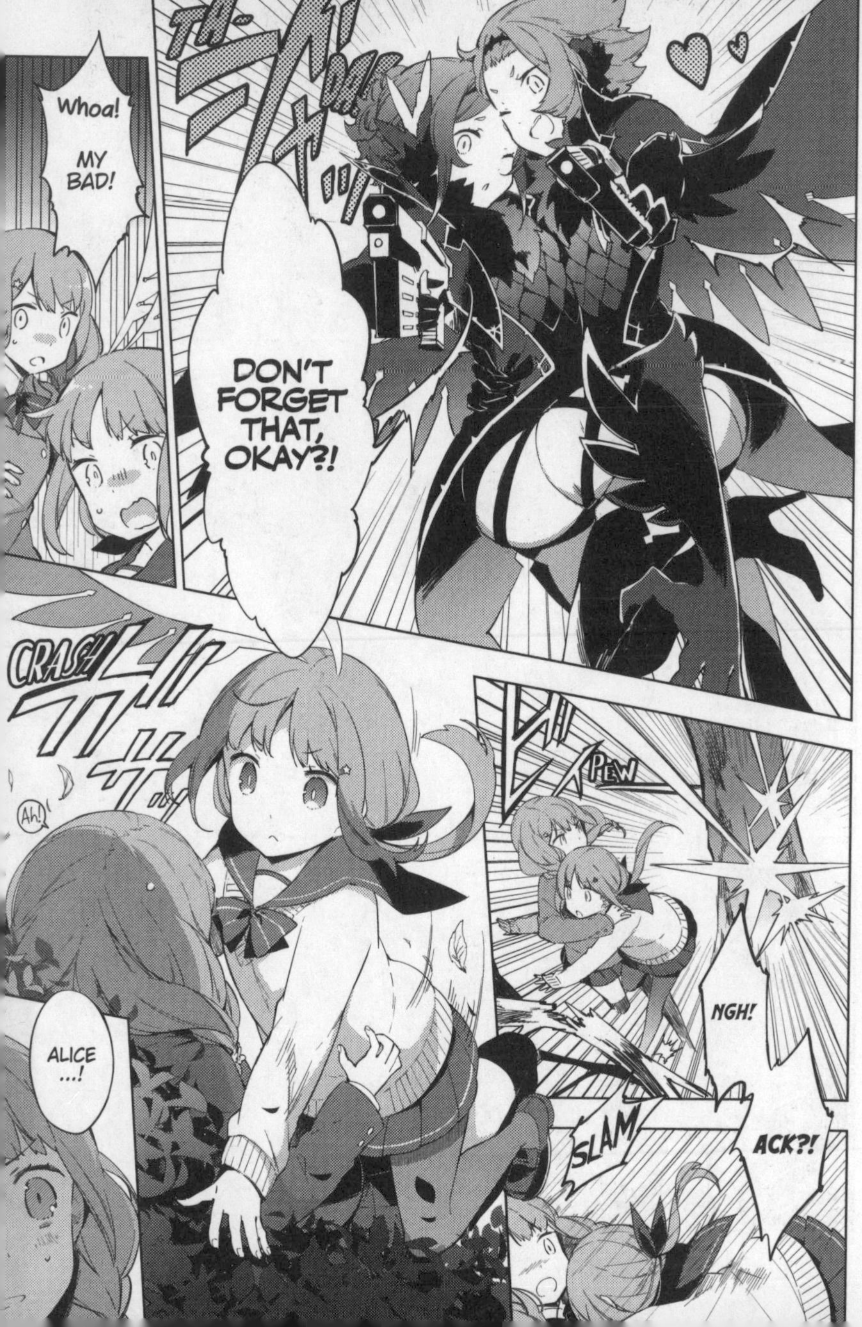

TH-DMP
DON'T FORGET THAT, OKAY?!
Whoa!
MY BAD!
PEW
NGH!
SLAM
ACK?!
CRASH
Ah!
ALICE ...!

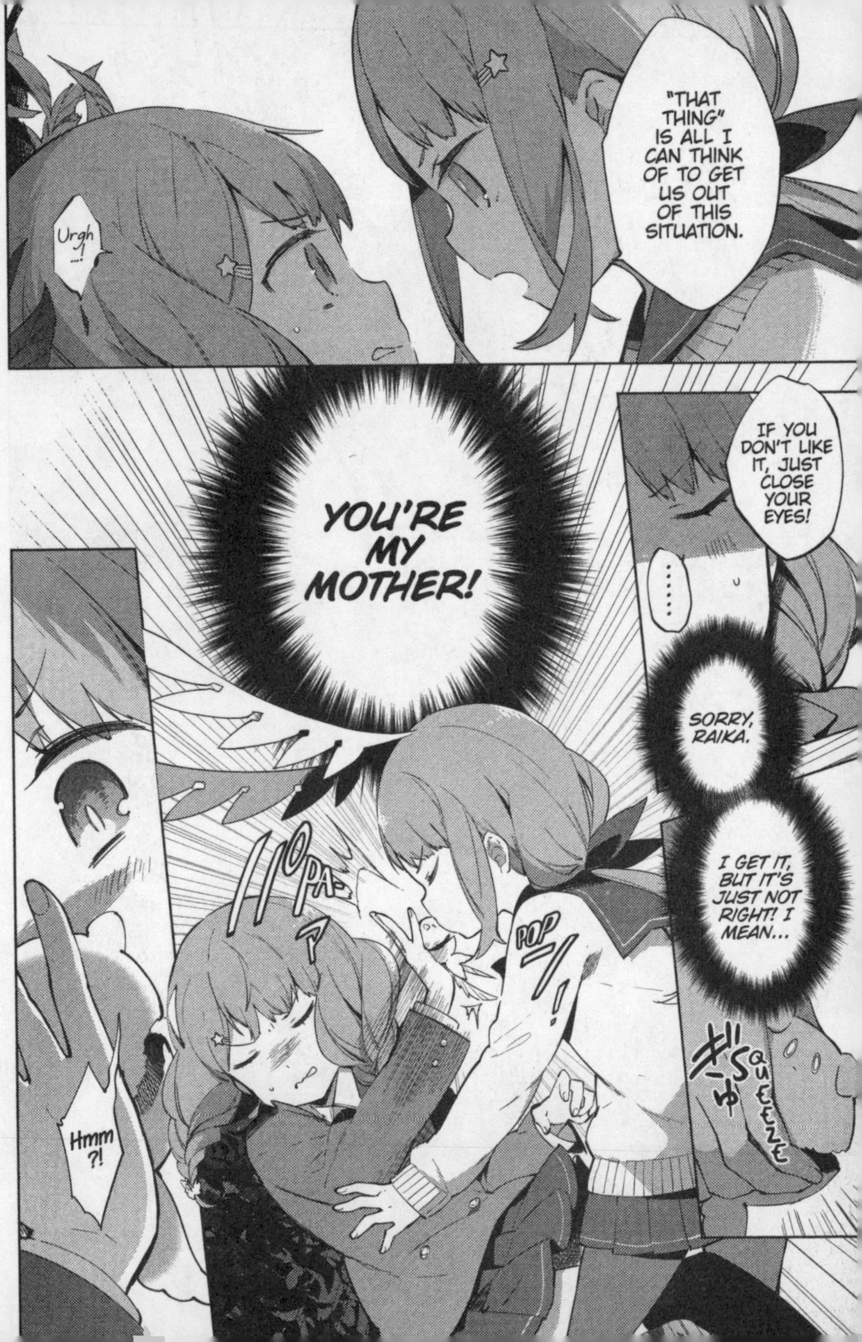
"THAT THING" IS ALL I CAN THINK OF TO GET US OUT OF THIS SITUATION.
Urgh...!
IF YOU DON'T LIKE IT, JUST CLOSE YOUR EYES!
......
YOU'RE MY MOTHER!
SORRY, RAIKA.
I GET IT, BUT IT'S JUST NOT RIGHT! I MEAN...
POP
OPA
SQUEEZE
Hmm?!

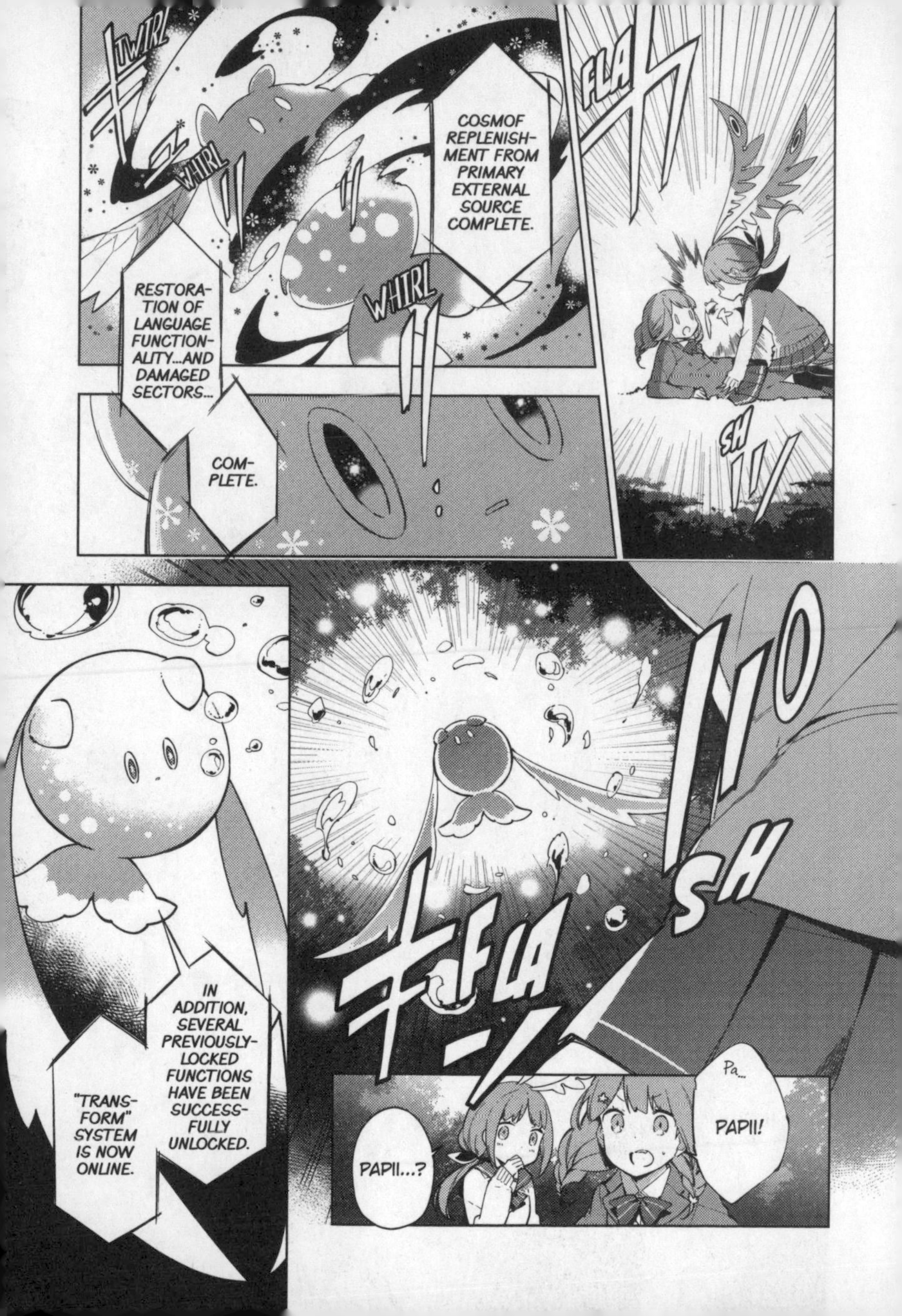
FLA
SH
COSMOF REPLENISHMENT FROM PRIMARY EXTERNAL SOURCE COMPLETE.
SWIRL
WHIRL
WHIRL
RESTORATION OF LANGUAGE FUNCTIONALITY...AND DAMAGED SECTORS...
COMPLETE.
SH
FLA
Pa...
PAPII!
PAPII...?
IN ADDITION, SEVERAL PREVIOUSLY-LOCKED FUNCTIONS HAVE BEEN SUCCESSFULLY UNLOCKED.
"TRANSFORM" SYSTEM IS NOW ONLINE.

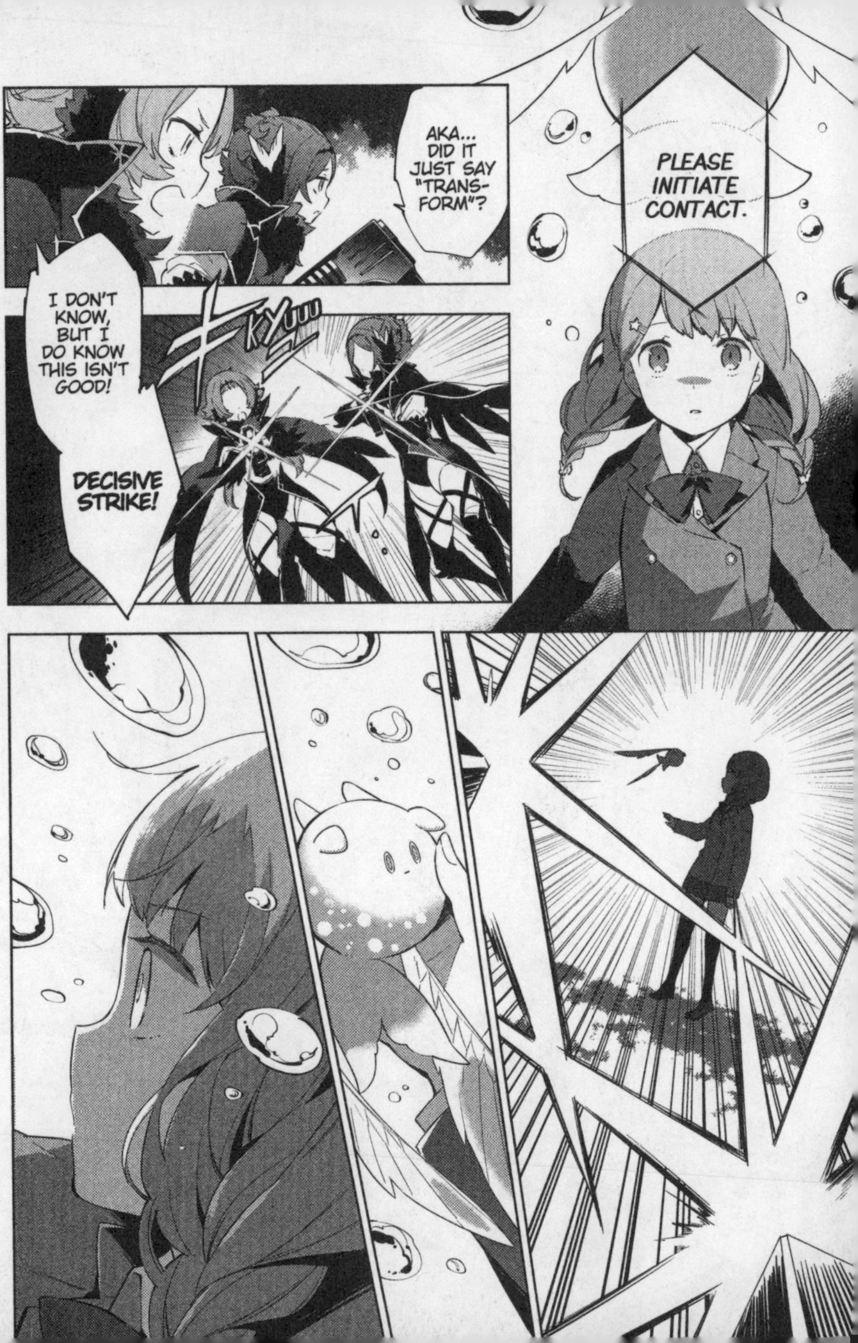

PLEASE INITIATE CONTACT.
AKA... DID IT JUST SAY "TRANS-FORM"?
I DON'T KNOW, BUT I DO KNOW THIS ISN'T GOOD!
KYUUU
DECISIVE STRIKE!

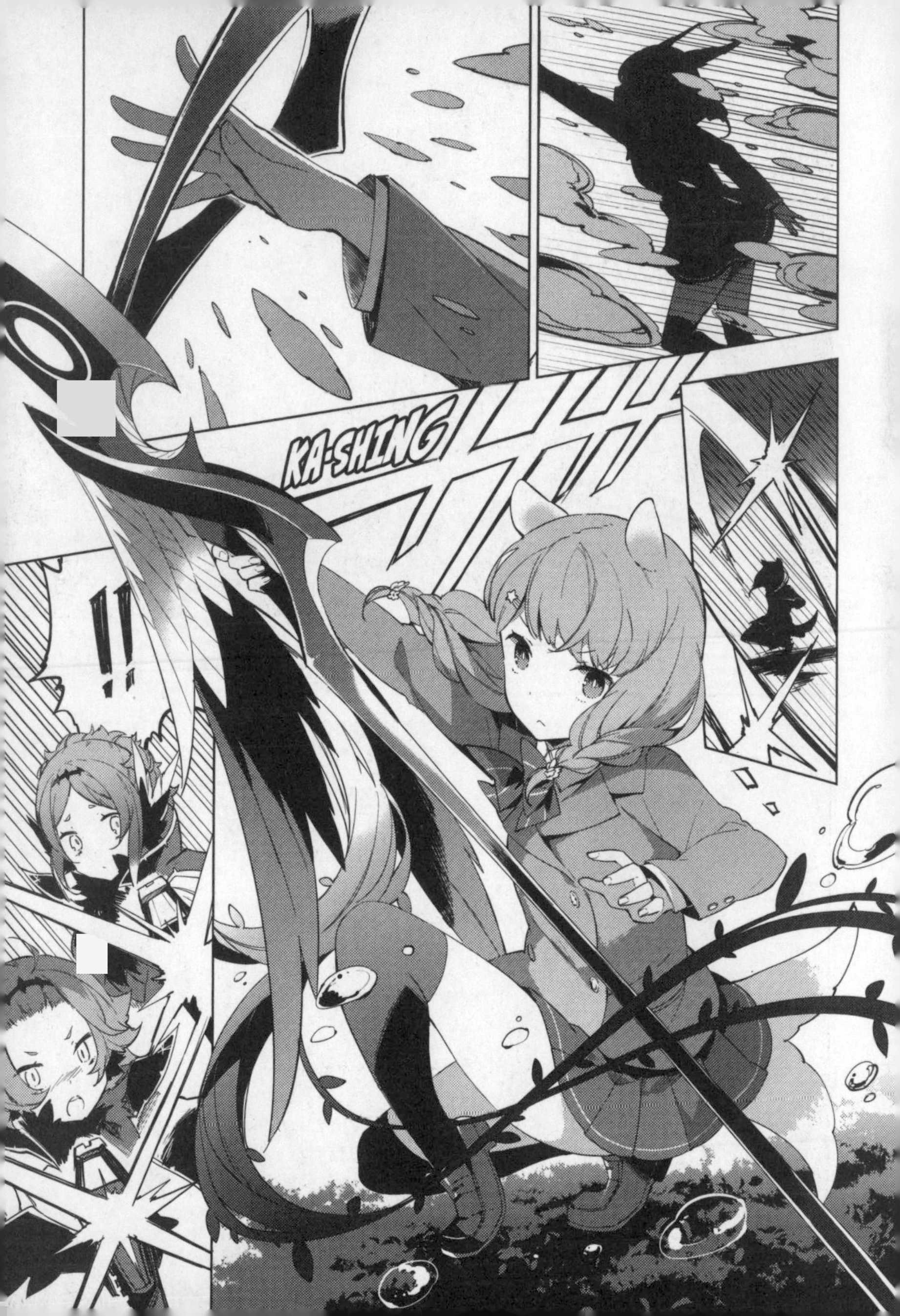
KA-SHING
!!

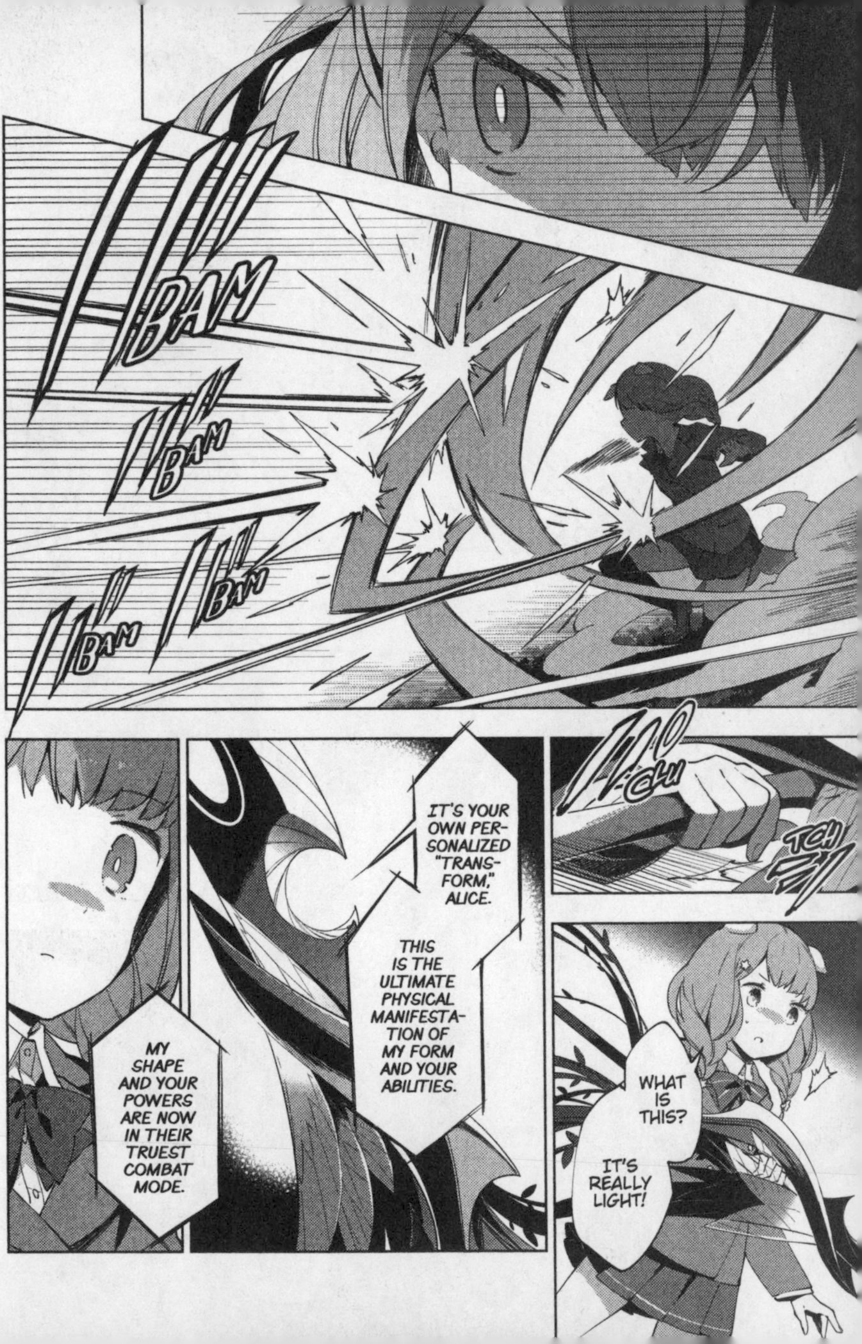
BAM
BAM
BAM
BAM
CLU
TCH
WHAT IS THIS?
IT'S REALLY LIGHT!
IT'S YOUR OWN PERSONALIZED "TRANSFORM," ALICE.
THIS IS THE ULTIMATE PHYSICAL MANIFESTATION OF MY FORM AND YOUR ABILITIES.
MY SHAPE AND YOUR POWERS ARE NOW IN THEIR TRUEST COMBAT MODE.

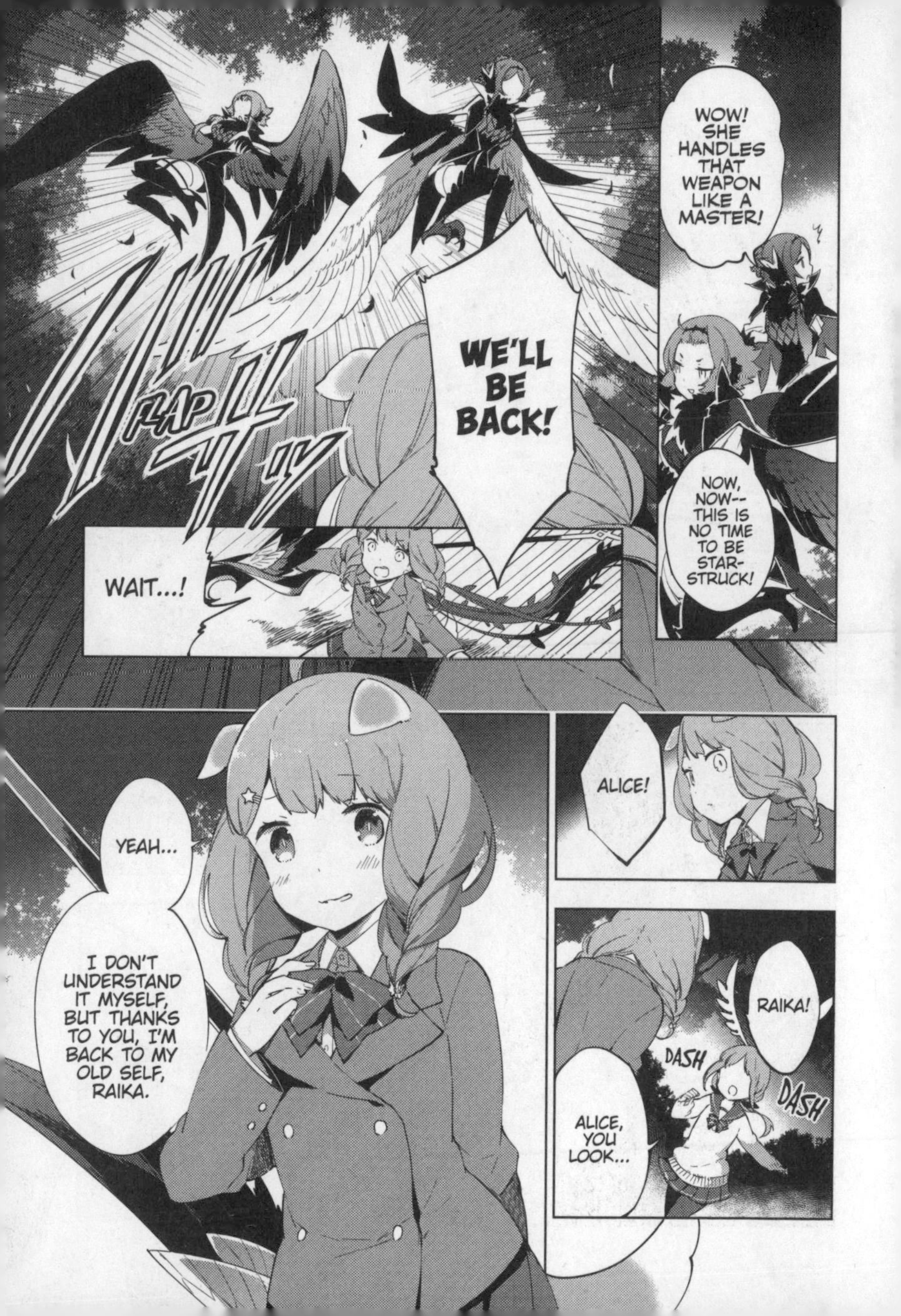
WOW! SHE HANDLES THAT WEAPON LIKE A MASTER!
NOW, NOW-- THIS IS NO TIME TO BE STAR-STRUCK!
WE'LL BE BACK!
FLAP
WAIT...!
ALICE!
RAIKA!
DASH
DASH
ALICE, YOU LOOK...
YEAH...
I DON'T UNDERSTAND IT MYSELF, BUT THANKS TO YOU, I'M BACK TO MY OLD SELF, RAIKA.

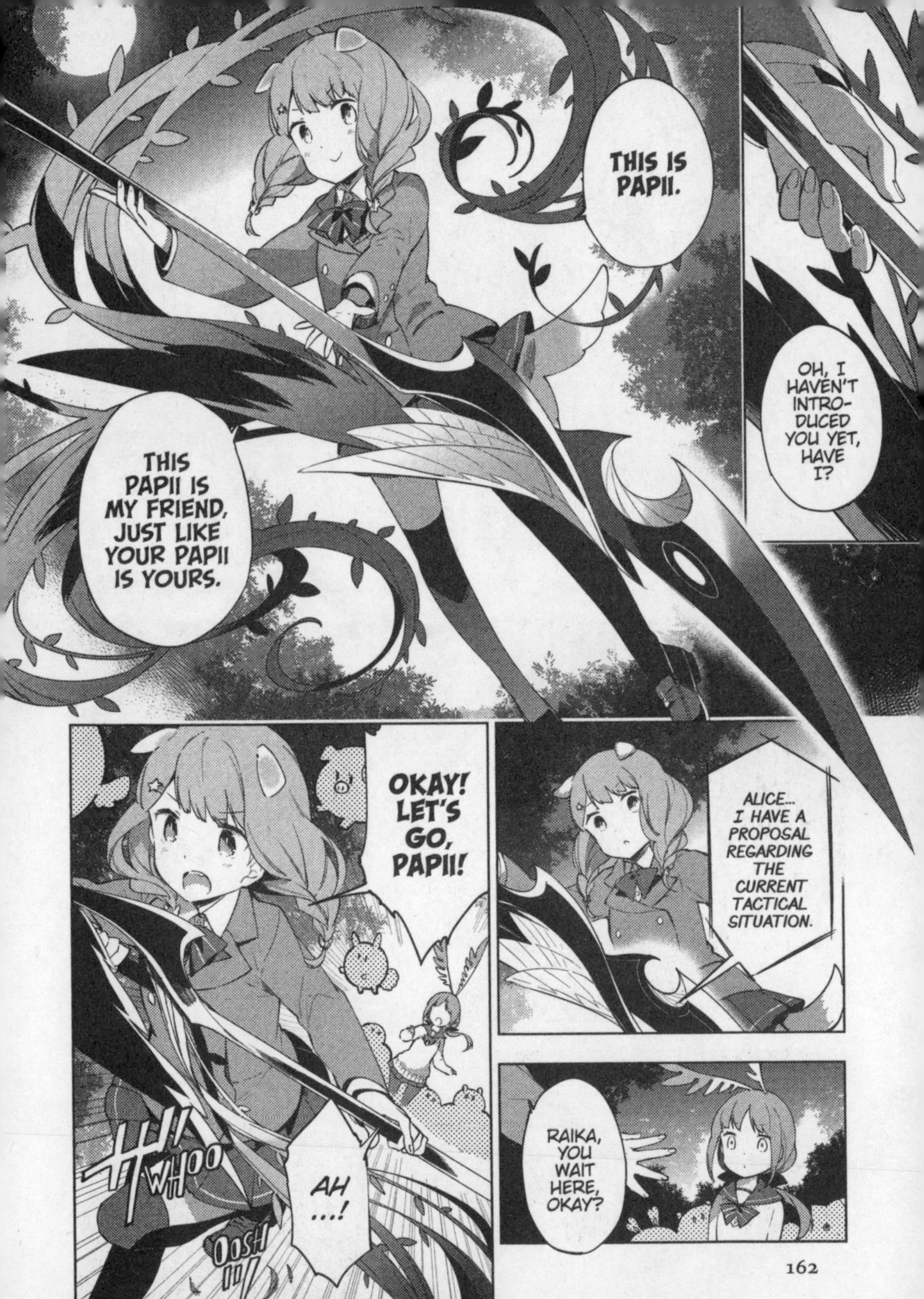
OH, I HAVEN'T INTRO-DUCED YOU YET, HAVE I?
THIS IS PAPII.
THIS PAPII IS MY FRIEND, JUST LIKE YOUR PAPII IS YOURS.
ALICE... I HAVE A PROPOSAL REGARDING THE CURRENT TACTICAL SITUATION.
RAIKA, YOU WAIT HERE, OKAY?
OKAY! LET'S GO, PAPII!
AH ...!
WHOO
OOSH

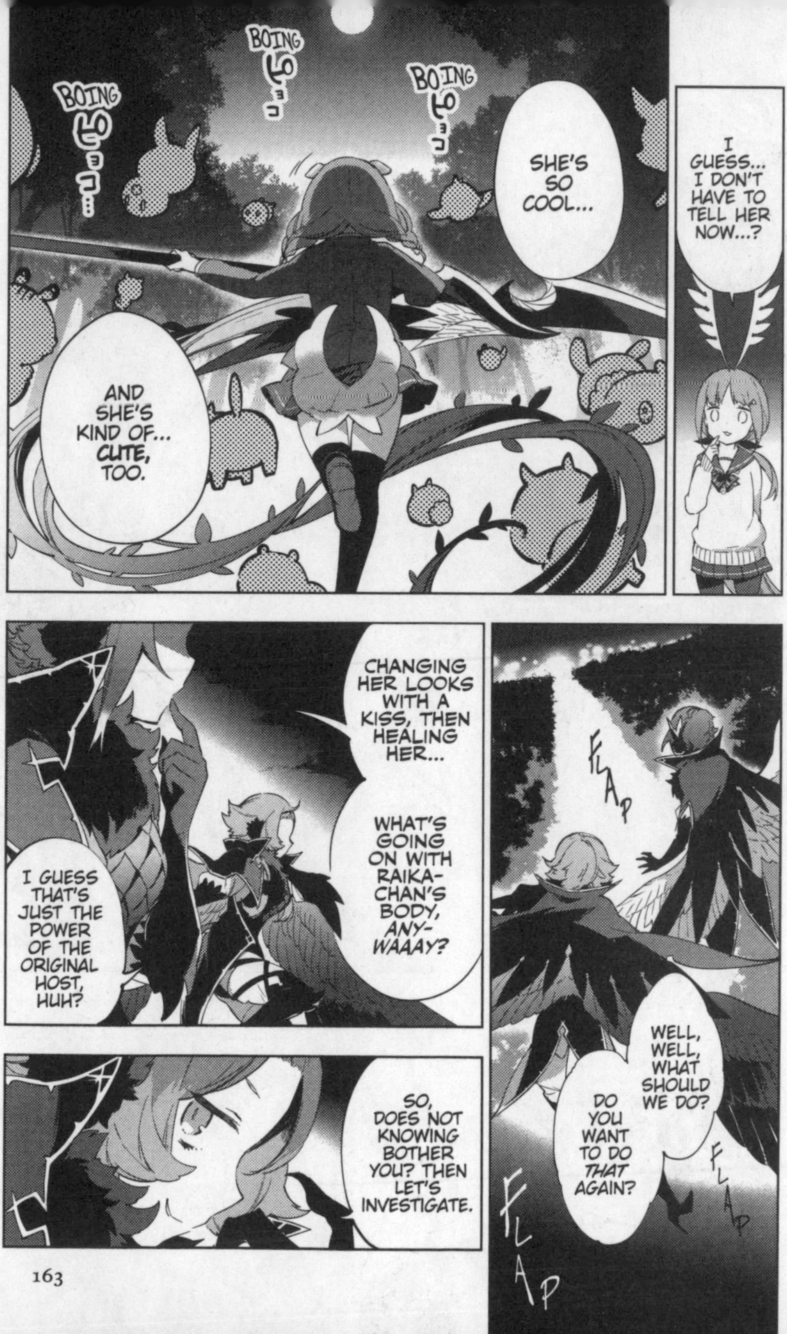
I GUESS... I DON'T HAVE TO TELL HER NOW...?
SHE'S SO COOL...
BOING ピョコ
BOING ピョコ
BOING ピョコ…
AND SHE'S KIND OF... CUTE, TOO.
FLAP
WELL, WELL, WHAT SHOULD WE DO?
DO YOU WANT TO DO *THAT* AGAIN?
FLAP
FLAP
CHANGING HER LOOKS WITH A KISS, THEN HEALING HER...
WHAT'S GOING ON WITH RAIKA-CHAN'S BODY, ANY-WAAAY?
I GUESS THAT'S JUST THE POWER OF THE ORIGINAL HOST, HUH?
SO, DOES NOT KNOWING BOTHER YOU? THEN LET'S INVESTIGATE.

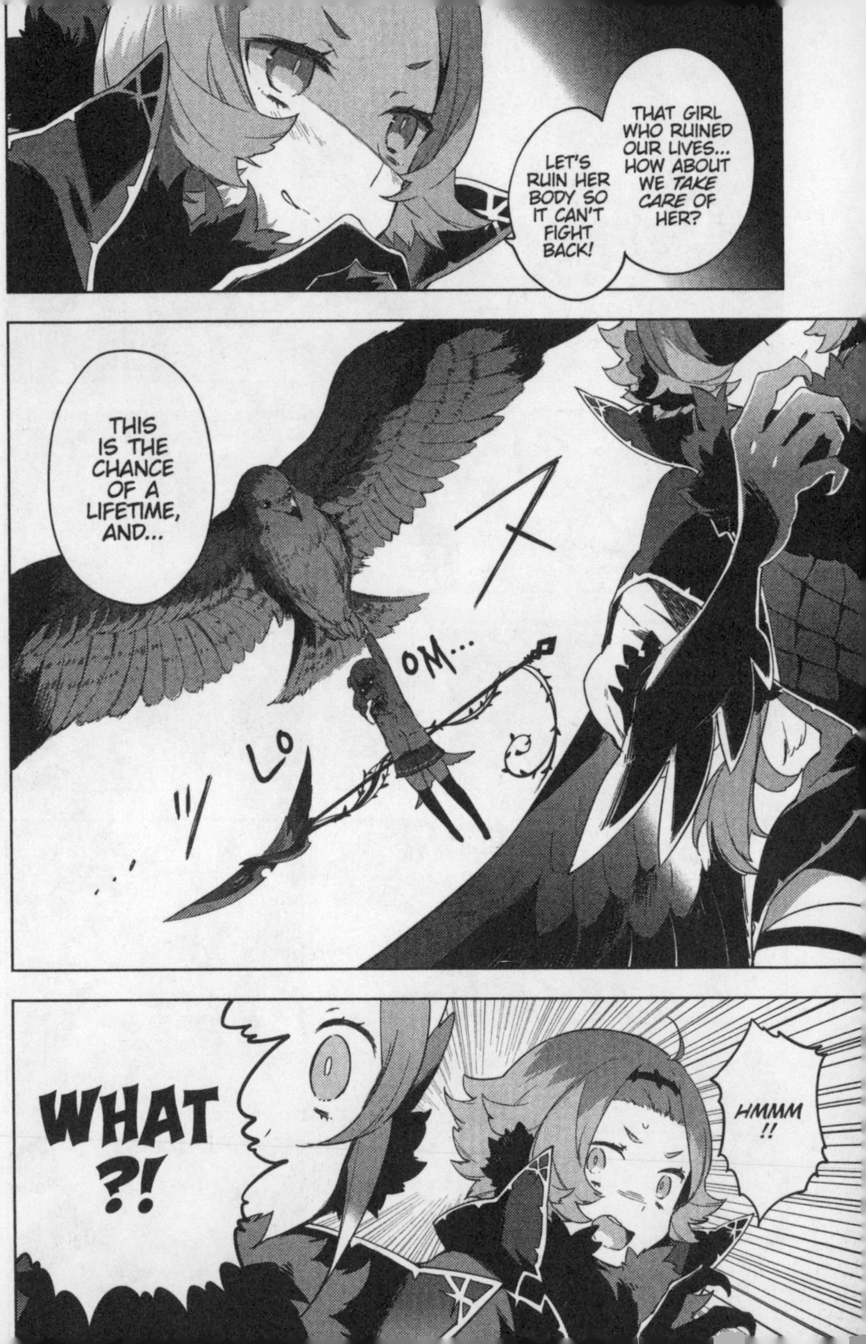
THAT GIRL WHO RUINED OUR LIVES... HOW ABOUT WE *TAKE CARE* OF HER?
LET'S RUIN HER BODY SO IT CAN'T FIGHT BACK!
THIS IS THE CHANCE OF A LIFETIME, AND...
OM...
HMMM !!
WHAT ?!

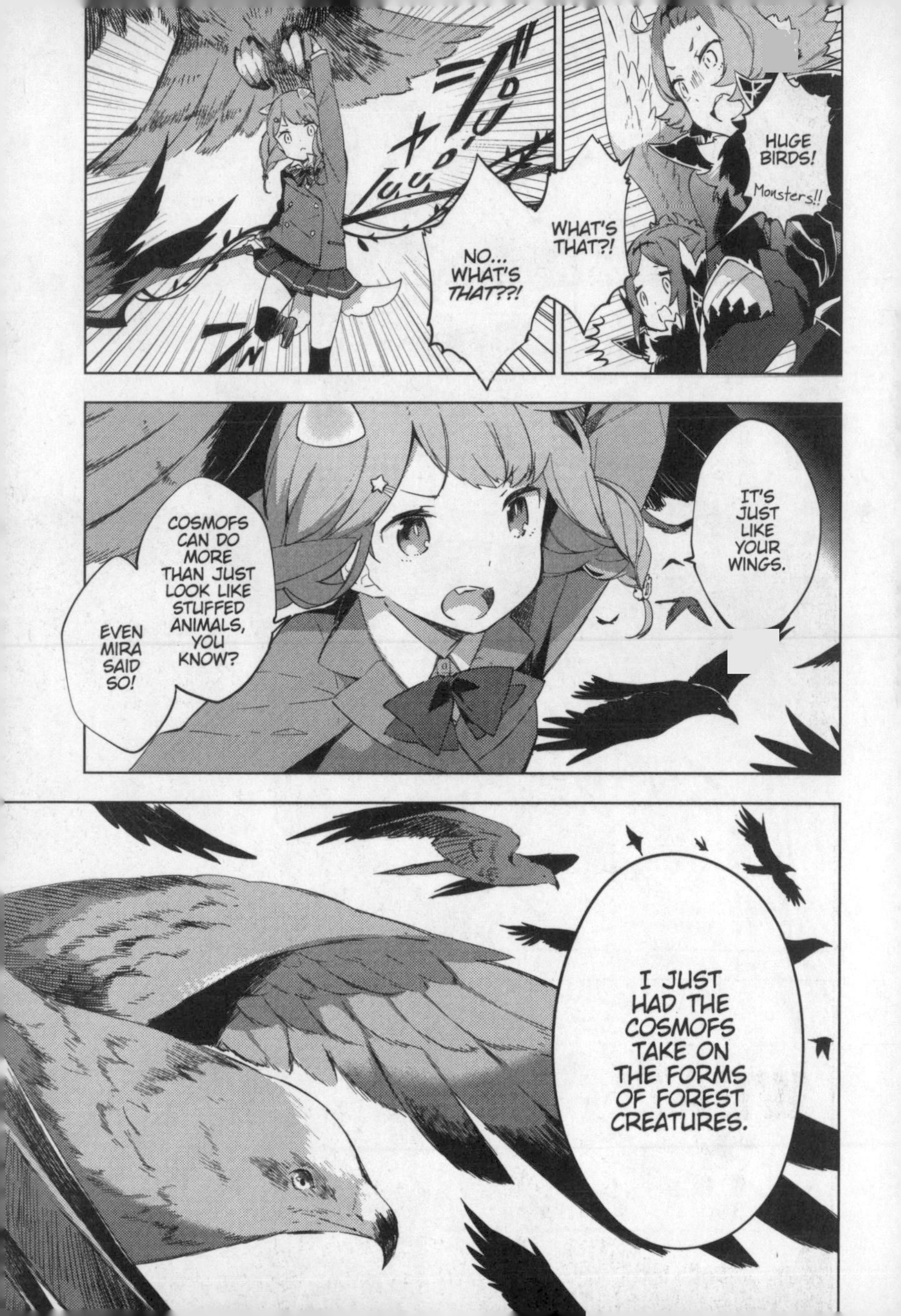
HUGE BIRDS!
Monsters!!
WHAT'S THAT?!
NO... WHAT'S *THAT??!*
IT'S JUST LIKE YOUR WINGS.
COSMOFS CAN DO MORE THAN JUST LOOK LIKE STUFFED ANIMALS, YOU KNOW?
EVEN MIRA SAID SO!
I JUST HAD THE COSMOFS TAKE ON THE FORMS OF FOREST CREATURES.

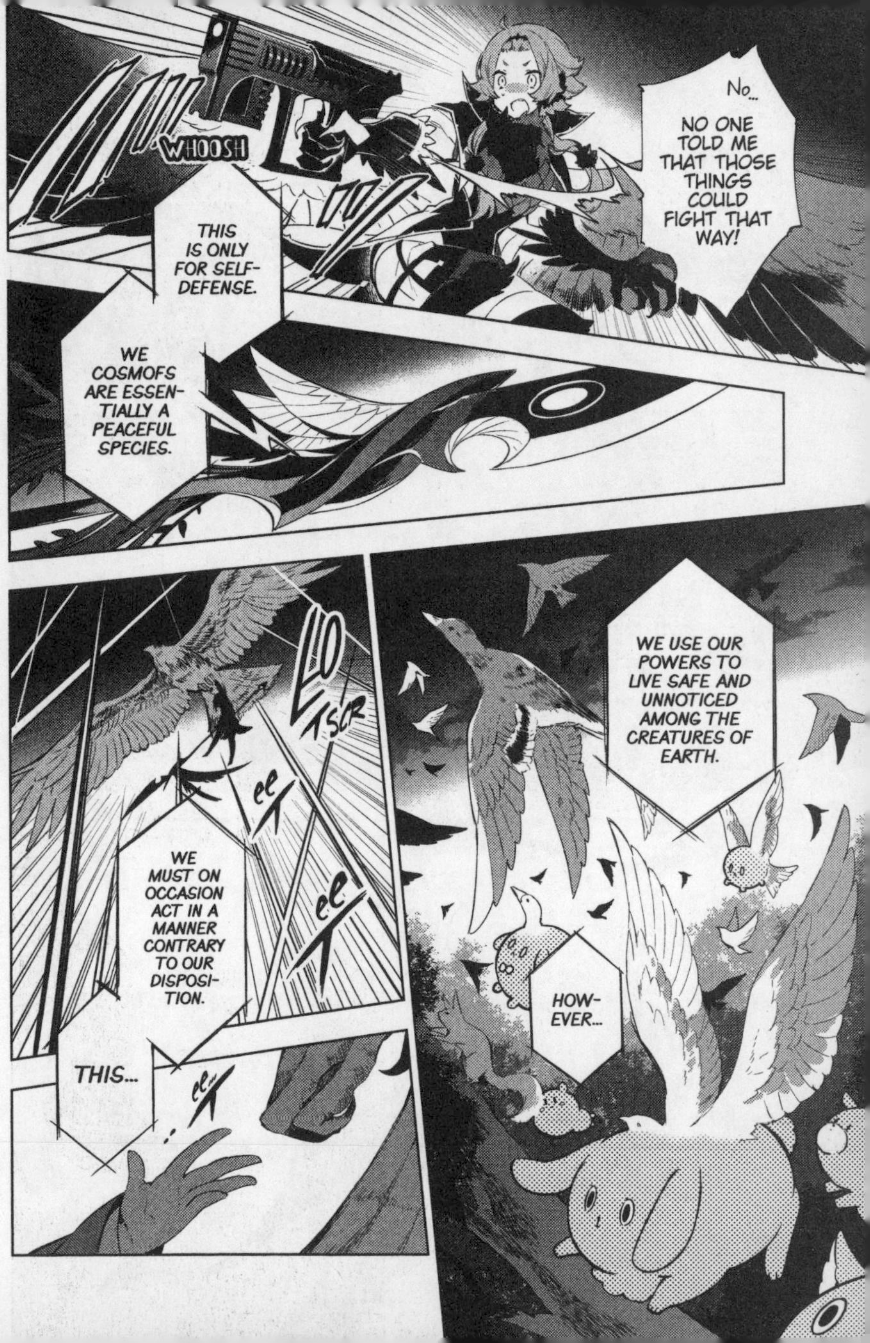
No...
NO ONE TOLD ME THAT THOSE THINGS COULD FIGHT THAT WAY!
WHOOSH
THIS IS ONLY FOR SELF-DEFENSE.
WE COSMOFS ARE ESSEN-TIALLY A PEACEFUL SPECIES.
WE USE OUR POWERS TO LIVE SAFE AND UNNOTICED AMONG THE CREATURES OF EARTH.
HOW-EVER...
SCR
ee
WE MUST ON OCCASION ACT IN A MANNER CONTRARY TO OUR DISPOSI-TION.
ee
THIS...
ee...

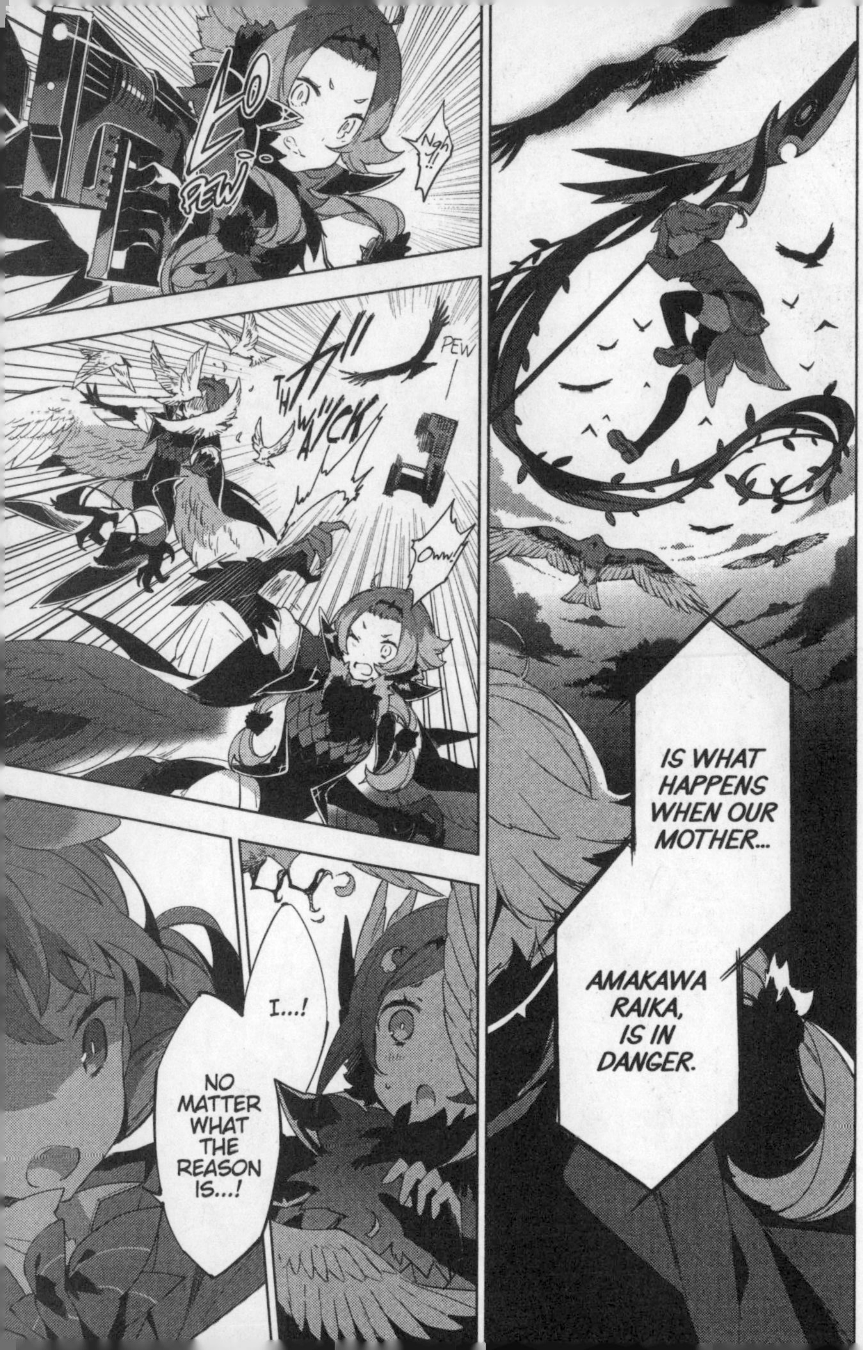
IS WHAT HAPPENS WHEN OUR MOTHER...
AMAKAWA RAIKA, IS IN DANGER.
Ngh!!
PEW
PEW
THWACK
Oww!!
I...!
NO MATTER WHAT THE REASON IS...!

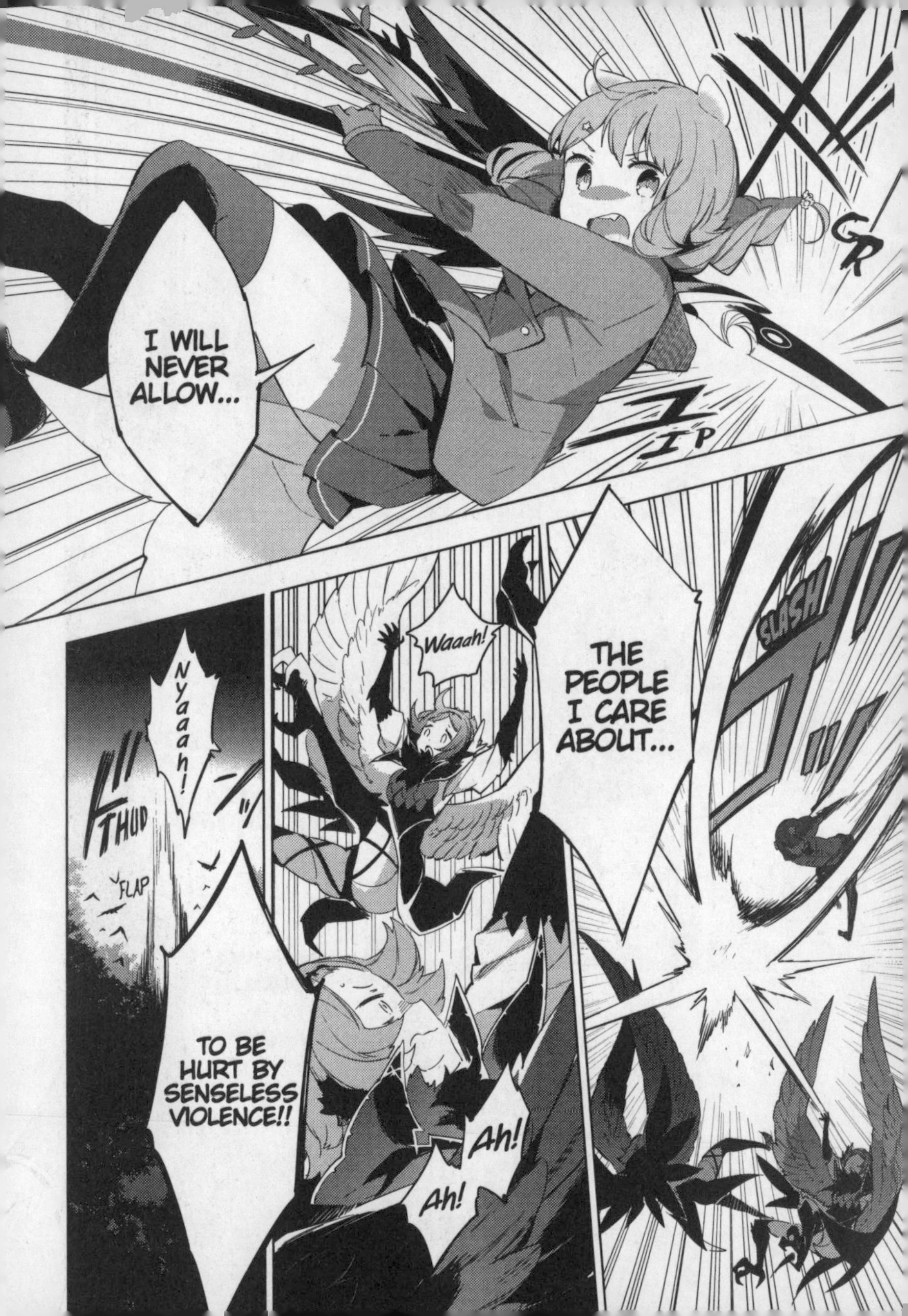
GR
ZIP
I WILL NEVER ALLOW...
SLASH!
THE PEOPLE I CARE ABOUT...
Waaah!
Nyaaah!
THUD
FLAP
TO BE HURT BY SENSELESS VIOLENCE!!
Ah!
Ah!

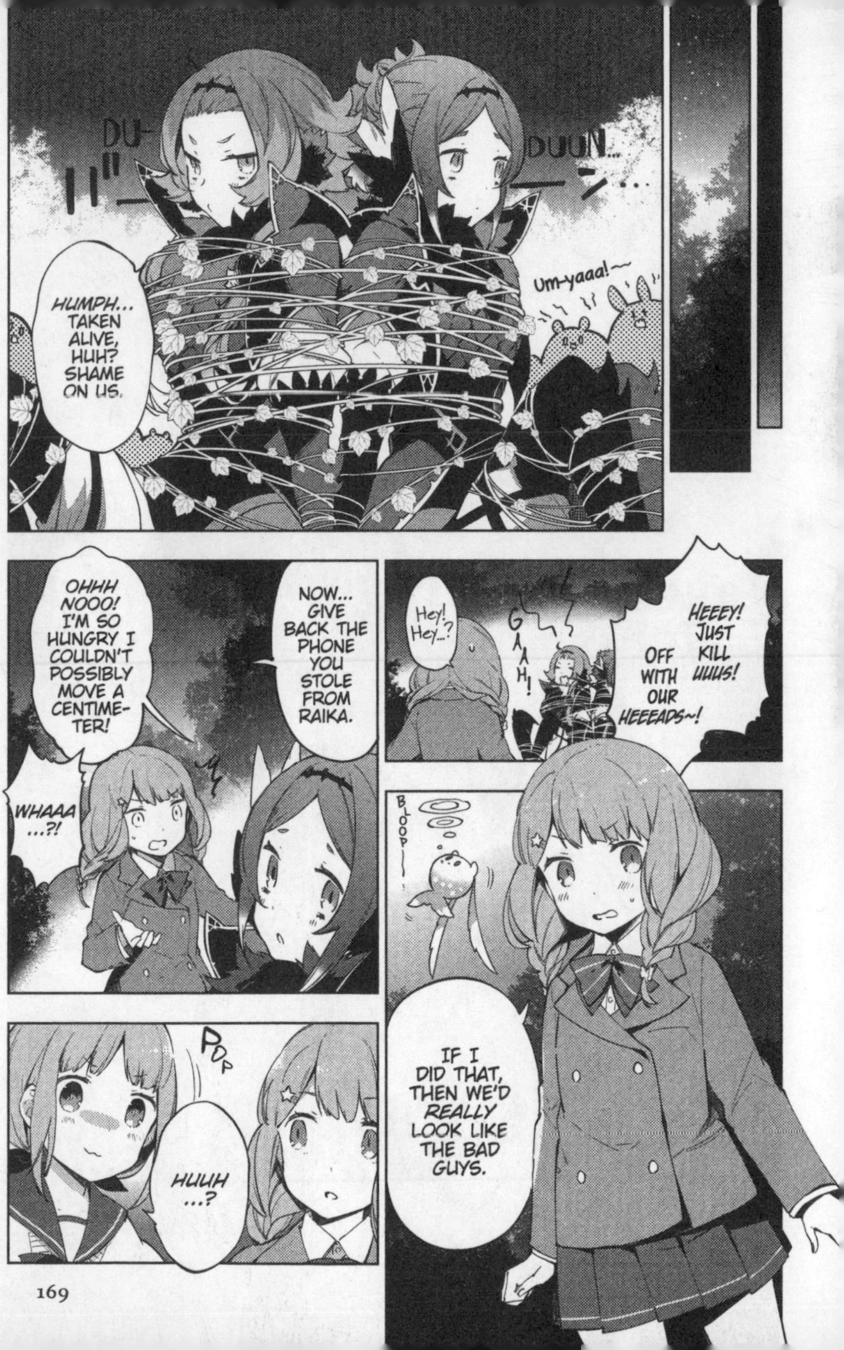
DU-
DUUN...
Um-yaaa!~
HUMPH... TAKEN ALIVE, HUH? SHAME ON US.
HEEEY! JUST KILL UUUS!
OFF WITH OUR HEEEADS~!
Hey! Hey...?
GAAAH!
NOW... GIVE BACK THE PHONE YOU STOLE FROM RAIKA.
OHHH NOOO! I'M SO HUNGRY I COULDN'T POSSIBLY MOVE A CENTIMETER!
WHAAA ...?!
BLOOP
IF I DID THAT, THEN WE'D *REALLY* LOOK LIKE THE BAD GUYS.
POP
HUUH ...?

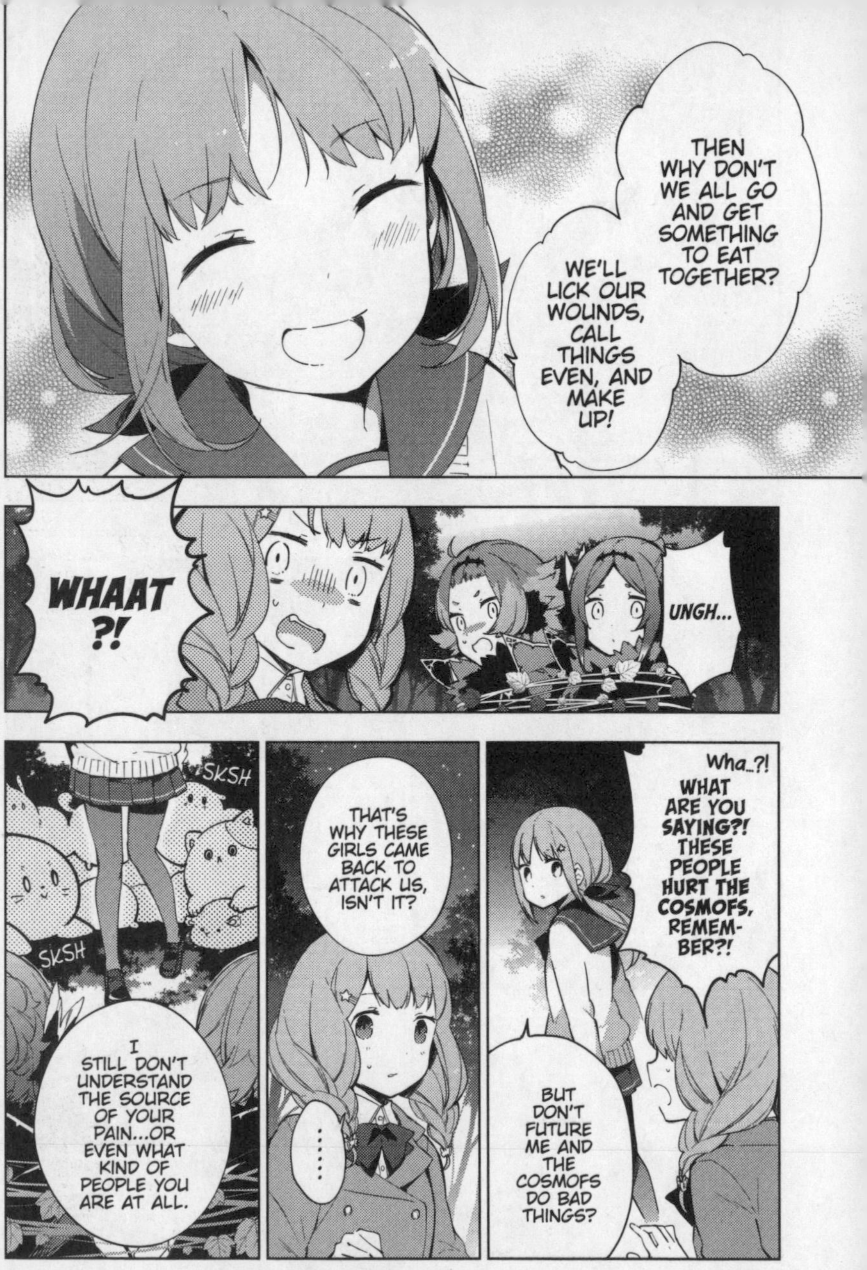
THEN WHY DON'T WE ALL GO AND GET SOMETHING TO EAT TOGETHER?
WE'LL LICK OUR WOUNDS, CALL THINGS EVEN, AND MAKE UP!
UNGH...
WHAAT ?!
Wha..?!
WHAT ARE YOU SAYING?! THESE PEOPLE HURT THE COSMOFS, REMEMBER?!
BUT DON'T FUTURE ME AND THE COSMOFS DO BAD THINGS?
THAT'S WHY THESE GIRLS CAME BACK TO ATTACK US, ISN'T IT?
......
SKSH
SKSH
I STILL DON'T UNDERSTAND THE SOURCE OF YOUR PAIN...OR EVEN WHAT KIND OF PEOPLE YOU ARE AT ALL.

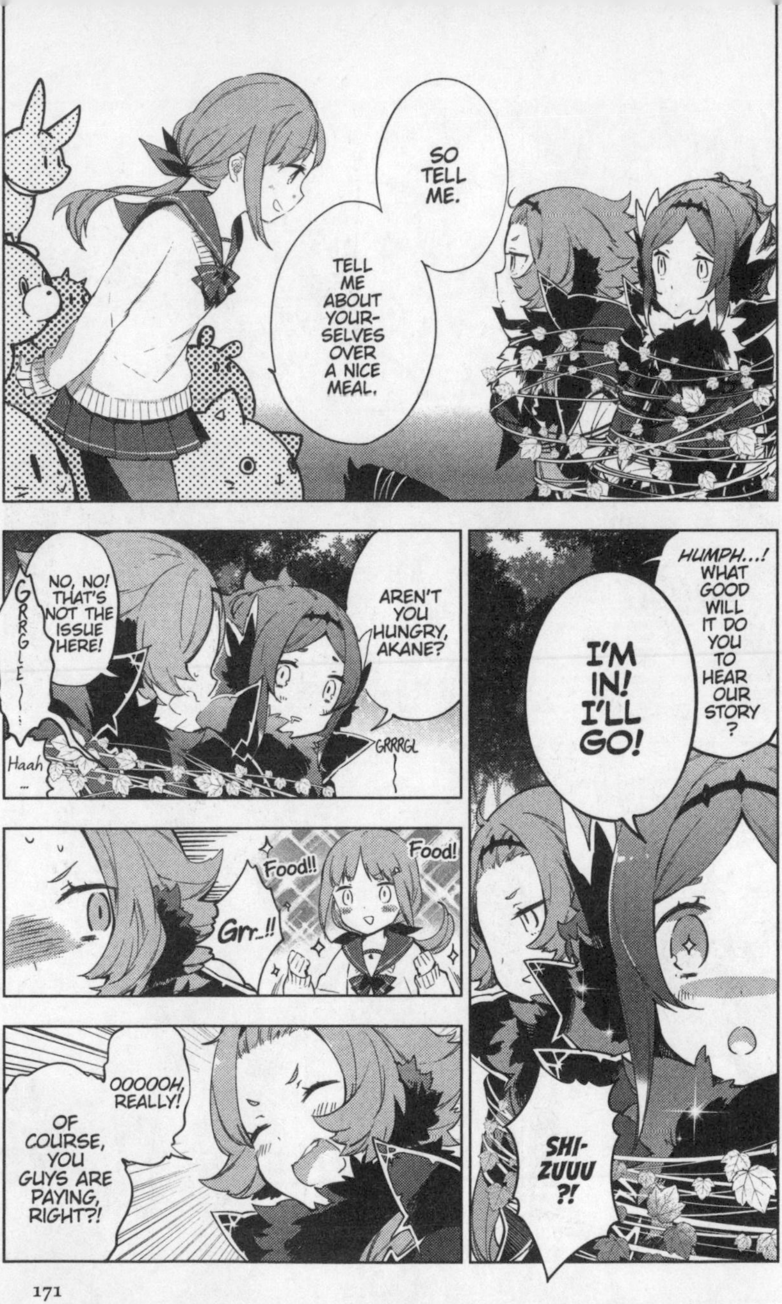
SO TELL ME.
TELL ME ABOUT YOUR-SELVES OVER A NICE MEAL.
HUMPH...! WHAT GOOD WILL IT DO YOU TO HEAR OUR STORY?
I'M IN! I'LL GO!
SHI-ZUUU?!
AREN'T YOU HUNGRY, AKANE?
GRRRGL
NO, NO! THAT'S NOT THE ISSUE HERE!
GRRGLE...
Haah...
Food!
Food!!
Grr...!!
OOOOOH, REALLY!
OF COURSE, YOU GUYS ARE PAYING, RIGHT?!

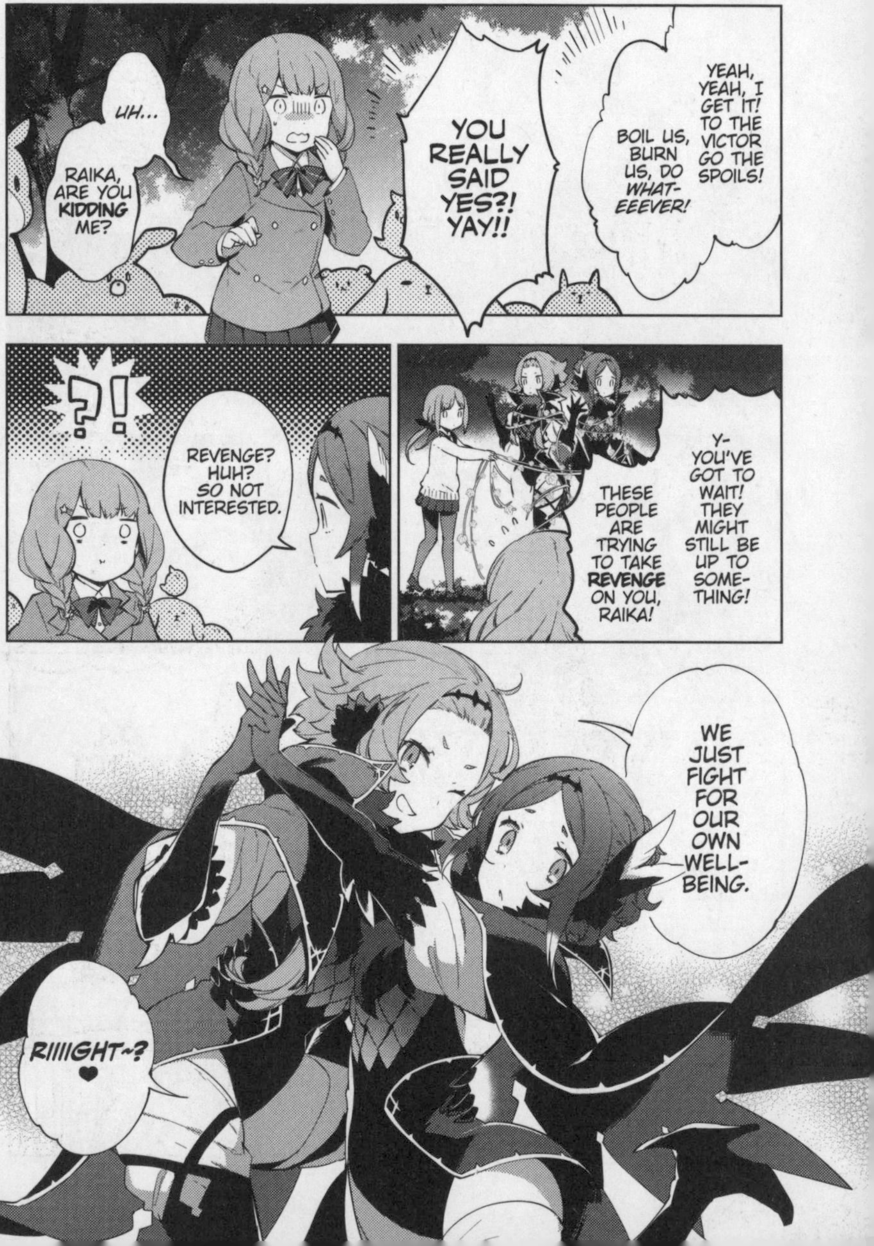
YEAH, YEAH, I GET IT! TO THE VICTOR GO THE SPOILS!
BOIL US, BURN US, DO WHAT-EEEVER!
YOU REALLY SAID YES?! YAY!!
UH...
RAIKA, ARE YOU KIDDING ME?
Y-YOU'VE GOT TO WAIT! THEY MIGHT STILL BE UP TO SOME-THING!
THESE PEOPLE ARE TRYING TO TAKE REVENGE ON YOU, RAIKA!
?!
REVENGE? HUH? SO NOT INTERESTED.
WE JUST FIGHT FOR OUR OWN WELL-BEING.
RIIIIGHT~? ♥

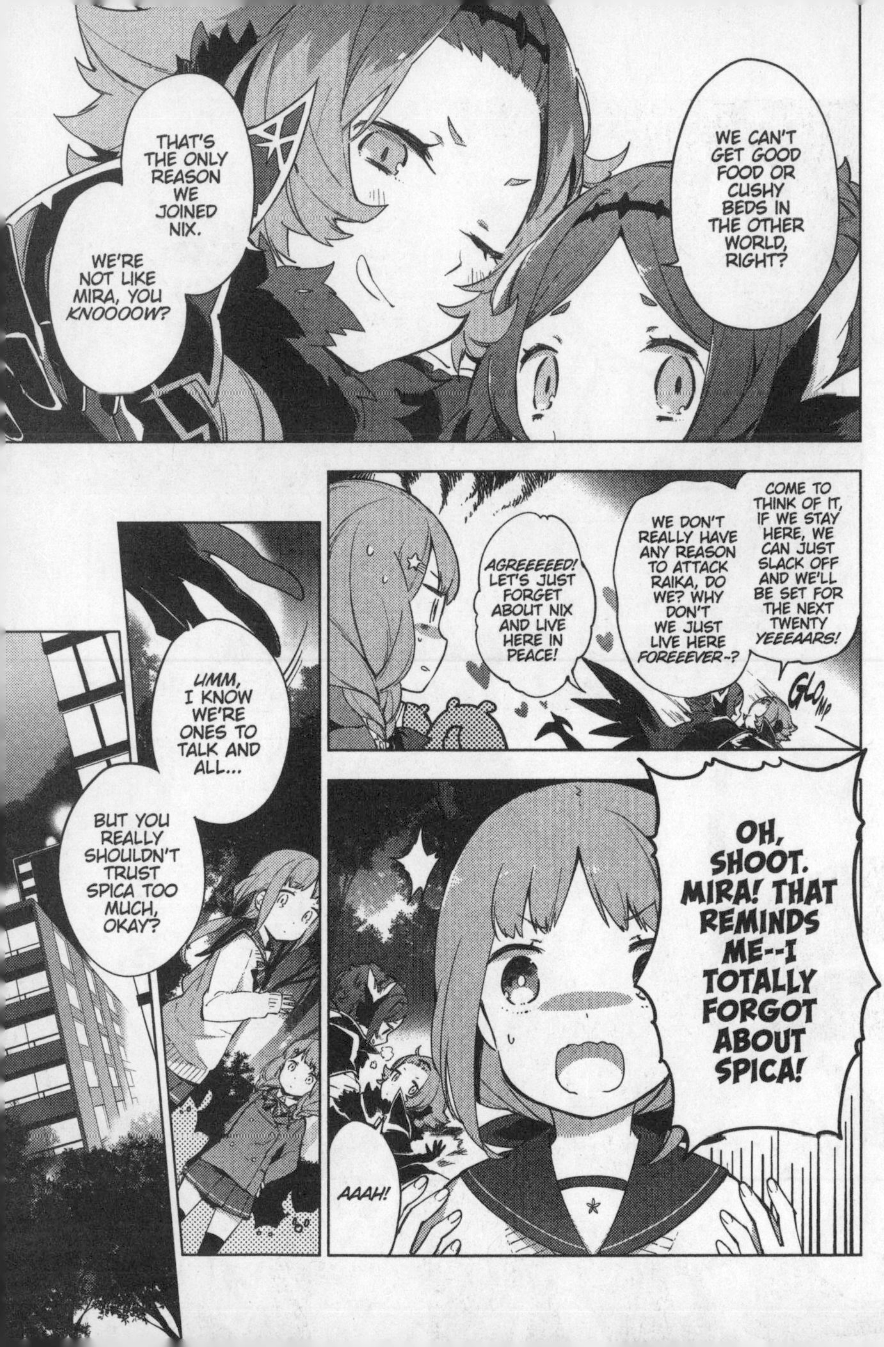
WE CAN'T GET GOOD FOOD OR CUSHY BEDS IN THE OTHER WORLD, RIGHT?
THAT'S THE ONLY REASON WE JOINED NIX.
WE'RE NOT LIKE MIRA, YOU *KNOOOOW*?
COME TO THINK OF IT, IF WE STAY HERE, WE CAN JUST SLACK OFF AND WE'LL BE SET FOR THE NEXT TWENTY *YEEEAARS!*
WE DON'T REALLY HAVE ANY REASON TO ATTACK RAIKA, DO WE? WHY DON'T WE JUST LIVE HERE *FOREEEVER*--?
*AGREEEEED!* LET'S JUST FORGET ABOUT NIX AND LIVE HERE IN PEACE!
GLOMP
OH, SHOOT. MIRA! THAT REMINDS ME--I TOTALLY FORGOT ABOUT SPICA!
*AAAH!*
*UMM*, I KNOW WE'RE ONES TO TALK AND ALL...
BUT YOU REALLY SHOULDN'T TRUST SPICA TOO MUCH, OKAY?

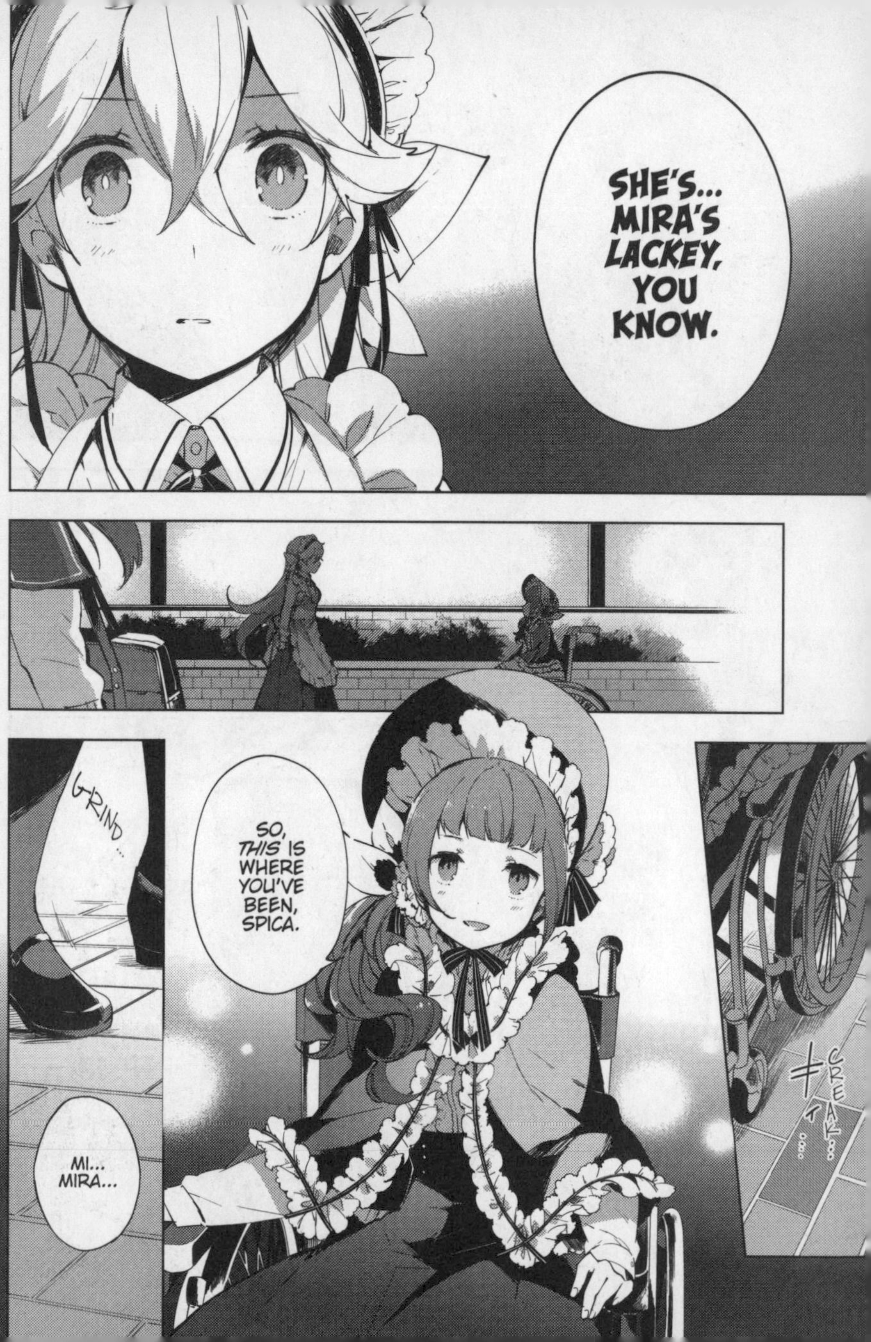
SHE'S... MIRA'S LACKEY, YOU KNOW.
CREAK...
SO, *THIS* IS WHERE YOU'VE BEEN, SPICA.
GRIND...
MI... MIRA...

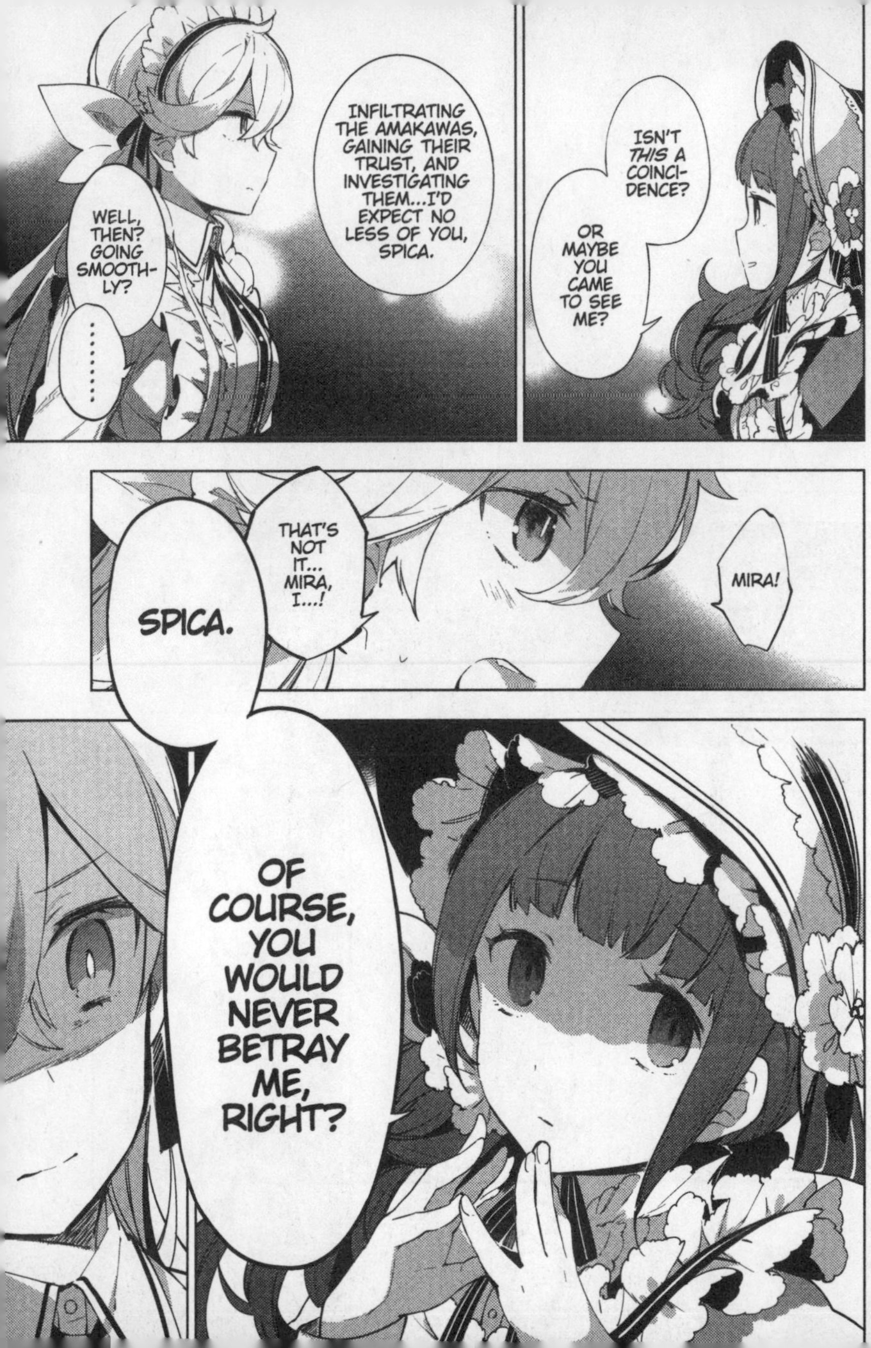
ISN'T THIS A COINCIDENCE?
OR MAYBE YOU CAME TO SEE ME?
INFILTRATING THE AMAKAWAS, GAINING THEIR TRUST, AND INVESTIGATING THEM...I'D EXPECT NO LESS OF YOU, SPICA.
WELL, THEN? GOING SMOOTHLY?
......
MIRA!
THAT'S NOT IT... MIRA, I...!
SPICA.
OF COURSE, YOU WOULD NEVER BETRAY ME, RIGHT?

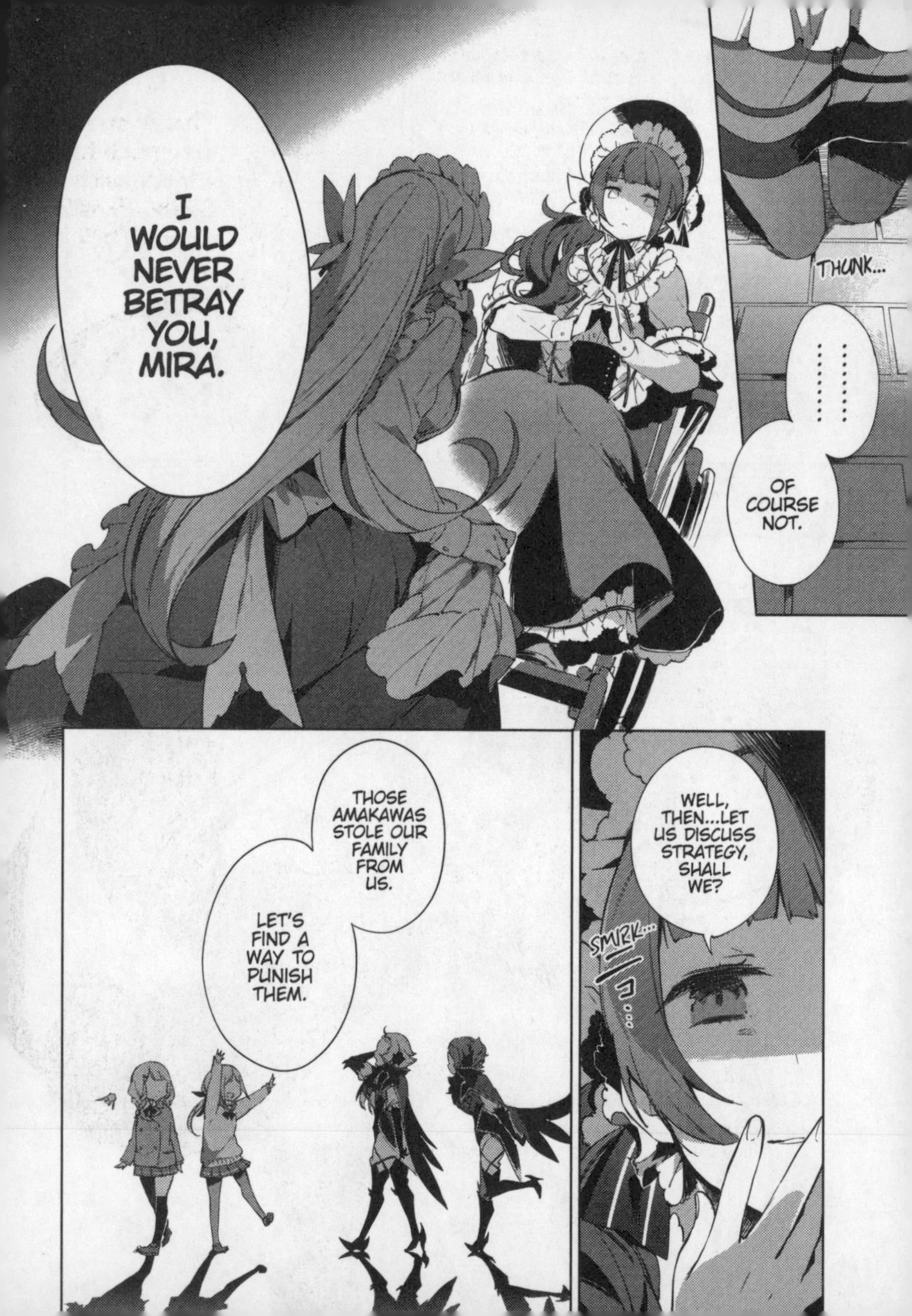
THUNK...
......
OF COURSE NOT.
I WOULD NEVER BETRAY YOU, MIRA.
WELL, THEN...LET US DISCUSS STRATEGY, SHALL WE?
SMIRK...
THOSE AMAKAWAS STOLE OUR FAMILY FROM US.
LET'S FIND A WAY TO PUNISH THEM.

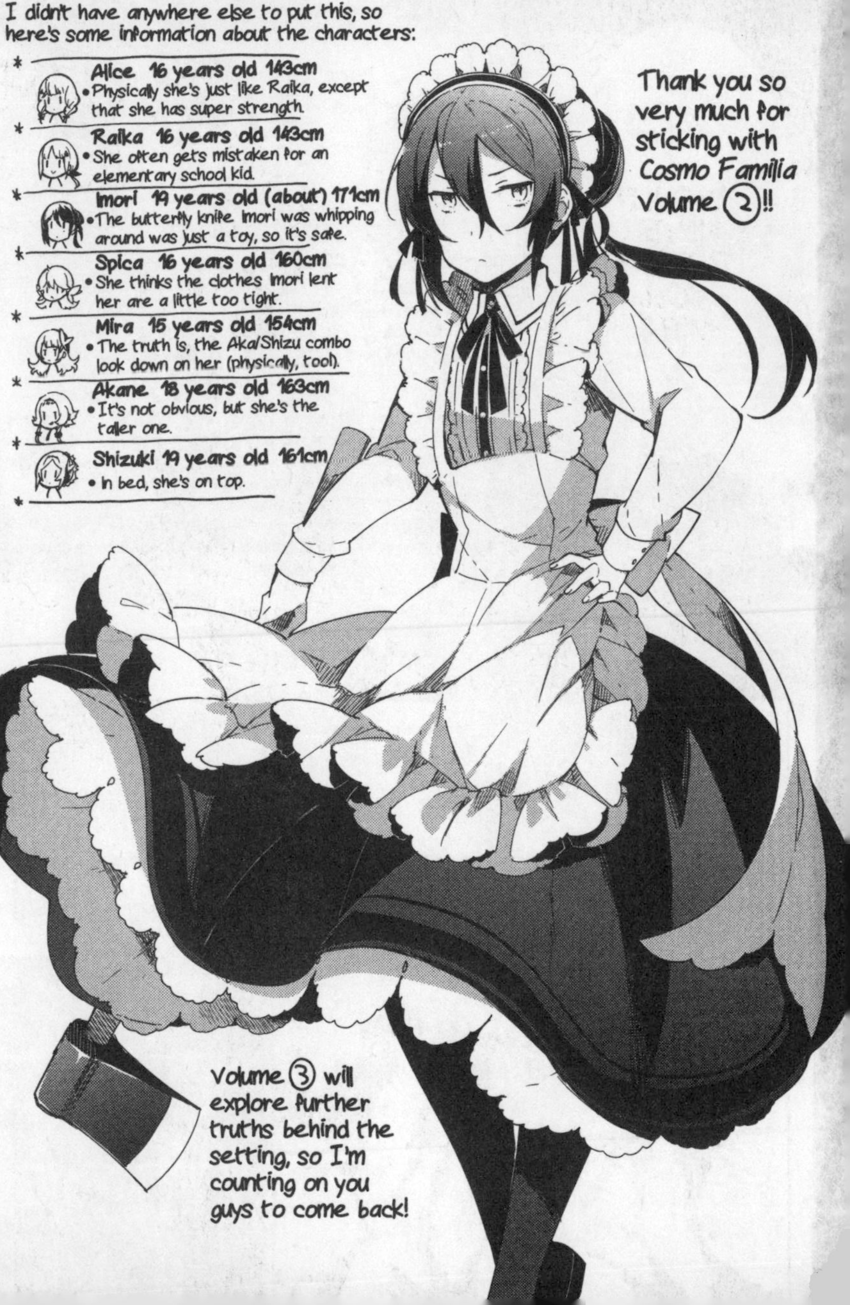
I didn't have anywhere else to put this, so here's some information about the characters:
Alice 16 years old 143cm
• Physically she's just like Raika, except that she has super strength.
Raika 16 years old 143cm
• She often gets mistaken for an elementary school kid.
Imori 19 years old (about) 171cm
• The butterfly knife Imori was whipping around was just a toy, so it's safe.
Spica 16 years old 160cm
• She thinks the clothes Imori lent her are a little too tight.
Mira 15 years old 154cm
• The truth is, the Aka/Shizu combo look down on her (physically, too!).
Akane 18 years old 163cm
• It's not obvious, but she's the taller one.
Shizuki 19 years old 161cm
• In bed, she's on top.
Thank you so very much for sticking with Cosmo Familia Volume 2!!
Volume 3 will explore further truths behind the setting, so I'm counting on you guys to come back!

SEVEN SEAS ENTERTAINMENT PRESENTS

# COSMO*FAMILIA

story and art by **Hanokage**

VOL. 2


TRANSLATION
**Beni Axia Conrad**

ADAPTATION
**Kim Kindya**

LETTERING AND LAYOUT
**Carolina Hernández Mendoza**

COVER DESIGN
**Nicky Lim**
**George Panella** (LOGO)

PROOFREADER
**Stephanie Cohen**

EDITOR
**Shanti Whitesides**

PREPRESS TECHNICIAN
**Rhiannon Rasmussen-Silverstein**

PRODUCTION MANAGER
**Lissa Pattillo**

MANAGING EDITOR
**Julie Davis**

ASSOCIATE PUBLISHER
**Adam Arnold**

PUBLISHER
**Jason DeAngelis**





Seven Seas press and purchase enquiries can be sent to Marketing Manager Lianne Sentar at press@gomanga.com. Information regarding the distribution and purchase of digital editions is available from Digital Manager CK Russell at digital@gomanga.com.





ISBN: 978-1-64505-490-0

Printed in Canada

First Printing: September 2020

10 9 8 7 6 5 4 3 2 1


FOLLOW US ONLINE: ***www.sevenseasentertainment.com***

## READING DIRECTIONS

This book reads from ***right to left***, Japanese style. If this is your first time reading manga, you start reading from the top right panel on each page and take it from there. If you get lost, just follow the numbered diagram here. It may seem backwards at first, but you'll get the hang of it! Have fun!!

1
2
3
4
5
6
7
8
9

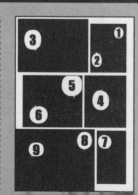